André Gorz
A Life

THE FRENCH LIST

André Gorz

A Life

WILLY GIANINAZZI

TRANSLATED BY CHRIS TURNER

LONDON NEW YORK CALCUTTA

Seagull Books, 2022

Originally published in French as *André Gorz, une vie* by Willy Gianinazzi
© Editions La Découverte, Paris, France, 2016

First published in English translation by Seagull Books, 2022
English translation © Chris Turner, 2022

ISBN 978 0 85742 988 9

British Library Cataloguing-in-Publication Data
A catalogue record for this book is available from the British Library

Typeset by Seagull Books, Calcutta, India
Printed and bound in USA by Integrated Books International

For Walter Riffel

CONTENTS

Paths to Postcapitalism

As a general principle, what matters about writers is their work. We might almost say that their lives are merely negligible background or fertile ground for anecdote. The analyst and depth psychologist Carl Gustav Jung used to say that his sedentary existence beside Lake Zurich was of no significance, whereas his spiritual life was a constant ferment of ideas. But how do things stand when writing is an urgent task which life itself commands, when it is the product of a quest pegged to an author's deepest torments and self-questionings? Can we, in that case, eschew 'the discovery of the everyday',[1] where the enigma of the human condition rumbles on constantly.

'When am I really "myself", that is, not just a product externally determined by alien forces and influences but responsible for my own actions, thoughts, feelings, values and so on?'[2] For André Gorz, only through a quest for meaning can an answer to this question be found. A quest that is simultaneously both existential and philosophical. Gorz was, then, twice a rebel: as an unassimilated individual who learned to live by overcoming his youthful refusal to exist through a rejection of social conformism; and, as a subversive writer rejecting the grip of the techno-capitalist machine on life and nature. On these two fronts he battled constantly. When one thinks about it, his favoured themes follow naturally: the critique of alienation, consumption, work and the destruction of the environment; praise for autonomy, free time, creative activity and the good life. And one might predict the authors who would inspire him: Jean-Paul Sartre, Edmund Husserl, Karl Marx, Ivan Illich.

Though exercising the privileged occupation of journalism, which kept him apart from the soul-destroying labour the mass of humanity has to

---

1 Bruce Bégout, *La Découverte du quotidien* (Paris: Allia, 2005).

2 André Gorz, 'Afterword: A Discussion with André Gorz on Alienation, Freedom, Utopia and Himself' (Hilary Pilkington trans.), interview conducted by Martin Jander and Rainer Maischein on 16 October 1983, in *The Traitor* (Richard Howard trans.) (London: Verso Books, [Second Edition] 1989), p. 274. *The Traitor* was originally published as *Le Traître* (Paris: Seuil, 1958).

perform, and though reluctant to commit to political activism for temperamental reasons, André Gorz naturally aligned his critical ideas with his life. There are few thinkers who have united theory and practice as closely as he did. The philosopher Simone Weil is certainly one such case and what has been said of her goes also for Gorz: 'Not being significantly grounded in social reality—and particularly in the world of work—the way they behave in their existence is, for intellectuals, the only touchstone of the authenticity of their convictions.'[3] The biography you are about to read will confirm this on almost every page.

Indeed, this back-and-forth movement between the work and the life will prompt us not to call our protagonist systematically by his established pseudonym, André Gorz, which corresponds to his role as a thinker, but by one or other of his names or pseudonyms as the context dictates. Let us simply list these here: Gerhart Hirsch, Gerhart Horst, Gérard Horst, which were his successive legal names; G. Bosquet, Michel Bosquet and André Gorz, which were assumed names, used respectively for his incursions into the translation of novels, journalism and literary or theoretical prose. So many names that shaped his uncertain identity.

André Gorz's *œuvre* is impressive. Born in 1923, he began writing during the Second World War and stopped only when he chose to end his life in 2007. With 18 books, 17 of these translated into other languages, he won a large audience at different times and in varied milieus: trade unions, the New Left, social democracy, political ecology and associations of the unemployed and insecurely employed. And probably more abroad than in France.

André Gorz was clearly every inch a thinker, but an unusual one. In Switzerland where he lived for 10 years—from 1939 to 1949—he was a reluctant, transient auditor on the benches of a philosophy faculty, going on to gain an engineering qualification in a scientific field that he never pursued professionally. In France he was in full-time employment for almost 20 years as a journalist at *Le Nouvel Observateur* and wrote for *Les Temps modernes* even longer, alongside a number of other non-university-trained writers like himself. Self-taught, he deliberately eschewed the image of the professional philosopher—even going so far as to disparage his own credentials: 'The truth is, I'm a *bricoleur*, a maverick—all in all, someone

---

3 Jacques Julliard, *Le Choc Simone Weil* (Paris: Flammarion, 2014), p. 24.

not really serious,' he confided in private in the last days of his life.[4] Half-philosopher and half-journalist, Gorz felt himself to be 'a sort of hybrid creature, something like a street musician', making no claim to virtuoso playing but offering his honest interpretation to an interested audience.[5]

Gorz was certainly not a 'functionary intellectual' working within the cosy confines of the university or specialist research institute and producing knowledge destined for the bookshelf or, at best, for demonstrating expertise in television studios (where he sometimes made appearances) and the corridors of power. Gorz saw it as his role not merely to deposit that knowledge and pass it on but to exploit it, interrogate it, reformulate it—in short, to *upturn* it, in order to 're-shape the way problems are conceived.'[6] To use his own words, the point was to bring out 'the need to unpick the weft of the dominant discourse that condemns lived experience to silence.'[7] *Betraying* order and society, it was the duty of the intellectual, with whom Gorz identified in his novel *The Traitor*, to use the tools of critical thought to help tease out the possibilities of another world that is humanly desirable. By contrast, decision-makers and experts—including those serving the cause of managerial socialism—are constantly battering the weary ears of worried and downtrodden employees, of the unemployed and of other incredulous, insecure workers with the theorems of competition, growth and employment for employment's sake. However, the fact that paths to salvation are possible outside of these illusory solutions is nowhere better illustrated than in the passionate but exacting *œuvre* assiduously constructed by André Gorz.

---

4 André Gorz to Françoise Gollain, 20–26 April 2007 (from the 'fonds Gorz' of the Institut Mémoires de l'édition contemporaine or IMEC; hereafter: GRZ).

5 André Gorz, interview in German by Martin Jander and Wolfgang Templin on 8 October 1989 (GRZ 10.26); published in *Die Tageszeitung* (31 January 1990) without this passage.

6 Christophe Fourel, 'De la politique du temps au revenu citoyen. Itinéraire d'un penseur de l'après-capitalisme', interview by Sarah Troche, *Geste* (6 October 2009), p. 57.

7 André Gorz, 'La vie, la nature, la technique' in *Le Fil rouge de l'écologie. Entretiens inédits en français* (Willy Gianinazzi ed., Erich Hörl after.) (Paris: Éditions de l'EHESS, 2015), pp. 19–81; here, p. 81; this is an augmented translation of ' "Archäologie" des philosophischen Fadens. Die Entpackung der verpackten Philosophie', interview by Erich Hörl, *Kurswechsel* [Vienna] 3 (1990): 5–36.

Writers sometimes produce a whole host of books and yet, after reaching the age of maturity and forming a settled set of ideas, just keep churning out the same one with more or less sterile variations. Gorz is not one of those authors. He went deep with his research and was just as determined in his willingness continuously to revise his ideas, exploring new intellectual territory, discovering new potential sources of rebellion, with, as his unchanging objective, to press reality to yield proposals that could give free rein to a concrete utopia. The task he stuck to stubbornly was that of 'imagining a non-capitalist, non-market society that could bring freedom and fire the imagination.'[8] The road was a long and winding one.

---

8 André Gorz to Denis Clerc, 19 May 1983 (GRZ).

PART ONE

The Alienation of Modern Man

The 1940s and 1950s: Comfort and Conformism

'Gamble on the will to live.'

Raoul Vaneigem, *Nous qui désirons sans fin*, p. 187

'This perpetual modification, this power
of initiative and transformation is freedom.'

André Gorz, *The Traitor*, p. 81

CHAPTER ONE

A Stranger to Himself

André Gorz describes his childhood in an autobiography of 1958 entitled *The Traitor*, in which, of necessity, he expresses a highly personal viewpoint and feelings. However, with the additional distance available to us, it is not impossible to form an image of the family he grew up in.

The central protagonist of our story was born in Vienna on 9 February 1923, 18 months after his sister Erika ('Helena' in *The Traitor*). His given names were Gerhart Robert Karl Jacob. His father Robert Hirsch ('Jacob' in *The Traitor*), born in Převov (Moravia) in 1880 to a wealthy Jewish family, worked first in the crate and barrel business of his rich brother-in-law Armin Bondi—married to Anna (described as 'beringed' and 'covered with pearls' in *The Traitor*)—where he met his future wife, a secretary. Then, when Bondi died, he took over and ran this substantial timber processing factory, which he attempted to hand over formally in 1938 to a nominal figurehead, a certain Josef Drexler, in order to avoid expropriation under the 'Aryanization' law.

On 19 July 1919 Robert Hirsch married Maria Starka, 15 years his junior, in the Roman Catholic Church, which presupposes his conversion to his wife's religion. She had been born in Nuremberg but grew up at Pilsen (Bohemia) in a humble Czech Catholic family that settled at Vienna in 1918, where the father Karl ('Yaroslav' in *The Traitor*) gave up his activity as a 'wandering' lyrical singer to open the Starka theatrical agency, which was bailed out by his Jewish in-laws but assured of long-term survival thanks to the son. It was with the German Naturalist dramaturge Gerhart Hauptmann in mind that the mother chose her son's name.

The family enjoyed a middle-class lifestyle in a flat in a smart district of the city, Ober-Sankt-Veit (Heitzinger Hauptstrasse, 116). They lived away from the city centre and, being relatively uncultured, despite the book collection and grand piano on view, the children grew up far removed from the artistic Vienna the son would later discover as a tourist.[1] Thus, by several

---

1 According to André Gorz's letter to Franz Schandl, 1 November 2004, in 'Über den Horizont unserer Handlungen. Aus den nachgelassenen Briefen des André Gorz', *Streifzüge* 41 (November 2007), p. 11.

accounts, he would remain devoid of any aesthetic sense. But his mother, who vested her love and excessive expectations in her children, saw to it that they were well educated. When he began school, Gerhart could read, write and count. The family's French nanny taught the children the rudiments of her own language.

Around 1930 or 1931, aged seven or eight years old, Gerhart who had, like his sister, been baptized, learned, either in the street or from within the family,[2] that his father was Jewish. On 19 May 1930, out of anxiety at the rise of anti-Semitism in Austria, Robert Hirsch changed his name: the family would now be called Horst. 'If one day you wonder why,' wrote his mother in her son's 'life-diary', 'here is the answer: daddy did it first and foremost out of love for you. Only later perhaps will you understand what a sacrifice it was for your father to take such a decision and carry it through, and I would like you to feel a special sense of gratitude for your father's self-denial on this score. You must not give a false explanation for the abandonment of the name Hirsch. Whatever their name, all honourable people are of equal value.'[3] On 12 June 1933 the father was baptized a Catholic. Following the Anschluss in 1938, these precautions neither prevented the factory being seized by an early member of the Nazi party, Paul Hudl, who was implicated in the assassination of Chancellor Dollfuss in 1934, nor their eviction from the attractive family apartment which was taken over by an 'Aryan' Nazi party member. Only one other member of his father's family seems to have been troubled by the regime's anti-Semitic drive. That was Gerhart's uncle Oskar Hirsch ('Oscar' in *The Traitor*), a professor at the University of Vienna and a well-known otolaryngologist, who was forced into exile; after the war, he recovered the paintings the Nazis had stolen from him, including a canvas by Egon Schiele (it so happened that the Horsts lived in the building adjoining the one where Schiele died in 1918). Now homeless, the mother took her two children off to live with her sister, while the father, as a safety measure, rented a modest room in a boarding house before joining her in November 1941. Immediately after the war, the couple reunited and the father recovered his position as a business owner.

---

2 *The Traitor* contradicts itself on this point within the space of a hundred pages (pp. 41–2 and 121–2).

3 Maria Starka-Horst, life-diary of her son, entry of June 1930, fo 77, GRZ 21.1.

These, then, are the more or less objective facts about his childhood that we can extract from the flood of scathing criticisms the son levels at his parents in his introspective essay, from his various later declarations, from the family papers he left at his death, from his mother's remarks in her son's life-diary[4] or from recent productive research in the Austrian archives.[5] It remains to be seen how Gerhart Hirsch/Horst experienced that childhood himself.

An 'Inauthentic Half-Caste'

Where his father was concerned, Gerhart could bear neither his authoritarianism—either at the factory or in the home—nor his subscribing to the values of order and hierarchy that supposedly still made him say, even in 1951, that he had nothing against Hitler apart from all the anti-Semitism. As for his mother, he attributed her marriage to social climbing and venal intent, which she pursued in the face of her anti-Semitic father's opposition; he was critical of her for having done all she could to suppress the Jewishness of her husband—with whom she barely got along at all—and consequently the half-Jewishness of her baptized children. Her brother, who made a success of the theatrical agency, displayed the swastika with pride. It was, then, an 'odd family', a family 'divided against itself and whose divisions he had to internalize.'[6] Looking back, he would say: 'I could not meet the expectations of either my father or my mother. I was condemned to betray one or the other of them or both of them at once, like one of those bastards who are central figures in Sartre's theatre.'[7] Convinced that he could not satisfy 'his mother's exorbitant requirements'[8] and that he could not live up to what the 'tribunal of his parents and ancestors' expected of him, Gerhart shrank back into himself as a child, 'stammering, silent, shy,

---

4 In October 1985, at the age of 90, the mother made a present of the *Tagebuch* to the son about whom it was written. It consisted of 78 pages and the last entry was dated 1930 (GRZ 21.1).

5 Wolfgang Stenke, 'Die Wege des André Gorz' in Claus Leggewie and Wolfgang Stenke (eds), *André Gorz und die zweite Linke. Die Aktualität eines fast vergessenen Denkers* (Berlin: Verlag K. Wagenbach, 2017), pp. 10–34.

6 Gorz, *Traitor*, p. 105.

7 Michel Contat and Thomas Ferenczi, 'Un entretien avec André Gorz', *Le Monde* (14 April 1992).

8 Gorz, *Traitor*, p. 117.

short-sighted and paralysed with guilty terror whenever a voice summoned him to show himself in the outside world.'[9] This is why 'he never lived his relation to the world and with others as a quasi-natural immediacy, his spontaneity is poisoned at the roots, he learned to keep a wary eye on his affective intentions as soon as they emerged.'[10] Consequently, he distrusted a hostile world that he found elusive and alien (was he not a laughing stock among his classmates for having changed his name?).[11] Admittedly, he loved his elementary school teacher Franz Spiroch, a 'red' who played the role of substitute father[12] and who instilled in him the certainty that 'human labour is the origin of the world that is given to us.'[13]

But at school and in the street he found reflected back to him a negative image as a Jew, which his mother strove to counteract with talk of a mythic aristocratic lineage from which she claimed descent. As for the ideals of strength and manliness, he couldn't receive these from an ageing, hen-pecked father who seemed to him to display, as a Jew, weakness and cowardice; the temptation was great to admire these things elsewhere in socially validated character types that would subsequently be embodied in the Hitler Youth, which he would obviously be unable to join, and the brownshirts of the SA. This mix of contradictory feelings would lead the author of *The Traitor* to say that his childhood was that of 'an inauthentic half-caste'[14] condemned to internal exile. Some pages written in 1946 would provide an account of his existential situation:

> This world is not *his* [. . .]. He has no life: his primordial engagement with the world has crumbled as a result of a series of displacements and misfortunes; his situation may perhaps even be said to have been originally torn in two, like that of the half-caste, stateless person or emigrant, so that the world does not appear to him in any definite perspective, so that he has no historical, social or ethnic

---

9 Unpublished fragment of *The Traitor* (GRZ 1.15).

10 André Gorz, *Fondements pour une morale* (Paris: Galilée, 1977), p. 464.

11 Remarks by his sister Erika, reported by Christophe Fourel in 2009. See Christophe Fourel (ed.), *André Gorz. Un penseur pour le XXIe siècle* (Paris: La Découverte, 2012), p. 18.

12 Gorz, 'La vie, la nature, la technique', p. 27.

13 André Gorz, undated manuscript (GRZ 8.32).

14 Gorz, *Traitor*, p. 121.

'ground' on which to stand. [. . .] As the baptized son of a Christian mother and a Jewish father, when he makes to act as a Christian he is rejected into the Jewish camp and when he tries to integrate with the Jews he is thrown back towards the Christians. Half-castes, whites and blacks all mutually reject him and repudiate him equally. Whatever he does, his behaviour will not manage—at least not manage quickly—to take on board and effectively move beyond his initial situation, in such a way as to totalize it.[15]

The importance André Gorz accords to the reconstitution of his childhood lends interest to the question which his mother, at the age of 87, will ask '[her] dear little one' in a spirited letter, written 'without any bitterness!' after her—now reconciled—son informed her of an autobiographical interview that had appeared in the press: 'How would you have developed, for example, if you had been the son of an extreme nationalist Sudeten German, for there was such a man among my suitors? If you had been spared the riven nature of your ancestry, what would the influence of such a father have been on your lively mind?'[16] It is idle to speculate on the answer, but there is a sense to the question and the underlying philosophical problematic is crucial, since it was from his *particular* experience that Gorz drew the *universal* principle of emancipation on which the whole of his social thinking was based. That principle was stated as follows:

Individuals have to construct their identities themselves, to find for themselves what is 'just', electively to form for themselves the communities they feel able to belong to [. . .]. This condemnation to autonomy is [their] common condition.[17]

The Choice of French

On 20 July 1939, Gerhart Horst arrived in Switzerland. He was 16 years old. His mother and sister were with him. His father, who came to see them off at Vienna station, had no inkling that he would not see his son for eight years and that after the years spent in Switzerland, Gerhart would choose France over a return to his native land. For the moment, what was in prospect were

---

15 Gorz, *Fondements pour une morale*, pp. 361–2.
16 Letter from Maria Horst-Starka to her son (in German), 2 September 1982 (GRZ).
17 Contat and Ferenczi, 'Un entretien avec André Gorz'.

long holidays, first at Montreux, the upmarket health resort on the banks of Lake Geneva where the adolescent observed that the 'lackeys' were more numerous than the rich clients for whom they worked, then in a family *pension* at Zurich, an affluent city where pleasures were muted and poverty seen as shameful.

The invasion of Poland on 1 September and the outbreak of war in Europe, which added to the trauma of the Anschluss the year before, drove his mother to make feverish efforts to find her son a place in a Swiss boarding school. Despite the financial restrictions on the family since the economic crisis of the 1930s, which deprived the Horsts of their holidays on the Adriatic beaches of Italy or Slovenia or in the hotels of Arosa in Grisons, followed by the charges imposed by the post-Anschluss anti-Jewish laws, his mother's hand was forced: she had necessarily to opt for an international educational establishment for the wealthy, which had become Switzerland's speciality. From the wife of a director of Daimler-Benz whom she met in a queue at the Aliens Bureau, his mother got wind of an institute that prepared young German, Dutch and Swiss pupils for the baccalaureate. It was in this notoriously iron-disciplined German-speaking school, accredited by the Greater *Reich* (and pro-Nazi through its headmaster),[18] situated near Saint-Moritz in Grisons some 1,700 metres above sea level, that the adolescent acquired concrete, objective—and not merely inner—experience of loneliness and exile. When one appreciates that Swiss patriotism, in search of its *Heimat*, was built around the naturalistic myth of the mountains, one can see the quasi-ontological significance of the memories that would remain with the one-time boarder at the ultra-select *Lyceum alpinum* of Zuoz:[19]

> At first the mountain thrilled him, then it weighed on him; he dreamed of the sea because the sea inspires dreams, while the mountain, unchanging, daunts imagination. Men crawl in its shadow, their thoughts short as the horizon, narrow as the valley, greedy as the rocky soil; because human activity does not affect it, the mountain is discouraging, nourishes introversion, conservatism.

---

18 Gorz, *Traitor*, p. 146.

19 The autobiographer conceals its identity (from his mother) by speaking of the Institut Montana at Klosters in another valley an hour's train ride away, but he refers correctly to the altitude of the school at Zuoz and he kept the certificates of his attendance at that establishment.

History washes over its feet without affecting it, and men of the mountain do not believe in history; for them there is only a lunar eternity, boredom articulated by the barber, tobacco and wine.[20]

It is as though, following Vidal de La Blache's geographical determinism, the proverbial conservatism of this country is forever set in its stone! It was, it seems, in the work of André Gide that Horst found literary corroboration of his abhorrence of the rocky heights.[21]

In all his school subjects Gerhart Horst achieved good, if not excellent, results. He was equally strong in French and English, in German and maths. He did not take religious studies, being conspicuously and definitively atheistic. One winter's evening of 1939–40, he resolved to throw himself body and soul into learning French. The language was not unfamiliar to him, having been a muffled melody of his childhood, in counterpoint to his mother tongue which he now rejected as such.

Objectively, however, the choice of French, which revived the fond memory of his nanny, could not, as he stated in an interview, have been a 'divorce from [his] mother',[22] who had also learnt the language. And Walter Riffel, who knew Horst from 1943 onwards, says his friend was not in any way ill-disposed towards his mother until she opposed his marrying Doreen[23] Keir in 1948, and that his father had told him she had been careful to choose French-speaking nannies, so as to prevent them from having the slightest contact with the father, who spoke only German.[24]

While the teachers warned Gerhart in his school record book that 'he would be well advised not to cut himself off so haughtily from the other students', his decision amounted to a secession. It was crucial, implying, as he saw it, a civilizational choice. 'He decided,' as he was to write in *The Traitor*, 'that the body of true thought and Reason was the French language, that the country where life was still and par excellence possible was France.'[25]

---

20 Gorz, *Traitor*, p. 146.

21 See Walter Riffel to André Gorz, 26 August 1990 (GRZ). Riffel is from the mountainous canton of Grisons and Gorz knew him from student days at Lausanne.

22 See André Gorz, *Penser l'avenir. Entretien avec François Noudelmann* (Paris: La Découverte, 2019), p. 30.

23 Keir's official birth name was 'Doreen'. She later became known as 'Dorine' in France.

24 Personal communication with Walter Riffel, 17 March 2016.

25 Gorz, *Traitor*, p. 152.

As soon as he could, he had people call him Gérard and this was a permanent decision (it is what his close circle would call him) and French would deliberately become his chosen language of expression (with concessions to English, relating to the demands of work and his romantic commitment): it would be a long time before he agreed to give interviews or lectures or write in his mother tongue, his fame playing a role in that. 'During more than 40 years (1940–1983),' he would write, cultivating the legend of his linguistic repulsion, 'I refused to speak, think or write in German.'[26] This move to devote himself—after France's fall to the Nazis—to French language and literature, which he would describe as 'passionate, disciplined, ascetic' and even involving 'masochism',[27] betrayed a hidden need to break with all that an overprotected but unhappy childhood had meant for him: 'France,' he would explain, 'was the Other of all that he was and knew [. . .] he fled the Austro-Germano-Judeo-Christian contradiction for the myth of the French absolute'[28]—a 'contradiction' which he internalized as a character flaw and which, as we have seen, had its origin in his family background. He would continue, then, to see himself as a half-Jew, an emigrant, a foreigner and rootless. He would regard himself as having 'no national identity': 'I have four Czech grandparents, two of whom were Jewish,' he was to tell a German interviewer in 1982. 'I am no more French than Wittgenstein is English, Feyerabend Californian or Ivan Illich Mexican—all three of them Viennese men who lived overseas.'[29]

---

26 Letter from André Gorz to Oskar Negt in English (because typed by his wife Doreen/Dorine) of 23 May 1990 (GRZ). In 1971 Gorz chose deliberately to express himself in English in a seminar at the University of Heidelberg. Though it is not certain that he accepted the invitation to speak on the German NDR radio station in 1969, he did take part, in 1970 and 1971, in German and Swiss German television programmes. In 1974 at Cuernavaca, he addressed a German interlocutor in his mother tongue, but affected a French accent (information supplied to the author by Jean Robert on 28 April 2013) . . . It was not until 1980 that he agreed to interviews with German-language publications, subsequently according many of them. If a psychoanalytic explanation is to be sought for this breaking of the taboo, it is noticeable that the decision coincides roughly with the date of his reconciliation with his mother some time around 1982.

27 Gorz, *Traitor*, pp. 152, 154.

28 Gorz, *Traitor*, pp. 152, 162–3.

29 André Gorz, 'Friedensbewegung—keine europäische Solidarität?', interview by Claus Leggewie, *Links* (special edition: 'Zeitung zum Frankfurter Friedenskongress 17–20

With his Swiss and Greater Reich baccalaureates in his pocket and determined to make good the break with his past, Horst left the German-speaking part of Switzerland for French-speaking 'Romandy'. But he was still a long way from knowing what direction to take in life. At 18 he knew only that, Jewish or not, he didn't want to be drafted into the German army. Even though his father saw no danger to himself and refused to emigrate (for a long time his wife had been trying to get him to leave for Brazil), the family approved their son's choice and financed his university studies, before a philanthropic childless couple from Zurich, won over by his mother's good qualities, took over that burden. The grateful Horst would visit the couple regularly during his student years in Switzerland.

The Swiss Case

Gérard Horst arrived at Lausanne in April 1941. He enrolled in chemistry at the university's School of Engineering. He did not consider the humanities because its degrees were not recognized abroad. He took little interest in his studies, but in 1945 he graduated in chemical engineering from the University of Lausanne.[30] Passing fancies of working in the Belgian Congo persisted for several months but came to nothing and, with his efforts to gain employment in Switzerland and, later, in France proving unsuccessful, he was never to work in that particular field. His true intellectual inclinations were of a quite different nature.

As soon as he arrived in the capital of the Canton of Vaud he began to read intensively in literature and philosophy. He devoured Gide, Raymond Ruyer and Dostoyevsky, developed a passion for Valéry, discovered Sartre's *Nausea* and *The Wall* (in a bookshop window display in Genoa, where he had gone in 1941 to see his mother), then made a thorough study of *Being and Nothingness*, which was published in 1943. His immersion in French literature led him to decline an offer he had received in 1942 to emigrate to the United States, where his uncle Oskar Hirsch, the otolaryngologist, had found refuge. But this reading did not fill the spiritual void that continued to beset him, nor did it remedy the isolation of his first 18 months at Lausanne.

June 1982') (June 1982): 8. It was probably this interview, which had already been published in the *Frankfurter Rundschau* of 14 June, that Gorz sent to his mother.

30 'Les nouveaux gradués de l'université de Lausanne', *Gazette de Lausanne* (15 June 1945).

He would later observe that none of his deliberations helped to bring him any closer to the Swiss. The incomprehension was total. What he saw in the press or in cinema newsreels were propaganda clichés that smacked of Petainism and a feigned neutral politics that in practice favoured the Axis. Was he aware that there was effectively censorship at all levels? While war raged on the eastern front and in Libya, among the Swiss whom he met in cafes or in the street he sensed unconcern allied with prosperity, each being based, as he was to remark sarcastically, on 'six years of food and fuel stocks'. But this Switzerland 'without truth' which 'exiled its inhabitants from history and locked them into security and comfort as though in a prison' was no more congenial to the Swiss students he would soon meet.[31]

If we read the autobiographical narrative of *The Traitor* from a historian's point of view,[32] we see that the light the young Horst cast on his host country did not provide total illumination. Another section of the population besides the privileged closed circle of student youth was also opposed to the God-fearing bourgeois order, though Horst knew little of it because it was not a milieu he frequented. And, moreover, that milieu knew little of the Swiss wealth that so dazzled a penniless student like himself. I am speaking of the workers. They bore the full brunt of wartime restrictions, particularly the food rationing that continued until 1947—and even beyond that in the case of bread—because of ongoing economic difficulties (in 1948 the Canton of Vaud resorted to compulsory labour for civil servants and youth, who were sent to work in the fields for three weeks!). To this we may add the chronic housing shortage and the continued existence of slums.

This austere picture of post-war Swiss reality is absent from *The Traitor*. Yet, without a sense of it, it is difficult to understand the repeated miners' and factory workers' strikes in Lausanne and its hinterland in this period. These strikes also remind us that Lausanne, like Geneva, was not just a middle-class university city, but also a working-class one with its Socialist and Communist bastions. The 'Reds' had already led the city council during the period of Comintern-backed Popular Fronts (1934–37). With the end of censorship and of the ban on Communists—which, in the canton of Vaud, dated from 1938—the Parti ouvrier et populaire (POP), created as an

---

31 Gorz, *Traitor*, pp. 176, 172, 176.

32 Drawing on Françoise Fornerod, *Lausanne, le temps des audaces. Les idées, les lettres et les arts de 1945 à 1955* (Lausanne: Payot, 1993); Pierre Jeanneret, *Popistes. Histoire du parti ouvrier et populaire vaudois. 1943–2001* (Lausanne: Éditions d'en bas, 2002).

underground organization in 1943, won the local elections of 1945 by some margin and, with the Socialists, formed the new majority on the city council (the start of the Cold War and the effects of the Prague *coup* of February 1948 would prevent that majority being re-elected in 1949). This post-war electoral advance of the workers' parties—a nationwide development that caused the 'bourgeois parties', as they styled themselves, to fear a recurrence of the revolutionary situation of 1918—brought the fulfilment of a long-standing demand of the Swiss labour movement when a pension scheme was introduced in 1948.

For those Swiss inclined to rebellion, there was, then, scope for manoeuvre in political action. For Horst, however, any prospect of revolutionary transformation in the country was illusory so long as the surrounding world did not change. He shared the gloomy outlook of his fellow students, one of whom exclaimed: 'What can we do in this Kafkaesque universe, given that we are as despairing as goldfish in a bowl? Impotent, we are impotent.'[33] With his student acquaintances providing his only horizon, he would write that 'their rebellion was helpless': 'either it stopped short or it poured out as literature.'[34] As for those who remained in the POP, 'out of resentment at this stifling society', they could only do so ensconced in the impotent embrace of Stalinism, 'fleeing in sectarian fashion from reality towards a prophetic system that denies it, but whose prophecy and dream of human brotherhood remained without any effect on their condition.'[35] Horst was tormented by this genuinely pathos-laden sense of revolutionary impossibility. After leaving Switzerland, he would at one point contemplate writing a pamphlet entitled *The Revolt of Swiss Youth*.[36]

A Bohemian, Student Life

Two concurrent events were to bring an end to Gérard Horst's loneliness: the start of a relationship with a young woman worker whom he saw at weekends ('L' in *The Traitor*) and, alongside his frequenting of Indian,

---

33 Charles Apothéloz, 'Idéologie et mystification' (1949) in *Cris et écrits. Textes sur le théâtre, 1944–1982* (Lausanne: Payot, 1990), p. 158.

34 Gorz, *Traitor*, p. 178.

35 Gorz, *Traitor*, p. 179. Only the last part of this passage is rendered in the current English translation [Trans.].

36 See letter from Gérard Horst to Walter Riffel, undated [1953?] (GRZ).

German, Italian or Austrian expatriates and exiles, his acceptance into a student society. This latter—intellectually significant—event is curiously neglected in his autobiography, but we should accord it its full importance.

On 30 October 1942 Horst was co-opted into Lausanne's Société de belles lettres. He became its secretary in 1944–45, before taking over the same role in 1945–46 for the whole of Switzerland, the other sections of the organization being located in Geneva, Neuchâtel and Fribourg. On 7 February 1947, he was appointed vice-president of the Lausanne society— a very striking token of his integration among his peers.[37] This student society, created in the early years of the nineteenth century, was very active at the time and embraced a wide range of opinion, its range of sensibilities running from the (Centre Left) 'Radicals' to some POP members. Having cast off the uniforms of their predecessors, its members pursued 'a rather joyful rebellion against all conformism.'[38] They were committed to staging a theatre performance once or twice a year. Writers, journalists and visual artists were invited to lecture to the society, and these lectures were followed by good-humoured drinking sessions.

Horst shunned these. He preferred the less worldly, more informal discussions that took place on Friday evenings, when the students presented a work or text of their own or declaimed poetry. This was the moment he was able to find an audience and intellectual moorings. In the family boarding house, where he lodged with students, an actress, a painter and a promising writer, he already 'dominated the conversation of the guests with his witty or sarcastic quips.'[39] By his eloquence, lofty thinking and superior knowledge, he mesmerized some students and impressed everyone. One of them taunted him with the charge: 'You stink from intelligence the way some people stink from under their arms.'[40] Later, Gorz would write in self-justification: 'I was totally unhappy at that time and I took my unhappiness

37 *Belles lettres de Lausanne. Livre d'or du 200e anniversaire, 1806–2006* (Lausanne: Société des belles lettres de Lausanne, 2007), p. 376; *Gazette de Lausanne* (18 February 1947).

38 Bertil Galland, 'Celui qui feuillète aujourd'hui la collection de *La Gazette littéraire* s'émerveille' in Jean-Pierre Moulin (ed.), *Présence de Franck Jotterand. Recueil de textes* (Lausanne: L'Âge d'homme, 1997), pp. 17–23; here, p. 19.

39 Walter Riffel, from his letter to André Gorz, 26 August 1990 (GRZ) and the author's personal communication with Walter Riffel, 17 March 2016.

40 Gorz, *Traitor*, p. 210.

out on others. I wore it as a form of superiority. I detached myself from the world and the judgement of others, and from that detached location I judged (and damned) everything and everyone.'[41] Horst introduced his fellow students to the writings of Camus, Queneau, Prévert and Nizan, and the novels of Sartre. Taciturn by nature, he was transformed when he spoke of philosophy and discoursed, in a quiet monotone, on the themes of existentialism, leaving his listeners mostly unable to follow him. He was also familiar with American realist and social literature, which he devoured in English. He had a weakness for James T. Farrell and, particularly, Dos Passos;[42] he also read Faulkner. And, for purely financial reasons, he translated two fashionable American novels for a local publisher, thus bolstering his mastery of the English language.[43]

Those who rubbed shoulders with Horst in his Lausanne exile agree in their depiction of him today. Their memories may be influenced by the reading of *The Traitor*, but little-known details come through in spite of all that. The point is forcefully made that Gérard was extremely cerebral and supremely indifferent to all but highly intellectual matters.[44] And in this 'obscure' period of his life he is remembered as being frosty, anything but effusive, not seeking friendship, austere and truly odd [*singulier*].[45] As a 'terrorist of the rational',[46] he didn't share in any of the usual hi-jinks of student life. He refused to engage in the *charriages* (hazings) practiced at the Société de belles lettres. He didn't drink or frequent bars much, preferring instead to play chess. This was both by taste and also for want of funds. He was unusual, too, for his lack of interest in jazz and his contempt for sport (he had thrown out his skis, bicycle and tennis racquet), that 'mind-numbing

---

41 Letter from André Gorz to Walter Riffel, 29 October 1990 (private archives), in answer to the letter cited above.

42 See Gérard Horst, 'La littérature américaine industrialisée', *Servir* (19 June 1947).

43 Ramona Stewart, . . . *Et le désert autour* [*Desert Town*] (Gérard Horst trans.) (Lausanne: Marguerat, 1946); Charles Mergendahl, *La Route aux étoiles* [*Don't Wait Up for Spring*] (translated and adapted by G. Bosquet [alias Gérard Horst]) (Lausanne: Marguerat, 1947). The pseudonym was no doubt employed because of the fierce criticism of this book in the article referenced in the preceding footnote.

44 Personal communication, Jean-Pierre Moulin, 9 December 2010.

45 Personal communication, Charles-Henri Favrod, 12 October 2010.

46 This expression was used by Gaston Cherpillod in a letter to the author, 15 December 2011.

discipline' imposed on him at Zuoz before he had himself excused games.[47] At the beach, however, 'in spite of what [he] say[s],' he exhibits an 'attachment to athletic physical values',[48] as his holiday snaps prove—and even in old age, he began his day with vigorous exercises![49] Nonetheless, at Lausanne he allowed himself five visits to the cinema a week and, smoked as everyone else did then, being only too happy to have unearthed the cheapest tobacconist's in the city—his miserliness was proverbial.[50]

Apart from the allusion to the fine velvets of his trousers and jackets (though he wore them until they were thoroughly threadbare), the outlines of the portrait drawn by a journalist colleague who would rub shoulders with him for almost 30 years were already there:

> He was quite an enigmatic bird, with folded wings and subdued plumage—though he chose good quality fabrics—speaking slowly and softly, always precisely and competently, at times giving a sense of being disconcerted, if not indeed distressed, at the ignorance of his interlocutors. In discussions he wore a patient smile, almost amused at the objections that might be levelled against him, but he invariably kept up his efforts at persuasion. It was at times as though he had managed to extricate himself from Plato's cave and accede to the universe of truth. Yet was he arrogant or scornful? Never. He liked to listen, to learn, to read everything, to devour information.[51]

After leaving the Wachsmuth family boarding house at 5, chemin de Boston and 'camping' at friends' places for a while, in the Autumn of 1946 Horst rented a little loft apartment in the old town at 6, rue du Tunnel, where prostitutes plied their trade amid a generally working-class population. Visitors recount even gloomier memories of the place than the description in *The Traitor*, and of the frugal life, verging on mortification that its occupant led there, built around a diet of oatmeal. They speak of an insalubrious bedroom

---

47 Recollections of remarks made in confidence to Walter Riffel, mentioned in his letter to Gorz of 26 August 1990.

48 André Gorz to Walter Riffel, 29 October 1990.

49 Reported by his translator Chris Turner.

50 The author of *The Traitor* does not seek to conceal this. Anyone who knew Gorz highlights this character trait.

51 Serge Lafaurie, 'Hommage à André Gorz', address delivered to a commemorative round table in Paris, 5 May 2009.

with black sheets on the walls and closed windows; a lack of heating; an electrical element to heat water; a single lightbulb hanging from a cord in the middle of the room. His disciple Freddy Buache remembers 'badly functioning plumbing, while a bowlful of water stood imposingly on the floor. During our conversations, Horst would take ladlefuls from it, which he swigged down in little gulps before continuing his critical commentary on some proposition.'[52]

Friends and Acquaintances in Lausanne

At the Société de belles-lettres, Horst had an osmotic relationship with the cream of the young intellectuals, who were fired with extraordinary post-war intellectual excitement and driven by the idea that there was a new world to be built. These people would effectively open up the culture of Francophone Switzerland to the outside world.[53] A large number operated out of Paris—a city Horst regarded as 'the centre of the world'—arriving there as frenziedly excited as birds newly released from their cages: they would later be Horst's first friends in Paris.

Among those he regarded as important, we find Jean-Pierre Moulin (who joined the society in 1942), a journalist and song-lyricist (and friend of Boris Vian) who settled in Paris in 1946, becoming an habitué of Saint-Germain-des-Prés, and Franck Jotterand (1943) who stung the city council in 1947 by denouncing Lausanne as closed-minded and anti-youth. Having also left Switzerland for the Paris of the Existentialists, the latter became a passionate follower of Jean Vilar and the stage plays of Albert Camus. In 1949, travelling back and forth between the two cities, he edited the extraordinarily diverse international kaleidoscope of arts and culture that was the literary supplement of the *Gazette de Lausanne*. It was this close friend of Horst's who told him that he stank of intelligence. Charles-Henri Favod (1946) also comes to mind, a senior correspondent and critic at the same newspaper, who went on to be a film producer (his films included Marcel Ophüls' *Le Chagrin et la pitié* in 1969). As does Charles Apothéloz (1942) who left his bourgeois family for bohemia and gave up law for the theatre.

---

52 Freddy Buache, *Derrière l'écran. Entretiens avec Christophe Gallaz et Jean-François Amiguet* (Lausanne: L'Âge d'homme, 2009), pp. 44–5.

53 See Jean-Pierre Moulin, 'Jean-Pierre Moulin, un "Amant américain" à Paris', interview by Jean-Jacques Roth (interviewer), *Le Nouveau Quotidien* (3 January 1993).

There are also those who, though not mentioned by name, find their hopeless rebellion described with affection in *The Traitor*, such as Jean-Pierre Schlunegger ('Jean-Marie' in the novel)[54] (1944), a poet of solitude who took his own life at the age of 39. Or Gaston Cherpillod ('A' in the novel)[55] (1945), the son of a worker and a farm-servant, who was dismissed from his teaching post in 1953 in the climate of the Cold War. Cherpillod, who was also a self-styled 'rebel' writer, as well as an activist and city councillor with the POP and later with the Alternative Left, remembers Horst hanging a red flag with a hammer and sickle motif in his window in May 1946, the anniversary of the armistice.[56] Or, lastly, such as the aforementioned Freddy Buache ('B' in the novel)[57] (1948), a fervent cinephile (one of the prime movers behind the Swiss Film Archive, the equivalent of the French Cinémathèque) and author of the post-Dadaist manifesto *Le Doigt*, a source of disquiet to the Communist-led city police force.[58] It was with Buache, who discovered André Breton at the same time as frequenting the Stalinists of the POP (who accused him of Trotskyism), that Horst perhaps felt the greatest affinity. Feeling, like Horst, something of a hybrid creature on account of his humble country origins which, at the university, left him 'feeling like a mongrel',[59] Buache became infatuated with existentialist philosophy and chose the young Austrian intellectual, one year his junior, as his 'guide'.

54 Gorz, *Traitor*, p. 178.

55 Gorz, *Traitor*.

56 Gaston Cherpillod (d. 2012) in a letter to the author, 15 December 2011. In his account, this took place at the armistice in rue de Bourg. However, as Horst only moved into that street in April–May 1946, we take this geographical fact as a firmer guide than human memory.

57 Gorz, *Traitor*, p. 178.

58 Sold in the street by sandwich-men and advertised with a banner stretched out across the city's only high-rise building (the Tour Bel-Air) one day in summer 1948, this provocative manifesto with its comical page layout, which involved other Belles Lettres students but not Horst, was reviewed by him in the newspaper he worked on. See G. H., 'Le Doigt. Un manifeste des étudiants lausannois', *Servir* (8 July 1948). It is reproduced in Fornerod, *Lausanne, le temps des audaces*, p. 199.

59 *Personnalités suisses*, 8 April 1969, a programme of Télévision suisse romande (TSR) on Freddy Buache. (available at: rts.ch/archives; last accessed: 23 July 2022); see also Gorz, *Traitor*, p. 178.

At Lausanne, Horst also moved advantageously in the milieu of radio, the most important of the French Swiss media in the years after the war. In particular, he frequented the couple Benjamin Romieux and Jane Rosier assiduously.[60] She was an actress with Radio-Théâtre, while he was head of international news at Radio-Lausanne (Sottens), lending it an exceptional documentary dimension. It is likely that this well-known local cultural figure contributed, by the extent of his knowledge in that area, to producing the political analyst Horst can be seen developing into in his articles from 1947 onwards.

Two of Horst's other acquaintances, similarly older than him, also had radio programmes. The journalist Léon Savary, highly respected as a speaker at the Société de belles-lettres, was adept at addressing rebellious youth, exhorting them not to give in to the siren calls of a career. While also awaiting the end of the war to leave for Paris, he lived in Berne, where he was correspondent for the *Tribune de Genève*. One day in the summer of 1944, Pierre Cordey, who had found a place for himself in radio too, asked him to intercede in Horst's favour with the head of the Aliens Directorate of the federal police to end the bureaucratic wrangling over his obtaining a residence permit. It was in an untypically tipsy state that Moulin and Cordey, another member of 'Belles-Lettres', had found a forlorn Gérard around midnight in a hostess nightclub in the Tour Bel-Air,[61] devastated by the receipt of an expulsion order! Savary prevailed after threatening to make an issue of the matter in the press[62] and Horst was granted an 18-month permit.[63]

In *The Traitor*, a bout of meticulous interrogation by police officers over a three-month residence permit is described at some length.[64] The fact is that there is no sympathy in Switzerland for the avoidance of military service. The administration, not understanding the danger Jews, who were not given political refugee status before July 1944, and hence also this half-Jew

---

60 Personal communication, Charles-Henri Favrod, 12 October 2010.

61 The building, which is part of the present-day Bel-Air Métropole complex, was Switzerland's first 'skyscraper' [Trans.].

62 Moulin, ' "Amant américain" à Paris'.

63 Provisional authorization to reside in the canton of Vaud, valid from 31 August 1944 to 28 February 1946 (GRZ, 21.2).

64 Gorz, *Traitor*, pp. 179–82.

would be running—he would soon be stripped of his Greater Reich passport as a draft dodger—saw it as normal and logical that he would return home to do his duty. However, despite militarism being the most widely shared ideological posture in that country where the armed forces were militia-based, it inevitably produced antibodies—to the point where Horst would take his first steps as an activist after the war in anti-militarist, pacifist circles. We shall return to this.

There was another occasion when Horst feared his residence permit might be suspended. During a boat trip on Lake Geneva in the company of Riffel and Alan Stace, Doreen's half-brother who had come to visit, their vessel was seized after cutting across a boat from the Compagnie générale de navigation. Riffel took responsibility for the incident and would subsequently succeed in having an exorbitant fine cancelled.

The other acquaintance whose voice was heard on the Swiss airwaves was the novelist and reporter Alexandre Metaxas, whom Horst had known at the family boarding house. He was the scion of a rich Greek family from Odessa, with whom he had severed all relations. After internment in a camp, he managed to leave France during the war to take up residence at Lausanne. His friends were envious of him because, at the age of 28, he was about to have a first novel published by Gallimard, *Le Nœud coulant* [The slipknot] (*Les Temps modernes* would review it). Though he shared a penchant for the American novel with Horst, he was his opposite in character—exuberant and voluble; they did not become close friends. His wife was Swiss and a most accomplished cook, but he treated her very disrespectfully, leaving her to stand watching guests eat after she had served them a meal. This description by a guest is not reported idly, since it was in fact at a meal at the Metaxas's that Horst, now without a girlfriend and just back from a journey to Italy (he had travelled alone and been bored to death), met the woman who would become the love of his life, Doreen Keir ('Kay' in *The Traitor*).

This young Englishwoman (her Scottish name was not her father's) was born in London 23 years earlier, on 12 April 1924. Having only recently arrived from England and stammering out a reedy-voiced French, she was working as an au pair for the Metaxas family. That evening, saying nothing and standing silently like Mme Metaxas, she impressed and intrigued the three guests who thought they knew the sad story of her past: her husband, a submariner in the British navy, was said to have been reported missing in action during the war.[65] She wasn't yet 20 years old when, in late 1943, she married Victor Henkers, an Englishman her own age, in the London suburbs.[66] She did not live with him, even though, contrary to the suppositions of our informant, we know that he was safe and well. Having re-married in 1950, he would subsequently emigrate to the US.[67]

The divorce was finalized on 23 September 1947. It was a free woman, then, that Gérard began to date a month later, taking her to the Belles-Lettres ball at the celebrated Beau-Rivage Palace (at the dance, he deputed his great friend Riffel to take care of his ex-girlfriend!). Doreen would not like to speak of her past and Gérard, who would employ his own images to reconstitute this very first meeting,[68] was to be silent on these sentimental vicissitudes. In a rough draft of *The Traitor*, in which he admits that by 'geography, upbringing and history', they initially formed an 'improbable' couple, he writes that, 'despite intimacy and habit', they 'each retained their mystery for the other'.[69] Doreen had married very young to escape an adolescence as disturbed as her childhood. Gérard would manage to get her to tell that from the age of four she had lived with her father—known as 'step-father'—whom constant quarrelling had separated from her mother, Elisabeth Coleman. Coleman was officially married to another man, James Keir, an institutionalized First World War invalid. In the twilight of a life lived together, Gérard would write of the childhood experience of loneliness that they shared and express in poignant words of love all that he owed to his partner in his sublime *Letter to D.*, subtitled *Histoire d'un Amour* [Story of a love].

---

65 Interview with Charles-Henri Favrod, though he speaks of a 'fiancé' rather than a husband. The two other guests are Favrod himself and José Bovay, another member of Belles-Lettres.

66 General Register Office, *England and Wales Civil Registration Indexes 1916–2005*, London, Oct.–Dec. 1943.

67 General Register Office, *England and Wales Civil Registration Indexes 1916–2005*, July–Sept. 1950; *US Naturalization Record Indexes, 1791–1992*.

68 See Gorz, *Letter to D.*, pp. 4–6.

69 Unpublished fragment of *The Traitor*, undated (GRZ 1.15).

CHAPTER TWO

The Construction of Self

As soon as he arrived in Lausanne, Horst made systematic efforts to acquire the best possible mastery of the French language. He quickly came to feel the need to write, since he suffered a 'continual craving to express in written words a fundamental silence, an original solitude from which the writer escapes only by the action of writing.'[1] Turning himself into pure mind through writing was, for the moment, his only way of existing: 'The writer's project entails an attitude that resolves an irresolvable situation by making the questioning of the meaning of life the very meaning of life: the writer's life becomes a life lived for questioning, and in that activity anxiety finds its cure.'[2]

Writing, a Saving Neurosis

Keeping a diary—from 1940 to 1946—wasn't enough. In late 1943, he wrote a philosophical study of love, which he called *La Comédie des sentiments ou le Traité des trois bonheurs.*[3] In 1945, he began a novel, entitled *Vie morte*, which he signed with the anagrammatic name Gérard Sorth. It aimed to be a 'description of Despair and the vanity of life which he wanted to make monumental.'[4] The nihilism was acknowledged and summed up as follows in the note he appended in old age to the manuscript he had preserved: 'Fragments of an anti-novel depicting the absurdity of everything, including of the sense of the absurdity of everything.' *The Traitor* also retains a trace of this destructive spirit that turns around against itself: 'if nothing has any importance, then the consciousness that nothing has any importance has

---

1 Gorz, *Traitor*, p. 59.

2 Gérard Horst, 'Kafka et le problème de la transcendance' (1945) in Fourel (ed.), *André Gorz. Un penseur pour le XXIe siècle*, p. 204.

3 GRZ 50.1.

4 Gorz, *Traitor*, p. 207 (translation modified to respect Gorz's capitalization of the word *Désespoir*); André Gorz, 'Vie morte (extraits)', *La Règle du jeu* 45 (January 2011): 167–9.

no importance.'[5] This writing project, which veers off into 'sub-Valéry and sub-*Nausea*'[6] comes to nothing, being swallowed up in the whirl of a tormented thinking.

Between two outbursts about the unjust nature of the world, did Horst never speak on the subject of suicide with his friend Schlunegger, a *poète maudit* and follower of Paul Valéry who was obsessed by his father's decision to take his own life? Haunted by this 'constant thought'—already embedded within *Vie morte*—writing saves Horst, being both a palliative that 'exempts him from living' and, in its creative aspect, a life-supporting act, though it forces the writer into a process of constant self-production.[7] Of this period, the image he will retain will be that of 'a neurotic writer who tried to blot out his existence—the experiences, the emotions, the feelings.'[8]

For one term during the war, Horst went to some lectures at the philosophy faculty. He derived nothing from them: they seemed so 'grotesque' that he publicly mocked the lecturers and never returned.[9] It was as a self-taught student that he increasingly laid the foundations for his philosophical quest. By 1945, he had incorporated Georges Bataille, Leon Chestov, Karl Jaspers and Sartre into his thinking and he began to learn something of Kierkegaard through Jean Wahl's 1938 book *Études kierkegaardiennes*. This reading helped him to prepare a lecture on the underpinnings of Kafka's work, which he delivered not at Belles-Lettres, whose platform was reserved for the older generation, but at the Société des études de lettres.[10] That institution, founded in 1926 and boasting 419 members, was an offshoot of the Arts Faculty of Lausanne University. It organized lecture series with invited speakers—both established scholars and interested amateurs—in the fields of literature, history and philosophy. Some 15 people attended the lecture, including a group of Austrian exiles with whom Horst mixed regularly.

---

5 Gorz, *Traitor*, p. 166.

6 Gorz, *Traitor*, p. 168.

7 Gorz, *Traitor*, pp. 59–60.

8 Letter to Franz Schandl, 1 November 2004, p. 9.

9 André Gorz, 'Oficios del saber y del trabajo', interview by Michel Zlotowski in December 1998, *Clarín* (Buenos Aires) (21 February 1999), supplement.

10 See the brief mention of the lecture in the society's journal: *Études de lettres* 19 (3) (July 1945): 184.

He did not choose the subject at random. He saw his own condition reflected in Kafka, a Moravian Jew (like his father): in Kafka's writings, he said, 'instead of revelatory acts we find an absence of acts; and the most significant of all seems to me to be Silence', which Valéry explains as reflecting his 'distress'.[11] The perspective he adopts is an existentialist—even Sartrean—one, since, as the lecturer sees it, Kafka's narrative symbolism gives free rein to the experience of the absurd by raising the unresolved dilemma of transcendence.

Existentialist Exercises

Towards the end of 1945, freed from his burdensome chemistry studies, Horst embarked on a never-ending essay that would occupy him three hours a night for the whole of his stay in Lausanne. Eight or nine years' effort left him with fifteen hundred pages covered in delicate handwriting. Only in 1977, and then cut down by more than one-third, would the manuscript be published, as *Fondements pour une morale* [Foundations for a morality].

In the beginning, the author's aim was to overcome the nihilism he had himself given into and thus to reject the asocial subjectivism of a Chestov, Nietzsche or Jaspers.[12] Not by denying the agonies that his excluded, lonely condition caused him, but rather by bringing to bear his singularity as 'a universally relevant insight into the human condition'; he had to 'reinvent everything human to justify not his own particular preferences but his refusal of this rotten, alien world.'[13] In a clearly autobiographical page in *Fondements pour une morale*, written in 1946, the figure of the 'rootless individual' prompts consideration of the specific state of consciousness that makes it possible to describe the artificial, conventional character of a world which 'integrated' human beings' experience as natural.[14] There follows a searching examination of all the attitudes that are complicit with this standardized reality, exposing their inauthenticity and their element of bad faith.

---

11 Horst, 'Kafka et le problème de la transcendance', p. 203.

12 See Gérard Horst, 'Qui est Sartre?', *Servir* (31 July 1947), reprinted in Fourel (ed.), *André Gorz. Un penseur pour le XXIe siècle*, p. 236. See also André Gorz, Preface to *Fondements pour une morale*, pp. 14–15.

13 Gorz, *Traitor*, pp. 202, 211.

14 Gorz, *Fondements pour une morale*, p. 463.

The categories developed by Sartre in *Being and Nothingness* would be employed in this gigantic operation of deconstruction. On a first reading, in 1943, Horst did not fully assimilate that work. He had first to gauge how it differed from—and how original it was in relation to—other closely related philosophical approaches, which he set about studying: the work of Heidegger (*What is Metaphysics?*), Husserl, (*Ideas, Cartesian Meditations, The Crisis of European Sciences*),[15] Merleau-Ponty (*Phenomenology of Perception*) and, a little later, Hegel (*The Phenomenology of Spirit*). In this way, he equipped himself to explore the philosophical underpinnings of the Sartrean reflexive method. That method consists in seizing upon the human being at the point where he produces the world before becoming its plaything. This requires, as Husserl puts it, a 'return to the naïveté of life', which is the 'constant ground of validity, an ever-available source of what is taken for granted' ('Thinking only becomes understanding', Gorz will repeat in 1990, 'if the lived relation to what is thought is itself understood in its underlying intentionality. If, on the other hand, thinking excludes any lived relation to its object, then we are speaking of a dogmatic-technical thinking which the subject cannot inhabit, which is inaccessible to self-criticism and potentially anti-human').[16] The author of the 'essay' (as it is called in *The Traitor*) therefore uses Sartre's method to give body to a philosophical project that is 'his own particular adventure'[17]—or, to put it another way, that satisfies the existential choices of the concrete individual at its origin.

This, as Gorz will be most eager to stress late in his life, should in no way be taken to mean that this project—as with any philosophical project centred on the subject—is a rationalization of the existential, psychological situation of its author. However, if it is to be grounded in—and invested with—a universal value, it must start out from a primary, 'irreducible' philosophical experience, which in this particular case is 'the experience of anxiety, *ennui* and contingency.'[18] Philosophy, as he understands it, helps us

---

15 Gérard Horst possessed, and would always use, the, original—though abridged—edition of *Die Krisis* published by Husserl in the Journal *Philosophia* at Belgrade in 1936. He probably came by it from Husserl's last assistant, Eugen Fink, whose address Heidegger gave him in the reply to his letter of 10 April 1946 (Letter from Martin Heidegger to Gérard Horst, 3 May 1946 [GRZ]).

16 Gorz, 'La vie, la nature, la technique', p. 21.

17 Gorz, *Fondements pour une morale*, p. 508.

18 André Gorz, 'Lettre à François George', *Les Temps modernes* 632-4 (July–October 2005): 59.

to live, in the sense that it asks the *vital questions* of the individual. 'It seems to me,' adds Gorz in this same connection, 'that the meaning of my life, the very possibility of living, depended on these questions.'[19] Philosophy plays a part in one's self-creation. In 1983, this conception, which underpins his entire existence as an involved writer [*écrivain impliqué*], was lent a definitive formulation:

> Here, the question of alienation and whether it is possible to overcome it arises. For me, philosophy is not Hegel or those great creators of philosophical systems, but the attempt to understand, to discover oneself and what one is, to take control of, liberate and create oneself.'[20]

This individual we have seen placed in the position of privileged observer is depicted, then, in *The Traitor* as a 'man confined in an alien and hostile world',[21] faced, in formal terms, with three possible ways out. The elaboration and axiological ranking of these three possibilities in fact lend *Fondements pour une morale* its structure—after a first, preliminary section which the author sets aside to ground his own phenomenology of freedom ontologically:[22]

1. *Vital Attitude.* It is possible to escape one's original condition by attempting to placate the imprisoning order by conforming to its demands, even at the price of disadaptation from oneself. The best way to do this is to allow oneself to give in to habit. Another way is to allow oneself to be 'haunted' by the values of power, wealth or security. This is not so much a 'sovereign choice' as a 'choice by default', which the unhappy consciousness of the rootless individual excludes from the outset.

2. *Aesthetic Attitude.* It is also possible to be resigned to one's fate by an escape into daydreaming. Not being able to live in the real world, you create an imaginary world and live in it.

---

19 André Gorz, 'Authenticité et valeur dans la première philosophie de Sartre', *Les Temps modernes* 632–4 (July–October 2005): 627.

20 Gorz, 'Afterword: A Discussion with André Gorz on Alienation, Freedom, Utopia and Himself', p. 274.

21 Gorz, *Traitor*, p. 147.

22 For a summing up, see *The Traitor*, p. 147 and *Fondements pour une morale*, pp. 127–38 and 504–08.

3. *Moral Attitude.* It is possible, lastly, to work at one's escape by choosing to construct the conditions of one's autonomy and liberation. In this case, we shall speak of 'moral conversion'.

The first and second attitudes have something of the nature of an alienation that cannot protect one from—at best, latent or muted—suffering, because they involve an inevitable measure of inauthenticity. Only the third attitude, presented in a final section entitled 'The Choice of Freedom', is acceptable. It is towards this we should strive because, by giving an ethical foundation to the necessary revolt against social alienation, it opens a path to human authenticity and, hence, to human freedom. The fact remains, however, that between oneself and freedom there is always a gap created by upbringing and culture, and it is therefore virtually impossible ever to register an absolute moral victory over the given.

Let us note here that a fourth possibility, advocated by Marxism, is not envisaged: the possibility of changing the world. However, as early as his first published book, Gorz will endorse this: 'Man is impossible in this world of ours, therefore it is this world which must be changed; imperatively.'[23] Let us note too, as Gorz himself does, that this pursuit centred on a ranking of values implying a disapproval of moral relativism isn't something Gorz takes from Sartre's *Being and Nothingness*—which comes to no great conclusions on this point—though it is echoed to some extent by Simone de Beauvoir (*Pour une morale de l'ambiguïté*, 1947) and Francis Jeanson (*Le problème moral et la pensée de Sartre*, 1947).[24] Gorz omits to mention, however, that between 1946 and 1948 Sartre also embarked on a series of reflections on morality, which he showed to his disciple in 1949 as a 2,000-page manuscript.[25] Hence, perhaps, the 'affinities' detected between Sartre's posthumously published *Cahiers pour une morale* and some of the analyses of alienation, freedom and moral conversion in *Fondements*.[26]

---

23 Gorz, *Traitor*, p. 51.
24 Gorz, Preface to *Fondements pour une morale*, p. 16 n.
25 Related by Gérard Horst in his letter to Walter Riffel, 7 July [1949] (GRZ).
26 See Arno Münster, *Sartre et la morale* (Paris: L'Harmattan, 2007), pp. 50–1.

First Thoughts on Work

André Gorz's philosophical choices, centred on the subject, led him from the outset to give consideration to questions relating to work. They would come to have a preponderant place in his writings.

Serious Work

Of all the life attitudes that undergo an existential critique in *Fondements*, there is one that will provide André Gorz with the starting point for his thinking on work. This is the trade or profession one chooses in order to enter the world of work.[27] It may happen, as in the typical example of the profession of engineer, described in opposition to artistic professions, that one makes a choice in order to be-in-the-world rather than to be oneself. With the result that, if it so happens that pleasure is the only motivation for the work one undertakes, one plays fast and loose with the 'seriousness' of a profession, which consists in maintaining a technical relation of effectiveness with the laws and the order of the universe. The only freedom this serious work offers is technical freedom, which is circumscribed in its relation of dependency on the world. That dependency has its apparent advantages: it provides security, protects one from oneself and frees one from one's own 'terrible "subjectivity"'. But this is a 'drowning in the objective', an 'abdication of self' and an abnegation of existing for oneself.

This conception of 'serious work', which is in fact no more than sketched out in *Fondements*,[28] is a reference to what Sartre calls 'the spirit of seriousness'. To elucidate the point, we may take Sartre's definition as it applies to 'values' and adapt it to the object that is 'work': 'The spirit of seriousness', he writes in *Being and Nothingness*, 'has two characteristics: it considers [. . .] [work] [. . .] as a transcendent given independent of human subjectivity and it transfers the quality of "desirable" from the ontological structure of [. . .] [work] [. . .] to its simple material constitution.'[29] What then, in counterpoint, is this original form of work that is shot through with subjectivity and fundamentally desirable?

---

27 Gorz, *Fondements pour une morale*, pp. 70–1.

28 It is, however, important to Gorz himself, who in 2005 republishes the relevant few pages. Gorz, 'Authenticité et valeur', pp. 629–35.

29 For the original definition, see Jean-Paul Sartre, *Being and Nothingness* (London: Methuen Publishing, 1958), p. 626.

The First Sense of Work

In an article in *Servir* in August 1947, Horst raises the question overtly:

> Originally, a man does not work to earn money or to sell his prod-
> uct. He works because life is work and you only realize yourself by
> making something which expresses you and in which you are rec-
> ognized. Of course, even the painter sells his canvases and the
> writer his books. But he does not create them to sell. It is creation
> that is endless. It is life, insofar as it is realized in that creation, that
> is the end for man.[30]

In this ideal vision of work, the artistic professions serve as a model, but
they are not the only ones under consideration: 'It is life again that the peasant conquers by cultivating the fields. It is future life he is sowing when he
seeds the land and reaps the harvest. [. . .] Like any free producer, he is
interdependent with the society for which he produces, and the society feels
interdependent with him.'[31]

There follows, by contrast, a description of the degradation of work under
Taylorism. The repetition and fragmentation of actions, the impenetrable
nature of ultimate goals, occupations that have not been freely chosen, the
interchangeability of workstations—everything conspires to make the
worker lose the meaning of what he is doing.

'Inward Unemployment'

The working man may, then, be shorn of his subjectivity. This finding is
made in a review Horst wrote a year later of a work by the young Genevan
sociologist Roger Girod, soon to be a fellow writer on *Servir*, which prefig-
ures the literature on the leisure society.[32] The contemporary malaise is
identified with an abeyance of the inclination and need to *do/make* things.
For man is what he does/makes.

---

30 Gérard Horst, 'Du libéralisme au communisme. Faire et avoir', *Servir* (14 August
1947).

31 Horst, 'Du libéralisme au communisme'.

32 G. H., '*Gagner son temps* par Roger Philippe', *Servir* (26 August 1948). Roger Philippe
was a pseudonym.

Engaged in mere drudgery or shackled to a production line, man cannot make himself. Work no longer offers any of those 'indeterminacies' that enable the worker to bring his 'creative freedom' to bear and to dominate the productive process rather than be its mere instrument. This is why we may describe the worker, as Girod does, as 'inwardly unemployed'. If he does not simply wither away, he longs to occupy his mind, left vacant by his work. Some seem to find a new *raison d'être* in sport, but Horst's preference runs in a different direction, expounded by the author: syndical activity, which could become genuinely essential and relegate mechanical work to the status of a distraction.

The Meeting with Sartre

While touring Switzerland with Simone de Beauvoir to deliver a series of lectures, Jean-Paul Sartre made an appearance at Lausanne's Capitole cinema on Saturday 1 June 1946. A young specialist in Sartrean existentialism in the auditorium could scarcely contain his admiration. The lecture had been announced seven months before.[33] There was feverish excitement around it and a great many people were curious to attend; the eventual audience numbered a thousand. Since the sensational Paris lecture 'Existentialism is a Humanism' of 29 October 1945 and the publication of that text at Geneva by the Nagel publishing house, there had been a lively debate on existentialism in the Swiss–French press.[34] The subject was very much in vogue. It was also fiercely controversial, so seriously did it seem to challenge both the religious and political conformism of the 'right-thinking'. However, stigmatizations of existentialism generally went hand in hand with an ignorance of Sartre's categories, leading to misconceived condemnations. Other voices, such as that of the Genevan philosopher Jeanne Hersch, a student and follower of Karl Jaspers, helped to promote an understanding of this new version of existentialism, receiving a particular welcome in *Servir*, the left-wing Lausanne magazine edited by Lucien de Dardel, who was himself attracted by Sartre's ideas and had already been to Geneva to hear him speak the previous week.

It was at the initiative of the local Poetry Society that 'the pope of existentialism' was brought to Lausanne. Founded in 1944 by Edmond Jaloux,

---

33 Without an exact date being set. See *Gazette de Lausanne* (26 October 1945).
34 See Fornerod, *Lausanne, le temps des audaces*, pp. 49–51.

a literary critic and French academician who had retired to the canton of Vaud, that society could hardly be seen as a left-wing conclave, thus proving that interest in Sartre's orations could also be a matter of open-minded curiosity. The society was at pains to invite Horst to the private drinks reception with Sartre that was planned to follow the lecture that evening, so as to show their guest that scholars at Lausanne were fully acquainted with his work. For two or three hours, the young man monopolized the discussion with the master. The author of *The Traitor* traces the difference in their existential attitudes to their very bodies: Morel (alias Sartre) occupies the space around him 'with his voluminous gestures', whereas *he* describes himself as having 'the gait of a fowl and parsimonious gestures, as if he were trying to contain his being within himself.'[35] In his first article on Sartre, he wrote:

> This first contact inspires confidence; you want to enter into this full world [of his] and it isn't too difficult to do so. For Sartre doesn't dismiss any question lightly, puts you at your ease and makes you want to spend hours discussing the topic you've just raised. [. . .] He doesn't thrust some theory on you from the outset, but tries to understand your position; it is quite possible he will do this better than you do.[36]

Horst would later note that 'he wasn't like the image a reader might form of him. He was lively, friendly, attentive. He was interested in everything and didn't take himself seriously. An ideal interlocutor.'[37] He absolutely wanted to see Sartre again. He also had questions for de Beauvoir and wrote to her. He went to Geneva the following Thursday, unaware that the lecturer was then away in Berne and thereby also missed meeting de Beauvoir who was giving a talk at Lausanne on that day.[38] Three days later, on Sunday 9 June, as the couple were preparing to travel back to France, he managed to obtain a half-hour interview with them in a Geneva café. The discussion

---

35 Gorz, *Traitor*, pp. 214–15, 67 [translation modified]. Gorz has some difficulty shaking off this fowl-like posture, as we can see from a film shot in the countryside around Vosnon in 1990 to accompany an interview by Marian Handwerker: only now the old man, puny as ever, is running through the open fields stretching out his long arms in an imaginary soaring to freedom.

36 Horst, 'Qui est Sartre?', p. 234.

37 Gorz, 'La vie, la nature, la technique', p. 28.

38 See letter of Marie Brindel to Gérard Horst, 6 June 1946 (GRZ).

hit a snag over the question of involvement [*implication*]: 'But even if the world were unjustifiable as you keep repeating, you have to make a choice,' Sartre told him.[39]

The disciple is impressed by the philosopher's relation to the concrete, by his ability to live fully and serenely in a world he cannot reject. These are all things he himself lacks. The interviews with Sartre have their effect. Horst seems to stop wallowing in his unhappy isolation. He wants to find happiness by opening up to himself and to a full awareness of the world he inhabits. This is what comes out of the first text on Sartre which he publishes in July 1947 in *Servir*, more than a year after their meeting, but only two months after beginning to write for that weekly.

In that long article, the budding Sartrean applies himself to refuting the hackneyed idea that existentialist philosophy is a doctrine of anguish and despair. After enlisting Hegel, Marx and Kierkegaard among the ranks of existentialist philosophers because they take human lived experience on board in its dynamic totality, he asserts that when existentialism speaks, with Hegel, of unhappy consciousness, loneliness and a lack of meaning for every individual, it is not a call for resignation. On the contrary, it is a call to freedom in a ceaseless search to move 'beyond the particular to the universal, beyond solitude to communication, beyond absurdity to meaning. [. . .] Anxiety, about which so much nonsense has been written, is simply this demand of freedom desiring itself; the awareness that every decision is a risk.'[40] Horst no longer indulges in the 'permanent disenchantment with Man', of which he accuses Albert Camus;[41] *The Outsider* (1946 [1942]) and *The Rebel* (1956 [1951]),[42] which typify this misanthropy, will not be references for the future author of *The Traitor*.

In another *Servir* article, written nine months later in April 1948, which is a riposte to the magazine's editor-in-chief, himself a Vaudois evangelical who saw echoes of Kierkegaard's Christian existentialism in Sartre's atheism, Horst prefers to set aside the Danish philosopher's 'mysticism' and stress

---

39 Gorz, *Traitor*, pp. 215–61.

40 Horst, 'Qui est Sartre?', pp. 236–7.

41 Gérard Horst, '*La Peste* d'Albert Camus', *Servir* (17 July 1947).

42 All dates enclosed within square parentheses that follow the titles of translated works refer to the date of the original-language publication rather than the publication date of the translated work.

that, if one must look for a God in existentialism, the reference has to be to Hegel's *Phenomenology of Spirit*. Like Man who, in Sartre's writings, has to *make himself*, Hegel's God, which takes the form of Spirit, 'must be revealed, must become manifest, must become the meaning of our acts and projects.' Hence, concludes Horst, in a surprising association of ideas, this perpetual construction of the human order in existentialism reminds us, all political views apart, of 'the Trotskyist formula of "permanent revolution" '.[43] To make such an allusion really was to speak freely in the Lausanne of the 'socialo-Stalinist bloc'.

Theatre was highly regarded at the Société des Belles-Lettres and performances were high points of its activity. For the annual event of 1948, one of Sartre's minor plays was chosen, *Les Faux nez*, the script having been published by the *Revue du cinéma* the year before.[44] The troupe of actors, formed under the direction of Charles Apothéloz, was made up of Horst's usual acquaintances among the students, though it also included his own partner Doreen, who made some friends among that group. After a first staging at Lausanne in November, which Horst diligently announced in *Servir*, pointing up the existentialist aspects,[45] the troupe formed themselves into the Compagnie des Faux-Nez and gave two further performances in which Doreen figured, though eventually she pulled out of the company since, in reality (and as other actors admitted), her deficient command of French robbed her performance of credibility.[46]

The next stage was participation in the Concours de jeunes compagnies (Young Companies' Competition) held at Paris in the early summer of 1949. The arrangements were done well: the programme, with original drawings by Cocteau and Picasso, contained a foreword of a philosophical nature and an afterword on the 'authentic' mode of life of the actors (in other words, a roaming, Bohemian existence). Horst took care of the foreword, polishing up the text he had published in *Servir*. The storyline of the play—which Sartre told Favrod, who came to ask his permission to stage

---

43 G. H., 'Sartre contre le chrétien?', *Servir* (29 April 1948). Lucien Dardel had written an article with the same title in the previous issue of 22 April.

44 Fornerod, *Lausanne, le temps des audaces*, pp. 181–4; Apothéloz, *Cris et écrits*, pp. 259–60.

45 G. H., 'Une première de Sartre à Lausanne', *Servir* (25 November 1948).

46 Author interviews with Freddy Buache, 11 October 2010, and Charles-Henri Favrod, 12 October 2010.

it, was 'unstageable'[47]—fitted perfectly with the existentialist theme, which presented human beings as functions of their 'mirrors': the courtiers wore false noses because the prince had a huge nose. For Apoth', Buache—who played the prince—and Horst, the three most Sartrean and politicized members of the group, the aim, through an earthy staging of the play, was to expose the hypocritical conventions and lies of society. 'The prince is you,' explains Horst. 'Perhaps you have grasped, as he has, that you had made a persona and beliefs for yourself on the basis of others' beliefs, that public opinion is merely the outcome of each person's belief, who believes that he is a particular way because all the others believe he believes he is that way!'[48] The play was performed at the Théâtre de l'Atelier on 22 and 23 June 1949 and the slick production won the prize for best direction. It is not certain, however, that the three cronies' demystifying intentions came over clearly to everyone, one snob in the audience being heard to mutter smugly that Surrealism was vastly more revolutionary . . . [49]

One important episode did unfold on the margins of these theatrical activities. Sartre didn't attend the performances, but Buache was able to visit him and spoke about the man Sartre had met in Lausanne, telling him Horst was eagerly looking for work in Paris and hoped to go and live there. Sartre remembered Horst clearly and agreed to facilitate this.[50] As a result, Horst was employed helping Marcel Duhamel translate thrillers for Gallimard/nrf's 'Série noire'. Though decently paid, the job would, however, provide him with only six weeks' work.

Gérard Horst and Doreen Keir, who had accompanied the actors, now found a place to live in Paris. A French friend, Cécile Béchaux, who was the daughter of a rich Tunisian settler and worked in a Lausanne publishing house (she would shortly afterwards open the Clairefontaine bookshop in Tunis), rented them her attic—with running water and a squatting toilet— under the eaves on the fifth floor at 74 rue des Saints-Pères.[51] With their cat

---

47 Above mentioned interview with Charles-Henri Favrod. He was at the time president of the Société des Belles-Lettres.

48 [Gérard Horst,] Preface to the Compagnie des Faux nez programme. Cited in Buache, *Derrière l'écran*, p. 62.

49 J.-P. M. [Jean-Pierre Moulin], 'Les Faux-nez à Paris', *Gazette littéraire* (supplement to the *Gazette de Lausanne*) (2 July 1949).

50 Author's interview with Freddy Buache.

51 Just off the rue de Sèvres in the Saint-Germain district [Trans.].

(the couple would always have cats!), they would keep it for three years. We shall see that, by working in an activist organization—Citoyens du Monde (the World Citizens movement)—Horst would find a more lasting financial solution than he had with Duhamel, and this would enable the couple to settle in France.

CHAPTER THREE

The Third Force

The introduction to 'Belles-Lettres' and the meeting with Sartre were crucial stages on the path that led Horst from nihilistic egotism to an opening-up to others. Exposure to certain realities through journalism marked a further, supplementary stage on that path.

The Budding Journalist

It was by chance that, one day in May 1947, Lucien de Dardel, the editor of *Servir* asked Gérard Horst to react to a news story which, it seemed, ought to concern him: the emigration to Palestine of Jews who had survived the concentration camps. He would continue to work for the magazine on a freelance basis until it ceased operation in January 1949. By that time, he would have written some 50 articles signed in his own name or with the initials G. H. or H.

At the Left-Wing Weekly Servir

Servir, launched in September 1944 at Lausanne, was a remarkable weekly of the non-Marxist intellectual Left, whose influence reached into all parts of French-speaking Switzerland. It was organized on a cooperative basis, the cooperative model having considerable traction in the country at the time, and aimed to extend its readership in trade union circles. It was not attached to any party and, though it decried Soviet policy, it was not actively anti-Communist. With an allegiance to democratic and cooperative socialism, as well as to a humanism that drew on Emmanuel Mounier and, to an even greater extent, on Sartre, the magazine's editor, a practising Protestant, deliberately positioned the publication as a third force that was neither capitalist nor Communist. With one exception, Horst's contributions conformed to the line of the magazine.

It is easy to understand why one of Horst's earliest articles, which covered the June 1947 strikes in France after the Communists had left the government, was not published by *Servir* but by the liberal *Gazette de Lausanne*. Quite anti-Communist in its tenor, the article was equally critical of the excesses of the strikers who enjoyed both Socialist and Christian support. The reasons given related to the strikers' economically unrealistic demands, given the underproductive state of the national economy.[1] It would not be the only occasion when Horst showed himself an economic realist . . .

In *Servir*, Horst held forth on literature (Camus, Malraux), cinema (Chaplin) or theatre (Sartre) and commented on current international political affairs. At times he was able to play the special correspondent, as at the Rencontres internationales de Genève in September 1947, where Personalists (Emmanuel Mounier and Nikolai Berdyaev) and Communists discussed humanism, Marxism and technical and moral progress. He also took advantage of a stay in Vienna—where, not having seen his family for eight years, he spent a month and a half with them at year's end in 1947—to deliver a striking report on the wrecked and occupied post-war city and to reflect on the banal everyday reality of Austrian collaboration with the Nazis.[2]

From Horst's—often intermingled—political and economic analyses, there emerges quite a personal picture of the state and balance of the world in the aftermath of war. The characterization of the two great powers, the USSR and US, stands out, but the attention paid to the situation in Palestine is also worthy of mention. The initial approach to the Jewish question is to point out that Hitler's persecutions had made an unprecedented contribution to the formation of a self-conscious Jewish community,[3] a point reminiscent of the Sartrean image of the Jew as someone who is only as he is because of the other's gaze (*Anti-Semite and Jew* [1946]).

If the Jews had a legitimate claim to land in Palestine—Horst left aside the colonial dimension[4]—that claim was necessarily expansionist, as the territory allocated to them was insufficient.[5] Yet, everything suggested that

---

1 See Gérard Horst, 'Opinions. Dessous de grève', *Gazette de Lausanne* (28 June 1947).

2 Gérard Horst, 'Vienne. Février 1948', *Servir* (19 February 1948); 'Problèmes autrichiens, problèmes universels', *Servir* (25 March 1948).

3 Gérard Horst, 'Le problème juif', *Servir* (29 May 1947).

4 On this question, see Yaël Dagan, 'Les mots du sionisme. Retour aux sources', *Mil neuf cent. Revue d'histoire intellectuelle* 27 (2009): 133–46.

5 Gérard Horst, 'L'enjeu palestinien', *Servir* (13 May 1948).

the expansion would be peaceful and would take place under the banner of social revolution, led by the 'Communist communities' (*kibbutzim*) of which Horst had heard idyllic accounts. Consequently, he interpreted the war between Jews and the Arab states of May 1948 as a phase in the class struggle.[6] The conflict between Jews and Palestinians, punctuated by acts of ethnic cleansing, was swept under the carpet, the Palestinian national cause being as yet embryonic. Horst would not return to these questions;[7] he left such matters to Sartre, from whom *Servir* would take a pro-Jewish article published in France in Jean Daniel's monthly *Caliban*.[8] In reality, the national question, wherever it arose, would never really concern him, except in the context of anti-imperialism or, as in the case of divided Germany, if it turned into anti-Soviet national consciousness.

The Soviets' Paradox and the Americans' Fetish

Horst ascribed the division of Europe, which began in early summer 1947, to the Soviet Union. If the USSR excluded its satellites from receiving American aid, in order to keep its hands on those countries' resources, that was because it was prey to an innate paradox. That backward country had carried through a revolution, but, unable to overcome its backwardness, it continued to favour economic considerations while drifting towards ugly dictatorship.[9] Not that the material imperative wasn't justified. It could even be said to be the order of the day throughout Europe: the state of crisis the continent had been in since the war meant the population's need could not be met and economic *dirigisme* was necessary, even if that meant sacrificing an element of democracy to it.[10] Hence Horst's above-mentioned condemnation of wage demands in France.

As for the United States, it was nonetheless guided by its economic objective of finding an outlet in Europe for its over-production. The generosity of the Marshall Plan went hand in glove with imperialism and had

---

6 Gérard Horst, 'Une nouvelle face de la guerre palestinienne', *Servir* (20 May 1948).

7 Except on the occasion of the Sabra and Chatila massacres in September 1982; see below, p. 228)

8 Jean-Paul Sartre, 'C'est pour tous que sonne le glas', *Servir* (24 June 1948); reprinted in *Situations*, VOL. 3 (Paris: Gallimard, 2013; new revised and augmented edition).

9 Gérard Horst, 'Le paradoxe soviétique', *Servir* (10 July 1947).

10 G. H., 'Les nouvelles maladies de la démocratie', *Servir* (6 November 1947).

echoes of the ambivalence of *potlatch*.[11] The system governing that prosperous country, emblematic of liberalism in general, consisted in eroding the anthropological meaning of work so that the worker's only goal was pay and the boss's only aim was profit. As he learned from the Marxist economist Jean Domarchi,[12] who in Gilles Martinet and Pierre Naville's *Revue internationale* combined value theory and phenomenology,[13] *money* was at the heart of this system: it was the 'supreme value', the 'fetish' that the proletariat chased after as it embourgeoised itself, and which capitalists and the middle classes wished to accumulate, so as not to have to work anymore.

By equating this spirit of capitalization with a 'mystique of saving', Horst denounced the selfish aspiration of the rentier to one day reach the stage 'where it [would] be possible to consume without producing and peacefully enjoy exquisite idleness in a subjugated world.'[14] We can see here that this young autodidact, not fully conversant with the mechanism of capital's reproduction but already identifying the underlying consumerist incentive, had put his finger on what, almost 50 years earlier, theorist of the leisure class Thorstein Veblen had dubbed America's 'pecuniary culture'.

Activist at 'Citoyens du Monde'

Because of Hiroshima, the return to peace in 1945 failed to put an end to the collective angst. In fact, it triggered a new form of war psychosis that would simply grow and grow. 'That is why we need fearless words [. . .]. And we shall divert the course of despair,' proclaimed his poet friend Schlunegger (in 'Plus jamais Hiroshima' [Never again Hiroshima]). To the threat of the nuclear destruction of humanity, the Cold War added the division of the world into two blocs, lending plausibility to a potentially apocalyptic Third World War. Writing in the January 1947 issue of *Esprit*, Emmanuel Mounier described the times as 'a warlike, atomic, crematory, concentrationary age' and, in his *1984*, penned in 1948, Orwell imagined a total dictatorship arising out of a nuclear cataclysm. Horst registered this

---

11 G. H., 'Que veut l'Amérique?', *Servir* (2 October 1947). Horst has read Georges Bataille who sees *potlatch* as a gift that obliges the recipient to make a larger counter-gift.

12 Gorz, *Traitor*, p. 218.

13 Jean Domarchi, 'Théorie de la valeur et phénoménologie', *Revue internationale* 2 (January–February 1946).

14 Horst, 'Du libéralisme au communisme'.

escalation of global dangers in his own way. He condemned the diversion of Marshall Plan funds into European rearmament and the increasing military aggression of the US, going so far as to say that he favoured—out of provocation or fierce anti-Americanism?—the USSR acquiring its own atom bomb to calm the whole situation: with death now in its own hands, humanity would perhaps prefer humaneness to the reign of power.[15]

It was through reading *Les Temps modernes* in October 1948 that Horst became aware of the positions of the Rassemblement démocratique révolutionnaire (RDR), which he would fully adopt as his own. That party, created in France in the February by Sartre and David Rousset and already faltering by the end of the year, positioned itself as a *third force*, though it was distinct from the anti-Gaullist and anti-Communist parliamentary party of that name (*Troisième Force*), being distinguished from it by its neutralism towards the two blocs of East and West. In terms of social policy, it advocated a middle way between capitalism and Stalinism. 'The only chance for Europe and peace,' argued Horst, 'is for us to make ourselves politically independent' of the two great powers; 'Socialist Europe can cease to trouble the United States if we stop taking Russian anti-capitalism for socialism and learn to see Soviet society as a broken socialism diverted from its initial goals and not likely to get back to them on the strength of historical inevitability alone.'[16]

The RDR's choices chimed with Horst's political sensibility, but this had no practical consequences where he was concerned. It was in the footsteps of another neutralist third-force movement that he was persuaded to walk. This was not to be the European federalists whom he encountered at Montreux when sent there as special correspondent in August 1947: he faulted them on regarding the USSR as an obstacle and yet overlooking the failings of the West, particularly its colonialism.[17] His preference went, rather, to the 'Mundialists', who wound up their first international congress at Montreux on 24 August three days before the Europeanists opened theirs, though Horst passed no comment on them at the time.

---

15 G. H., 'Arrière-plan Marshall', *Servir* (10 June 1948); G. H., 'Préparatifs d'invasion', *Servir* (21 October 1948), Gérard Horst, 'Vaincre la Russie par la persuasion?', *Servir* (30 September 1948).

16 G. H., 'La défense de l'Europe se passe de canons', *Servir* (14 October 1948).

17 Gérard Horst, 'Pour une Europe fédéraliste, mais comment ?', *Servir* (4 September 1947).

The 'Mundialists' formed a heterogeneous movement that remained divided over the very notion of world government and the steps to be taken to achieve it.[18] At Montreux, the adherents of the—heavily Anglo-Saxon—Universal Movement for a Global Confederation (UMGC) took the view, in a federalist perspective, that the way to maintain a peace that seemed threatened by antagonisms between nation-states was to move quickly to convene a World Constituent Assembly that would transform the United Nations Organization (UNO) into a confederation with enhanced powers and authority. Another tendency, present in France, advocated the creation of a Peoples' Constituent Assembly that would establish a unitary government for the world that went way beyond federal governance by states. Beyond the divergences, the Mundialist movement managed to move itself centre stage by dint of the individual initiative of a pragmatic, resolute American.

Garry Davis, a former bomber pilot won over to the peace plans of Albert Einstein and Bertrand Russell (*One World or None*), surrendered his passport and declared himself a citizen of the world. Then, in order to avoid expulsion from France, he encamped on the steps of the Palais de Chaillot on 12 September 1948, taking advantage of the international status of the site that housed the UN Assembly. Davis, then aged 28, hit the headlines for quite a period, while at the same time attracting all kinds of activists who wished to recruit him to their various causes. The French Mundialists, led by Robert Sarrazac,[19] a serviceman and former resistance fighter at the head of *maquis-écoles*, emerged as the most prominent among these and pulled off a new media coup alongside Davis in November, when they interrupted the proceedings of the UN Assembly. Public meetings ensued, on 3 December at the Salle Pleyel and 9 December at the Vél d'Hiv before an audience of 20,000.

There was prestigious support, comparable (at times the names were identical) to the support the intellectuals' RDR received: others to speak, apart from Davis, were Jean Paulhan, abbé Pierre, Mounier, Vercors, Bourdet, Rousset, Breton and Camus (the last four were also at the Salle Pleyel on the 13th for the RDR meeting). An agreement of 25 December with Claude Bourdet, the director of *Combat*, saw the launch of a double-sided insert

---

18 Rolf Paul Haegler, *Histoire et idéologie du mondialisme* (Zurich: Europa Verlag, 1972).

19 See Nicolas Barret, 'Les Citoyens du Monde, 1948–1951', MA thesis, University Paris I, 1992.

in that newspaper entitled *Peuple du monde*. Edited by Sarrazac, it served as the official French organ of Citoyens du Monde [World Citizens] (CDM), the organization that arose out of the movement that formed around Davis. Above and beyond the expected contributors (such as the British Labour MP Henry Usborne and the abbé Pierre, both members of the UMGC), the prestigious ones (Thomas Mann) or those of anecdotal interest (Jean Daniel), we should perhaps mention the unusual plea for peace made by Jacques Duboin in the issue of 5 March 1949, which argued for an 'abundancist' economy.[20]

It is worth noting that at that same moment, on 23 December 1948, *Servir* also began to run a page in the magazine entitled 'Tribune de la paix' [Platform for Peace] in support of Davis. In addition to the extracts from French articles that appeared there, there were also original contributions, including articles signed by Metaxas, who covered the mass meeting at the Vél d'Hiv, Buache, René Bovard, whom we shall discuss below, and Horst. The latter's article was clearly in tune with the peace plan, but it raised a thorny issue by asking, 'Does Garry Davis's action have a political coloration?' The answer was to be found in the aversion that the first 'world citizen' provoked among the 'enemies of the people', whom he referred to as follows:

> In every country there are functionaries, racketeers, military cliques, industrialists or corporations whose particular interests stand opposed to the interests of the majority. And in every country it is this minority that centralizes power in its hands, subverts the normal operation of institutions and substitutes a will and logic of state for the will and common sense of the people.[21]

On 20 January 1949 *Servir* suddenly ceased publication. Financial reasons were cited. The decision came after behind-the-scenes negotiations had broken down with the trade unions, which declined to take a share in the enterprise. It was a harsh blow for everyone. Davis's cause lost its Swiss–French platform and Horst his income. A meeting with a pro-Davis activist would enable him to bounce back.

---

20 On Jean Daniel, see chapter 8. We shall speak of the theoretical affinities between Gorz and Jacques Duboin in chapter 15.

21 Gérard Horst, 'L'action de Garry Davis a-t-elle une couleur politique?', *Servir* (20 January 1949).

The Case for Conscientious Objection

As editor of an important journal of social affairs, *Suisse contemporaine*, René Bovard was in contact with a pro-Davis group that emerged at Geneva in April 1949. He could also count on an even more active, like-minded group which, on the initiative of the Dardels and Horst, had already been formed at Lausanne, where Davis went to speak to the People's Cooperatives Festival on 3 July.[22] At that time, Horst—who, with Doreen, was selling the *Peuple du monde* on street corners—was again seeing Bovard, whom he had run into at the *Rencontres internationales* of 1947. Bovard, a Gandhian pacifist and conscientious objector, was sentenced to three months in prison in 1947. He was also a Quaker. This affiliation facilitated his contact with Davis, who was himself taken in by Quakers after being removed from his protest camp by the police. Bovard got on well with the American activist and this led him to begin procedures that would lead to Davis potentially being allowed to settle in Switzerland.[23] The relationship became firmer at the time of the trial, on 6 May 1949, of the French conscientious objector Jean-Bernard Moreau, to whose cause Davis lent his support. *Peuple du monde* printed two articles in favour of conscientious objection by the 'Swiss' writers Bovard and Horst, the latter devoted to exposing the inner workings of the trial.[24]

Horst's interest in this issue was not accidental. At the same point, Apothéloz was preparing to defend himself in a second conscientious objection trial. With his friend Buache, he ate his meals at Gérard and Doreen's flat, where they discussed Sartre's rejection of 'seriousness', the refusal to play the game of the bourgeois states that 'oppressed' proletarians and hence the refusal to serve in the armed forces, but also proletarian violence against those *salauds*, the 'bourgeois'.[25] It has to be said that, from Lucien de Dardel

22 See Garry Davis's letter to Isabelle de Dardel and Gérard Horst of 4 April 1949 (GRZ). The group formed officially on 20 June 1949 (Lucien de Dardel, *Gazette de Lausanne* [12 September 1949]).

23 René Bovard to Gérard Horst, 12 August 1949 (CENAC, Bibliothèque de la Chaux-de-Fonds).

24 René Bovard, 'Situation de l'objecteur de conscience dans le monde', *Peuple du monde* (21 May 1949); G. H., 'Un Citoyen du Monde en prison: Jean-Bernard Moreau', *Peuple du monde* (21 May 1949).

25 See extracts from the long *mémoire* submitted to the judges in Charles Apothéloz, 'Idéologie et mystification', pp. 145–62. With its acerbic description of the Swiss and their boring comfort, this text seems to foreshadow the themes of *The Traitor*.

to Horst, neither non-violence nor the 'contemplative quietism' of Gandhi's disciples[26] found favour with the Lausanne pacifists, despite their 'strange audiences'[27] made up of Catholics, Protestants, Quakers etc. Non-violence, a moral absolute that exists only through its opposite which comes to serve as its foil, was even a source of irritation that would stay with Horst throughout his life, as he remembered some of his Swiss acquaintances.[28] He would, however, continue to defend conscientious objection, which he saw as an act of rebellion.[29]

At Citoyens du Monde (CDM), the pacifist attitude to conscientious objection was not supported unanimously. It has to be said that the idea of a World Security Force, raised initially by the conscientious objector Moreau, which justified the interest the CDM showed in it, had been dropped, both during his trial and by his supporters. This was too much for the Sarrazac group, which feared a political and anti-militarist deviation from the original supra-national objective. The dissension led Davis to take a back seat in mid-July 1949. For all that, the pacifists, whom Sarrazac had had in his sights for some time, were not removed from leading roles, since Bovard became the CDM's international secretary at a meeting organized at Paris on 14–15 May 1949. Being unable to take up residence in the French capital while the internal crisis was at its height, Bovard asked Horst to become his right-hand man with the French secretariat. Horst was already in Paris since, on 22 June, two days after the public meeting officially establishing the Lausanne CDM, he had gone there with the Faux-Nez troupe and had not left. During July, Horst took up the post, which was a paid role, but did not declare his income to the authorities.

World Citizenship: A Social Myth

Quite apart from the divergent views that were a cause of division, the Citoyens du Monde had only vague, distant objectives. This was the criticism Sartre levelled at them. He didn't share either the downright hostility

---

26 Gorz, *Fondements pour une morale*, p. 411.

27 Gorz, *Traitor*, p. 246.

28 See, for example, André Gorz and François Châtelet, 'Et si la politique redécouvrait la morale . . . ' (dialogue), *Les Nouvelles littéraires* (5 May 1977).

29 See Michel Bosquet [André Gorz], 'Le droit de désobéir', *Le Nouvel Observateur* (26 November 1979).

that François Mauriac or Robert Aron showed towards them or the friendly fellow-feeling of Bourdet, but he took the view the CDM was a mere talking shop. When invited to make the opening contribution to a debate within their own newssheet, he argued that world government was of the order of an ideal or 'myth in the Sorelian sense of the term' and, as such, it absolved them of concrete commitments for peace alongside the Palestinians, the Indochinese or the Madagascans etc.[30] The Sarrazac group, adopting this idea of myth forged by Sorel, replied that 'modern history finds itself faced with a new social myth', that of 'world citizenship', which opened 'the gates of an active dream, capable of coinciding with the innermost aspirations of the individual.'[31] Bovard's position was similar, when he argued—while taking the view that the creation of global structures would be premature so long as the hegemony of the US and USSR was not counterbalanced by the rise of other powers, such as China, India and Europe—that the 'spirit' of world unity had to be fostered right now, as it was essential to the future achievement of that unity.[32]

In coming to Paris, Horst was fulfilling his fondest wish. But his enthusiasm rapidly faded. He rushed to the RDR National Congress on 28–29 June 1949 only to witness the quarrels of a dying movement. Disenchanted, he felt he was being 'carried along and swallowed up by the world, without any great hope of acting on it.'[33] Having lost the throng of admirers he had begun to develop a liking for ('I am used to being regarded as an impressive sort of man. At Lausanne, that was generally the way of it. But since then [. . .]'),[34] he had, together with Doreen, to reconstruct his social life with almost nothing to build on—it was not until late 1955 that he would begin to see Sartre and de Beauvoir frequently again.

And then, most importantly, there was the unpleasant surprise. When he arrived at the Secretariat of the Citoyens du Monde for France and associated countries, he not only discovered that nothing had really been done, but also that the whole operation was a 'shambles' and Davis

---

30 Jean-Paul Sartre, 'Jean-Paul Sartre ouvre un dialogue', *Peuple du monde* (18 June 1949).

31 'Garry Davis et la citoyenneté mondiale seront-ils une nouvelle mystification de l'après-guerre?', *Peuple du monde* (18 June 1949).

32 René Bovard, 'Citoyen du monde', *Suisse contemporaine* 9 (9 September 1949): 445.

33 Horst to Walter Riffel, 7 July [1949] (GRZ).

34 Horst to Walter Riffel, 21 January 1953 (GRZ).

decidedly naïve. There was a backlog of tens of thousands of outstanding applications for 'world citizen' registration; the foreign groups—to be found mainly in the three defeated countries Germany, Austria and Italy, where there was a greater appetite for neutralism and where former Nazis and fascists were recycling themselves—did not obey any directives. Worse than that, the German organization, which accounted for half of all registrations with CDM, was in the hands of Atlanticists working for the Americans. Horst, sickened by the situation, threatened to resign.[35] The only happy note that brightened his life at this time came in the private sphere: on 20 September 1949, he overcame his principled reservations and married Doreen in a civil ceremony at Lausanne.

The salaried appointment turned out ultimately to be a sterile experience for Horst, as he drifted into a role as a subordinate pen-pusher in a cluttered office, spending his time collecting stamps or, between visits from foreign affiliates, composing circulars, communiqués and assorted admonitions. As the international context became unfavourable to proposals of global neutralism, the decline of the CDM was inevitable. On its last legs by then, the CDM made Horst redundant on 24 April 1950 after nine months with the organization. A weary Davis returned to the US on 20 May, just a few days before the start of the Korean War, which revealed the untimeliness of the dream of a world assembly of peoples.

35 See the exchange of letters between Gérard Horst and René Bovard of August 1949 (CENAC).

CHAPTER FOUR

Journalism as Compromise

'Here Paris is a sad city, Claude Bourdet is done with *Combat* and the Citoyens du Monde are done with Gérard! We're eating oatflakes and hoping to find something—tomorrow, always tomorrow. And we're reading *Le Figaro* and the *New York Herald*. Yes, the world is so sad!'[1] These few despondent words from Doreen Horst to their Swiss friend Walter Riffel in April 1950 echo the general atmosphere of intellectual gloom (the thrill of Liberation had worn off) and the material difficulties with which the couple was battling in the year of unemployment that loomed before them. Doreen and Gérard both took a string of casual jobs. She worked as a model at the École des beaux-arts, gave private English lessons, turned archivist in the service of a private individual and guided groups of British students around the French capital.

Gérard also transformed himself into a guide, an insurance salesman (his two-day trial was never going to lead anywhere) and a paid correspondent for *L'Illustré*, the Swiss magazine he had read eagerly in the dining room of his Lausanne *pension* (the job came through his connection with Jotterand).[2] He also tried unsuccessfully to get work as a German translator at UNESCO (the United Nations Education, Science and Culture Organization), where Roger Girod was employed, and successfully, thanks to that same contact, to become private secretary to General Thakar, the military attaché of the Indian Embassy. For seven months, Horst wrote reports on the international situation in Europe and gave daily lessons to Thakar's daughters. 'We are perhaps going to get rich,' he wrote ironically to Walter Riffel, who had stayed behind in Switzerland. 'Because we are unemployed, we are working more than ever before. From morning till night. Like idiots.'[3]

---

1 Doreen Horst to Walter Riffel, 14 April [1950] (GRZ).

2 See, for example, 'Comment on vit à Paris avec un salaire moyen', a typewritten article no doubt intended for that popular magazine (GRZ, Riffel folder).

3 Gérard Horst to Walter Riffel, undated [1950] (GRZ).

He had already asked that friend, whom he first got to know at the family *pension* in Lausanne, to send powdered milk and coffee, sugar and rice . . .

Employment at Paris-presse

On 15 April 1951 Gérard Horst, then aged 28, was taken on by *Paris-presse L'Intransigeant*, a mass-circulation evening newspaper. He gave his close friend the news:

> I am about to be engulfed by the rottenness of the world. In [this instance], the rottenness of the world has assumed the face of *Paris-presse*, where I have eagerly accepted a writing job on an as yet unknown salary. I begin next week and my system is beginning to be poisoned by all the compromises I shall be asked to make with myself.[4]

Horst got this job thanks to 'a famous journalist' to whom he was introduced by Betty, an American friend ('Jane' in *Letter to D.*).[5] We assume the journalist in question to be Jean-Jacques Servan-Schreiber, an occasional columnist at that daily. *Paris-presse*, founded in 1944, was a conservative newspaper. From 1952 onwards, it was controlled by the group that owned *France-Soir* and by Gaullist businessmen (its director Édouard Corniglion-Molinier, who would shortly be a minister in the Laniel government, and the 50 per cent shareholder Marcel Dassault). Horst was assigned the task, from 18 May onwards, of co-writing the roundup of the foreign press, which would be given greater space as the years went by. Doreen helped him to sift through the mass of Anglo-Saxon publications, thereby beginning a research activity that would enable her to support her partner throughout his journalistic career. Gérard did, however, prevent her from learning the language of the German civilization he detested.

The most diverse subjects were covered: social questions, the techno-sciences (atomic tests, electric cars), public health (ionizing waves with unknown effects, radioactivity); or the happy (the growing of wheat in Siberia or Alaska) and unhappy prospects (rising sea levels) ensuing from

---

4 Gérard Horst to Walter Riffel, 22 April [1951] (GRZ).
5 Gorz, *Letter to D.*, p. 45.

the climate change that CO_2 emissions from industry were causing.[6] From 1954 onwards, Horst occasionally worked on the foreign desk too. His first foreign affairs 'story' had been a reportage in March 1953 from Vienna which he signed as Gérard Horst. He was asked to change this by-line on account of its German appearance and he chose Michel as a given name and Bosquet as a surname, the latter being a translation of 'Horst' (we know that he had already used this *nom de plume* in Switzerland for personal reasons).[7]

In his articles, he learned the 'tricks of objectivity',[8] 'each containing a discreet dose of poison, the materials of an indictment omitted so that the facts could speak for themselves.'[9] In them he described the methods of McCarthyism and the FBI, the Americans' manoeuvres in Italy to undermine the Communist CGIL [Confederazione Generale Italiana del Lavoro] union, and the aims of the Arbenz government in Guatemala, which was just then being overthrown in the interests of United Fruit. Gorz, who saw these articles as subversive, would later write to a female student that they were, nonetheless, unassailable, since similar analyses were to be found in other 'right-thinking' newspapers, such as the *New York Times*. Yet, as he would also confide in that letter, 'I couldn't after all write what I wanted, and still cannot: journalism isn't a means of expression. It's a compromise.'[10]

Bosquet's self-image in the *Paris-presse* days, the one he conveyed to his friend and confidant, remained 'that of a traitor and *salaud* compromised by the lousy reactionary press', where, 'with bad conscience and resentment [he] pursues a policy of choosing the lesser evil.' 'So,' he concluded, 'I go around with a long face all day.'[11]

---

6 'La Terre se réchauffe d'un degré par siècle', *Paris-presse L'Intransigeant* (5 March 1954).

7 See above p. 15n43.

8 Gorz, *Letter to D.*, p. 47.

9 Gorz, *Traitor*, p. 245.

10 Letter from André Gorz to an (unidentified) female student, 17 March 1967, published as 'André Gorz intellectuel et journaliste. Lettre à une étudiante (1967)', *EcoRev'* 46 (Summer 2018): 131–7. On this subject in general, see Cyril Lemieux (ed.), *La Subjectivité journalistique. Onze leçons sur le rôle de l'individualité dans la production de l'information* (Paris: Éditions de l'EHESS, 2010).

11 Gérard Horst to Walter Riffel, 20 June [1954] (GRZ).

Mendesism and Modernism at *L'Express*

A ten-minute interview in July 1955 was enough to open up a nine-year-long career for Bosquet at *L'Express*, beginning that October. As soon as he arrived, as a journalist who later became a friend would remember, 'we immediately saw we were dealing with someone out of the ordinary . . . he wasn't at all the typical hard-bitten pressman.'[12] His recruitment, which had the magazine's founder and managing editor behind it, can be explained by the need for journalists created by the (temporary) transformation of the weekly into a daily, to support Pierre Mendès France, the candidate in the 1956 legislative elections. 'I was delighted to go to *L'Express*,' Gorz would recall in 1967, 'because it was after all a more intelligent publication than the daily paper I'd been at before and, though one couldn't actually express oneself, one could say more things there, though always with lots of caution and concessions.'[13]

L'Express, a magazine of information and opinion created in 1953, was intended as a political platform placed by its managing editor at the disposal of Mendès France, whom he was trying to steer in the most reformist direction possible.[14] With the connivance of a young sub-editor by the name of Serge Lafaurie, who was already at *L'Express*, Bosquet, who was tasked with covering international news, also set about modifying the image of the Radical leader, though in a direction different from Servan-Schreiber, the champion of Americanism: with 'hairy-chested Serge [who] thinks like me,' he wrote privately, 'we have done such good work that the Yankee embassy has already concluded that Mendès is neutralist [and] *Time* magazine has attacked him for it.'[15] Bosquet respected Mendès, whom he met during the election campaign. Already in his *Paris-presse* days, he had placed him, with Bourdet, among the men who were doing 'better work' than those who chose the Communist Party.[16] Just like Jean Daniel, who covered the acutely

---

12 Serge Lafaurie, 'Hommage à André Gorz'.

13 Gorz, 'André Gorz intellectuel et journaliste'.

14 Christian Delporte, '*L'Express*, Mendès France et la modernité politique (1953–1955)', *Matériaux pour l'histoire de notre temps* 63–4 (July–December 2001): 96–103; Michel Jamet, *Les Défis de L'Express* (Paris: Cerf, 1981).

15 Gérard Horst to Walter Riffel, 2 January [1956] (GRZ). His most recent signed article at that point was Michel Bosquet, 'L'URSS propose: "Fixons immédiatement une date pour arrêter les expériences atomiques" ', *L'Express* (30 November 1955).

16 Gérard Horst to Walter Riffel, undated [1953?] (GRZ).

topical events in North Africa for the magazine, he was won over to the Mendesist policy of colonial disengagement.

But that policy did not entirely define Mendès France—or L'Express. He also embodied 'modernism', for which anti-colonialism was a precondition. By this, we mean the ideology and practices which, in the 1950s, drove the progressive sectors of the middle classes and the state's senior civil servants, politically in thrall to Radicalism and Social Christianity, to rationalize and energize the French economy on the American model, while advocating redistribution of the benefits of growth.[17] The appearance of finance pages in L'Express—and in the then left-wing daily Le Monde—were part of this same trend: it was a response to the pedagogical, democratic concern to provide the public with information on questions felt to be crucial to the country's future (later on, Jean Boissonnat's L'Expansion would fully perform this same function).[18]

With enormous reluctance, Bosquet played a part in this. When he signed his first article on economics in L'Express on 20 November 1958, he became the specialist in a field of journalism he was to cultivate for almost 25 years. While initially sharing the column with Jean Cau, Sartre's former secretary, and the demographer Alfred Sauvy, who alternated with the Eastearn Europe specialist K. S. Karol on foreign policy, he made a name for himself with his field research. With those studies, he brought subtlety and intelligence to the examination of situations, conjunctures and issues, though ultimately not without an approving nod towards the idea of progress and the discourse of economic rationality, sometimes under the guise of the rationality of (French-style) indicative planning.

For example, when invited on several occasions by the grocery-chain owner Édouard Leclerc to visit his shops—he admired the humanistic ideas of this Breton ex-seminarian, with whom he discussed politics freely—he praised the elimination of intermediaries in distribution and the process of concentration as a rationalization that made smaller margins and low prices

---

17 Luc Boltanski, 'America, America . . .', Actes de la recherche en sciences sociales 38 (May 1981): 19–41.

18 Philippe Riutort, 'Le journalisme au service de l'économie. Les conditions d'émergence de l'information économique en France à partir des années 50', Actes de la recherche en sciences sociales 131–2 (March 2000): 41–55.

possible. And this led him to characterize the small shopkeepers' protests against the Leclerc system as going against 'progress'.[19]

Even when he was listening to trade unionists, Bosquet was dependent on sources gleaned from the French Planning Commission and from business people. He also attended (with Dorine) meetings of the Club Jean Moulin at the home of the *mendésiste* Stéphane Hessel, its founder, where he met high-ranking civil servants. At *L'Express*, he reproduced the ambient discourse of a period and an elite, which boiled down to Keynesianism and planning. Even before he was handed the Economics column, he conceded in *The Traitor* that his 'weakness for world demographic problems, statistics on the world's resources, strategic theories [and] five-year plans' would make him 'a good official of the Planning Ministry or the Population Service'.[20] And in 1993 he would recognize that, when dealing with 'very high-level' economists in the various ministries and government departments, it was important first to *understand* what was being said, and that his—in fact, rather unsystematic—reading of Marx was mainly of use in helping him to develop 'keys for interpretation' in his journalistic work— in other words, not so much to criticize as to understand.[21] There was, then, in Bosquet–Gorz a definite kind of intellectual dualism that saw him split 'between a moralist attentive to the realm of ends and an economist fascinated by the logic of things'.[22]

On another level, that of his professional position, Bosquet was more aware of the barriers preventing him from applying his critical faculties. These reduced the scope for manoeuvre granted him by the magazine. In 1967, replying to a student, he assessed these clear-sightedly:

---

19 See Michel Bosquet, 'Vie quotidienne. L'aventure de Grenoble', *L'Express* (2 April 1959); 'Économie. Le "circuit du pauvre"', *L'Express* (3 March 1960); 'Reportage. Leclerc et la liberté', *L'Express* (11 October 1962). *A contrario*, see 'La mort des "petits"', *Le Nouvel Observateur* (4 May 1970). This last article is reprinted as 'Small Tradesmen: The End of the Line' in *Capitalism in Crisis and Everyday Life* (John Howe trans.) (Hassocks: Harvester Press, 1977), pp. 57–63.

20 Gorz, *Traitor*, p. 71.

21 Jeremy Tatman, 'A Dialogue with Gorz'. Reprinted in Conrad Lodziak and Jeremy Tatman, *André Gorz: A Critical Introduction* (London: Pluto Press, 1997), p. 124. The interview was carried out in November 1993.

22 Louis Pinto, 'Un théoricien du *Nouvel Observateur*' in *L'Intelligence en action: Le Nouvel Observateur* (Paris: Métailié, 1984), p. 157.

I didn't come to journalism through activism, but to earn my living in a way that kept me informed, helped me to think and forced me constantly to learn. It was through working as a journalist that I became a bit of an activist. But [. . .] a journalist always writes for his editor. In other words, depending on the way the editor sees the tastes and opinions of the public, he writes articles likely to please his audience, to bring him a certain audience. The 'line' of a publication or its 'manner' are always *strumentali*: the truth or accuracy of the analysis come second to the commercial value of the article, its 'pull' [. . .]. If you ask me, then, what I think of my work as Bosquet, I'd say I don't recognize myself in it. I can count the articles I'd be willing to countersign with all my names: [he enumerates six].[23] Out of the hundreds of articles I did, that's a very small number.'[24]

In these circumstances, it is easier to understand why Gorz was scrupulously careful not to allow his pseudonym as a social philosopher to become associated with his *nom de plume* as a journalist: in the former case, he was a subject; in the latter, 'he didn't exist.' And that was what he found unpleasant about journalism: 'Mobilizing all the resources of your thinking to produce a thinking from which your thinking is absent.'[25]

Early in 1963, *L'Express* took a centrist turn by combining, unabashed, the productivist myth and an appeal to a 'middle management' readership, who were the advertisers' target group. Enshrining his break with Mendès France, whom he had still supported in the 1962 elections, Servan-Schreiber began to ease out the journalists committed to the earlier line. Jean Daniel, the editor, was dismissed in January 1964 and picked up by *Le Monde*. No longer recognizing himself in the spirit of the publication, moved from the sensitive Economics page and, with his operational autonomy constrained,

---

23 We have identified them precisely: Michel Bosquet: 'Reportage. Grève à l'italienne', *L'Express* (27 September 1962); 'Communistes. Les premiers pas', *L'Express* (20 December 1962); 'Le "socialisme" et la bagnole', *Le Nouvel Observateur* (11 May 1966) (translated as ' "Socialism" and the Motor Car' in *Capitalism in Crisis and Everyday Life*, pp. 27–8); 'Les chômeurs de la relance', *Le Nouvel Observateur* (17 August 1966); 'Et si on nationalisait la Bourse [. . .] ', *Le Nouvel Observateur* (12 October 1966); 'Cent mille morts par jour', *Le Nouvel Observateur* (21 December 1966) (translated as 'Other People's Hunger' in *Capitalism in Crisis and Everyday Life*, pp. 129–33).

24 Gorz, 'André Gorz intellectuel et journaliste.'

25 André Gorz, ' "Je n'existe pas." Note sur le journalisme' (circa 1960) in Christophe Fourel (ed.), *André Gorz en personne* (Lormont: Le Bord de l'eau, 2013), p. 94.

Bosquet in turn resigned in September at the point when the repositioning strategy found its new formula in the words 'news magazine'.[26] Settled at an industrial tribunal (with a letter from Mendès France to support his case), his long-delayed departure can be explained by the fact that, in his case, the solution of the offer of an alternative post proved a lengthy process.[27]

He could have taken the editorship of a journal on the international experiences of the labour movement, such as the bilingual *International Socialist Journal/Revue internationale du socialisme*, which Lelio Basso was preparing to launch and to which he would lend his full support.[28] Or he could have agreed to edit the magazine of the Christian CFTC trade union (Confédération française des travailleurs chrétiens), which was at that point transforming itself into a secular organization, the CFDT (Confédération française démocratique du travail), but he declined that offer too, certain that it would mean forfeiting his political independence. His Italian trade-unionist friend Bruno Trentin (who maintained a filial friendship with the CFTC intellectual Paul Vignaux, with whom he had spent time in France in his youth) wrote to him on the subject:

> Despite its very great value and its great significance, I agree with you that, to accept it would in fact have forced you to become—at least for quite some time—a functionary of the CFTC, with all the limitations and pressures that entails. And that would very probably have limited your scope for action and the influence your writings may have on the French labour movement and the CFTC itself.[29]

In the end, he joined with the other defectors from *L'Express*, Jean Daniel, K. S. Karol, Claude Krief, Serge Lafaurie and Lafaurie's uncle Jacques-Laurent Bost, in founding *Le Nouvel Observateur* in November 1964. Another dramatic phase of his life as a journalist was beginning.

---

26 See his long resignation letter in Fourel (ed.), *André Gorz. Un penseur pour le XXIe siècle*, pp. 238–46.
27 Letter from Pierre Mendès France to Michel Bosquet, 17 November 1964 (GRZ). The dispute was over the redundancy payments that would ensue as a result of the legal application of the conscience clause in Gorz's contract.
28 Bruno Trentin alludes to this proposal in a letter to André Gorz of 13 October 1964 (GRZ).
29 Trentin, letter to Gorz, 13 October 1964 (GRZ).

CHAPTER FIVE

Alienation in the Affluent Society

Horst presented the manuscript of *Fondements pour une morale* to Sartre on 1 December 1955, having put the final touches to it some time before. Almost five months were needed for the philosopher, consumed by other theoretical issues, to get a sense of it and, in the end, to recommend it to three publishers.[1] In the preface to the work, published in 1977, Gorz, who reduces this waiting period to some six to eight weeks, relates Sartre's perplexed reaction to the vast work, which he doubtless only skimmed, whose ontological and moral framework seemed dated. It was without any illusions that Sartre provided his protégé with a note of recommendation to Jean Hyppolite, the editor of a philosophical collection at the Presses Universitaires de France (PUF). In hindsight, it was predictable that the manuscript would be rejected. Its author was, however, surprised—contrary to what he would later claim.[2] In a letter to Walter Riffel of 2 January 1956, he expressed optimism about what he referred to humorously as '*leuvre*' (a play on *l'œuvre*—the work—and *couleuvre*, which, used figuratively, connects with notions of humiliation and being deceived): 'When JPS [Sartre] has read it, I think it will be published; next winter perhaps.'[3] However, Horst was not thrown by this failure, as he had already launched upon another project that was, in some ways, its continuation. I am referring to the writing of *The Traitor*.

Freedom and Existential Analysis

The Traitor, an atypical autobiographical novel, is simply the application to a particular case of the phenomenological typology of attitudes and situations elaborated in the lengthy theoretical tome.[4] The development and

---

1 See Gérard Horst to Walter Riffel, 2 January and 5 April [1956] (GRZ).

2 See Gorz, Preface to *Fondements pour une morale*, p. 18.

3 Horst to Walter Riffel, 2 January [1956].

4 For a broad contextualization, see Michael Mundhenk, 'Appropriating Life-History through Autobiographical Writing: André Gorz's *The Traitor*, a Dialectical Inquiry into the Self', *Prose Studies: History, Theory, Criticism* 8(2) (1985): 81–96.

aim of the work are the same as for *Fondements*: it is about carving out the path which, at the end of a labyrinthine tangle of inauthentic, alienated motivations and relationships, leads the subject to freedom. Sartre remains the central reference. Just as *Fondements* was modelled on *Being and Nothingness*, *The Traitor* now had the example of Sartre's *Saint Genet* (1952) to work from, a book that exalted social secession and betrayal, an aspect reflected in Gorz's choice of title.

This kind of biographical account has three stages to it: a period of youthful development is followed by trials and tribulations, then by resolution. Unlike Camus's *The Fall* [1956], in which the protagonist tells his own story and bares his soul without intermediary, *The Traitor* is written in the third person, in order to maintain the distance between how the man is and the way he sees himself. But once again unlike Camus, what is striking is the language used, which is fairly informal, and the often tortuous reasoning, which introduces intimacy and sincerity into a story that is primarily a dialogue with himself.

The novel consists of four parts with pronouns for titles—'We', 'They', 'You' and 'I'. The first part confronts the great question of the moment—how the individual is to position himself with respect to Marxist and analytic theories—in 1957, Sartre published *The Problem of Method* in *Les Temps modernes*, in which he replied to Georg Lukács on 'Existentialism and Marxism'. The next two parts depict 'He' grappling with others to express the rejection of self and of the image the others project back to him. In the final, resolution-bringing section, 'I' overcomes the 'terror of identification' by coming to accept himself.[5]

Expressing himself informally, Gorz presented his project to Riffel as 'a new thingummyjig I've begun to hatch, and which is to show pretty much from real life, from my own example, how a chap—yes, indeed—can manage to understand himself and get a grip on himself, psychoanalyze and Marxize himself off his own bat.' In the same letter, in which he mentions the meetings with Sartre to hand over the manuscript of *Fondements*, Horst

5 See the fine, though very different, analyses by Norio Inoue, 'Il—Je—Sujet de l'énonciation', *Memoirs of the Faculty of Liberal Arts and Education* (Yamanashi University, Japan) 33 (December 1982): 75–83 (an offprint was sent to Gorz; GRZ, Inoue file); and Frédéric Worms, 'André Gorz ou l'autre issue' in Fourel (ed.), *André Gorz en personne*, pp. 39–50.

observes that his mentor's concerns are similar to his own and he can see how to take advantage of that:

> He explained to me that, personally, phenomenology didn't excite him all that much anymore and what was important for him was to find a perspective from which the unity of psychoanalysis and Marxism could be underpinned—I rather suspected this was the case—and that the thing was to understand how 'Society' fitted together, where it came from that there was such a thing, and to reconcile its historical meaning with its lived meaning [...] which enabled me to see that I'd de-railed at a certain point from the new thingummyjig.[6]

What Is a Traitor? The Marginal and the Intellectual

The title of the work receives little elucidation in the course of the text and its meaning is blurred in the 2005 edition by an extract on the cover from the conclusion[7] in which Gorz foregrounds the betrayal suffered by the 'traitors' of his ilk. Betrayed from the outset by a reality that assigns them a role and a place they did not consciously wish for, 'ill adapted to our reality, devoured by needs which our civilization cannot satisfy', some men become 'traitors' to society.[8] Exactly like Jean Genet, as depicted by Sartre. They are those who cannot ignore their 'definitive flaw'[9] which makes it impossible for them to recognize themselves in the image of their situation in society. Treason then comes to be embodied in the 'opposition and contestation'[10] through which the individual seeks and shapes his authenticity. The traitor is the rebellious and excluded individual.

Every society bears within it, as its own negation, this figure of otherness. It represses it with the implicit pledge of its members to confine themselves only to what is lawful and hounds it out with generalized suspicion when, in holistic ('archaic') or authoritarian ('McCarthyite') fashion, it dictates each individual's place.[11] In 2004, Gorz would press the point again: 'It's only in

---

6 Gérard Horst to Walter Riffel, 2 January [1956].

7 The passage in question appears on page 272 of the English edition of *The Traitor*.

8 Gorz, *Traitor*, p. 266.

9 Gorz, *Traitor*.

10 Gorz, *Traitor*, p. 247.

11 André Gorz, *La Morale de l'histoire* (Paris: Seuil, 1959), pp. 86–7n.

the interstices of this logic, its misfirings and margins, that autonomous subjects emerge, through whom moral questions may be posed'.[12] It is surprising
that, in order to assess the social influence of the non-conformist subject,
Gorz never had occasion to refer to the incisive study by the social psychologist Serge Moscovici, *Social Influence and Social Change* (original English
publication 1976). He preferred, on this point, to appeal to the authority of
another researcher, the sociologist Alain Touraine, whom he would study
attentively.

There is one case in which the 'marginal' individual has a special social
visibility. This is when, on the one hand, he accepts his solitude and thereby
the solitude of others, and, on the other, chooses to evaluate the world on
the basis of his 'demand for humanity': in that case, he is an *intellectual*.[13]
By dint of his distance from society, the intellectual is the 'traitor' par excellence.[14] Embodying the 'spirit of autonomy', he 'says no to the world of alienation and inhuman necessities. But, in doing so, he does not prevent that
world from existing, nor does he forge the instruments of its transformation'.[15] His role is not to deny the imperatives of everyday life. He is not
well placed, for example, to criticize, either from within or outside the
Communist Party, 'the action of the revolutionary class' while making light
of its 'objective conditions'.[16] His role is, rather, to keep alive the negativity,
the 'nostalgia for a human world' that is in each of us, so that one day, by
becoming aware of this, human beings will free themselves. The intellectual,
whose natural calling is the revolt of the mind and who is sometimes isolated by his temptation to judge real movements from a position of
superiority, will then find himself alongside those who, like him, are critics
of general alienation and will necessarily 'be on the "Left"'.[17]

In 1960, in an issue of the journal *Arguments* devoted to intellectuals,
Edgar Morin, who had in the previous year published a self-criticism of his

---

12 André Gorz, *Ecologica* (Chris Turner trans.) (London: Seagull Books, 2010), pp.
4–5.

13 Gorz, *La Morale de l'histoire*, p. 141.

14 Gorz, *Traitor*, pp. 266–8.

15 Gorz, *La Morale de l'histoire*, pp. 141–2.

16 Gorz, *Le Traître*, p. 258 n.

17 Gorz, *La Morale de l'histoire*, pp. 143–4.

past commitment to the Communist Party,[18] indirectly discussed the dilemma raised by Gorz. He points out that the left-wing intellectual—of a naturally dissident cast of mind and an Enlightenment thinker—who poses an 'absolute' (in this case, the 'demand for humanity') so as to set up a tension between that absolute and 'realism' (in this case, 'objective conditions'), evinces a weakness of judgement by comparison with the 'Marxist vulgate' that inculcates that same realism.[19] We shall, then, have to examine this pre-1960 'weakness' on Gorz's part with regard to the matter at hand here: namely, official Communist ideology.

From the Standpoint of Psychoanalysis and Marxism

From the outset, the narration of *The Traitor*, which depicts a man struggling with the torments of his unfulfilled being, raises as crucial the question of the relation between objective determinations, which relate both to his past and his social milieu, and the personal choice in which his freedom plays itself out. This relation would forever underlie the emancipatory project of André Gorz, who regarded human beings as the subjects of their actions. It invites comparison with the problematics that diverge in part from the existential approach: Freudian psychoanalysis and Marxism.

Existential psychoanalysis, which is neither a speech-based psychotherapy nor a form of introspection but a *narrative technique of disclosure*, sets out from personal choice—a key concept—to 'understand how you have arrived at your condition, how you have chosen yourself starting from there, how you have let yourself be infected by it, half victim, half accomplice, how it has been possible that you have agreed to live it. [. . .] His idea, then,' is that there is an objective bent to the personal choice [. . .].'[20] Gorz, following Sartre,[21] is dismissive of both the notion of unconscious and of libido, with the result that, as he sees it, the complex of the personality, which contains nothing buried in the impenetrable depths of being, is best revealed by a phenomenological approach. This neither excludes points of

---

18 Edgar Morin, *Autocritique* (Paris: Le Seuil, 1959).

19 Edgar Morin, 'Intellectuels. Critique du mythe et mythe de la critique', *Arguments* 20 (October–December 1960). Reprinted in *Arguments 3* (Paris: UGE, 1978), pp. 137–8.

20 Gorz, *Traitor*, pp. 43, 47.

21 See Betty Cannon, *Sartre and Psychoanalysis: An Existentialist Challenge to Clinical Metatheory* (Lawrence: University Press of Kansas, 1991).

agreement with psychoanalysis proper nor, indeed, does it rule out effects on clinical practice: at this same time, Ronald Laing's study in existential psychiatry *The Divided Self* (1959), which owed as much to the Swiss psychiatrist Ludwig Binswanger as it did to Sartre, developed a phenomenology of the Self whose clinical and political significance would soon give birth to the extraordinary, explosive anti-psychiatry reform movement.

One of the convergences with Sigmund Freud's theory concerns the recognition of the original determination by childhood, which is that of a choice or a complex imposed by family relations (Sartre speaks of an 'original contingency of choice')[22] and which, from the outset, gives rise to an incompleteness or lack in the individual. Hence this image from Merleau-Ponty which strikes Gorz in *Fondements pour une morale*: the past 'remains like a wound through which our strength ebbs away.'[23] In that book, he lays out his conception:

> We became bound to ourselves and to the world in childhood [. . .] the way we disclose the world is always motivated by the way we are already situated by the choice we have made regarding our corporeity, our childhood past, the immediately perceptible world [. . .] our adult behaviours are the sublimations or symbolizations of our infantile complexes, our relations with others remain oriented by the choice we made of ourselves in our relations with our father or mother, and that original choice is like the subjective *fatum* which leads to our always finding ourselves in the same type of situation.[24]

The other—equally fundamental—convergence concerns the liberatory possibility of choosing, at a later stage, to re-appropriate this enforced choice in a modified way.[25] Which means that the individual is not irremediably confined to his/her original determination. In concrete terms, this means one will refrain from over-hastily explaining some revolutionary behaviour, for example, by reference to an infantile complex of rebellion against

---

22 Jean-Paul Sartre, 'Existential Psychoanalysis' in *Being and Nothingness*, pp. 557–75.

23 Maurice Merleau-Ponty, *Phenomenology of Perception* (London: Routledge & Kegan Paul, 1962), p. 85; Gorz, *Fondements pour une morale*, p. 460.

24 Gorz, *Fondements pour une morale*, pp. 459–60.

25 On the psychoanalytic perspective, see Claude Rabant, 'Un choix renversant' in Max Bensasson and Annick Feissel (eds), *La Question du choix inconscient. Déterminisme et responsabilité du sujet* (Marseille: Éditions du Hasard, 1997), pp. 37–45.

the father[26]—or, in Gorz's case, his future choice of the economics of self-limitation by reference to his avarice . . . 'For, as soon as a complex has managed to transcend itself and become an objectively grounded commitment, and to own that commitment in the name of the demand for freedom historically asserted within it, that complex is liquidated *as* complex.'[27]

As Gorz will say later, discussing the notion of autobiography with his Sartrean friend Michel Contat, there comes a moment when 'the propositions one advances hold up independently of the original motivation.' Conceiving the autobiographical story as a construction legitimating the 'already present' identity of the author is also something that will be avoided. From this standpoint, *The Traitor* is a 'different undertaking', which tries 'to understand the "original choice" in its conditioning and its meaning . . . to be able to rework it, to reshape the situation and become the subject of one's endeavours.'[28] If then, as Gorz would explain in an important article on Sartre, the initial 'affective constitution, which is the way in which originally, before any possible reflection and retroaction, we bound ourselves in childhood to our bodies, to others and to the world' remains as the matrix of experience, that does not mean we are prisoners to it: you never let this go but you always pass beyond it, 'forming, on that basis, *true* relations with historical reality.'[29]

Besides, the 'situation' that presents itself to the individual is not the product solely of his existential path, which is freighted with the past. The incompleteness of the human being, who is born dependent and subsequently acquires free will (Gorz does not reject the comparison with the free will of the Christians),[30] is rooted in a wider—social and economic—context which is active at every moment and in the present, and which only *Marxism* grasps as the form of essential determination the adult human

---

26 Gorz, *Fondements pour une morale*, pp. 438–9.

27 Gorz, *Fondements pour une morale*, p. 439.

28 André Gorz to Michel Contat, undated [September 1988] (GRZ).

29 André Gorz, 'Sartre malgré lui?', *Le Nouvel Observateur* (6 December 1976). The article is a review of François George's book *Deux Études sur Sartre* (Paris: Christian Bourgois, 1976).

30 In fact, in 1976 he is waiting for someone 'finally to discover the troubling similarities between Sartre's ontology and left-wing Christian theology—similarities confirmed by ethical and political convergences of which neither Sartre nor the Christian Left seem entirely aware.' (Gorz, 'Sartre malgré lui?')

being is subject to in his choices. That the functions and social roles of the individual define his identity by preventing him from existing by himself will, for Gorz, be an unshakeable verity: 'It's not "I" who acts, but the automated logic of social systems that works through me as Other, that makes me participate in the production and reproduction of the social megamachine.'[31] There is no freedom that can free itself from this world; it is, of necessity, 'situated' in the world. This also means that the encounter between subject and context is constitutive of a situation that is not settled in advance and always offers, potentially, the possibility of revolt and a reorientation towards freedom. The moral injunction prompted by the subject's permanent collusion with this twofold—individual and social—determination is simple: one must, in a single sweep, change oneself and change the external conditions of one's existence.[32] A synchronic, dialectical axiom that both Marxism and Christianity oppose, each privileging a different one of the terms in play.

Narrative deconstruction helps in this work, since it does not regard the human being as the passive, constrained outcome of a collection of subjective and objective causes merely added together. Purely causal explanations are wide of the mark. They are to be set aside for the obvious reason that, stated retrospectively, they provide too simple an explanation for the choice as it should be made. This standpoint rejects both Marxist and psychoanalytic theory:

> Both, although they are on different levels, explain man by his condition (material, infantile). This explanation is always true, but that is also its weakness; since every choice is conditioned, you can always prove it was 'given in advance' as a possibility or an objective probability, but you can never prove it was fatal or necessary, or foresee it [...].[33]

That the socialism that is to be built must respond to the same dialectic of conditions and choices is something we shall shortly discover in Gorz's more political writings.

---

31 Gorz, *Ecologica*, p. 4.
32 Gorz, *Traitor*, pp. 45, 53–4, 73–4.
33 Gorz, *Traitor*, p. 80.

An Author Is Born

In September 1956, the manuscript of *The Traitor* was completed and quickly delivered to Francis Jeanson, editor at Les Éditions du Seuil and a philosopher close to Sartre. The latter had already promised Horst a preface. However, publication was not assured at that point: Jeanson (knowing he was imminently about to leave the publishing house) had to threaten to resign to secure it. The manuscript was accepted only narrowly, the publisher ultimately being persuaded by the prospect of Sartre's indirect collaboration.[34] The book, with Sartre's long, laudatory introduction, came out in the late winter of 1958. Extracts were published before that in *Les Temps modernes* of October 1957 and March 1958.

The moment chosen was of particular significance: the author had just lost his father in September. Not wishing to associate the introspective, subversive writer with the political journalist now known as Michel Bosquet, nor to upset his mother, whom he treats even more harshly in the book than his father, Horst chose a new pseudonym that he used for the first time in the extracts.[35] The fear of compromising his naturalization, for which he had applied two years earlier (with the assistance of Mendès France), ultimately played no role, since he had obtained it by decree, as Dorine had also done, on 12 April 1957. In seeking a pseudonym, he opted for 'André', another French Christian name (was he echoing André Gide here, his first literary love, whose pursuit of perfect simplicity he had admired?),[36] and 'Gorz', which was phonetically close to his surname 'Horst'. He took it after noticing the brand name Goerz (from the name of the company's founder) on the field glasses bequeathed to him by his father, which he had brought back from the funeral (mistakenly) believing this to refer to the town of Gorizia (Görz in German), an Italo-Austrian 'bastard town, which was for

---

34 See André Gorz to Madeleine Lafaurie, 2 November 1958 (GRZ).

35 It was also to preserve his anonymity, which he was particularly concerned to do vis-à-vis his mother, that he took care to employ a false birth date in all his books. His first, *Le Traître* (1958), gave him out to be three years younger (and had him coming to France at the Liberation); for another, he pretended to be six years younger (see *Stratégie ouvrière et néocapitalisme* [Paris: Seuil, 1964])! It wasn't until 1982 that he decided to reveal his pseudonym to his mother, then aged 87.

36 See Gorz, *Traitor*, pp. 103–04. Another hypothesis has the origin as André Malraux. See Christophe Fourel, 'Itinéraire d'un penseur' in *André Gorz, un penseur pour le XXIe siècle*, p. 16.

many years unclear as to its true identity.'[37] We may note that the writers of 'unhappy consciousness', Carlo Michelstaedter and Italo Svevo were natives of that region.

This first publication put an end to years of solipsistic writing. Admittedly, the failure of a later manuscript to find a publisher—we shall come to this— led Gorz to write, in a letter to an admirer of *The Traitor*, that he felt 'neither triumphant, nor admirable, nor destined for a bright future,' but his entry into the bookshops gradually gave him confidence and a place in the world.[38] He was now an author (on 21 May 1959 *L'Express* would publish extracts from his next work *La Morale de l'histoire* and would boast, in its publicity, of having on its staff André Gorz, rather than Michel Bosquet . . .). And an author honoured to have been reviewed by Maurice Blanchot, who drew a parallel with Robert Musil's *Man Without Qualities*, another book by an Austrian exiled to the shores of Lake Geneva.[39] With *The Traitor* selling some tens of thousands of copies and being quickly translated into English, for the first time in his life its author pocketed a tidy sum (three million old francs over the year). It would be his bestselling book until, at the end of his life, he wrote *Letter to D.*, the story of his love for Dorine.

In French-speaking Switzerland, where the story is set, the book was well received. As soon as it came out, passages on Swiss youth were studied in secondary schools thanks to Jeanlouis Cornuz, a Sartrean teacher and POP member, who had very likely spent time with Horst in Lausanne and had led a small study circle with affiliations to the RDR.[40] Michel Contat, a pupil of Cherpillod and Cornuz and himself a future Sartre specialist, read *The Traitor* during his final year at the *lycée* in Lausanne. The New Left, in gestation following the defections affecting the POP after 1956, was to take from this work of Gorz's—and even more from the following two books of

---

37 Gorz, 'André Gorz intellectuel et journaliste'. See also a radio interview with François Noudelmann on France Culture in 2005: *Penser l'avenir*, p. 35. In 1926 the family had spent seaside holidays at Grado in Gorizia province.

38 The aforementioned letter to Madeleine Lafaurie (1958). The addressee was the mother of Serge Lafaurie, Gorz's colleague at *L'Express*.

39 Maurice Blanchot, 'The Terror of Identification' in *Friendship* (Elizabeth Rottenberg trans.) (Stanford, CA: Stanford University Press, 1997), pp. 208–16. First published as 'La passion de l'indifférence', *La Nouvelle Revue française* 67 (July 1958): 93–101.

40 Jeanlouis Cornuz, 'D'une lecture faite en classe', *Études de lettres* 2, 1 (3) (July–September 1958): 95–103.

1959 and 1964—the tools for its humanist, revolutionary socialism, and this would contribute to distinguishing it from the Swiss–German Extreme Left[41] that remained mired in neo-Stalinism.

Marxism and Socialism

There were several events in the 1950s that would make for a tempering of the polarization between the two geopolitical blocs and, as a knock-on effect, a climate in the West more favourable to both Marxism and Soviet Communism, though not to seeing a perfect overlap between the two. Now that the Korean War had ended, the appearance of anti-colonial demands in Africa (Guy Mollet's policy at Suez and in Algeria acted to boost these), the death of Stalin and the hope that an end had truly been put to Stalinism with Khrushchev's report to the Twentieth Congress of the CPSU, functioned to shift European—and particularly French—intellectuals towards the Communist parties and their ideologies. The Jesuit Sovietologist Henri Chambre bears witness to this changed climate with his dispassionate 1955 study of Marxism in the Soviet Union,[42] whereas Merleau-Ponty, representing a counter-tendency alongside Claude Lefort of the 'Socialisme ou Barbarie' group, took a firm stand against it with *The Adventures of the Dialectic* [1955], which confirmed his falling out with Sartre. The Soviet suppression of the Hungarian revolution in 1956 curtailed this trend by encouraging a sharp distinction between Eastern European 'socialism' and the emancipatory, anti-imperialist ideal of authentic Marxism. In this sense, Herbert Marcuse's *Soviet Marxism* (1958), which underscored the distinction, was a timely intervention.

The thinking of Sartre was typical in the way it followed this course.[43] Gorz was not to be outdone. He developed in a 'pro-Communist' direction, which, as he tells it, ended with new acquaintances and new reading in 1957.[44] However, like Sartre, he persisted for a while in cherishing illusions over a 'de-Stalinization' that 'might herald an authentic socialism'.[45] And

---

41 The Zurich POCH [Progressive Organizations of Switzerland] and the POB [Progressive Organizations of Basel].

42 Henri Chambre, *Le Marxisme en union soviétique* (Paris: Éditions du Seuil, 1955).

43 Emmanuel Barot (ed.), *Sartre et le marxisme* (Paris: La Dispute, 2011).

44 Gorz, *Letter to D.*, p. 80.

45 Gorz, *La Morale de l'histoire*, cover text.

when, in 1959, on a study trip to the GDR, he was horrified by the conformism of the workers and the brainwashing the regime subjected them
to, he put these aberrations down to . . . 'the German character'.[46] In the
1960s, it seems he even took the view that the French Parti socialiste unifié
(PSU) was inferior to the Swiss (Communist) Parti du travail [Swiss Labour
Party]—probably because it was less of a *workers'* party.[47]

When, much later, Cornelius Castoriadis, a fellow member, with Lefort,
of the Socialisme ou Barbarie group, would recall Sartre's pro-Soviet ambi-
guities in this period—comments which brought down Gorz's wrath upon
him—it was in fact Castoriadis who was right and not the master's defender
and sometime accomplice.[48]

Moreover, it is certain that Gorz's interest in the 'philosophy of Marx',
which he distinguishes from the vulgate of his followers (Engels included),
kept on growing and that he was able to say, as Sartre did, that 'there is no
other philosophy for this age.'[49] This attraction to Marxism was preceded
by an attraction to the proletariat: during winter 1949–50, he had himself
photographed with Dorine outside the Renault factories at Billancourt by
their Swiss friend, the professional photographer Suzi Pilet, whom Gorz
knew through his former girlfriend ('L' in *The Traitor*).[50] It arises initially
in the shadow of Sartre's development: in a manuscript of a hundred or so
pages written in 1958, Gorz tries to show 'the completion of existentialism

---

46 Michel Bosquet, 'Reportage. La perspective à l'Est', *L'Express* (11 June 1959).

47 According to Philippe Ivernel, then a PSU activist, in his undated letter to Gorz
(GRZ).

48 See Cornelius Castoriadis, 'The Diversionists', *Telos* 33 (1977): 102–06 (originally
published as 'Les divertisseurs', *Le Nouvel Observateur* [20 June 1977]); André Gorz,
'Sartre and the Deaf', *Telos* 33 (1977): 106–08 (originally published as 'Sartre et les
sourds', *Le Nouvel Observateur* [27 June 1977]); Cornelius Castoriadis, 'Reply to André
Gorz', *Telos* 33 (1977): 108–09 (originally published as 'Réponse à André Gorz', *Le
Nouvel Observateur* [4 July 1977]).

49 André Gorz, 'Force et faiblesse du marxisme d'aujourd'hui', undated [1960?] (GRZ
8.26). See Jean-Paul Sartre, *The Problem of Method* (London: Methuen Publishing,
1963), p. 29, this work being a translation of the first section of Sartre's *Critique de la
raison dialectique* (Paris: Gallimard, 1960); published in English as *Critique of Dialectical
Reason* (Alan Sheridan-Smith trans.) (London: Verso Books, 2004).

50 One of the photographs was published in *Libération* of 5 October 2006 in connection
with an article, though it appeared with the erroneous (and impossible) date of February
1947. [This photograph appears on the cover of the present work].

in a renovated Marxism.' That—excessively technical—text was turned down by the editors at Seuil, who criticized it for its 'deadly dull, jargon-ridden' character.[51] But Gorz already had another book underway.

The 1950s saw a proliferation of studies of Marxism entirely outside of standard Communist orthodoxy. A humanist reading of Marx acquired free rein with the work, in France, of the Thomist Pierre Bigo (*Marxisme et humanisme*, 1953), the Jesuit Jean-Yves Calvez (*La Pensée de Karl Marx*, 1956), Maximilien Rubel (*Marx*, 1957), Pierre Naville (*De l'Aliénation à la jouissance*, 1957), Lucien Goldmann (*Recherches dialectiques*, 1958) and, in the United States, Erich Fromm (*Marx's Concept of Man*, 1961) etc. It is as part of this broad general movement that we must situate Gorz when he publishes his first work of theory in June 1959, *La Morale de l'histoire*. He said that he had read Calvez's book (almost a mandatory reference), the writings of the young Marx (key texts for all these writers) and the Trotskyist Isaac Deutscher's *Stalin*,[52] to which must be added Lenin's *What Is to Be Done*?

Written between 1956 and 1958, in the hybrid style of philosophical journalism, *La Morale de l'Histoire* mingles the visions of existentialism and Marxism, affirming the fruitfulness of the encounter between the two. The title cleaves to the concerns of the times, as echoed in the manuscript on morality that Sartre passed to Gorz in 1958 for comparison.[53] It was not, however, very felicitous in terms of the overall content of the argument. The title of the Spanish translation, which translates as 'history and alienation'[54] gives a better sense of the problems addressed in the book—alienation in capitalist society and the prospect of socialism.

When Enjoyment [jouissance] *Takes Precedence over Efficiency*

In some of the pages of *Fondements pour une morale*, Marxism is discussed as a philosophy of history and hence as a theory of the building of socialism. The existentialist premiss of the choice of ends governs the principle

---

51 The aforementioned letter from Gorz to Madeleine Lafaurie (1958). The manuscript is mentioned only generically in the letter, but we believe we have identified it: consisting of 96 sheets, it is preserved as GRZ 1.1.

52 Gorz, *Letter to D.*, p. 79.

53 These working notes were placed by Gorz, through Michel Contat, in the French National Library in 1988.

54 André Gorz, *Historia y Enajenación* (México: Fondo de Cultura Económica, 1964).

adopted: the path liberating the proletariat is valid not so much as part of an objective process—the process of history—but of a conscious project that produces 'possibles'.[55] As for the means-ends dialectic which Merleau-Ponty calls on, following Trotsky (*Their Morals and Ours*), in his trenchant articles on 'The Yogi and the Proletarian',[56] this finds a subtle application in *Fondements*, where ends merge with means, the principle being that ends can be implemented and illustrated as much as possible in practice—without, for all that, means being shorn of the constraints of the present state of affairs. In an alienated world, these constraints are the product of an unavoidable evil. Subsequently, Gorz will be all too ready to revert to this argument to temper his critique of Eastern European regimes bogged down in the travails of a 'socialism of shortages and accumulation'.

However, in a 'happy' situation, in which the project has reached fruition, things present themselves differently. The anti-productivism present deep within Marxism is an ideal. It then becomes a question of not putting off enjoyment until later. In an authentically socialist society, he explains in the conclusion to *Fondements*, 'a construction plan will be valid insofar as its execution can be achieved without overwork and constraint, for there is no hurry, and even if the future it is leading to will be better than the present, there is no reason to sacrifice the joy of the present to it through unjustified haste.'[57]

The adherence to Marxism should not be based on the historic role of the proletariat that ensues from economic conditions, but should rest on a project focussed on a humanism, a project which is, in the words of (the young) Marx, a 'total re-conquest of man'.[58] It follows ideally, in a socialist society under construction, that efficiency and rationalization are not primary criteria for judging the moral authenticity of current action, since the routine, conformism and bureaucratization that threaten that authenticity erode freedom and lead to a new conservatism. 'The world in which freedom reigns is not the world of maximum rationalization,'[59] but the one in which

---

55 Gorz, *Fondements pour une morale*, pp. 113–18.

56 Gorz quotes Maurice Merleau-Ponty, 'Le yogi et le prolétaire (II)', *Les Temps modernes* 14 (November 1946): 253–87. Translated in Merleau-Ponty, *Humanism and Terror: The Communist Problem* (London: Routledge, 2017).

57 Gorz, *Fondements pour une morale*, p. 569.

58 Gorz, *Fondements pour une morale*, p. 587. The German expression is *die völlige Wiedergewinnung des Menschen* [Trans.].

which that rationalization enables the full development of human resources, even at the expense of immediate efficiency.

Gorz's humanist utopianism stops at this point. Pierre Naville, with his Surrealist and Trotskyist background, goes further in his book, contending that the Marxian critical standpoint that makes it possible for enjoyment to be grounded as freedom is the standpoint of non-work, a disinterested activity that has no value—and invokes Marx's son-in-law Paul Lafargue's famous *Right to Be Lazy*.

Socialism Is an Optional Necessity

La Morale de l'Histoire takes up the theme of the subject in history, a theme we encountered at the end of *Fondements*. Though, as Gorz sees it, history has no *direction* to it that is set in stone—an opinion shared by the ex-Trotskyist Castoriadis at this same point—a moral orientation may be embodied in a powerful social force that aspires to freedom: namely, the proletariat. This morality of the proletariat cannot be grounded in material and contingent *interests* in the form of work or wages, which are the very negation of their free being; it has to be grounded, rather, in *needs* posited in their 'autonomy', and in demands for humanity as *ends*.[60] We shall come back to this point.

Gorz is not far removed here from the case for proletarian autonomy and morality that the Council Communist and Marxologist Maximilien Rubel took from revolutionary syndicalist Georges Sorel, but his reference is, in fact, to Lenin and his problematic of workers' consciousness. The incongruity of the connection we are making here is merely apparent, the common ground between Sorel and Lenin being their rejection of spontaneism. Gorz takes the view that this revolutionary disposition, which mingles morality and needs, is not immanent to the labour movement and is, in appearance, introduced from the outside by its theorists. That revolutionary disposition does, however, assert itself in the workers' struggle when that struggle comes up against the impossibility of them making a life for themselves. From that point, the necessity of socialism is expressly willed by the proletarians and demands 'the explicit consciousness of their human ends': their praxis 'will have no other reasons than the ones it gives itself; in

---

59 Gorz, *Fondements pour une morale*, p. 589.
60 Gorz, *La Morale de l'Histoire*, pp. 147–56.

short, it will be *autonomous.*' If the demand for socialism must be backed by a conscious project—on which Lenin opportunely insisted—this also means that socialism isn't inevitable and is the response to a will: 'it is only an *optional* necessity.'[61] This is even truer now, since the attenuation of cyclical crises has eliminated the vital necessity for socialism that followed from pauperism.[62]

The Theory of Alienation

Gorz wrote on one occasion: 'My starting point has always been the experience of alienation.'[63] In that respect, he was following those of his generation. Whatever he may have said as a result of his disappointment with the failure of his *Morale* to make an impact in France (the print run was 4,000 copies and it was a long time before the book sold out), believing it to be exceptional in its themes,[64] many authors in the period 1956–68 made alienation a cardinal category of the Marxist philosophy they studied. The historian Pierre Nora described it as the 'buzzword' of the age.[65] These writers homed in on the critique of 'alienated labour' in Marx's *Economic and Philosophic Manuscripts* of 1844, which were published in Moscow in 1932: Marcuse commented on them immediately in Germany and Henri Lefebvre presented extracts from them in a volume of selected writings published in 1934.[66] The authors in question read that work with reference to Hegel, whose thought was given scholarly exposition in France by Alexandre Kojève and Jean Hyppolite: to get to grips with Marxism, as they saw it, you had to know Hegel. In a similar spirit, Gorz, visiting the GDR, was astonished that Hegel was not taught in that country (and that Ernst Bloch, the mediator of the young Marx, had been banned there since 1956).[67]

---

61 Gorz, *La Morale de l'Histoire*, pp. 166, 167, 172.

62 Gorz, *La Morale de l'Histoire*, pp. 163–81.

63 Letter in English from André Gorz to Josué Pereira da Silva, 29 January 2006 (GRZ).

64 See Gorz, Preface to *Fondements pour une morale*, p. 19n. According to Gorz, the Italian (1960) and Spanish (1964) translations received greater attention.

65 Pierre Nora, 'Aliénation' in *Le Débat, Les Idées en France 1945–1988* (Paris: Gallimard, 1989), pp. 493–500.

66 On the importance of these *1844 Manuscripts* for the Western Marxism of the period, see Perry Anderson, *Considerations on Western Marxism* (London: New Left Books, 1979), pp. 50–1.

67 See Bosquet, 'Reportage. La perspective à l'Est'.

For these authors not in hock to Stalinism, the issue was to demolish what some regarded as the anti-dialectical, positivistic 'reflection theory' of consciousness on which Communists drew in their claim to possess scientific truth. Henri Lefebvre, who had come to Communism through Surrealism and retained a degree of independence, had already cast doubt on this theory before the war; at odds with the party since the Budapest events of 1956, he set the tone by problematizing the discrepancy between what people think and how they act in the first volume of his *Critique of Everyday Life* [second edition 1958], which was a prelude to the critique of advertising and the consumer society contained in the second [1961].

Other authors followed, reserving a crucial place for the concept of alienation. As we have already mentioned, these included Father Jean-Yves Calvez, who was nonetheless hostile to an accord between Christians and Marxists; Pierre Naville who, after noting that Hegel founded political economy on the 'system of needs', drew inspiration from the *1844 Manuscripts* to situate disalienation beyond the realm of work; Lucien Goldmann, who studied reification on the basis of the Hungarian Communist György Lukács's *History and Class Consciousness* (a text disavowed in 1960 by its long-since 'officially approved' author, as it endangered the idea of reflection); and the psycho-sociologist Joseph Gabel who, basing himself also on Lukács and on the phenomenology of the psychiatrists Binswanger and Minkowski, interrogated the concept of political alienation', drawing on 'false consciousness' as illustrated by clinical cases of schizophrenia (*False Consciousness* [1962]. The philosopher Kostas Axelos, who was working alongside Edgar Morin to tease out a 'meta-Marxism' in the journal *Arguments*, at the same time as he was editing Gabel and translating the 'outlawed' young Lukács for the Éditions de Minuit's 'Arguments' collection, was well aware of how things stood when, by deconstructing the concept of alienation, he rebranded Marx as a 'thinker of technology' (*Marx, penseur de la technique*, 1961).

If Gorz neglects the *economic* critique that lends the *1844 Manuscripts* their vigour, preferring the philosophical views of Marx and Engels' *German Ideology*, and if he makes no serious effort at a detailed study of Hegel, that is because he continues to be steeped in existentialist phenomenology. For him, that philosophy is sufficient for reflecting on alienation, *having as its object the ends and needs of man.*[68]

---

68 For a long account of the theory of alienation in Gorz, see Josué Pereira de Silva, *André Gorz. Trabalho e política* (São Paulo: Annablume, 2002). Pereira de Silva does,

The Non-accomplishment of Ends

Summing up Hegel, Gorz writes (doubtless on the basis of Marx's interpretation) that the essence of man for him is work [*le travail*] and that it is through work that man realizes himself. Hegel mainly sees alienation as the externalization of the subject in the products of his work. What is involved is an objectification (*Entäusserung*—a becoming-other) that is of the order of control, with no contradiction between the subject and the matter transformed. As for Marx, he takes an opposite version from Hegel, in which alienation means the loss of self into the object produced, which acquires an independent quality. This is an estrangement (*Entfremdung*—becoming alien) that is of the order of servitude and it brings the individual's ends into contradiction with the observed outcome.[69]

Existentialism, concerned less with the economic act of producing than with the generic act of the socialization of the individual, describes this phenomenon in its way as an 'alienation mediated by others': the aims of what I do end up drowned in the system because my action is limited by the actions of others.[70] Marxism explains this as 'social alienation': human activity is deployed in a fragmented, uncoordinated way, with the consequence that the result achieved at the level of society is independent of individual ends.[71] In all cases, the basic initial postulate is the same: the non-accomplishment of the human in objectification is possible because 'we are always action towards our ends'[72] and there is no guarantee that these will be realized. For all that vulgar (and Stalinist) Marxism may keep on saying that man is the product of objective conditions and that alienation is a passively experienced state and subjectively non-existent, those conditions were produced by human beings with ends which we are very much bound to investigate.

These ends which humanity sets itself are there to satisfy a specific demand which precedes its action and governs the whole of its behaviour. For existentialist philosophy, prior demand is the product of a *choice*. From a social and economic standpoint, it may be defined as a *need*. The question

however, obscure the place of the notion of *need* in the underpinning of that theory, perhaps because Portuguese makes no distinction between 'need' and 'necessity' (*necessidade* covering both concepts).

69 Gorz, *La Morale de l'histoire*, p. 54.

70 Gorz, *La Morale de l'histoire*, pp. 67–74.

71 Gorz, *La Morale de l'histoire*, pp. 83–92.

72 Gorz, *La Morale de l'histoire*, p. 55.

of what needs are, how they are differentiated and how they intervene in the working of a social system turns out, then, to be essential for measuring the alienation in a society. It is all the more essential for the fact that Western societies—and American society foremost among them—have reached such a degree of wealth that they give the—erroneous—impression that they can satisfy the needs of all and have begun the process of lifting the proletariat into the middle class.

What Is a Need in the Affluent Society? The American Case

The great advantage of the analyses Gorz develops on alienation lies in the fact that his theoretical critique of the phenomenon involves a consideration of the contemporary forms it takes. The anthropological critique has a sociological critique running alongside it that lends it concrete form. As in the past, Gorz looks towards the United States. His two-pronged experience of the Swiss case—a comfort and alienation which he found unbearable, but also a puritanical, autarkic phobia of waste which he internalized— leaves him well-placed to grasp the American situation.

He studied this through two works which, though unknown in France, were having an enormous impact on the other side of the Atlantic: *White Collar* (1951) by C. Wright Mills and David Riesman's *The Lonely Crowd* (1950). The first of these, reminiscent, in its psychological approach, of Karen Horney's *The Neurotic Personality of our Time* (1937), describes the behavioural alienation of employees in the labour market and in service jobs. The second, its themes echoing those of another book by another émigré German psychoanalyst, Erich Fromm's *Fear of Freedom* (1941), explains the modernity of the US in terms of an emergent 'social character'. This consists, for the atomized individual who is shorn of his traditional references, in seeking behavioural norms in how others see him, in calming his anxiety through social proprieties, the herd instinct and consumption. His own needs will, therefore, be those of his peers. But what is the nature of those needs?

Needs, observes Gorz, are always socially conditioned and should not be classed as artificial on the grounds that they did not exist before the arrival 'of the gadgets and innumerable tools of technological civilization': 'The richer a civilization, the richer and more diverse will human needs be.'[73] But

---

73 Gorz, *La Morale de l'histoire*, pp. 234–5.

if need, for Marx, far from reducing to a physiological datum, corresponds to a lack that is embedded at every moment in a social context, this is because it is an 'autonomous exigency' the subject gives himself at the very moment when he is caught in the net of 'alienating objectivation'. It is at this level of the analysis that Axelos, left out of account by Gorz, deplores in Marx's writings an indeterminate and 'metaphysical' underside of the concept of alienation. This is why, Gorz goes on undaunted, 'Marxists implicitly found an ethic on need':

> They see negativity in it: need and the needy human being contest the existing society—and the penury that society installs—in the name of need and the needy and that alone. Need is incipiently revolutionary; it implicitly calls for a society that makes its satisfaction and enrichment possible.[74]

But everything changes if need, instead of providing the grounds for social demands, is generated by existing society simply to perpetuate itself: 'If men do not plan a society according to *their* needs, but if society shapes men according to *its* needs.' It seems, then, that we have to distinguish between autonomous and heteronomous, authentic and inauthentic needs. But how are they to be distinguished? And *who* will draw this distinction?'[75] This muddle, which brings into play the difficult definition of the subject working at his own disalienation, is left hanging for the moment. On the other hand, basing himself on the American case presented by Riesman, Gorz readily identifies the logics and techniques put to work to generate and orient needs.

In order to shift the goods created by mass production, the economic system produces desires which, as it happens, are those of conformity, social adaptation and recognition by one's peers. Thus, advertising incites us to consume so as to keep up appearances and be like others.

By satisfying the quest for uniformity, this marketing strategy ultimately applied only to a definite cycle of the American—and subsequently, European—economy: that of the 'one-dimensional man' derided by Marcuse. Gorz also uncovers a more substantial strategy which was going to characterize capitalist growth in the long term. This is the increase in ephemeral needs that are renewable as a result of the artificial obsolescence

---

74 Gorz, *La Morale de l'histoire*, p. 235.
75 Gorz, *La Morale de l'histoire*, pp. 235–6.

of products; thus 'wastefulness' is pre-arranged by decking out products with symbolic values that make them obsolete even as they are still physically viable. As the American advertising executive Stanley Resor, whom Gorz cites at length, pointed out in 1957, the full utilization of production capacities requires the growth of consumption, something that isn't given automatically by income growth but is made possible thanks to the 'force of education' that advertising represents.[76] We have here 'the fundamental alienation of the capitalist affluent society':

> The obligation to consume to keep the economy going; the fact that we will have to consume in order to be able to work, and not the other way about; the fact that the existence of millions of workers can only be assured by the systematic squandering of the wealth they produce; the fact, therefore, that their work, which is destined to be squandered, has no meaning and remains enslaved to its products.[77]

The 'critique of the affluent model of consumption' emanating from these pages anticipates the themes which Jean Baudrillard, returning from the US, will develop so strikingly in his *The Consumer Society* of 1970.[78] Most importantly, it makes of Gorz an 'ecologist before the term even existed', as he will himself claim in an interview carried out in 2004.[79] Indissociable from a critical theory of needs, it is indeed the starting point for his future conversion to an anti-capitalist political ecology.

---

76 Gorz, *La Morale de l'histoire*, pp. 246–7 and 250–1.

77 Gorz, *La Morale de l'histoire*, pp. 254–5.

78 Jean Baudrillard, *The Consumer Society: Myths and Structures* (Chris Turner trans.) (London: Sage Publications, 1998).

79 Gorz, *Ecologica*, p. 6.

PART TWO

Liberation from Work in the Age of Automation

The 1960s: Fordism and the Welfare State

'Revolution is simply the movement that imposes the reality of life on the economic reality which negates it.'

Raoul Vaneigem, *Nous qui désirons sans fin*, p. 179

'The problem becomes that of the kind and content of the life to be produced.'

André Gorz, *Strategy for Labor*, p. 101

CHAPTER SIX

Revolutionary Reformism

Scrutinizing the different ages of life is something existentialism does.[1] Sartre had expatiated at length on childhood and death and Simone de Beauvoir would do the same with regard to old age (*La Vieillesse*, 1970). Between the two there remains 'working' age, that long period of adult life separating youth from old age which, when compared with these, poses the problem of autonomy in an incommensurably different way: the dependency on others inherent in childhood and looming over the third age is far removed from the situation of the adult in the prime of life, whose power Gorz, as a good existentialist, undertakes to de-mythify.

The End of Youth, and Social Integration

At the turn of the 1950s, Gorz felt the need to write a follow-up to *The Traitor* that would reflect his new situation in life. He called it 'Le vieillissement'—ageing.[2] As early as 1958, the book's cover blurb stated: 'A man discovers that it is too late: *he is who he is* [il est fait]. Without noticing it and while still thinking he was keeping the future open, he has begun to have a life'. 'He reaches the age when there is no starting again, the age when you begin to grow old, when you have to accept taking up a place in society that will make you Other among Others'[3]—that is to say, in prosaic terms—you 'would have to take a job and, for the most part, lead an *ordinary* life.'[4]

At the age of 38, the man had forged a career for himself, with two books published, together with articles that had gained some notice. He was

---

1 Éric Deschavanne and Pierre-Henri Tavoillot, *Philosophie des âges de la vie* (Paris: Grasset, 2007).

2 André Gorz, *Le Traître* suivi *de Le Vieillissement* (Paris: Gallimard 'Collection Folio essais', 2008 [2005]), pp. 375–405. Original version published as 'Le vieillissement', *Les Temps modernes* 187 (December 1961): 638–65, and *Les Temps modernes* 188 (January 1962): 829–52.

3 Gorz, 'Le vieillissement', *Le Traître*, p. 375.

4 Gorz, *Traitor*, p. 238.

married (since 1949) and naturalized French (since 1957). He was beginning to experience a degree of material comfort. He was better housed (since 1956 he had been living in a fourth-floor flat at 65, rue du Bac, where he co-habited with cockroaches but had the use of a bathtub . . .) and he went on regular summer holidays (to Italy, Nerja on the Andalusian coast or Yugoslavia), initially on the back of a motorcycle, then in a car in which he clocked up thousands of miles. Emotionally, he felt he had reached adulthood, having successfully smoothed things out with his parents, starting with his mother:

> I have no grievances towards her anymore and, when I see her again once a year, I appreciate her good sides which are remarkable, the way I appreciate anyone else's good sides. I had, similarly, forgiven my father for being my father shortly before his death in 1957: in the end he had told me his—very sorry—life story. I believe a person only becomes an adult when he has so entirely emancipated himself from his parents—in our societies this always involves a rebellious phase—that he can try to understand their lives like those of any other individual close to him.[5]

And with his wife, he felt the stability of what he envisaged as a lifelong union: 'After 15 years of life together, they formed what is called a devoted couple. The magic of desire had vanished between them, except sporadically, and they had [sic] faithful to each other.[6] As far as they could see, they would remain so till the end of their lives. They were on the way to dying together.'[7] Though reluctant to follow the prevailing consumer model in inventing needs for themselves—they had as a couple 'never spent anything like what [they] could have spent on [their] standard of living or level of consumption'[8]—Gorz was ready to enquire into the conformism and routine of his life and the weakening of his ideals, into the compromises[9] and alienation[10] of his journalistic occupation, into the life he was losing/wasting

---

5 Gorz, 'André Gorz intellectuel et journaliste'.

6 The text is defective here.

7 Fragment of an unpublished follow-up to *The Traitor*, undated [1962?] (GRZ 50.3).

8 Gorz, *Letter to D.*, p. 82.

9 See an unpublished imaginary dialogue by André Gorz, undated, reflecting his early days at *Paris-presse* (GRZ 50.3).

10 See André Gorz's notes on journalism, contemporary with 'Le vieillissement', which are published in Fourel (ed.), *André Gorz en personne*, pp. 92–9.

as he earned his living ('all work consisting in selling one's time to have the remaining time for oneself')[11]—in other words, into his 'ageing' and the meaning of the word 'integration'.

At that same moment, the filmmaker Jacques Demy was portraying the malaise afflicting young people reaching adulthood with the film *Lola*, whose protagonist is bored and disaffected with work. In reference to another film that offended conventional opinion by portraying a group of disoriented young people rejecting both work and social integration, Marcel Carné's *Young Sinners*, Gorz had already developed some thoughts on the difficulties his generation of immediate post-war youth had finding a way forward. It seemed to him that, steeped as they were in existentialist ideas, they shared with their elders in the Resistance generation the reforming zeal that came out of the Liberation. By 1950, that zeal was exhausted, leaving an ideological void in the following generation described by Carné, a void reinforced by the absence of a revolutionary perspective in the developed West.[12] Gorz noticed that in the Soviet Union too, young people were seeking meaning in their lives.[13] He had great expectations of the transformative fervour of young people in other parts of the world, particularly in 1960 in Cuba and Algeria. As a Third Worldist, like all progressives at the time, he shared those expectations with most French intellectuals who were to be rather disconcerted by the youthful effervescence of May 1968 in France.

But Gorz, who rubbed shoulders with the perspicacious Alfred Sauvy at *L'Express,* was looking also to the changes the baby-boomers might bring 'from 1965 onwards'.[14] This proved to be a good intuition, since '68, as Edgar Morin would stress in the thick of the events, would also be a demographic/generational phenomenon. The *mal d'époque* specific to the West seemed to him the sickness of a deadlocked world:

> It is the monstrous inertia of its [the world's] petrified structures; it is our powerlessness to change it and the impossibility of finding a meaning for it; it is the death of traditional values and revolutionary values *at one and the same time*. What is left? A life without

---

11 Fourel (ed.), *André Gorz en personne.*, p. 96.

12 André Gorz, 'Le point de vue d'André Gorz, auteur du *Traître*', *Gazette littéraire* (supplement to *La Gazette de Lausanne*) (18 October 1958).

13 Manuscript of an unidentified article [from second half of 1960] (GRZ 7.2).

14 André Gorz, 'Le vieillissement', pp. 388, 390.

significance, this transitional state of availability that we call 'youth', which we take advantage of (if we can) without believing in it; this gloomy future the collective apparatuses have pre-established for everyone.[15]

If, for Gorz, youth is the period in which 'the individual regards society as a contingent hindrance and believes he can build his life against it or in the margins', the loss of that illusion expresses arrival at adulthood: the individual is no longer free to choose another path than that which his past has already marked out for him. This 'excess of conditioning'[16] corresponds to what Sartre, in the *Critique of Dialectical Reason*, which Gorz had just read, calls the weight of the 'practico-inert': 'one is produced in passivity by what the practico-inert ensemble makes out of what one has just made'[17] (referring to 'Le vieillissement', an expert on Sartre's work would tell Gorz, 'You have drawn the pith out of the *Critique* here.')[18] The consequence of this is the restriction of the domains of what is possible and a paralysis of the imagination. While the lack of means for action confines young people to pure oppositional protest [*contestation*], adulthood is, admittedly, the moment for action but not of omnipotence: action is immediately frustrated by the discovery that 'each individual has a purchase on the world only through the instruments provided by the social field and those instruments, even when he reshapes them for his own use, mark out like a destiny the sense and unsurpassable limits of his action.'[19]

Gorz concluded that the transition to adulthood and ageing are less about a biological process and more about the sanction of society (Beauvoir, who immediately spotted the fruitfulness of Gorz's analysis, would say the same thing of old age, which is only such in the eyes of the other), since it isn't so much the individuals' bodies that dictate their age as their relation to society: adulthood is the 'social age' when the individual is socially integrated.

That integration is signified by the place of producer and consumer carved out for him within a social machinery in which he has no purchase

---

15 Gorz, 'Le point de vue d'André Gorz, auteur du *Traître*'.

16 Gorz, 'Le vieillissement', pp. 386, 392.

17 Sartre, *Critique of Dialectical Reason*, VOL. 1, p. 337.

18 François George to André Gorz, 9 October 2005 (GRZ) subsequent to Gorz sending him the new edition of *Le Traître* containing 'Le vieillissement'.

19 Gorz, 'Le vieillissement', p. 395.

on anything whatever, but, through self-censorship and habit, assumes his function with the ease of a well-oiled cog in a machine: 'You are no longer oppressed: you oppress yourselves.'[20] This kind of observation does not relate to the diffuse mass of the excluded—the poor students and the jobless, wageless, homeless etc.—which, for that reason are potentially oppositional, as he had already suggested in 1946 with respect to the rootless.[21] Integration occurs both through the *career* and the *financial solvency* it makes possible. This twofold alienation is reflected in the mirror of the commodity illusion, defined as follows:

> [P]roducing these cosmetic, false objects which, in our conformity-inducing consumer societies, have to carefully conceal beneath their flawless veneer the *sweat, fatigue* and *dirtiness* of work, the *asperities, resistance and wear* of material, in order to reflect to the duped and fascinated consumer [. . .] the mythic, fetishized world of affluence: that is to say, the absolutely false world of painless elegance in which commodities are born instantaneously and by magic thanks to the simple casual gesture of taking a note from one's wallet, and in which *money* is the shortest path from need to enjoyment, wealth is *purchasing power* and the scarcity of products, scarcity of cash.[22]

Les Temps modernes **and the Italian Horizon**

Gorz's thinking deepened during the 1960s. Having been essentially philosophical, it now took a more economic form, as though existential critique could derive its legitimacy only from a concrete, empirical approach to the techno-material structure of society. With the intensification of capitalism's economic and technical advances, on which the idea of progress had rested since Condorcet's *Esquisse d'un tableau historique,* came pressure to situate rationality on that terrain. It was there, as a consequence, that those who claimed to undermine that rationality were required to pitch their arguments.

The spectacular penetration of structuralism into the social sciences, including Marxism (Louis Althusser published his *For Marx* in 1965), attests

---

20 Gorz, 'Le vieillissement', p. 401.

21 Gorz, *Fondements pour une morale*, p. 463.

22 Gorz, 'Le vieillissement', pp. 401–02.

to this trend aspiring to scientificity; the decline—already underway—of existentialism, which gave precedence to life and history, was a pendant to it.[23] Gorz remained impervious to this fashion which transformed the subject into a 'bearer' of structures and left out of account the *praxis* that brought about radical breaks. He showed this in June 1967 during a broadcast of the radio programme *Le Masque et la plume* in which, with Mikel Dufrenne, he inveighed against the structuralist thought of Foucault, Lévi-Strauss, Althusser and the rest.[24] Later Gorz would relate that he had objected that Lévi-Strauss was definitely conversing freely with him, to which the anthropologist had replied, 'smiling, that his words were merely neuronal activities in "his" brain, confirming once again that he was a "perfect virtuoso of subjectless, formalizing thought".'[25] Gorz would be just as critical of the postmodernists who downplayed the subject in the same way.[26]

In a way, though, this reorientation, reflective of the times, would show up all the same in Gorz's thinking—to be precise, in a reading of Marx that left aside his youthful philosophical writings to concentrate on his critique of political economy. *Capital* and, to an even greater extent, Marx's preparatory work on that book which was published in Moscow in 1939, then in a facsimile edition in Berlin as *Grundrisse der Kritik der politischen Ökonomie* (1953), were now among the books he kept closest by him. Consequently, the 'Marxist humanism' that was seen as deriving from the *1844 Manuscripts* and abhorred by Althusser was specifically rejected by Gorz on the grounds that it was based on a generic human nature with needs that can be rediscovered, rather than needs seen as 'overdetermined' in historical production.[27]

---

23 See Anna Boschetti, *The Intellectual Enterprise: Sartre and Les Temps modernes* (Evanston, IL: Northwestern University Press, 1988), pp. 229–30.

24 'Sartre et le structuralisme', *Le Masque et la plume* (France Inter, 11 June 1967) (available at: https://bit.ly/3wEa87C; last accessed: 25 July 2022) See also André Gorz, *Réforme et révolution* (Paris: Seuil, 1969), pp. 18–19.

25 André Gorz, *Wissen, Wert und Kapital. Zur Kritik der Wissensökonomie* (Zurich: Rotpunkt, 2005 [2004]), p. 118. This is the revised and augmented German edition of *L'Immatériel* (Paris: Galilée, 2003); published in English as *The Immaterial: Knowledge, Value and Capital* (Chris Turner trans.) (London: Seagull Books, 2010).

26 See Gorz, 'La vie, la nature, la technique', pp. 30–2.

27 See his interview with Ilija Bojović in *Socijalizam*, June 1967, reprinted in Ilija Bojović, *1968. Archéologie d'une pensée*. Text established and presented by Boško Bojović (Vevey: La Valsainte, 2008), pp. 124–5.

This was an important point of disagreement with the 'naturalist conception' that appeared to him to underlie the idea of alienation in the writings of the Freudo–Marxist Herbert Marcuse, and Gorz was now able to make it explicit.[28] Hence the de facto proximity to the accusation of 'biologism' which that other American Frankfurtian Erich Fromm relentlessly levelled against his colleague and rival.

This development in Gorz's thinking went hand in hand with his editorial activity at *Les Temps modernes*. It was because Sartre sensed that the influence of his philosophy was waning and wished, as a result, to broaden the thematic base of the journal that he decided in November 1960 to co-opt Gorz on to the editorial board at the same time as he recruited the psychoanalyst Jean-Bertrand Pontalis and Bernard Pingaud from the world of letters. Covering international events (after a first article published in April 1960), Gorz brought a socioeconomic dimension to the political section, which had the backing of Marcel Péju, the journal's general secretary, and Claude Lanzmann.

The expansion of the editorial board occurred in the wake of the 'Manifesto of the 121' in support of the Jeanson network. The *Temps modernes* team were involved in shaping this manifesto which argued for the right to refuse the draft for the Algerian war. Unlike the other two new members of the editorial board, Gorz did not sign it. At *L'Express*, this was also the case with Servan-Schreiber and Jean Daniel, whereas the cartoonist Siné, Lafaurie and Bost appended their names. We do not know why Gorz did not. There can, however, be no doubt that he was resolutely on the side of the new Algeria,[29] as indeed were many other non-signatories (including Bourdet and Martinet at *France-Observateur*), who were concerned not to increase the political divisions within the Left. This would seem to represent a 'rift between practice and theory', further confirmed by his refusal, 'despite his stated principles, to "carry suitcases" ', according to Olivier Todd who

---

28 See Gorz, *Réforme et révolution*, p. 17.

29 Michel Bosquet signed an article on Algeria and its future in the first issue of the Genevan monthly *Dire* (April 1960) alongside Jotterand, Favrod, Moulin, Apothéloz and Bovard. Swiss friends of Gorz's worked behind the scenes for Algerian independence, such as Favrod, who actually argued the case for the whole of Africa, or Freddy Buache's wife Marie-Magdeleine Brumagne, who visited Gorz on clandestine trips to Paris. Michel Contat, with whom Gorz would subsequently associate, was a member of this Swiss branch of the Jeanson network.

rubbed shoulders on the editorial team with 'the ever strange Gorz'.[30] In reality, this attitude chimes with what seems to us to have been this intellectual's 'uncommitted involvement', which we shall explain below.

Péju was accused of being too close to the Algerian FLN (it was alleged, in fact, that he was in their pay) and left the journal in 1962. That episode has been interpreted as the effect of a succession struggle between the publication's Sartrean disciples (including Jean Pouillon) and an interloper. Gorz, who would never fully be a member of the in-group, did not engage in it. However, following the ousting of Péju, his political authority within the newly formed management committee continued to grow to the point where it became preponderant in 1968, with the proportion of articles of a political cast increasing almost to 50 per cent in this period. This was not so much because of the closeness of his ideas to those of Sartre—though that was something he did cultivate, as attested by a lecture on 'Sartre's current thought' which he gave at the Théâtre du Faux-Nez, Lausanne, at Jotterand's invitation, on 18 February 1961.[31] He owed his aura, rather, to his expertise in economics: 'He influenced Sartre,' remembers Olivier Todd, 'coming out with lots of figures, all of them pointing in the right direction. Since no one—absolutely no one—with the possible exception of Lefort, had even the most basic economic knowledge, [he] could freely exert an economic terrorism that was all the more readily accepted for the fact that it corresponded to progressivism and the prevailing desires.'[32] In 1963, he managed to have two dense economic articles on the Common Market published, one by himself and another by Lazare Rozensztroch.

Yet it wasn't so much his few articles on economic and social themes in the years before 1968 that brought him power in *Les Temps modernes* as his coordination of thematic issues for which he supplied introductions, such as those of Autumn 1962 and February 1967 on the labour movement or of May 1963 on the Sino-Soviet conflict. The very first of these issues drew on Italian authors for half of the articles: Lelio Basso, Vittorio Foa and the

---

30 Olivier Todd, *Un fils rebelle* (Paris: Grasset, 1981), pp. 113–4. The 'suitcases' in question contained money and documents for the Algerian National Liberation Front (FLN) [Trans.].

31 See also André Gorz, 'Sartre and Marx', *New Left Review* 37 (May–June 1966): 33–52.

32 Todd, *Un fils rebelle*, p. 113. Lefort's participation in *Les Temps modernes* ended in 1953.

Communists Bruno Trentin, Lucio Magri and Giorgio Amendola. It reveals that Gorz was now charting his political course by orientations that emerged from the Italian labour movement, within whose ranks a radicalized Left of a new type was forming.

Gorz was extending his intellectual network at the time. In 1962, he was already in contact with Marcuse. He also maintained relations—politically closer at that point—with the Trotskyists Ernest Mandel and Jean-Marie Vincent. Mandel, who was to become the leading figure in the Fourth International, was engaged in 'entryism' into the Belgian Socialist Party. He had published an encyclopaedic treatise on Marxist economics in 1962[33] and Gorz both cited this enthusiastically and called regularly on its author for articles on Marxist theory in *Les Temps modernes*. Vincent was a young leader of the Parti socialiste unifié (PSU), who dazzled Gorz with his erudition in the social sciences and who, when *La Morale de l'histoire* came out, had pointed out to him the passages he should read in the *Grundrisse*, which Gorz was discovering at the time. In 1963, Vincent invited Gorz to the international conference on 'European Integration and the Labour Movement' organized by the Centre d'études socialistes, close to the PSU, and Gorz, attending a conference for the first time, made a long presentation there.[34] Gorz also struck up a relationship with Perry Anderson's *New Left Review*, in which he would publish from time to time. It was he who, in early 1964, used his influence to have his friend Ronald Fraser, whom he had met on holiday in Andalusia in 1957, taken on to the staff of *New Left Review*, where Fraser would become a mainstay. Thanks also to Vincent, who introduced him to his own circle of acquaintances—including Germans—and with whom he went to Italy in 1963, Gorz operated as an international journalist, something which brought him closer to Italian theorists who would have a great influence on him.

Among these, Lelio Basso (the future founder, with Sartre, of the Russell Tribunal) did not realize that he was laying the foundations of a friendship when he wrote to *L'Express* in 1962 to dispute a poorly informed investigation into the Italian socialist Left under the by-line Michel Bosquet.[35] Basso,

---

33 Translated into English as Ernest Mandel, *Marxist Economic Theory* (Delhi: Aakar Books, 2008).

34 Gorz, *Strategy for Labor*, pp. 135–90.

35 See Michel Bosquet, 'Italie. Le grand pari', *L'Express* (1 February 1962). Bosquet had got his information from Pietro Nenni, the leader of the Italian Socialist Party, whom

who moved in PSU circles (frequenting Gilles Martinet, Marc Heurgon and Vincent) even before the birth of that party in 1960, was keen on international exchanges.[36] A left-wing, Luxemburgist Socialist (and scholarly publisher of Rosa Luxemburg), opposed to the Italian Centre-Left government that had arisen from Socialist participation, he co-founded the PSIUP (Italian Socialist Proletarian Unity Party) in 1964, whose position on the Italian political spectrum was comparable to that of the PSU in France. It was his attention to the political and democratic pre-requisites of the transition to socialism that fed into Gorz's thinking.

Contributions to that thinking on a different level came from Lucio Magri, a young Catholic who had joined the Italian Communist Party (PCI) in 1956, becoming one of its leaders before being expelled in 1969; from Vittorio Foa, a former liberal-democratic resistance fighter, a Socialist dissident and founder of the PSIUP, a leader of the CGIL trade union confederation, described plausibly by Gorz as an 'anarcho-syndicalist'[37] and a respected thinker of the Extreme Left;[38] or from Trentin, who was born in France into an exiled anti-fascist family, a former resistance fighter and the talented Secretary General of FIOM, the metalworkers' union, whom Gorz got to know well on seaside holidays in Apulia in 1963. The thinking of these three men was forged, in each case, in *reflection from a workerist angle* on the nature of the struggle the working class tends to wage against the capitalist labour process. This is what interested Gorz, who in 1963 began writing *Stratégie ouvrière et néocapitalisme*, subsequently translated as *Strategy for Labor: A Radical Proposal*.

From 1962 onwards, Gorz increased the number of trips to Italy and the people he met with there. At the very beginning of the year he came back from Rome highly impressed by his visit to the headquarters of the

---

he had met at Megève. See Michel Bosquet's reply to Lelio Basso of 9 February 1962 (LLB: Fondazione Lelio e Lisli Basso, Rome).

36 See Roberto Colozza, 'Une affinité intellectuelle, une proximité politique. Lelio Basso, Gilles Martinet et la "deuxième gauche" ', *Histoire@Politique* 16 (January–April 2012): 1–12, (available at: histoire-politique.fr; last accessed: 25 July 2022).

37 In the post-war period, he worked together effectively with the one-time revolutionary syndicalist Giuseppe Di Vittorio at the head of the CGIL.

38 The journals *Quaderni rossi* and *Il Manifesto*, to which we shall turn later, began with an article by Foa.

CGIL, where he talked with Foa, a 'massive intellectual figure' in his fifties, who reminded him of Jean Hyppolite, and with Trentin, 'who seemed just as intellectual'.[39] The first words he remembered Foa saying to him fore-shadowed a whole new strategy and social project: 'It is the workers' struggle against alienation that will keep trade unionism alive, not just the struggle against exploitation.'[40] In September he witnessed for himself the originality of the strikes by the Turin and Milan metalworkers, who were not so much calling for wage rises as targeting the 'despotism' exerted over working conditions 'by capital'. He reported Trentin's declaration that: 'The more the workers' living standards rise, the more the other aspects of labour relations become unbearable.'[41]

When, for *L'Express*, he went with Karol to the tenth PCI Congress in Rome in December, he came across such dynamic, open-minded leaders as Rossana Rossanda (Karol's future companion), with whom he would soon come to share the adventurous ideas of '68. It was also an opportunity for him to size up the 'Italian path' to socialism, which was distinct both from Stalinism and from French reformism: it was both distant from the 'real socialism' that had been denounced since 1956 and careful not to dissociate reforms from the thoroughgoing transformation of society.[42] He made detailed analyses of it, such as the one that appeared in the first issue of *The Socialist Register*, edited by the Marxist theorist Ralph Miliband.[43] As for his article in the inaugural number of *Le Nouvel Observateur* in 1964, it was the product of an interview with Trentin in Rome, which heralded other trips to Italy.[44]

The intense relations with the Italian Marxists also showed up in reciprocal collaboration on magazines and journals. At times Gorz had their articles translated for *Les Temps modernes*. Before 1968, he himself collaborated on Basso's *Problemi del socialismo*; on *Mondo nuovo*, the PSIUP

---

39 Michel Bosquet, 'Socialisme. Le laboratoire italien', *L'Express* (4 January 1962).

40 André Gorz to Jacques Robin, 12–4 September 1997 (GRZ). Gorz dates the episode to 1960 (?).

41 Bosquet, 'Reportage. Grève à l'italienne'.

42 See Bosquet, 'Communistes. Les premiers pas'.

43 Michel Bosquet, 'Aspects of Italian Communism', *The Socialist Register* (October 1964): 82–91.

44 Michel Bosquet, 'L'automobile en crise', *Le Nouvel Observateur* (19 November 1964).

publication edited by Lucio Libertini; on the *International Socialist Journal*, a French–English bilingual bi-monthly created by Basso in 1964 in Milan (Martinet and Vincent were the French and Ken Coates and Jim Mortimer the British representatives on the editorial board), working (in 1967) to find Scandinavian collaborators for it; and even on *Critica marxista*, the PCI's journal, commenting on the thought of Marcuse or defending that of Sartre.

Workers' Control and Workers' Autonomy

Between 1946 and 1973, the standard of living increased by a factor of three in France, social inequalities decreased and the way of life underwent a thorough transformation.[45] The economist Jean Fourastié dubbed these years the *trente glorieuses*, the 30 glorious years (the riposte of the ecologists would be that they were 30 disastrous ones).[46] The social compromise prevailing in Europe at the time consisted in rationalizing work by Fordist methods in exchange for full employment and redistributive policies. The docile worker, who was at one and the same time—in line with Ford and Keynes's intentions—a consumer, was to have 'purchasing power' and comfort as his sole horizons. The 1960s represent the high point of this model of economic expansion, which was backed up, in France and Italy in particular, by a tendency towards economic planning on the part of a welfare state. It was precisely in the course of that decade that the challenge to the Fordist social contract began to emerge on the workers' side—timidly in France through the CFTC and then the CFDT,[47] but very strongly in Italy through the CGIL. Not to mention the awakening to activism of the youth in those countries, which gave rise to the New Left and heralded 1968.

By publishing the 'half-Italian' issue of *Les Temps modernes* entitled 'Données et problèmes de la lutte ouvrière' in 1962, then in spring of 1964 his new book *Stratégie ouvrière et néocapitalisme* and, lastly in 1967 *Le Socialisme difficile* [*Socialism and Revolution*, 1973], a book structured

---

45 Jean Fourastié, *Les Trente Glorieuses ou la révolution invisible de 1946 à 1975* (Paris: Fayard, 1979).

46 Alain Hervé, the founder of the French branch of Friends of the Earth, coined this phrase.

47 A large majority of the CFTC, a Christian trade union federation, transformed itself into the—secular—CFDT in November 1964.

largely around two lectures he delivered in Mexico City in 1966,[48] Gorz presented himself forcefully as the harbinger of this rising wave of protest.

He observed that, however legitimate they might be, wage demands within the framework of a contractual incomes policy assisted in the reproduction of the system, because they placed 'industrial action from the outset on the terrain of the dominant ideology and consumption structures.'[49] But the satisfaction of these quantitative needs in no way prevented rebellion against the intolerable state of the workers' condition. Not, as the CGT [Confédération générale du travail (General Confederation of Labour)] and the French Communist Party continued to believe, because poverty (in relative terms) continued to exist, but because, as an Italian worker explained, replying to a survey undertaken by *Quaderni rossi*—a workerist journal that was a product of the dissident Socialist faction—'the worker, no matter what his pay, feels that no price, however high, will compensate him for the time' he wastes working in conditions—and towards a goal—that are imposed on him.[50] It wasn't so much exploitation as alienation, in the broad sense of oppression and the de-humanization of working relations and conditions, that prompted the rejection of capitalism as a system of 'authoritarian' and 'anti-democratic' social relations.[51]

Consumerism and the political social-democratization of the working class were thus counteracted by the emergence of *qualitative needs*. Since Marx, we have known generally that these radical needs are for 'a free and many-sided development of the human faculties', but they now took on the precise form of an aspiration to control the modes and contents of labour and, subsequently, consumption and leisure activities. This demand, which goes to the heart of the conditioning undergone by the producer-consumer, is of the order of *workers' control* in the dual sense of the right of oversight[52] and counter-power. That control can only be exerted in the context of a labour movement that takes trade-union action as its priority. It presupposes,

48 André Gorz, 'Unions and Politics' and 'Arduous Socialism' in *Socialism and Revolution* (Norman Denny trans.) (New York: Anchor Books, 1973), pp. 71–107, 179–214.

49 André Gorz, 'Avant-propos', *Les Temps modernes* 196–7 ('Données et problèmes de la lutte ouvrière') (September–October 1962): 392.

50 Gorz, *Socialism and Revolution*, p. 90.

51 Gorz, *Strategy for Labor*, p. 31.

52 The verb *contrôler* in French also means to monitor or oversee [Trans.].

in parallel, the *autonomy of the working class* vis-à-vis the capitalist management of enterprises, not to ignore this latter (as the CGT did), but so that trade union negotiation could pitch solutions against it that were compatible with the life-demands of the workers. More broadly, that autonomy expresses itself as a contesting of capitalist civilization in its entirety—'its priorities, its hierarchy of values and its culture.'[53] It is also political in nature, since 'workers' freedom', to use the expression of the anti-Stalinist Vittorio Foa,[54] is always in danger of being stifled by a management which, though socialized, might be bureaucratic and centralized. The lessons of 'socialism' in Eastern Europe were being drawn.

Structural Reforms

With the Communists' catastrophism having produced an *attentiste* stance and with insurrection inconceivable in Europe, the only question was whether it was possible, within capitalism, to 'impose anti-capitalist solutions that would not immediately be incorporated and subsumed into the system.'[55] The old 'reform or revolution' debate within the labour movement no longer had any meaning.

On the other hand, it was necessary to define the difference between 'reformist reforms' and 'revolutionary reforms'. The former represented submission to established rationality. The latter, based on deep human exigencies and needs, could be recognized by the way they prepared the working masses to take charge of society through decentralization and the increased number of instances of decision-making and enabled them to determine the direction of development. These 'non-reformist' or 'anti-capitalist' reforms were, precisely, structural reforms, by way of which the workers conquered *positions of power* or asserted *power*.'[56] This is why:

> [T]he struggle for autonomous partial powers and *their exercise* must present the masses with socialism as a reality that is *already* at work, acting on capitalism from the inside and demanding its free flowering. Instead of setting the present against the future in a dichotomous way, like Evil against Good, and present impotence

53 Gorz, *Strategy for Labor*, p. 24.
54 Gorz, *Strategy for Labor*, p. 41.
55 Gorz, *Strategy for Labor*, p. 12.
56 Gorz, *Strategy for Labor*, pp. 12–13.

against future power, the future must be made present and power already tangible through actions that reflect back to the workers their positive strength.[57]

The Beginnings of a Political and Trade Union Audience

In this way, Gorz was having his say in the political debate that was beginning in this period within the PSU, a party to which he felt close. Section heads in Paris or the provinces (such as Philippe Ivernel, or Alain Badiou with whom he would stay in contact long after their paths had diverged) were keen to invite him to meetings to question him on 'workers' strategy'. Thanks also to the intellectually stimulating discussions he had with most of the party's leaders, whom he knew personally, he played his part in shaping the idea of a 'revolutionary reformism'. That idea was taken up by other intellectuals of PSU sensibilities, such as the journalist and sociologist Serge Mallet, who published a lengthy review of *Stratégie ouvrière et néocapitalisme*, and the philosopher and sociologist of literature Lucien Goldmann who frequently cited Gorz's work.[58]

Going beyond the traditional trade unionism of 'pay and conditions', Gorz's analyses also found an initial resonance within the CFDT which, as we should remember, had, at its inception, wished to make Gorz its spokesman. Around 1960, in what were still the days of the CFTC, Gorz was in regular—and, indeed, friendly—contact with a number of the leaders, such as Michel Rolant, Frédo Krumnow, Jean Auger and Gilbert Declercq. Declercq invited him to lead two training seminars for the Nantes area of the CFTC. Gorz was struck at the time by the fact that ' "socialist humanism" often found more combative mouthpieces in France in certain trade unions of Christian origin (CFTC) than in others that were Communist in inspiration.'[59] It was hardly surprising, then, that the reports read at CFDT conferences were studded with his name—such as the report by Secretary General Eugène Descamps in 1964 or the Secretary General of the Metalworkers' Federation Jean Maire in 1965. A comradeship was beginning.

---

57 Gorz, *Strategy for Labor*, p. 16.

58 Serge Mallet, 'Un réformisme révolutionnaire', *France Observateur* (21 May 1964).

59 André Gorz, 'Force et faiblesse du marxisme aujourd'hui', undated (GRZ 8.26).

CHAPTER SEVEN

Automation and the New Working Class

Before being a social pact that caused workers to 'swallow' the rationalization of work, Fordism *was* the very process of rationalization that was implemented in major industry in the advanced capitalist countries. The system of fragmented tasks to be performed at a predetermined rate, which was put in place by Taylorism, served as a framework for the introduction of the assembly lines and mass production characteristic of Fordism, to which, in certain sectors, were added the automation of machines and/or the proliferation of technical studies departments. This changed the nature of work and the workers' relation to it. The 'white-coated worker'—an engineer or technician responsible for design, management or supervision—became an emblematic figure of the modern factory.

It is difficult to generalize about such structural transformations, which remain partial and unequal,[1] but they raise questions of a sociological and political order which, in the first instance, concern the labour movement. If it is true that the proletariat is at once 'a social situation and a lived experience', as the apt expression coined by a prolific and already influential French sociologist by the name of Alain Touraine had it, then the question is: what becomes of the workers' consciousness in the specific conditions of this neo-capitalism.[2]

Neo-capitalism in the Factory

The debate, which in another form also took place in Italy (as we have already glimpsed) and in the Anglo-Saxon world (as we shall see) stirred both sociologists and trade unionists into action.[3] In France, it had an exceptionally

---

1 Jean-Daniel Reynaud, 'La nouvelle classe ouvrière. La technologie et l'histoire', *Revue française de science politique* 22 (3) (1972): 529–42.

2 Alain Touraine, 'Situation du mouvement ouvrier', *Arguments* 12–13 (January–March 1959). Reprinted in *Arguments* 4 (Paris: UGE, 1978), p. 230.

3 See Gérard Adam, 'Où en est le débat sur "la nouvelle classe ouvrière"? État des travaux', *Revue française de science politique* 18 (5) (1968): 1003–23; Gerd-Rainer Horn,

broad reach and was enthusiastically joined by activists, to the point where, on occasion, the social actors themselves pursued and justified their struggles using political arguments arising out of this controversy. The debate, which was started by an issue of *Arguments* (12–13 [1959]) entitled 'Qu'est-ce que la classe ouvrière française?' [What is the French working class?] and was very much in evidence in the voluminous *Traité de sociologie du travail* (1962) edited by Georges Friedmann and Pierre Naville, went on intensely for some ten years or so, until the new social patterns that came out of the explosion of '68 captured the attention of the sociologists and futurologists of the labour movement, who saw in these either refutation or confirmation of the existence of this new working class.

Three antagonistic positions emerged in that debate.

1. The position taken by Touraine, which was expressed in *Arguments*, in the *Traité de sociologie du travail*, and subsequently in some dense tomes by Touraine: *Sociologie de l'action* (1965) and *La Conscience ouvrière* (1966). Without proposing a historical chronology, Touraine modelled three successive phases characterizing the development of the system of industrial production: a phase A, in which the skilled worker masters his trade and aspires to take control of production (the trade system); a phase B in which Taylorism and Fordism eliminate the autonomy of the different trades and raise technique over execution (the technical system); and a phase C, incorporating the previous phase, in which automation puts technique in the service of management, thus promoting a company spirit—or spirit of 'participation'—which replaces the old workers' consciousness and encourages political reformism (the programmed system).

2. The defensive position of the French Communist Party and its CGT trade union federation, which viewed current developments from a lofty distance. According no importance to the existence of a 'labour aristocracy' which the 'new-working-class' theorists tended to seize on, this position asserts the tangibility of a cohesive working class which, far from withering away and replenishing the ranks of the middle classes, was allegedly seeing a worsening of its material situation. In arguing for the changelessly revolutionary

---

'The Changing Nature of the European Working Class: The Rise and Fall of the "New Working Class" (France, Italy, Spain, Czechoslovakia)' in Carole Fink, Philipp Gassert and Detlef Junker (eds), *1968: The World Transformed* (Cambridge: Cambridge University Press, 1998), pp. 351–71.

character of the working class, the members of the Socialisme ou Barbarie group, Daniel Mothé and Cornelius Castoriadis, very hostile to the 'pontificating' sociology of work of the Touraine sort, also took this more distant attitude.

3. Lastly, a position which, while in agreement with Touraine's historical sequencing, drew different political conclusions, favouring workers' self-management. This is expressed, with various different nuances, by Serge Mallet, who published *La Nouvelle classe ouvrière* [The new working class] in 1963, Pierre Belleville of the CFTC who called his own 1963 book *Une Nouvelle classe ouvrière* [A new working class], André Barjonet, who wasn't yet a member of the PSU (unlike the other two) but was at odds with his own CGT trade union, and Gorz who, after masterminding the famous issue of *Les Temps modernes* in 1962, joined the debate fully in 1964 with his *Stratégie ouvrière et néocapitalisme* [*Strategy for Labor*, 1967]. Let us pause to examine the analyses of Mallet and Gorz, the most characteristic and forceful expressions of this third position.[4]

Theorizing Workers' Self-Management

Serge Mallet and Workers' Self-Management

Though it is not empirically verifiable across all enterprises, Serge Mallet's thesis has the advantage of simplicity, which explains the popularity it enjoyed in the 1960s. Where Touraine establishes a typological succession, Mallet sees a linear historical evolution leading to automation and to greater skilling of labour in what he describes as 'high-end' sectors. He infers from this that skilled workers, who are decreasingly required to carry out fragmentary operations, acquire a 'synthetic vision of a complex task'[5] that prepares them for company syndicalism and self-management—hence the comparison of the present phase with the Phase A that found expression, at the political level, in the revolutionary syndicalists' aspirations to self-government.[6]

---

4 See Dick Howard, 'New situation, new strategy: Serge Mallet and André Gorz' in Dick Howard and Karl Klare (eds), *The Unknown Dimension: European Marxism since Lenin* (New York: Basic Books, 1972), pp. 388–413.

5 Serge Mallet, *The New Working Class* (Nottingham: Spokesman Books, 1977), p. 67.

6 For an introduction to revolutionary syndicalism by a historian who was also a CFDT official, see Jacques Julliard, *Autonomie ouvrière. Études sur le syndicalisme d'action*

Writing in the second edition of *La Nouvelle classe ouvrière* in 1969, Mallet reiterates that:

> The more the importance of the research, creation and oversight sector increases, the more there is a concentration of human work on the preparation and organization of production and the more the sense of initiative and responsibility grows—in a word, the more the modern worker regains *at the collective level* the professional autonomy he had lost in the phase of the mechanization of labour—then the more do tendencies towards managerial demands develop. Today modern conditions of production offer objective possibilities for the development of the generalized worker self-management of production and the economy by those who bear the burden of it.[7]

André Gorz and Creative Praxis

In *Strategy for Labor: A Radical Proposal* (1964), Gorz starts out from a principle that comes to him from Marxism—namely, that the capacity of the workers depends on the organization of labour and the class composition that derives from it. That question, on which he grounds his strategy of anti-capitalist struggle, was to occupy his mind as an activist for nearly ten years. He developed it particularly in a paper with the exacting title 'Capitalist Relations of Production and the Socially Necessary Labour Force',[8] which he presented to a conference on 'The Trends of European Capitalism' held in June 1965 by the Istituto Gramsci in Rome (that text, which includes an analysis of the intellectual training of labour—in other words, of the student condition—was to enjoy quite a large audience, as it would be translated into English, French, Italian and German).

---

directe (Paris: Seuil/Gallimard, 1988) and the issue of *Mil neuf cent* introduced by Julliard, 'Le syndicalisme révolutionnaire', 24, 2006.

7 Serge Mallet, 'Mai-juin 68: première grève pour la gestion' in *La Nouvelle classe ouvrière* (Paris: Seuil, 1969 [second edition]), p. 41.

8 André Gorz, 'Capitalist Relations of Production and the Socially Necessary Labour Force', *International Socialist Journal* (Milan) 10 (August 1965): 463–80. Reprinted in Arthur Lothstein (ed.), *All We Are Saying: The Philosophy of the New Left* (New York: Putnam, 1970), pp. 155–71.

In his book, Gorz draws on Mallet and Belleville to define the contours of the new working class. He too thinks that it is the most skilled workers who manifest a 'need for autonomous activity, for creation and communication.'[9] But the technicians find it tedious to be merely looking at 'dials', overseeing the smooth operation of automated production. The aim was always for them to be highly skilled but ignorant of the areas outside their particular functions, and hence they have no chance of finding fulfilment in work whose ultimate meaning exceeds their grasp.

What is new, however, is to see the rejection of this amputation of their creativity emerging. The specific, new nature of the labour power that goes along with a system of production in which automation is destined to be generalized explains this change in attitude. For that labour power, less and less freighted with the physical energy that made it 'interchangeable' and hence increasingly charged with intelligence, now tends to escape 'quantitative evaluations'[10]—we can feel the burgeoning influence of Marx's *Grundrisse* here, a prophetic text on the potentialities within machinism driven to its logical ends, which Gorz cites for the first time in this work as a legitimation for workers' self-management.[11] The workers have the

---

9 Gorz, *Strategy for Labor*, p. 106.

10 Gorz, *Strategy for Labor*, p. 105.

11 Karl Marx, *Grundrisse* (Martin Nicolaus trans.) (Harmondsworth: Penguin Books in association with *New Left Review*, 1973), pp. 120–1. Let us cite some passages from the fragment of the *Grundrisse* 'on machinery, science and creative leisure', which Gorz translated himself and would quote throughout his work, commenting upon them as his own thinking developed: '[T]o the degree that large industry develops, the creation of real wealth comes to depend less on labour time and on the amount of labour employed than on the power of the agencies set in motion [. . .] whose 'powerful effectiveness' is itself in turn out of all proportion to the direct labour time spent on their production, but depends rather on the general state of science and on the progress of technology, or the application of this science to production [. . .] Real wealth manifests itself, rather—and large industry reveals this—in the monstrous disproportion between the labour time applied, and its product, as well as in the qualitative imbalance between labour, reduced to a pure abstraction, and the power of the production process it superintends. Labour no longer appears so much to be included within the production process; rather, the human being comes to relate more as watchman and regulator to the production process itself [. . .] In this transformation, it is neither the direct human labour he himself performs, nor the time during which he works, but rather the appropriation of his own general productive power, his understanding of nature and his mastery over it by virtue of his presence as a social body—it is, in a word, the development of the social

impression that they possess this capacity for labour because they have acquired it by their own training and they are best placed to know how to use it: '[The worker] is at the same time both labour power and the owner of labour power; he is a *praxis subject*'. He thus tends to 'understand himself as creative praxis which contains its own sovereign purposefulness'.[12] Beyond the immediate demand for workers' control, self-management becomes the perspective that will permit of that mastery.

The point is that the contradiction the worker experiences in the era of advanced capitalism is a contradiction over the purpose of work, which for the worker is to produce, 'by the application of his labour power to materials [. . .] wealth which has a human value', whereas for capital the aim is to generate surplus value by producing 'something, no matter what.' Thus the problem that arises for the worker is 'the kind and content of the life to be produced'.[13] This leads to the contesting of capitalist rule right across the board—that is to say, not only for its grip on the production phase, but as provider of oriented leisure and consumption.

Tailor-Made Consumers and Social Needs

Gorz's opposition to the current order was, then, as sweeping as it was radical, since in his writings it was an entire 'model of civilization' with inhuman and irrational ends that was deserving of the workers' critique. To show that these ends were systematically wrong-headed, Gorz drew on Marx but also found confirmation in the works of the North American Democratic economist John K. Galbraith who, in a book whose title encapsulated an era, *The Age of Affluence* (1958), had critically analysed the newly inverted

---

individual which appears as the great foundation-stone of production and of wealth [. . .] As soon as labour in the direct form has ceased to be the great well-spring of wealth, labour time ceases and must cease to be its measure, and hence exchange value [must cease to be the measure] of use value. The *surplus labour of the mass* has ceased to be the condition for the development of general wealth, just as the *non-labour of the few*, for the development of the general powers of the human head [. . .] The free development of individualities and [. . .] the general reduction of the necessary labour of society to a minimum [become the goal of production], which then corresponds to the artistic, scientific etc. development of the individuals in the time set free, and with the means created [. . .] The measure of wealth is then not any longer, in any way, labour time, but rather disposable time.' Marx, *Grundrisse*, pp. 704–08.

12 Gorz, *Strategy for Labor*, pp. 112, 115.

13 Gorz, *Strategy for Labor*, pp. 55, 101.

relation of dependency between corporations and consumers. In *Strategy for Labor*, Gorz writes:

> Instead of putting production at the service of society, society is put at the service of capitalist production: the latter endeavours with all its ingenuity to offer to *individuals* ever-new means of evading this intolerable social reality; and the implementation on a grand scale of these *individual means of escape* (automobiles, private houses, camping, passive leisure) thereby recreates a new anarchic *social process*, new miseries, inverted priorities and new alienation.[14]

Neo-capitalism sets itself the task, then, 'of shaping subjects for the objects to be marketed; not of adjusting supply to demand, but demand to supply'[15]—the effect of this being to maintain a permanent sense of dissatisfaction, if not indeed poverty, relative to a constantly renewed supply.

Given the thoroughgoing humanism on view in his *Morale de l'histoire*, it is understandable that Gorz should frame his new critique in terms of *human needs*. The critique of capitalism must be made in the name of 'the subordination of production to needs, both in terms of what is produced and the way it is produced.' And the same goes for the idea of 'socialism'. If, politically, socialism is the class power of the workers and, economically, the socialization of the means of production, it will be meaningless unless it is also 'a new type of relationship among men, a new order of priorities, a new model of life and of culture'[16]—in other words, if it promotes the development of 'qualitative' needs.

Gorz strives to provide a concrete list of these needs. Against the individual consumption needs prompted by capitalist supply, which atomize and isolate individuals in their daily lives, may be ranged 'collective (or social) needs', which relate to a vast swathe of collective services and facilities in the fields of transport, housing, town planning, health, education and culture which, as Gorz sees it, are all outside market imperatives and, for that reason, are important elements in the argument for restricting the logic and field of action of capitalism.

---

14 Gorz, *Strategy for Labor*, p. 67.
15 Gorz, *Strategy for Labor*, p. 70.
16 Gorz, *Strategy for Labor*, p. 12.

A First International Impact

It was because *Strategy for Labor* took as its subject a neo-capitalism that had reached the evolved stage, at which it entrenched its domination both through labour and consumption, that it found an audience in the most developed European countries, which rushed to translate it: Sweden (in 1965), Denmark and West Germany (in 1967). With the exception of the latter, for the moment, these and other similar countries approached Gorz to give talks. In 1966, he held an important series of lectures in Sweden, which were published by the Far Left weekly *Tidsignal* (and reprinted in *Le Socialisme difficile*).[17] In 1967, he agreed to talk with Norwegian students in Oslo and Social Democrats proposed that he extend the trip to Uppsala in Sweden. That same year, he was invited to a seminar in Malmo, having already spoken about his book at the University of Southampton (England) and travelled to Copenhagen to give a presentation. We may add that, still in 1967, invited on one occasion by Swiss socialists and, on another, by his old politically engaged friends (Cherpillod), he gave two lectures on workers' issues at Lausanne. He was said to be read as widely as Lefebvre and Mandel among the radical youth of the canton of Vaud,[18] while Swiss television sent the reporter Jean-Pierre Goretta to interview him on the May '68 events as they unfolded.

After 1968, with the aura he acquired from having had a ringside seat to May's events, as it were, German radio and television also came calling. Between 1969 and 1972, more and more of Gorz's articles were translated in German journals and collective works. Lastly, it should be noted that, in Germany, *Stratégie ouvrière et néocapitalisme* was widely read by the Young Socialists (JUSOS),[19] and the Left within the Social Democrats (SPD) fought against the 'small steps' policy of Willy Brandt precisely by brandishing

---

17 André Gorz, 'Reform and Revolution' in *Socialism and Revolution*, pp. 133–77.

18 Detailed reviews of his two books helped locally to spread his ideas: see Maurice Maschino, 'La morale de l'histoire', *Gazette littéraire* (supplement to the *Gazette de Lausanne*) (10 October 1959) (the author is actually a contributor to *Les Temps modernes*) and Charles-Henri Favrod, 'Une étude magistrale d'André Gorz', *Gazette littéraire* (29 August 1964).

19 According to Gorz (in his aforementioned letter to Jacques Robin), who was in contact with their leader Eberhard Schmidt.

Gorz's arguments on the 'structural reforms' that would open up a path towards 'a decentralized, collective economy'.[20]

In Italy, on the other hand, the book was not translated, probably because its themes were already well-worn in that country. If he was invited—as he was to Genoa and Milan in 1967—it was to speak about Vietnam . . . . As for his theory of needs, which remained unknown, it had no impact on the hedonist subjectivity of the autonomist movement of 1977. He thus left the field open for the Budapest School's not dissimilar theory of 'radical needs' laid out originally by Ágnes Heller in Italy (*The Theory of Need in Marx* [1974]), which was popularized by the Marxist phenomenologist Pier Aldo Rovatti in his magazine *Aut Aut*. This was a genuinely lost opportunity for Gorz, since the same Rovatti's plan to translate his writings for the political paperback series he was then publishing with Feltrinelli—'Opuscoli marxisti' (which included several titles by Antonio Negri)—came to naught.[21] His writings found greater resonance within Christian political and trade-union circles: *Settegiorni*, the weekly of the left wing of Christian Democracy, printed 40 articles by Michel Bosquet between 1967 and 1974 and the Edizioni Lavoro, the publishing house of the Catholic CISL trade union, published *Farewell to the Working Class* (1982), *Paths to Paradise* (1984) and, in 1994, an anthology of Gorz's writings on moving beyond wage-based society.

Lastly, in Franco's Spain, Gorz's writings—though systematically censored—were passed around in the backrooms of bookshops and had a dominant influence on the Frente de liberación popular, which was close to the PSU and PSIUP.[22] And *Stratégie ouvrière et néocapitalisme* was published in Catalan in 1967 in a translation by Jordi Solé Tura, despite his being a Communist exiled in France. And between 1966 and 1980 the anti-Franco Madrid weekly *Triunfo* translated some 40 journalistic pieces by Michel Bosquet. Once the post-Franco transition was complete, Gorz's proposals on a guaranteed income and reduced working hours attracted

---

20 Manuel Lucbert, 'L'aile gauche du parti en quête d'une "nouvelle société" ', *Le Monde* (15 May 1970).

21 See the letter from the man who had been lined up as translator, Marco Macciò, to André Gorz of 26 February 1974 (GRZ).

22 Julio Antonio García Alcalá, 'Un modelo en la oposición al franquismo. Las organizaciones Frente (FLP-EOC-ESWA)', VOL. 1, MA thesis, Universidad Complutense, Madrid, 1997, pp. 51–2, 365–6, 394.

the attention of the main democratic daily *El País*, which twice opened its columns to him, in 1983 and 1985.

In 1967, Gorz published another book, *Le Socialisme difficile*, which quickly gained international traction on account of the translations that appeared in 1968 (Swedish, Dutch, Brazilian, Italian) and 1969 (Japanese). We shall see below that Gorz's thought also found its way into Marxist circles in North and South America.

Leisure and the Integration of the Working Class

During the 1960s in Europe and North America, the attraction of new ways of consuming time, as well as the raised standard of living that made them possible, gave sociologists much food for thought. Some saw a leisure society in gestation, while others wrote of a broad middle class now including workers, each of these theories culminating in an axiomatic belief that all desire for social change had now disappeared. Gorz stood out against both conceptions.

Alienation of Free Time

Though working hours in France had not diminished between 1946 and 1968 (they still stood at 46.2 hours per week in 1968), expenditure on leisure time and holidays had actually grown very strongly (in summer 1969, more than half of French people spent at least 25 nights away from their homes purely for pleasure). It was this that enabled French observers to rally, with varying degrees of optimism, around the American promise of a 'leisure civilisation'. For the sociologist Joffre Dumazedier in *Vers une civilisation du loisir?* (1962) and the economist Jean Fourastié in *Des loisirs: pour quoi faire?* (1970), the use of disposable time exempt from social and domestic obligations—the definition of leisure—was quite simply a feature consubstantial with the modern human condition. For Gorz, it was evidence, primarily, of the alienation of the worker/consumer.

Capitalism, he notes, which imposes on society 'the need to consume what capital needs to have produced so as to maximize its profit' sets about, 'from the production phase, transforming the worker into a consumer— that is to say, into a person whose reality isn't work but passive consumption, whose "real" life is not what he does in the workplace and the local community, but what enables him to escape from them.'[23] As a result, the individual who falls back into his consumption-saturated private life, which he feels to be his only sphere of sovereignty, does not display 'first, or predominantly, *the attitude* of a citizen confronted by society but that of a worker, deprived of initiative, responsibility and the possibility of self-development in his work, who seeks *compensation* in non-work.'[24]

Things would be different 'if the forces of production have been so highly developed that a man's leisure occupations may be regarded as his *main social activity*, and his directly productive work as merely accessory (not only because of the short time it takes, but because of the power of the automatic processes)'. But with social relations continuing to be subject to the centrality of labour, free-time activities—DIY and various other pastimes—isolate the individual and prevent him from engaging in effective social activities: 'Marx was thinking of something very different from the growth of leisure considered as socially meaningless time when he envisaged "the free development of the human faculties" as being the full development of the social individual.' And Gorz concludes that 'there can, then, be no proletarian culture until the barrier dividing the world of work from the world of leisure has been broken down.'[25]

This circumspection with regard to leisure that is seen as merely extending the worker's alienation beyond work is neither new nor original. It is akin to the disillusioned findings of the philo-Communist sociologist Georges Friedmann who, as early as 1960, condemned the 'corruption of free time' in one of the studies in his *Sept études sur l'homme et la technique* (1966). It also attracted the attention of the Communist Party's monthly *Démocratie nouvelle*, edited by Paul Noirot (expelled from the party in 1969), which published extracts from *Strategy for Labor*—while dissociating itself from the book's other arguments—and called on Gorz to take part in a survey on the subject.[26]

---

23 Gorz, 'Avant-propos', p. 395.

24 Gorz, *Socialism and Revolution*, p. 199.

25 Gorz, *Socialism and Revolution*, pp. 200–2.

26 See André Gorz, 'Civilisation opulente et massification', *Démocratie nouvelle* 9 (September 1964): 75–6 and the survey 'Loisirs et sociétés industrielles', *Démocratie nouvelle* 5 (May 1966): 84–5, 89–91.

Critique of Herbert Marcuse

In the Anglo-Saxon world, the debate on 'the new working class' turned into a debate on 'the affluent society'. The emphasis was less on the possible consequences of automation for worker participation or self-management and more on the effects of greater prosperity for workers, bringing them more into line with the middle class. In publishing *One-Dimensional Man* (1964), Herbert Marcuse was following in this tradition. Marcuse, a Frankfurt School philosopher who had lived in the US since 1934, took an uncompromising stance. In his view, the masses' desire to contest the status quo in 'advanced industrial society' was fading not just because of material comfort and the assurance that it would continue to increase, but also on account of the manipulation of needs, which were reducing the individual to the role of a consumer in pursuit of work, even if that work was stupefying, and the ideological uniformity maintained by the media. The result was that exploitation was accepted, alienation imperceptible and criticism absorbed into the system.

Marcuse, who had already written the Freudo–Marxian study *Eros and Civilization* (1955) which had passed unnoticed in France, was not entirely unknown to French academics. He had been published in *Arguments* in 1960–61 and also by Kostas Axelos, who edited the *Arguments* series of books for Éditions de Minuit. Lucien Goldmann, whose 'genetic structuralism' was certainly closer to Marcuse's method than to that of the structuralists, invited him first to Paris in 1958–59, and then again in December 1961–January 1962 to lecture at the École pratique des hautes études, where he advanced the idea of 'organized capitalism'. Marcuse also visited a personal friend in Paris, the academic Paul Vignaux, who was pushing within the CFTC for its secularization.[27]

As for Gorz, he has a note in his 1962 diary of an evening spent with Marcuse on 22 March.[28] If this did take place, then it didn't exactly etch itself into his memory.[29] Of Marcuse's latest analyses he just knew the

27 Personal communication to the author, Jacques Julliard, 10 February 2014.

28 Loose sheet (GRZ 1.15).

29 He would later state that he hadn't known Marcuse personally in this period: Jean-Marcel Bouguereau, 'André Gorz: "Il avait raison sur toute la ligne" ', *Libération* (31 July 1979). A letter in English from Marcuse to Gorz of 2 December 1962 (GRZ), which ends with the words 'With best wishes to both of you', implies that Marcuse knew the couple and that they had therefore met.

brief overview provided in France in the journal *Médiations* (5 [Summer 1962]). In *Stratégie ouvrière et néocapitalisme* he writes in a footnote that he is sorry that he was only able to take the 'remarkable' *One-Dimensional Man* into account in the last pages of his own book. He did, however, rush to review it for the progressive New York–based magazine *The Nation*. While welcoming Marcuse's caustic account of the forms of soft repression that governed the technologically advanced societies, he wondered whether, in the light of the struggles of the labour movements in France and Italy, the author wasn't exaggerating the extent of those and the strength of the hold they exerted. He was sceptical, in particular, of Marcuse's central thesis that it was pointless to look to the Western working classes for the forces capable of achieving liberation.[30] That thesis, which overemphasized the potential role of deprived minorities (Marcuse had Black Americans in mind), resembled the line taken by Sartre in 1961 in his preface to the French edition of Frantz Fanon's *Wretched of the Earth*, which looked towards an uprising among the colonized. It was also reminiscent of Gorz's downbeat thoughts around 1960 on the integration and self-oppression of the 'Western' individual which he felt could be saved by 'marginals' or by the youth of the new countries (see above, pp. 81–83).

However, since the labour movement had acquired renewed vigour in Europe—and, particularly, in Italy—Gorz had overcome his pessimism. It was not for want of feeling the weight of Marcuse's arguments. Reacting to being sent the Foreword to the special issue of *Les Temps modernes* on 'the workers' struggle', Marcuse wrote personally to him on 2 December 1962 to say that he agreed totally on 'the fact' of alienation, but, as he saw it, one question remained unanswered:

> How can alienation become, concretely, the driving force in the struggle for power, the 'motive' for revolution? Seen from the conditions in the US: the (relatively but still) high and ever higher level of consumption is so oppressive and so beneficial that it makes alienation as well as the possibility of its abolition an *abstract* idea [...] the consciousness of alienation (without which there is no alienation) is arrested in its development. The 'subjective factor' is suffocated. Or: in becoming total and totalitarian, alienation is losing (absorbing?) its opposite. I am indeed the Other, and being the other

---

30 André Gorz, 'Call for Intellectual Subversion', *The Nation* (25 May 1964), p. 536.

is not so bad after all [...] ! It pays. If the refusal is that of the whole, who and where is the subject which refuses?[31]

Gorz stuck to his guns here. In his review, he argued that the US, on which Marcuse focuses exclusively, was a case apart (for historical and cultural reasons which blunt class consciousness in that country) and, contrary to Marcuse's belief, there was no contagion between it and the whole of the West. Gorz remained, moreover, convinced that the forms assumed by alienation, which is never complete, might, given the specific configuration of the European labour movement, offer greater revolutionary potential than poverty or colonial oppression. In taking this view, he was aligning himself with others among Marcuse's detractors, such as Lefebvre, Mallet and even Goldmann who, in summer 1964, debated with the author of *One-Dimensional Man* on the Dalmatian island of Korčula at an international symposium on the prospects for socialism.

In a lecture series organized by the political and social sciences faculty of the University of Mexico City in February 1966 around the issues raised by his latest work, Marcuse reviewed at some length his differences of opinion with Gorz, whom he referred to as 'his friend'.[32] The two points that posed a problem, as we have already seen, bore on the question of alienation and the specific character of the US. Marcuse discussed these in front of an audience of invited lecturers, who were subsequently gathered in a round-table discussion made up of Erich Fromm, Irving L. Horowitz, Karel Kosik, Mallet and Gorz himself. As the text of one of his own lectures—further fleshed out after the event[33]—attests, Gorz was not convinced by Marcuse's reasoning. Their intellectual affinity did, however, turn out to be greater than their divergences and these would, indeed, slip into the background after the '68 events, though they would not entirely disappear. In an exchange of letters in 1972, Gorz would still cling to some specious arguments. He would conjure up a 'historical and cultural difference' that separated them, Marcuse belonging, as he saw it, to an Anglo-Saxon and

---

31 Aforementioned letter from Herbert Marcuse to Gorz.

32 Herbert Marcuse, 'Libertad y agresión en la sociedad tecnológica' in Erich Fromm, Irving L. Horowitz, Herbert Marcuse, Victor Flores Olea and André Gorz, *La Sociedad industrial contemporánea* (Mexico City: Siglo Veintiuno, 1968), pp. 60–89.

33 See Gorz, *Socialism and Revolution*, pp. 78–83.

German tradition that was mistrustful of the masses, whereas he was part of an anarchistic Latin tradition inclined to be against the bosses![34]

It was, however, the case that this Mexican meeting between the two theorists of alienation—who, with their partners Inge and Dorine, shared happy moments in the streets of Mexico City, where they took photographs of each other—gave rise to a friendship that would last until the American philosopher's death in 1979.

---

34 See the letter in English from André Gorz to Herbert Marcuse of 17 December 1972 (HM: Herbert Marcuse Collection of the University of Frankfurt-am-Main).

CHAPTER EIGHT

Arduous Socialism

Le Nouvel Observateur, which succeeded *France Observateur* on 19 November 1964, was the product of a long negotiation. On the one side sat the industrialist Claude Perdriel, who financed it and became its managing director, with his friend Jean Daniel who was propelled into the editor's chair, and on the other side was Gilles Martinet, who, being backed into a corner by the old title's financial liabilities, agreed to hand over control of the magazine, including control of its political line.[1]

The austere nature and barely veiled pro-PSU line of the earlier publication gave way to a more approachable style and a non-partisan, but nonetheless left-wing stance. The magazine, which was read more by intellectual professionals in the public sector than private-sector executives, aimed to oppose *L'Express* all along the line. It was solidly anti-Atlanticist and displayed a sincere hope of seeing the Communist Party evolve, that party being an indispensable element in any potential left-wing government. The weekly placed itself under the patronage of Mendès France and Sartre, with whom there was a four-page interview in the first issue. However, the political heterogeneity of the writers, which did not, we may note, coincide with their diverse professional backgrounds, produced some friction within the team, which Jean Daniel's unifying authority took some time to smooth out.

Early Days at Le Nouvel Observateur

The early days of the new undertaking saw three different sensibilities in play alongside each other.[2] First, there was the PSU tendency, in the form of Gilles Martinet and Serge Mallet, who were seen as ideologues to be monitored carefully. Second, there was a Centre Left tendency represented by François Furet and Claude Krief, the latter supporting the programme

1 Louis Pinto, *L'Intelligence en action*; Jacqueline Rémy, *Le 'Nouvel Observateur'. 50 ans de passions* (Paris: Pygmalion, 2014).

2 Roland Cayrol, 'Nouvel *Express* et *Nouvel Observateur*', *Revue française de science politique* 16 (3) (1966): 493–520.

of Gaston Defferre against the views of the other journalists, including Michel Bosquet who leapt to the defence of the alliance with the Communists.[3] Third, there was the 'Third Worldist' tendency, close to *Les Temps modernes*. This included Olivier Todd, Jacques-Laurent Bost, Serge Lafaurie and K. S. Karol. It was supplemented in very short order by the arrival of Albert-Paul Lentin and was headed up by Michel Bosquet—'the most erudite' and 'most secretive' of all, whose 'jealously-guarded solitude,' as Jean Daniel was to write, 'both troubled and impressed us.'[4] Bosquet was the only one of this last group to be a member of the management board. That board, which would remain unchanged for many years, was small. The numbers were made up by Perdriel, Jean Daniel and the old guard from *France Observateur*: Gilles Martinet, Hector de Galard and Philippe Viannay. Subsequently, Jean Daniel—who really had the whip hand over the direction taken by the publication—would only have the Bosquet 'faction' to deal with.

Unsurprisingly, Bosquet took on the economic and social section of the magazine, covering issues at both the national and international level. Before 1968 he frequently singled out the question of unemployment, which was not high in France but did exist, despite being concealed by claims of full employment. Noting that it was constantly growing (360,000 people 'available for work' in 1968, as against 113,000 in 1961), he came to see that this could not all be ascribed to the flight from the land and to population growth. 1960s economic growth had the peculiar—and absolutely new—feature that it was based on an increase in productivity that reduced the need for labour, with investment actually increasing automation.[5] He was thus the first person to bring to light the phenomenon of 'jobless growth', long before the economists, who would not begin to speak of that troubling phenomenon until the 1990s.

At *Le Nouvel Observateur*, Bosquet undeniably had greater power and freedom as a journalist than before. Among the editorial team, he was recognized as having specific political/economic skills and an intellectual vision of things that was known to have solid philosophical foundations.

---

3 Michel Bosquet and Claude Krief, 'Que faire avec la "fédération"', *Le Nouvel Observateur* (10 June 1965).

4 Jean Daniel, 'Partir avec elle', *Le Nouvel Observateur* (27 September 2007).

5 See, for example, Bosquet, 'Les chômeurs de la relance'.

Was the way he viewed his profession changed by this? And how did the writer-intellectual that was the Bosquet–Gorz hybrid see himself?

The Involved Intellectual

In a 1967 letter in which he was replying to a student who asked him what political grouping he felt he belonged to, Gorz reviewed his journalistic activity, noting that there are 'militant publications', in which intellectual activists write analyses which they regard as correct'. *Le Nouvel Observateur* was, however, not of that type:

> I did not come to journalism through activism but to earn my living in a way that would keep me informed, help me think and force me constantly to learn. It was by working as a journalist that I became something of an activist. But, as Bosquet, I have never written in militant publications. [. . .] You cannot, therefore, say that I am part of any kind of community or group.[6]

This is, indeed, something he always refused to do. He described himself as 'allergic' to membership of a party—even of the PSU, to which he was close and on which he exerted influence.[7] Admittedly, he did, from time to time, attend meetings of the CFDT, which was gradually won over to the idea of worker self-management, and he regularly paid his trade union dues in the 1960s and 70s. He was even invited to speak at the union's 'Federal Council' on 3 September 1969 by its president Michel Rolant. And this undoubtedly qualified him to declare, in an interview for foreign consumption, that he had been an 'organic intellectual' of the CFDT.[8] In the 1980s he would be as much—if not more—of an influential intellectual with the German trade unions. But that was not an expression of real activism. Though he admired and learned a great deal from 'organic' thinkers (his own definition), such as the Italian trade unionists Foa and Trentin, he always took the view that the role of intellectuals was not to involve themselves directly in leading or organizing the labour movement. In a highly political footnote in *The*

6 Gorz, 'André Gorz intellectuel et journaliste'.
7 Interview with Mitchell Cohen, 18 June 1980. Cited in Mitchell Cohen, *The Wager of Lucien Goldmann: Tragedy, Dialectics, and a Hidden God* (Princeton, NJ: Princeton University Press, 1994), p. 258.
8 André Gorz, 'Oficios del saber y del trabajo'.

Traitor, which he was later to cut, he explained that to challenge 'the action of the revolutionary class' in order to change its direction would be inappropriate for a philosopher, mainly because such lofty criticism 'inevitably assumes the aspect of a class critique, weakening the cohesion, discipline and *politics* of the revolutionary party' and also because, as external criticism, it is ineffective, negative. And what if, by contrast, the philosopher joins the Communist Party?

> He will immediately feel both the political inappropriateness of his criticism and its necessity, but will not necessarily be better placed to render it effective, since (1) as a member of the Communist Party he will be held to its discipline and (2) as a bourgeois philosopher, he will be subject to understandable suspicion, which he will only be able to dispel by pledging to maintain party discipline even more assiduously than others. [. . .] His situation, outside or inside the CP, thus remains an unhappy one and shows up the objective fact that there is no place, in a class society, for a philosophy that is both right and effective.[9]

In an earlier letter to his friend Walter Riffel, in which he discusses his own case, he offers the following clarification:

> [Since] the bourgeois (and worse) order is solidly established and I am a member of the dominant class, one has to do something other than renounce one's class [*se faire transfuge*]—that is to say, in this case, turn into a bohemian, an anarchist or a derelict. It won't be about carrying on the proletarian struggle, which in any event has no need of us. But one can engage in another struggle in one's own social position, on condition that one accepts that position and, as a consequence, feels responsible rather than guilty.[10]

He therefore takes the view that there are politicians and 'obscure bourgeois holding down positions in ministries or government departments, or statisticians [and] journalists (though I'm not yet one of them)' who 'do better, more honest and more effective work than those who join the Communist Party or work themselves to death out of a love of self-denial.'[11] In 1967,

---

9 Gorz, *Le Traître*, pp. 258–9n [This passage was not retained in the English translation, which was made from a later edition. (Trans.)].

10 Gérard Horst to Walter Riffel, undated [1953?] (GRZ).

11 Gorz, *Le Traître*.

confirming that he intends neither to join the PSU or any other party whatsoever, he adds: 'In the present French and European context, a Marxist intellectual has greater freedom of doing research, of exerting influence, and of maintaining friendly relations with the various brands of socialists and labor leaders at home and abroad if he has no party affiliation.'[12]

It was, ultimately, in the contemporary letter to the female student that Gorz fully and calmly laid out his own situation as an involved intellectual and the sense of his commitment:

> You know (this is a thing psychoanalysts have understood), we never change. 'Authenticity' (which isn't a concept) never consists in becoming a 'universal man' but in learning to accept and make the best of your limitations, of the possibilities and impossibilities your particular history creates for you. My authenticity, as you know, excludes any form of integration into established communities and contains, as a possibility, on the one hand, a critical distance from environing reality and, on the other, an openness to alien experiences and realities which may be greater than in those who are directly involved in immediate reality. What I want to do, then, is to make that critical capacity available to those who act inside groups or established communities, so that they can use elements of thought or analysis to afford themselves a broader perspective. [. . .] My commitment remains intellectual, then, and is effective and impactful only through the mediation of those who act, seek to act and can, for the purposes of their action, make use of a piece of intellectual work. I am not in any way an activist.[13]

By this writerly engagement, which is not so much a withdrawal from the world as a step back from it to free the critical eye, Gorz was taking a position akin to many of his—equally rebellious—peers, such as Blanchot, Mascolo and Leiris, who were all involved to some extent in '68. That attitude in no way excluded the idea—in fact, it presupposed it—that, as Gorz would always assert, 'the mission of intellectuals is to contest things'.[14] It was

---

12 André Gorz, 'State of Mind', *The New York Review of Books* (14 September 1967).

13 Gorz, 'André Gorz intellectuel et journaliste'.

14 Radio interview. *À voix nue. Grands entretiens d'hier et d'aujourd'hui*, France Culture, broadcast 4–8 March 1991. This was also published on CD in *André Gorz. Vers la société libérée*, with a commentary by Michel Contat (Paris/Bry-sur-Marne: INA/Textuel, 2009).

precisely around this principle that Sartre would structure his famous *Plaidoyer pour les intellectuels* of 1972,[15] a talk he delivered in Japan in 1965, which consummately expresses the committed spirit of the generation of writers and thinkers who set the trend in the 1960s.

Building Socialism in the World

Socialist Realism

In the eponymous chapter of *Le Socialisme difficile*, 'Arduous Socialism', Gorz reminds the reader that Marx conceived Communism as the abolition of work imposed by scarcity. Now, he observed, that prospect was even further away in the 1960s than it appeared to Marx 110 years earlier: the fact was that, for historical reasons, the building of socialism had been begun in the countries with the lowest level of economic development. Socialism then presented itself as a method of accumulation—if not, indeed, of 'catching up' with the West (as Khrushchev wished to do), the effectiveness of which lay in the planned state direction of the economy. As a result, popular democracy was prevented from functioning. And even if exploitation was abolished, alienation remained total. In such a centralized, bureaucratized system, the needs of individuals had no way of being expressed. They were supplanted by objectives which, decided on high, aimed to meet the structural needs of the economy and the vital needs of the population, but were incapable of incorporating a *socialist* criterion of consumption based on the non-necessary. It was for this reason that, in attempting to respond to the supposed expectations of consumers, the range of consumer goods in the Soviet Union unimaginatively aped that in the capitalist countries. The most flagrant and disheartening case of this, as Gorz saw it, was the promotion of the private car.[16]

For Gorz, the vertical policy of the regimes of Central Europe ensues from an objective 'necessity' that relates to the 'socialism of scarcity' characterizing them.[17] After visiting Czechoslovakia in 1963, when he met the

---

15 Jean-Paul Sartre, 'A Plea for Intellectuals' in *Between Existentialism and Marxism* (London: Verso Books, 1983).

16 Bosquet, *Capitalism in Crisis and Everyday Life*, pp. 27–8; Gorz, 'Arduous Socialism', pp. 179–95.

17 Gorz, 'Arduous Socialism', p. 186.

economist Ota Šik and offered to open the columns of *Les Temps modernes* to him, and after taking on board Šik's reform proposals that heralded the Prague Spring, he refined his diagnosis. He listed a set of failings that were inevitably *immanent* to the demands of this type of state-led development which had to be *dialectically* corrected: first, neglect of quality and the sterilization of creative research due to planning based on accounting norms; second, the lack of democratic concertation; third, the de-politicization that ensues, leaving the desire for individual consumption to fill the space so vacated; and, fourth, the overlap between party and state, which prevents the party from being a vehicle for the popular aspirations that might ripen collectively in the grassroots assemblies.[18] After the Prague Spring was crushed in the summer of 1968, Gorz would continue the dialogue with the Czech Left (with Petr Pithart in particular), publishing his analyses in *Les Temps modernes*, and would sign a number of petitions against the ongoing repression.

Yugoslav Self-Management

Were the problems different in the Yugoslavia of self-management? Gorz constantly racked his brains over the Yugoslav 'heresy'. In 1948, when Tito was condemned by the USSR, he implicitly signed up to the Soviet arguments, seeing the postponement of collectivization as an 'ideological risk' and defending the idea that centralization, on certain conditions, 'allows for economic organization and a standard of living that are broadly superior to what is achievable in a free economy'.[19]

The establishment of self-management from 1950 onwards, combined with flexible state planning, began an original experiment that culminated in 1957 in the first Yugoslav Congress of Workers' Councils. The non-Stalinist European Left followed the experiment closely. In 1958, *Les Temps modernes* published *The Programme of the League of Communists of Yugoslavia* in book format. The CFTC—and subsequently the CFDT—took a close interest in it. As for Gorz, he gathered material for *L'Express* from the Yugoslav Information Centre in Paris. There he found an informant, soon to be the first secretary at the embassy, who would become a friend and go-between with the intellectuals of Central Europe ('Branko' in *Letter*

---

18 Gorz, 'Arduous Socialism', pp. 179–214.
19 Gérard Horst, 'Y a-t-il un communisme yougoslave?', *Servir* (5 August 1948).

to D.).[20] In 1959, upon his return from a one-month summer trip to Yugoslavia, he was delighted to have found no trace of the 'bluster' he had encountered in the GDR and was pleased to note that decentralized planning 'respected diversity, the art of living and the sense of beauty':

> This practice of the self-management of communes and enterprises is the chief original feature of the Yugoslav experiment. It has got rid not only of centralized bodies, but also bureaucratic high-handedness and unprofitable enterprises. It has reduced the Plan to being merely a regulatory framework, guiding, through selective credits and fiscal stimuli, initiatives that come from below.[21]

However, Gorz's naïve infatuation fizzled out during the 1960s. As the system's dysfunctions grew, despite the attempts of the 1965 reforms to remedy them by introducing competition between enterprises, his ingenuousness gave way to critical analysis of Yugoslav-style self-management.

Within the country, a group of Marxist academics (including the sociologist Rudi Supek and the philosopher Gajo Petrovič) shared the same concerns and eventually developed a dissident strain of thinking critical of the official line of the League of Communists that found expression in the Zagreb-based theoretical journal *Praxis*. This publication had already featured a review of *Stratégie ouvrière et néocapitalisme* [*Strategy for Labor*] penned by Supek. Having links to the outside world through its multilingual edition, the journal organized an international seminar each summer at Korčula. In 1967, the *Praxis* group extended an invitation to Gorz to discuss self-management, but nothing came of it. They did, however, manage to get him into that *Who's who?* of international Marxism that was its support committee. In 1972 *Le Socialisme difficile* [Arduous socialism], a title which also applied to the Yugoslav situation, was translated into Serbo-Croat.

That book contained the doubts Gorz had expressed in 1966 and 1967. Though, in his eyes, self-management still had promise for the future, he wrote that it 'isn't a panacea'.[22] At a stage of development in which accumulation remains an imperative, 'economic self-management' amounted to having workers' collectives take on productivist policies that were in

---

20 Gorz, *Letter to D.*, p. 53.

21 Michel Bosquet, 'Est-Ouest. La tentative yougoslave', *L'Express* (20 August 1959).

22 André Gorz, 'L'auto-gestion n'est pas une panacée' in *Le Socialisme difficile* (Paris: Seuil, 1967), pp. 137–42.

contradiction with the 'technical self-management', which had as its goal 'to transform the workers' condition, to abolish the degradation, mutilation and robotization of the worker and work entailed in production techniques of American origin'.[23] The crunch came, then, at the point where self-management met state planning, since, if the object was to guarantee 'that development would take place towards a socialist model of civilization and of life,'[24] the choice of priorities could not be left to the production units, which were always tempted by their own selfish aims. That antagonism was one of the dilemmas inevitably faced by a society in transition to socialism. It had, therefore, to be accepted. However, this implied a recasting of institutional roles: to the Party, *kept separate from the administration*, must go the—democratically debated—task of steering the major future choices expressed in planning; to the trade union, *kept separate from management*, must go the task of defending the aspirations and needs of the workers in the here and now.[25]

Cuban Internationalism

Covering international events for *L'Express*, Bosquet reported on the Castroist guerrilla war (February 1958), its victory with 'strong overtones of anti-Americanism' (January 1959) and the 'intolerable cancer' that Cuba represented for the Americans, who were threatening to overthrow Castro as they had Arbenz in Guatemala (October 1960). For *Les Temps modernes*, writing as Gorz, he also reported on the Bay of Pigs fiasco (May 1961).

Sartre visited Fidel Castro in 1960 and came back delighted. The following year, Karol attended the May Day festivities in Havana and was suddenly full of praise for the revolution. That revolution, seen as pragmatic and resourceful by C. Wright Mills and as 'romantically heroic' by Sartre, fascinated the progressive intellectuals of Europe and America from the outset. What subsequently captivated them was not so much the establishment of a socialist system tethered to the Soviet Union as the internationalist aura assumed by the regime through the diplomatic activism of one of its ministers, Ernesto Guevara, who, with Mehdi Ben Barka, had initiated the Tricontinental Conference. After the Argentinian's mysterious departure

---

23 Ilija Bojovič, Interview with André Gorz reprinted in Ilija Bojovič, *1968*, p. 119.
24 Bojovič, Interview with Gorz, p. 121.
25 Gorz, 'Arduous Socialism', pp. 205–14.

in 1965 to go and fight at some unspecified location, the Cuban authorities consolidated their solidarity network by organizing international jamborees on their blockaded island. At the time, every revolutionary intellectual in the West aspired to receive an official invitation to the revolution underway in the Caribbean.

When Gorz, accompanied by Dorine, landed at Cuba in the dying days of 1967, the Salon de Mai[26] had already taken place five months before and, with it, the Latin American Solidarity Conference which welcomed five hundred participants. Some 50 French artists, writers and intellectuals, such as Marguerite Duras, Michel Leiris, Dionys Mascolo, Maurice Nadeau and Jorge Semprún had made the trip. Bosquet's colleagues at *Le Nouvel Observateur* Karol and Lentin gave him an account of that first gigantic gathering, also bringing back photographs.

This time, promoted by Leiris among others, it was the turn of the Cultural Congress, which drew intellectuals from across the world to Havana, calling on them to take a stance on the Third World. Among the 400–600 guests (depending on the source consulted)—some of whom had already made the trip in July—were, from France, Pierre Naville, Kostas Axelos, Gisèle Halimi, Christiane Rochefort and the Chilean painter Roberto Matta, along with K. S. Karol and Rossana Rossanda. The Congress, which lasted a week, opened on 4 January 1968. Gorz's turn to speak came on 9 January. On first making contact with the Cubans in October 1967, he had already confided that 'he had been a constant admirer of [the Cuban revolution] from a distance.'[27] Though he had confirmed that it was easy to discuss with Fidel, whatever the circumstances, he was intimidated when he got up to speak. His intelligence seemed paralyzed. He knew that it was the calling of intellectuals to deal in words, whereas 'revolutionaries'—sometimes in the mould of 'organic intellectuals' like Castro—dealt in acts. This was what he would speak of, laying out the role allotted to the diffusers of culture, whom he saw only as bearers of 'universal values'. 'A European intellectual,' he said, 'can only address this Congress with modesty.' That was how he opened his talk, which, in scholarly fashion, he entitled 'Class Culture, National Culture and Universality', though he treated his subject summarily:

26 The annual Parisian exhibition of paintings, which was moved to Cuba that year under the aegis of Wilfredo Lam.

27 Letter from André Gorz to Manuel Gallich, Deputy Director of *La Casa de las Américas*, 10 October 1967 (GRZ).

A culture only acquires this universality when it merges with the intellectual and moral weapons being forged by a class struggling for its total emancipation. [. . .] The only thing we can aspire to is being agents of the subversion of our cultures and societies. [. . .] The only part of culture that is living and deserves to survive is the part that induces oppressed peoples to rebel against the oppressors. [. . .] Wherever it occurs, and provided that it is radical and total, the revolution not only engenders an authentic national culture, it also restores its universal influence and scope to the national culture. That is why it is true—as is magnificently illustrated by the internationalism of the Cuban revolutionaries and the example of Ernesto Che Guevara—that revolutionaries have no fatherland.[28]

In the early days of 1968, the Cuban journal *La Casa de las Américas* paid homage to Guevara, who had been assassinated in Bolivia on 9 October 1967. Gorz was invited to contribute a piece and did so, as did Jorge Semprún, Claude Julien and Anne Philipe from France. Most of the offerings were striking at once for their lyricism and paucity of content. Gorz's contribution, which had both the honour and the responsibility of being the opening piece, was no great exception to this, employing a tone of pathos reinforced by the rhythmic repetition of the poetic form of address to the dear departed: 'I write to you from a distant continent, comrade.'

Homage no doubt has its stylistic constraints,[29] but in this case formal vacuity and rhetoric reflected the difficulty of grasping Che's volatile personality and ephemeral career. By his geographical disappearance, long before he disappeared physically, Che became an elusive figure, the subject of all kinds of speculation: he was already a myth.[30] That myth also had a body, which an already famous photograph (taken in 1960 at a public funeral) undertook to magnify—the body of a man in his thirties with long

---

28 Congresso Cultural de La Habana, *Reunion de intelectuales de todo el mundo sobre problemas de Asia, Africa y América Latina* (Havana: Instituto del Libro, 1968). The French manuscript of this article is preserved at GRZ 9.22.

29 See, by contrast, the sober style of the article investigating Guevara's death by the same author: Michel Bosquet, 'L'assassin de "Che" Guevara', *Le Nouvel Observateur* (1 November 1967).

30 At *Le Nouvel Observateur*, it was Albert-Paul Lentin, who had been close to Ben Barka, who maintained the myth with his fiery articles (see the last of these, 'La victoire de Guevara', *Le Nouvel Observateur* [18 October 1967]).

hair and an inspired look in his eyes. The comparison with the Christic icon was too obvious for Gorz not to add his two penn'orth to it:

> I who am not a Christian tell you that your assassins labour under the same illusions as the Romans some 930 years ago when, alongside two thieves, they executed a Jewish agitator who had only twelve men with him: his ideas nevertheless got the better of the empire which at the time dominated the world.[31]

In his elegy, Gorz gives thorough voice to the pain of the survivor; it is strange that he should do so by appealing first to his own greatest emotional concern—alienation in work:

> I write to you from a distant continent, comrade, where men are not happy. We suffer there from toiling without knowing for whom or to what end; we suffer there from producing things measured only in terms of money or comfort. We suffer there from working eight or nine hours a day for a wage which, however high it is, will never make up for the monotony of our meaningless occupations.[32]

Back in Paris, what was Gorz's takeaway from the revolution in Cuba? First, that everything seemed possible. Over there, economic improvisation, disorder and rationing were transcended by a full-on idealism that was presumed to override material incentives. To a group of Europeans, among whom Gorz was all ears, Castro roared:

> In your countries, you entice the workers with money. [. . .] We think [. . .] there are things that are much more crucial in their lives than material needs: the—moral and spiritual—needs of dignity, culture, fraternity and justice.' Second, he told them that productivity wasn't everything, since the liberation of workers also meant not forcing them to work 'by imposing rationing on them through money.[33]

---

31 André Gorz, 'Al camarada Che Guevara', *Casa de las Américas* 46 (Jan–Feb 1968): 11. Reprinted in French translation in Fourel (ed.), *André Gorz. Un penseur pour le XXIe siècle*, p. 248. (The French original, which we follow here, is preserved at GRZ 8.24). The parallel with the Christ figure is also present in the above mentioned *Nouvel Observateur* article.

32 Gorz, 'Al camarada Che Guevara', p. 10. Reprinted in Fourel (ed.), *André Gorz*, p. 247.

33 Michel Bosquet, 'Fidel Castro est-il fou?', *Le Nouvel Observateur* (28 February 1968).

As a member of the management committee of the—virtually phantom—International Association of the friends of the Cuban Revolution, created following the Havana Congress with Michel Leiris as its chairman, Gorz had the 'Havana Appeal' (passed at the Congress) published in the February issue of *Les Temps modernes*. The Trotskyist Mandel was quite alone in imparting to him his concerns about political developments on the island.[34] In March Gorz coordinated an issue on Cuba that included extracts from Castro's speech to the Cultural Congress. In late September he was not named among the eight members of the above-mentioned Association (Antelme, Blanchot, Duras, Mascolo and some other minor figures) who took the initiative of writing an open letter to Castro, published by *Le Nouvel Observateur*, in protest at Cuban approval of the Soviet invasion of Czechoslovakia.

However, the reality principle would soon kick in with Gorz and most of the other sycophants. In 1971, along with Sartre, Beauvoir, Leiris, Nadeau, Semprún, Rossanda and others of their ilk (though Karol and Lentin were not on the list), Gorz broke with the Castroist regime, denouncing the iniquity of the trial to which the poet Heberto Padilla was subjected ('we should like,' the intellectuals' letter concluded, 'the Cuban revolution to return to what, at one time, led us to regard it as a model within socialism.').[35] He was prepared to recognize that in Cuba it was a foregone conclusion that 'in an order governed by scarcity, blockade, external terror and, shall we say, a form of popular movement that was never able to self-organize and was organized from above—by the charismatic leader, in particular—the whole thing would come toppling down on the leaders of the Cuban revolution and they were heading for horrendously hard times.'[36]

Armed Struggles in the Third World

Beyond Cuban internationalism, subscribing wholly to the Tricontinental Conference and its line, what did Gorz actually think of the battles fought by the peoples of the periphery against 'yankee imperialism'? We already

---

34 Ernest Mandel to André Gorz, 29 February 1968 (GRZ).

35 'La Lettre des intellectuels à M. Fidel Castro' (60 signatures), *Le Monde* (22 May 1971).

36 Gorz in dialogue with Sartre in 1972 in the film *Sartre par lui-même*. See Michel Contat and Alexandre Astruc, *Sartre* (Paris: Gallimard, 1977), pp. 118–9.

know he was convinced—and would remain lastingly persuaded—that the Western masses were the key element in the anti-capitalist fight. In that sense, he wasn't a Third Worldist. That is why, when he turned his attention to the Sino-Soviet quarrel, then at its height, he pronounced himself more attached to the principle of peaceful coexistence advocated by the Soviets than the warlike Third Worldist gesticulations of the Chinese, which were based, furthermore, on the erroneous forecast that capitalism would collapse in very short order.[37]

In one of the three lectures he gave at Mexico City in February 1966 entitled 'Colonialism at Home and Abroad', he articulated that point of view, ruling out the idea of a dividing line between imperialist nations and oppressed ones, given that there was, within each nation, a border discriminating against dominated groups. Internationalist solidarity and convergence were more the affair of—both developed and underdeveloped—peoples' struggles against capitalism, which imposed a single, monopolistic model of development on the world, based primarily on the subordination of agriculture to industry—on this latter point, he invoked the counter-arguments of René Dumont, Frantz Fanon and Mao Zedong.[38]

Gorz wasn't an unknown when he gave this talk in Mexico City (the text can be found in the Mexican publication in which most of the lectures in the series first appeared).[39] His *Morale de l'Histoire* had been published in Mexico in 1964 and had been studied in the Sociology and Economics Faculty of the University of Mexico City. And in Mexico Gorz wasn't an exceptional case, the structuralists Louis Althusser and Maurice Godelier and other French thinkers having also been translated there. All the progressive circles of Latin America were indeed highly attentive to the theoretical production of French-speaking Marxists. In the 1960s, for example, Lefebvre, Mandel and Vincent were translated in Argentina and Lefebvre, Goldmann and Jean-François Lyotard in Brazil, where *Stratégie ouvrière et néocapitalisme* and *Le Socialisme difficile* were also translated in 1968 (*Réforme et révolution* appearing in Mexico in 1969). Gorz's thoughts on

---

37 Gorz, *Le Socialisme difficile*, pp. 175–94. Originally published as the Introduction to *Les Temps modernes* 204 ('Le débat sino-soviétique') (May 1963): 1923–42.

38 Gorz, *Socialism and Revolution*, pp. 215–36.

39 Fromm, et al., *La Sociedad industrial contemporánea*, pp. 168–88. Like *Socialism and Revolution*, this publication contained also, in the same more fleshed-out form, Gorz's other two Mexican lectures to which we have alluded in the preceding chapters.

May '68 were laid out in the Argentine magazine *Pasado y presente* and articles of his were published that same year in the Brazilian opposition periodical *Revista civilização brasileira*. It will be clear, then, that this lecture, which undercut the certainties of the Third Worldists, did not pass unnoticed among the intellectuals of the South American Left, who criticized Gorz for his imperviousness to the 'national question'.[40]

He was not, however, rigid in his thinking. His meeting with Brazilian revolutionaries and the appearance of armed actions in Latin America would change the way he saw things to some degree. The example of the anti-imperialist resistance of the Vietcong also played a part in this—on 26 November 1966 he took part in the 'Six heures pour le Vietnam' [Six hours for Vietnam] at La Mutualité in Paris, which was the launch pad for the French National Vietnam Committee (CVN) and, like Marcuse, he also took part in public debates. It was in Mexico City, in fact, that he talked with exiled advocates of Liberation Theology—including the famous leader of the Peasant Leagues [*ligas camponesas*] in north-eastern Brazil Francisco Julião—who, though they were Catholics, helped him to see that, when fighting dictatorship, one has the right to use violence.[41] In 1969 and 1970 he popularized the issues underlying the Guevara-inspired Brazilian guerrilla war by meeting Jamil (alias Ladislas Dowbor) in Paris, by obtaining articles from the three active movements for *Les Temps modernes*[42] and by speaking about it sympathetically in *Le Nouvel Observateur*.[43]

From this point on, he granted a primary role to the Third World— through China and Vietnam and the armed avant-gardes that were trying to mobilize poor peasants more oppressed by imperialist dependency than

40 See Carlos P. Mastrorilli and Fernando Alvarez, *Marcuse Sartre Nizan Gorz y el Tercer Mundo* (Buenos Aires: Carlos Pérez Editor, 1969), pp. 44–55.

41 Michel Bosquet, 'Brazil: The Right to Violence' in *Capitalism in Crisis and Everyday Life*, pp. 134–40. First published in French, *Le Nouvel Observateur* (9 March 1966).

42 The Vanguarda Popular Revolucionário (Popular Revolutionary Vanguard) of João Quartim de Moraes and 'Jamil'; Ação Libertadora Nacional (National Liberation Action); and MR8 (The 8th October Revolutionary Movement). See the issues of May and November 1968 and November 1970.

43 Michel Bosquet, *Critique du capitalisme quotidien* (Paris: Galilée, 1973), pp. 242–7. First published as '1970: L'année des otages', *Le Nouvel Observateur* (28 December 1970). This article does not seem to have been included in the English translation published by Harvester Press.

by direct relations of exploitation—in the destabilization of empire, although they were unsuited to shift relations of production from within in the direction of Communism.[44] It was in this regard that Gorz supported the Third Worldism that permeated the period. Ultimately, we may say that he subscribed to a kind of Guevarism (yes to violence and guerrilla warfare), crossed tactically with Maoism (yes to support for the peasantry of the Periphery), and tempered strategically with workerism (yes to the labour struggles in the Heartlands). This ultra-Leftism, quite close to the neo-Trotskyist positions of the Jeunesse communiste révolutionnaire (JCR)[45] in France, was fully in tune with the revolutionary euphoria spreading around the world in 1968.

---

44 André Gorz, Introduction to *I Protagonisti della Storia universale, Volume 14: Il Mondo contemporaneo. La pace e la rivoluzione* (Milan: CEI, 1971), pp. xi–xxx.

45 The JCR was a forerunner of the Ligue communiste, which later became the Ligue communiste révolutionnaire. [Trans.]

CHAPTER NINE

The Ferment of '68

André Gorz was 45 in 1968. Though working outside academia, he took part, like everyone else, in the carnival of debate and discussion that submerged the streets of Paris that year. But he was not to be found on the barricades, in the student assemblies. He was at the factory gates, but not to hand out leaflets. The terms and limits of his political engagement, as he had defined them in the past, were also to apply to the way he approached May '68. In other words, in his own sphere, to which he consciously committed himself, his *intellectual involvement* was total. The signing of petitions, which had quite a substantial impact in the media, was one of his chosen instruments of intervention. At the height of the movement, Gorz signed a solemn declaration by prominent personalities that urged the students to muster and maintain a 'power of refusal' of great future significance. It was published on 9 May by *Le Monde* under the aegis of Sartre and Lefebvre, but it seemed to represent the spirit—and was perhaps the work— of Blanchot, Gorz, Mascolo, Nadeau, Leiris and their ilk.

> It is scandalous not to recognize in this movement the things it is straining after and which are at issue in it: the will to escape by every means possible from an alienated order, an order so highly structured and integrated that simple contestation always risks merely serving it.[1]

It would be difficult not to sense, also, the spirit of Marcuse in the framing of this sentence.[2] Quite logically, Gorz would later figure among the 180

---

1 'Il est capital que le mouvement des étudiants oppose et maintienne une puissance de refus déclarent MM. Jean-Paul Sartre, Henri Lefebvre et un groupe d'écrivains et de philosophes', *Le Monde* (10 May 1968). The first version was drafted by Blanchot. This petition is also signed by Robert Antelme, Marguerite Duras, Nathalie Sarraute, Jacques Lacan, Marthe Robert, Pierre Klossowski, François Châtelet etc. (35 signatures in all).

2 And indeed Marcuse approved this declaration and referred to it in an interview with Michel Bosquet: 'Les étudiants se révoltent contre un mode de vie', *Le Nouvel Observateur* (20 May 1968).

writers and artists who signed the petition, incriminating themselves by supporting the actions for which the *gauchiste* organizations involved in the May movement would be disbanded by the French Interior Ministry on 12 June.[3]

At **Nanterre** and at Le Nouvel Observateur

It was at the University of Nanterre, hastily created to cope with an excess of student numbers, that things began. Journalists on *Le Nouvel Observateur*, particularly the young René Backmann who was close to the students, were frequent visitors. However, in the late afternoon of Thursday, 25 April, Gorz went to Nanterre not as a sympathetic investigative journalist, but to debate. A political studies group, created by the Jeunesse communiste révolutionnaire, but filled with members of the 22nd March Movement (the protest group that originated at Nanterre), had invited him to discuss 'the social function of the university', a theme he had broached on many occasions in the pages of *Le Nouvel Observateur*. Two journalists from *Le Monde*, passing unnoticed among the students in what had been renamed the 'Che Guevara Lecture Theatre', reported on the proceedings.[4] The snapshot they provided offers a wonderful account of the psycho-intellectual ferment that was '68.

To begin with, a hothead from the Trotskyist (Lambertist) student committee threatened to consign the other guest, the mathematician and 'pro-selection'[5] academic Laurent Schwartz, 'who was not a member of the working class', to the same fate that had befallen the Communist apparatchik Pierre Juquin half an hour earlier, when pro-Chinese elements had thrown him out of a meeting called by his student acolytes, which they had managed to disrupt. Jumping up like a jack-in-the-box, cheery and bouncy, with his mane of red hair flowing, Daniel Cohn-Bendit, rebel leader of the 22nd March Movement, emerged from the melee on the stage to shout, off microphone, 'Laurent Schwartz must be allowed to speak. Let him speak and we'll

---

3 'De nombreuses personnalités se solidarisent avec les responsables des mouvements dissous', *Le Monde* (26 June 1968).

4 Published when the protest movement reached the streets and became a news item: Frédéric Gaussen and Guy Herzlich, 'L' explosion de colère des étudiants a surpris tous les observateurs', *Le Monde* (7 May 1968).

5 That is to say, he was in favour of the new selective university entrance measures the government had decided to introduce.

try afterwards, in the discussion, to take him down politically. If, after that, we come to the conclusion he's a filthy swine, we'll tell him.'

As they faced this crowd alone, were Schwartz—who had already founded the PSU and the CVN—and Gorz there to act as guiding lights or were they being put in the dock? Were they teachers open to dialoguing with their students, political tribunes, or simply adults offered up to the anger of youths ready to tear them limb from limb? It was an ambiguous situation. The speakers were bombarded with political questions. They were hesitant. They didn't seem to have ready, 'scholarly' answers. They were barely given time to react. One voice in the hall cut through with the fierce irony of a prosecutor: 'Let them think. You can see Monsieur Schwartz is thinking. Let's wait till he's finished, it might prove interesting.' Yet the hall wasn't entirely united against the speakers: there were too many sectarian divisions for that. The invective and insults were rapidly counterbalanced. When a 'pro-Chinese' or 'anarchist' student let rip, the room, suddenly outraged, shut them up.

Gorz, his thin, muffled voice aided by use of the microphone, broke through to the audience: at no point, according to the report, was he discomfited in his answers. He had, admittedly, been invited because he had opposed Schwartz's restrictive approach to university entrance in the columns of *Le Nouvel Observateur*,[6] which was very widely read by students, and because his extremely radical analyses of the university system ran very much in a direction approved by the movement—we shall return to this point below.

Things were a bit different at *Le Nouvel Observateur*, which lined up with the rioters and strikers in 1968. With 'that strange smile that cuts his long inquisitor's face in two',[7] Bosquet was reserved in his opinions. He did not feel entirely free to express himself. The balanced distribution of responsibilities within the management board, of which he was a member, means that we can describe the magazine, under Jean Daniel's leadership, as collegial. He also tended to talk at great length in editorial meetings. But he knew, for example, that his 'response' to Schwartz was a concession the majority of the writers had granted him. He always maintained a degree of

---

6 See Michel Bosquet, 'Réponse à Laurent Schwartz', *Le Nouvel Observateur* (8 November 1967).

7 Todd, *Un fils rebelle*, p. 114.

distance from Jean Daniel. He never acted like Gorz-the-philosopher at the magazine (though Daniel instinctively saw him that way: 'Something tells me that he will be significant in the history of ideas and that some pages of his will become standard references,' he noted in 1979).[8] Nor did he give vent to his feelings relating to the difficulties of being-in-the-world or, more pertinently, to the erasure of subjectivity involved in journalism—even 'opinion journalism'.[9] We may recall, incidentally, that he cut the pages referring to the practice of journalism from his essay on ageing—'Le vieillissement'—and he would leave them unpublished.

His best friend at the magazine, the one who had known him since their close collaboration at L'Express, Serge Lafaurie, would always describe him as 'rather enigmatic'.[10] For his part, Jean Daniel confessed an inability to understand him. As late as 1979, he wrote: 'I've seen him every day for 20 years, I've had a thousand opportunities for intimate conversations and, as close as I am to him, his face seems impenetrable to me.' In May 1968, for the editor-in-chief, 'his Trotskyist's conspirator's face [sic] becomes increasingly Asiatic', as he sees history accelerating in ongoing events. But it is simply the case that his situation at Le Nouvel Observateur is not without ambiguity: 'he belongs to the "management" or, at any rate, to what others regard as the "top of the organization": he isn't comfortable.'[11]

For discontent was also being expressed in the corridors of the magazine in the rue Royale. Le Nouvel Observateur was well represented in the heretical journalists' assemblies at the Sorbonne. After another night on the barricades, which all the writers had experienced in their various ways, they met up at the magazine (except for those in management) early on the morning of 25 May[12] with one precise intention in mind: power must come back to the base, the management committee must be paritaire—i.e. have equal worker representation—and the director must be elected. Lentin, the unwavering Che supporter, and Todd, turned gauchiste for this brief period, led the secessionist forces, with the support of Backmann, Claude Angeli

---

8 Jean Daniel, L'Ère des ruptures (Paris: Grasset, 1979), p. 50.

9 On this subject, see Willy Gianinazzi, 'Michel Bosquet ou le journalisme comme compromis' in Fourel (ed.), André Gorz en personne, pp. 81–6.

10 Serge Lafaurie, 'Hommage à André Gorz'.

11 All quotations here from Daniel, L'Ère des ruptures, p. 50.

12 And not on 11 May, as some sources suggest. Our dating, which we believe to be fully reliable, is contextual.

and CGT official Jean Moreau, while Mallet lay in ambush. Were they trying to impose a homemade version of the much-vaunted workers' control? Was worker self-management in prospect?

Bosquet had to choose which camp he was in, even if it meant going out on a limb. His decision was quickly made: that very morning he made it known that he was putting his vote at the disposal of the writers' assembly (he would resign definitively from the board of directors). Management with equal representation of the *writers* was, in fact, a possible political solution (a writers' company, with a holding of 10 per cent of the capital, would in fact eventually be created in 1970 under the chairmanship of Backmann): it would have introduced democracy among those who wrote the magazine and helped to shape its political line. That solution did not consist in granting power to the employees' general meeting, which actually convened in the afternoon amid a hubbub of escalating demands. This was because the press represents a particular case: it owes its soul to its pluralism, which has to be safeguarded on pain of producing a second-rate product. Employee oversight not just of working conditions but also of the *purposes* of work— as advocated in *Strategy for Labor*—would in effect have posed the political problem of respect for the freedom of the press, a precondition for pluralism. Sartre, the 'in-house sage' whom Jean Daniel met two days later, did however apply pressure in that direction. Bosquet, who understood that his own arguments couldn't apply in a case like this, found himself obliged to plead the cause of the contested editor with Sartre.[13] Since Daniel refused to embark on the desired adventure, the debate went no further.

It was not reopened in 1973 when Serge July's new Maoist–Sartrean newspaper *Libération* was created on the basis of co-management between directors and staff, since everyone there was agreed on a single political line. The question did, however, return to the agenda in 1975 after the Carnation Revolution in Portugal, when workers' control had been imposed by its employees on the Lisbon socialist daily *República*. It would be debated in France by the—pro-worker self-management—CFDT and by the Trotskyist Ligue communiste révolutionnaire (LCR),[14] which would manage to condemn such interference despite their own stated principles.

13 Daniel, *L'Ère des ruptures*, pp. 56–8; and 'Je me souviens', *Le Monde* (27 September 2007).

14 The LCR was the successor organization to the Ligue communiste in 1974, which had itself succeeded the JCR in 1969.

Nor did Bosquet follow *Le Nouvel Observateur*'s most left-wing jour-
nalists, who ended up jumping ship, like Karol, to work on the Italian Far
Left's new publication *Il Manifesto* (he would later return) or, like Mallet,
Lentin and Angeli, to take part, under the editorship of the ex-Communist
Paul Noirot, in founding *Politique Hebdo* in 1970. He remained, as it were,
the guardian of the magazine's good conscience. He thus appeared to
Jean-Luc Godard—the politically committed director of the film *La
Chinoise* (1967), who sent him a crotchety note after hearing him debate on
television—as the man who embodied 'the honesty of the dishonest
[*Nouvel*] *Obs*'.[15] If Bosquet seemed willing to put up with his employment
as a journalist, that was because he found fulfilment elsewhere, his double
having a leading role at *Les Temps modernes*. We shall come to this shortly.

Marcuse in Paris

In April 1968, Herbert Marcuse wrote to his friend André Gorz: 'I expect
to be in Paris from 7 May to approximately 11 May, where I am supposed
to participate in the UNESCO symposium on Marx. I hope to be able to
reduce my attendance to the bare minimum and to see you—or will you
again be out of town?'[16] Gorz would not be spending the weekend away, as
had been his habit; and Marcuse had no idea that he'd be landing in France
right in the middle of the student protests, for which he would be regarded
as a mentor, as he had been the previous year in a more overt way for the
German students who chanted the names of the three M's on their marches:
'Marx, Mao, Marcuse'.

However that might be, in France the rush was on to read *One-
Dimensional Man*, the translation rolling off the presses on 28 April and selling at a thousand copies a week. At *Le Nouvel Observateur*, Mallet was tasked
with providing an exhaustive account of the career and thought of the 70-
year-old professor. In an article entitled 'The Idol of the Rebel Students', the
theorist of worker self-management nonetheless attacked his pessimism and
happily drew on the criticisms Gorz had levelled at him previously[17] to conclude that it was Marcuse's system that was 'one-dimensional', since he relied

15 Jean-Luc Godard to André Gorz, 13 June 1972 (GRZ).
16 Herbert Marcuse to André Gorz (in English), 17 April 1968 (GRZ).
17 See Gorz, *Socialism and Revolution*, p. 80.

exclusively on 'those outside the production process'.[18] For its special issue of 20 May, *Le Nouvel Observateur* handed out the various tasks: it sent Sartre to interview the student leader Cohn-Bendit, with Bosquet also present, in an article with a title that would become emblematic—'L'imagination au pouvoir' [The Imagination in power]—and deputed Bosquet to to sound out Marcuse, who argued strongly that the students were in revolt against an alienating way of life. Marcuse and Bosquet–Gorz were in total agreement at the time on the exemplary, rousing value of the students' 'Great Refusal'. Indeed, the two held each other in growing esteem. In an interview that appeared in the Italian press in March, Marcuse had not hesitated, in fact, to raise Gorz—alongside Lelio Basso—to the rank of sole European representatives of 'authentic Marxism'![19]

Destroy[ing] the University!

Gorz and *Les Temps modernes* were interested in the student question very early on. In 1964 and 1965, in articles written by leaders of the student unions and mutual organizations (Màrc Kravetz, Antoine Griset, Jean-Pierre Milbergue etc.),[20] the journal provided a platform for contesting the universities and the way they operated.

If Gorz was overtly influenced by the critical analyses produced by French student organizations (UNEF [the National Union of Students of France] and MNEF [the National Mutual Benefit Society of French Students] and their German counterpart SDS [The German Socialist Students' Union]), he also contributed, through his last two books, *Stratégie ouvrière* [. . .] and *Le Socialisme difficile*, his articles and the articles he obtained from Italy for *Les Temps modernes*, to forging the theoretical 'Italian line' within France's student organizations. This he did precisely within the Union of Communist Students (UEC) before the so-called 'Italians', who claimed allegiance to that line (they were, in fact, Khruschevian) were excluded in 1965 and, more particularly, within the main student union

---

18 Serge Mallet, 'L'idole des étudiants rebelles: Herbert Marcuse', *Le Nouvel Observateur* (8 May 1968).

19 Ugo Stille, 'Marcuse, il teorico della protesta' (interview), *Corriere della Sera* (5 March 1968).

20 *Le Nouvel Observateur* did the same in December 1966 with a UNEF supplement entitled 'Contre l'université de classe' [Against the Class-based University].

UNEF, by way of the so-called *gauche syndicale*, then of the PSU students (known as the Étudiants socialistes unifiés) who, in 1967, provided a conduit from the *gauche syndicale* to leadership of the PSU.

This Italian 'line' was defined by anti-Stalinism and by showing the connection between the 'qualitative' needs of the new intellectual workers and the parallel aspirations of the students. It was through the impact on these milieus of politicized youth that Gorz and Sartre's *Temps modernes*, with a circulation of 10,000–15,000 copies, played an appreciable role in the ideological fermentation that was a prelude to '1968'. The influence of Gorz's writings on the American and German student organizations was not negligible either.[21]

Kravetz, the student union leader for the Paris humanities departments (the Fédération des groupes d'études de lettres) and Secretary General of UNEF was very much steeped in the Gorzian analyses of neo-capitalism. In his turn, Gorz drew inspiration from Kravetz's writings to interpret the contradictions and deadlock the university system found itself in from 1964 onwards. Between 1961 and 1967, student numbers increased by 232 per cent, but students received an ill-designed, lecture-based style of education: it vacillated between a disembodied teaching of the humanities and material that could provide some preparation for working life, but in a fragmented way and isolated from any social context. The students' desire for knowledge was at odds with a passive form of learning that prevented students from engaging in 'an autonomous labour of assimilation and research'. Gorz predicted that it was: 'In the realm of education that industrial capitalism will provoke the revolts it is trying to avoid in its factories.'[22]

And if the economy increasingly required a skilled workforce to be trained, it would be in the nature of things to see the cost of that training fully socialized. Hence the demand advanced by UNEF and the German

---

21 See, respectively, Andrea Levy, 'Reframing Socialism from the Fifties to the Fin-de-siècle: The Intellectual Odyssey of André Gorz', MA thesis, Concordia University, Montreal, 1998, pp. 115, 201n18; Claus Leggewie, 'A Laboratory of Postindustrial Society' in Carole Fink, Philipp Gassert and Detlef Junker (eds), *1968: The World Transformed*, p. 290. The American student leaders Greg Calvert and Carl Davidson refer explicitly to Gorz, 'Capitalist Relations of Production and the Socially Necessary Labour Force'; the SDS's German magazine published an abridged version of this text: 'Studium und Facharbeit heute', *Neue Kritik* 35 (April 1966): 19–23.

22 Gorz, *Strategy for Labor* [1964], p. 107.

SDS for *a universal student grant*, which would make all students without distinction *autonomous*, both with respect to their families and to the conditions laid down by the scholarship-issuing state. And they would be so not only materially, but also in terms of the choice of studies and the determination of their own criterion of usefulness.[23]

For this was, indeed, the fundamental question for anyone who came at pedagogy not from the egalitarian standpoint of republican democracy but from the Socratic standpoint of anarchism. In the former—meritocratic—case, making university studies open to all simply meant equality of opportunity with respect to the jobs market; in the latter—acratic—case, it meant the opportunity for everyone to acquire an education through the maieutics developed by pro-self-management pedagogues like Georges Lapassade, a leading figure at the experimental university of Vincennes, which was founded at the beginning of the 1968 academic year. In two articles in *Les Temps modernes*, published in 1968 and 1970—the latter bearing the outrageous title 'Destroy[ing] the University'—Gorz clearly laid out the alternatives: if it is about defending the inalienable right to study, is this with an eye to producing job prospects that cannot possibly be made available for everyone or, in contrast to this 'culture of utility' approach, to promote disinterested study that has an intrinsic value and is motivated by a 'rebel culture' that opens on to a life which the university, by definition, cannot make available?[24] Gorz's question brooked only one logical answer as Sartre saw it, having himself told *Le Nouvel Observateur* that the purpose of education is 'to produce dissenters'.[25]

An original reaction emerged from the pen of Jacques Julliard in that magazine. The historian had compared the practices of May '68 with the direct-action methods of revolutionary syndicalism. Julliard was already an official of the SGEN (Syndicat general de l'enseignement national), the education trade union affiliated to the CFDT, and a publisher at Seuil of Gorz's

---

23 Gorz, 'Capitalist Relations of Production and the Socially Necessary Labour Force'.

24 André Gorz, 'The Way Forward', *New Left Review* 52 (November–December 1968): 47–66 (first published as 'Limites et potentialités du mouvement de mai', *Les Temps modernes* 266–7 [August–September 1968]: 260–1); 'Destroy the University', *Partisan Review* 38(3) (Summer 1971): 314–18 (first published as 'Détruire l'Université', *Les Temps modernes* 285 [April 1970]: 1553–8).

25 Jean-Paul Sartre, 'Les bastilles de Raymond Aron', *Le Nouvel Observateur* (19 June 1968).

latest book, though he had not worked long at *Le Nouvel Observateur*, having been co-opted at Bosquet's instigation. In advancing his position, which was relegated diplomatically to an opinion column, he opposed Gorz by arguing that even from a revolutionary point of view, the university had to be saved for the role it played in 'the development and spread of knowledge'; he did, however, advocate eliminating the 'condition of teacher', so that each professor could acquire a different form of knowledge through contact with an activity that was not so removed from society.[26]

For his part, Marcuse had other reservations. To Bosquet's question whether the system didn't provide itself with the intellectuals that it alone needed, he replied that, in any event, the university must not be destroyed, but radically reformed so that the rebellion could continue to arm itself with the weapons of intellectual critique;[27] as Bosquet himself would let slip years later, ' "Destroy the University" was a slogan Marcuse viewed as stupid.'[28]

Already discomfited by the publication of other articles—that of Kravetz in 1964 and another ranged against the psychoanalytic *doxa* in 1969—Pingaud and Pontalis were repelled by Gorz's latest iconoclastic text to which Sartre lent his approval, positioning it as the lead article of the issue. They resigned from the magazine, disavowing the ultra-Leftism expressed in it, whose anti-institutional irreverence they were not prepared to countenance. At *Les Temps modernes*, which became more than ever a journal for the non-academic, the Workerist and Maoist credos were now to rule the roost—and be free to clash in its pages.

The Ultra-Leftist

'68 and Its Political Lessons

In France and throughout the world, the events of 1968 were a climactic moment. They were not the whole of '68, which has to be regarded as a set of ideologies and practices that were both political and socio-cultural,

---

26 Jacques Julliard, 'Save the University', *Partisan Review* 38(3) (Summer 1971) (first published as 'Sauver l'Université', *Le Nouvel Observateur* [4 May 1970]).

27 Herbert Marcuse, 'Socialisme ou barbarie' (interview by Jean Daniel and Michel Bosquet of 15 June 1972), *Le Nouvel Observateur* (8 January 1973).

28 Michel Bosquet, 'Herbert Marcuse, professeur de liberté', *Le Nouvel Observateur* (6 August 1979).

stretching over a longer period which, in reference to Gorz's case, we see as running from 1966 to 1972. It is by coming to an understanding of this period that it is possible to elucidate the historical meaning of '68 and to understand what was dying away and what was being born at that moment.[29]

In doing so, it seems to us that Gorz's thinking is specific in the following respect: it perfectly embodies the spirit of '68, that spirit not being a total break with the past, but having within it an ambivalence, a mix of old and new that was part of an intoxicating sociopolitical cocktail which unapologetically combined both 'Che' and 'the pill'. With hindsight, it is striking to see how the novel anti-authoritarian, existential, spontaneist trends in the social ferment that was then bubbling up against the consumer society were counterbalanced by an older, minority-interest process of politicization that led concomitantly to the proliferation of hyper-political groups posing questions of organization and power (with an element of violence thrown in). For the members of the former camp, 'everything was political', while for the latter group 'politics was all that counted'.

This duality would be ignored from the 1980s onwards by interpreters of '68 who were either disenchanted with it or settled back into established political ways (Cohn-Bendit, Bernard Kouchner, Serge July etc.), following Alain Touraine who retracted his initial view.[30] They would gloss over the ambivalent *political* essence of the celebrated event and retain only the *cultural* dimension, as though there had not been a general rebellion against the established order.[31] It is true that, over the long term, the cultural contribution (easing of moral standards, de-hierarchization etc.) eventually assumed greater importance than political attitudes that were swept away when the wave of protest 'ebbed', when people retreated back into 'private life' and the 'money-grubbing' Mitterrand years arrived. We must remember, however, that, at the time, this duality was properly *political*: it marked the return of the vexed question that has run through the whole

---

29 Out of an inexhaustible range of books and articles on the subject, see Isabelle Sommier, 'Les gauchismes' in Dominique Damamme, Boris Gobille, Frédérique Matonti and Bernard Pudal (eds), *Mai-juin 68* (Ivry-sur-Seine: Éditions de l'Atelier, 2008), pp. 295–305.

30 See Alain Touraine, 'Itinéraires intellectuels des années 1970', *Revue française d'histoire des idées politiques* 2 (1995): 394. We shall summarize his original analysis of May 68 in the following chapter.

31 Kristin Ross, *May 68 and Its Afterlives* (Chicago: University of Chicago Press, 2002).

history of the labour movement: the problematical relationship between civil society and politics, spontaneity and organization, movement and party. This is something that ranged Bakunin against Marx, Bernstein against Kautsky, Sorel against Jaurès or even Luxemburg against Lenin (this latter opposition often being raised in the debates on '68).

In a captivating reportage by Swiss television on the ongoing events, admirably filmed by Alain Tanner, Michel Bosquet explained that the students had implemented a 'Guevarist strategy' of 'not counting on the established parties', which were 'by their very history, conservative apparatuses', but rather on 'active minorities' which produced a contagious explosion of protest. 'The students were not organized. They began as a collection of tiny groups [. . .] which did not get on together'. Then Cohn-Bendit came along, a political animal of genius, advocating unity through action. 'It was action itself that was the main means of mobilizing the mass of the students.'[32]

As May 1968 subsided and in response to the electoral rout of the left-wing parties in June, which were incapable of providing the movement with a political outcome, the protagonists asked themselves what lessons were to be drawn. While Cohn-Bendit and Claude Lefort didn't see a problem since, in their view, what had been at stake was not the seizure of power, the books produced in the heat of the moment by writers of a Trotskyist[33] or Maoist[34] persuasion lamented the lost opportunity.

Gorz's viewpoint related to this latter political register, but the question he raised wasn't so much about power as about the logically prior question of the modalities of the organization of the masses. He was broadly in agreement with the intellectuals—whether members of the PSU or not (Heurgon, Vincent, Jacques Sauvageot, Emmanuel Terray, Maurice Najman, Jean-Paul Deléage etc.)—with whom he founded an ephemeral Centre for Revolutionary Initiative and Studies in 1970, which published the journal with the Leninist title *Que faire?* [What is to be Done?]. In *Les Temps Modernes*, Gorz invited Barjonet (who had broken with the CGT), Vincent, Mandel and the disgraced Italian Communists Rossanda and Magri to give

---

32 Jean-Pierre Goretta, 'Mai 68 à Paris', *Continents sans visa* (RTS, 6 June 1968) (available at: rts.ch/archives; last accessed: 26 July 2022).

33 Daniel Bensaïd and Henri Weber, *Mai 68: une répétition générale* (Paris: Maspero, 1968).

34 André Glucksmann, *Stratégie de la révolution* (Paris: Christian Bourgois, 1968).

their interpretation, while he gave his own views on the subject in editorials and long articles. It was clear for him that the May–June movement, powerful as it had been, had revealed the limits of spontaneity while at the same time sounding the death-knell for the Leninist model of the centralized vanguard party. He registered all this in his articles[35] and, in 1969, in *Réforme et révolution*[36] (a republication, with a new preface, of the essential elements of *Strategy for Labor*, with the addition of the eponymous chapter of the new work that was taken and re-worked from *Socialisme difficile*).

Two years before 1968 he had already raised the question of the party. Since the Social Democratic and Stalinist parties had thrown themselves headlong into the political institutions, he had proposed, with Basso, opting for a new model: a mass party, receptive to a direct democracy issuing from local experiences of a co-operative or self-managed type, that bore within it—by its embeddedness in the social fabric—a process of learning that helped to pose problems in ways that encouraged moving beyond the existing system.[37] That party, as he began to say at this point, would also function to develop orientations and work up demands coming from the base into an overall project and prepare a strategy for gaining power.[38] It would not, as the Trotskyists of the Ligue Communiste (the former JCR) were doing, turn itself into a high-flown vanguard laying down the line for the movement.[39] This concern to organize the labour movement upsurge in explicitly Luxemburgist terms can be easily explained, since in France the nine-million-strong strike movement was unable to develop the autonomy of action that would have enabled it to escape being brought back under the control of the CGT and Communist Party machines, these latter having put a brake on the upsurge of militancy and channelled it into the Grenelle Accords, where it ultimately fizzled out, and into pay rises that were soon eaten away by inflation.

---

35 Gorz, 'The Way Forward'; 'Ni trade-unionistes, ni bolcheviks', *Les Temps modernes* 279 (October 1969): 385–94.

36 Gorz, *Réforme et révolution*, pp. 9–56 (Preface) and 246–8 ('Réforme et révolution', included in *Socialism and Revolution*, pp. 175–7).

37 Gorz, *Socialism and Revolution*, pp. 104–06, 164.

38 Gorz, *Réforme et révolution*, pp. 43–56. Included and modified as 'Functions of a Revolutionary Party' in *Socialism and Revolution*, pp. 53–69.

39 André Gorz, 'Quattro domande ad André Gorz', *Giovane critica* 20 (Spring 1969): 50–6.

The Italian case was different. We have to pause to examine this, as Gorz referred now more than ever to the experience of the Italian Extreme Left, to which he gave copious space in Sartre's magazine and in his own thinking.

The Italian Horizon Again: Il Manifesto *and Lotta Continua*

'From spring 1968 to spring 1970 Italy saw the largest, longest and, in many respects, most radical movement of workers' struggles that the capitalist world has known outside periods of acute crisis. The "rejection" of work advocated from 1968 onwards by small political groups became a reality.'[40] That movement was characterized, on the one hand, by the intensity of the struggle, facilitated by the rebellious mass of young southern workers, who were, so to speak, 'internal immigrants'; and, on the other, by the modes of operation employed, which consisted in circumventing the established trade union machinery and developing councils of factory delegates that produced internal militant vanguards.

The Communist Left, with Luigi Pintor, Rossana Rossanda and subsequently Lucio Magri, soon saw how outdated the Italian Communist Party's strategy was. As early as June 1969 the first issue of a new monthly, *Il Manifesto*, appeared, seeking to provide the blueprint for a fresh approach. In late August, Sartre debated with the dissidents in Rome on the subject of 'Masses, Spontaneity and the Party'.[41] This study group, which turned itself into a party in 1972 after first being expelled from the PCI in November 1969 for factionalism, advocated moving beyond Leninism through a reading of Rosa Luxemburg that focused on not imposing an external consciousness on the workers' movement. It held up the example of the relationship between masses and party that supposedly applied in the China of the 'Cultural Revolution'.

Between 1968 and 1971, Gorz was happy to include a number of texts by *Il Manifesto* thinkers in *Les Temps modernes*. He also presented *Il Manifesto*'s 'Theses' in *Le Nouvel Observateur*.[42] As for *Il Manifesto*, they called on Gorz to work steadily with them[43] and translated his broadside

40 André Gorz, Présentation to *Les Temps modernes* 279 ('Italie') (October 1969): 332.

41 Jean-Paul Sartre, 'Masses, spontanéité, parti', *Les Temps modernes* 282 (January 1970): 1043–63. Taken from *Il Manifesto* (4 September 1969).

42 Bosquet, *Critique du capitalisme quotidien*, pp. 311–20.

43 Letter from Rossana Rossanda to André Gorz, 10 October 1970 (GRZ).

against the university system. Gorz also provided a home in *Les Temps modernes* for articles by the Sinologist and Maoist Edoardo Masi. He forged relations with other Italian Maoists, particularly Giampiero Mughini, the editor of the former cinema magazine *Giovane critica*, to which he granted an interview in 1969. He asked Mughini to put together an issue (August–September 1970) on the groups of the Italian Extreme Left. Under the influence of Mughini, who joined *Il Manifesto*, Gorz initially took the view that, among those groups, Potere operaio and Lotta Continua had no interesting strategic features.[44] This was not for want of meeting activists from Potere operaio very early on, as he did on holiday at Pugnochiuso in Apulia in the second half of June 1968 or at Milan in September 1969 when he talked with Antonio Negri, Sergio Bologna, Giairo Daghini, Franco Piperno and Oreste Scalzone (who had already visited him in Paris in May 1968)[45] and it wasn't for want of agreeing to Sartre publishing an article on the revolutionary vanguard by Adriano Sofri of Lotta Continua in his magazine in October 1969. From 1971 onwards, however, his interest in Lotta Continua increased as it became structured politically thanks to its involvement in various struggles. Gorz admitted to Sartre that he had been wrong about the group and that Sartre was right.[46]

Lotta Continua belonged to a new strain of Italian Marxism that emerged in the 1960s and whose origins we should trace here. The philosopher Galvano Della Volpe provides the distant theoretical reference point for the group (though Gorz denied being a 'DellaVolpist', he did quote him in 1967).[47] Della Volpe's major writings were published in Italy in the volume *Logic as a Positive Science* [1969], which, by its anti-humanism and its claim about the scientificity of Marxism, was the Italian pendant to Althusser's *For Marx*. But, unlike Althusser, Della Volpe reread *Capital* without evacuating either the subject or history (which would enable the only major French expert on his work, Jean-Marie Vincent, to train his guns on the structuralism of the École normale supérieure in the rue d'Ulm):[48] the

44 Gorz, Présentation to *Les Temps modernes* 279.

45 Personal communication from Oreste Scalzone, 23 November 2019.

46 Letter from Gorz to Jean-Paul Sartre, August [1971] (GRZ).

47 Paul Noirot, Jean-Marie Vincent, Manuel Ballestero and André Gorz, 'Sujet, structures, science et action politique. Discussion', *Démocratie nouvelle* 4 (April 1967): 58.

48 See Jean-Marie Vincent, 'Le théoricisme et sa rectification' in Jean-Marie Vincent, Jean-Marie Brohm, Catherine Colliot-Thélène et al., *Contre Althusser* (Paris: UGE, 1974), pp. 215–59.

engine of the class struggle was not, Della Volpe argued, the *structural* opposition between capital and labour, but the *living* opposition between capital and workers.

In 1961, one of Della Volpe's students, the dissident socialist Raniero Panzieri, an advocate of workers' control, founded *Quaderni rossi*. His intention was to conduct surveys among workers to gather their specific 'viewpoints'. It was at the *Quaderni* that the real founder of this tendency, the Communist rebel Mario Tronti, under the influence of the writings of Claude Lefort in *Socialisme ou Barbarie*, deepened Panzieri's analysis of the *enslavement* of the workers to the alleged technical rationality of capital— but also their *refractoriness* to that rationality. The originality of that analysis, though it echoed the idea of 'separation' in Georges Sorel,[49] consisted in postulating, not without exaggerated certainty, the autonomy of the working class from the rule of capital and its constitution as a political subject intrinsically resistant to class collaboration (*Workers and Capital* [1966]). As early as 1963, Tronti broke with Panzieri to set up a new magazine, *Classe operaia*. He took with him other intellectuals, such as Alberto Asor Rosa and the philosophers Massimo Cacciari and Antonio Negri.

This new publication must be regarded as the 'birthplace' of what would come to be called operaism (*operaismo*), a jargon term employed to make the distinction from the generic support for workers of earlier times, which is known in English more usually as autonomist Marxism. Having gambled on placing themselves at the heart of the working class through entryism into the PCI—a position Tronti developed in 1966—they saw their strategy fall apart in the upheaval of 1968, which led Negri to look to new groupings. These gave rise to the geographically dispersed centres of a movement of students and workers named (in imitation of the French 'Pouvoir ouvrier' that came out of the Socialisme ou Barbarie group) Potere operaio (PO).

However, the Pisa group, schooled in the workers' struggles at FIAT in Turin, diverged from the ultra-operaist option—indifferent to Third Worldism and tending towards militarism—of the Negrists (who, under

---

49 See George Ciccariello-Maher, 'Detached Irony Towards the Rest: Working-Class One-Sidedness from Sorel to Tronti', *The Commoner* 11 (Spring 2006): 54–73. This political current has often been dubbed 'Sorelian', though it has always denied the charge (see, for example, 'Anche Toni Negri è uno di quelli che vengono da lontano, da Sorel', *Quotidiano dei lavoratori* [19–20 February 1978]). In the 1980s, Negri, in exile in Paris, occasionally attended debates of the Société d'études soréliennes.

threat of repression, sought a gesture of solidarity from Gorz)[50] and went on to form Lotta Continua (LC) in 1969. The theorization of workers' autonomy acquired some precise watchwords: a single category of worker, a guaranteed wage (themes shared with PO), free transport and housing for all (hence the slogan: 'Let's take the city!'). LC became the largest extra-parliamentary group on the Italian Left. Gorz was attracted, as he wrote to Sartre, by its social practice, which had no equivalent in the intellectual *Il Manifesto* group,[51] and, as he wrote to Rossanda, by its refusal to pose the question of power in an *a priori* way.[52]

In mid-1971, Gorz made contact with Gianni Sofri of Lotta Continua who taught at the University of Bologna. Though he did not go to the Red City in July for the massive LC congress (6,000 participants), he obtained some of the group's writings, which he translated for the October issue of *Les Temps modernes*. Between 1971 and 1973, Gorz and Sofri exchanged several letters and met up. In November 1973, Gorz published an article in *Lotta Continua* on the class character of science.[53] At the same time, he received from Adriano Sofri, Gianni's younger brother and a leader of LC, a projected table of contents for an issue of *Les Temps modernes* that he had invited him to prepare. With the collaboration of the other LC leader Guido Viale (a future ecologist practitioner of recycling), that issue would appear in 1974 with the title 'Lotta Continua: la leçon italienne'.

Maoism and Les Temps modernes

Gorz first made contact with LC through the French Maoist Tiennot Grumbach, whom he befriended, visiting him several times in his activitist community at Mantes-la-Jolie. He warmed to Grumbach's zest for life and pursuit of happiness—a subject to make Althusserians shudder—and appreciated his awareness of the dilemma inherent in the relationship

---

50 See Giairo Daghini to André Gorz, 4 December 1969 (GRZ), in which this PO official announces that they are sending two emissaries to Paris (himself and Sergio Bologna) to obtain his support.

51 The aforementioned letter from Gorz to Jean-Paul Sartre.

52 André Gorz to Rossana Rossanda, June 1973, to which Rossanda refers in her reply of 10 August 1973 (GRZ).

53 André Gorz, 'Sul carattere di classe della scienza e dei lavoratori scientifici', *Lotta Continua* (10–11 November 1973).

between the activist and the worker in thrall to the socially prevailing ideas. 'Being "immersed" in the masses,' writes Grumbach in a memoir that is an assessment of his experience as an activist, 'we see ourselves as the agents of the subversion of that dominant ideology in the lives of people them-selves. In other words, we are never "like" ordinary people. If we thought that, we would be deceiving ourselves or deceiving them.'[54] Grumbach, who for his part treated Gorz as something of a guru, was agitating at that point at the gates of the Renault factory at Flins.[55] It was as a journalist on the look out for new forms of labour protest that Gorz had bumped into him there a number of times. In that activity, he drew on the experience accumu-lated from several trips to Turin to meet with Lotta Continua activists.

A nephew of Pierre Mendès France, Grumbach had a substantial record as a political activist. For three years he was a *pied rouge* in Algeria,[56] meeting Guevara there. Then, on returning to France in 1965, he became—alongside Robert Linhart—a leader of the Maoist group the UJC (ml) (Union des jeu-nesses communistes marxistes-léninistes), before 'establishing himself' as the jargon had it, like Linhart, in autumn 1968 in a Citroen factory in Paris, where he continued to work for several months. Grumbach was also one of the founders, with the former 'Italian' Roland Castro, of Vive la Révolution (VLR), the least dogmatic of all the French Maoist groups, whose aim was 'to change life', though inspired in that more by the Californian countercul-ture than the Chinese Red Guards.[57] Some feminists also joined the group, such as Françoise d'Eaubonne, giving impetus to the Women's Liberation Movement (MLF), as did Guy Hocquenghem who, with d'Eaubonne, cre-ated the Homosexual Front for Revolutionary Action (FHAR).

---

54 Tiennot Grumbach, 'En cherchant l'unité de la politique et de la vie', *Les Temps modernes* 307 (February 1972): 1215–16.

55 About 15 kms from Mantes-la-Jolie [Trans.].

56 The term *pied-rouge* was applied to those French left-wing activists who went to Algeria after independence to help in the reconstruction and development of the country. The expression was a play on the better-known *pied-noir*, a term that referred to Europeans born in colonial Algeria who 'returned' to France after independence [Trans.].

57 'Changer la vie' was a phrase attributed to Arthur Rimbaud, which the group used long before the Socialist Party took it over and made it the epigraph of their 1972 elec-tion manifesto.

Like the Gauche Prolétarienne (GP: Proletarian Left), the other so-called 'Mao-spontex' group,[58] VLR engaged in violence in the form of targeted street fighting. Unlike the GP, which won Sartre to its cause, VLR, which was very receptive to Lotta Continua both in terms of slogans and articles that it reprinted in its periodical, had Gorz's full support during its brief existence (1969–71). VLR's newspaper, which was itself simply called *Vive la Révolution*, gave way in September 1970 to the bi-monthly *Tout!*, printed under the banner 'Ce que nous voulons: tout' [What we want: Everything], a slogan first heard at FIAT in Turin. This was striking both by its 'underground' aspect (VLR was hatched at the Beaux-Arts art school in Paris) and by the emphasis on sexual liberation (questioning family structures, minors' sexual rights, feminist and homosexual demands relating to the body). As with the GP's *La Cause du Peuple*, Sartre was the nominal editor, as a shield against legal action. The Éditions Gît-le-Cœur publishing house, a shop-window for VLR, republished two heterodox Marxist classics of '68 Leftism: Paul Lafargue's *Droit à la paresse* [The right to be lazy] and the German Communist and psychoanalyst Wilhelm Reich's *Der sexuelle Kampf der Jugend* [The sexual struggle of youth].

Somewhat audaciously, but also with some justification, this *sui generis* Maoism was at times compared with anarchism or Situationism;[59] later, the Maoist element would be glossed over by Gorz, who preferred to speak of the 'libertarian opponents' of the GP.[60] Whatever the truth of the matter, it was these various movements that would, as they formally dissolved themselves, serve as the incubator for the most innovative social movements of the 1970s, movements with which Gorz would largely sympathize.

While an admirer of VLR, Gorz also had links with another Maoist current of feeling, which also looked to the Italian Far Left. Led by Marc Heurgon and Alain Lipietz, this tendency within the PSU was expelled by Michel Rocard in 1972 and formed itself into the Gauche ouvrière et paysanne (GOP). Many activists from this part of the Left, heavily involved in the Larzac struggle to conserve peasant land, would join Les Verts [The Greens]

58 Within French Maoism, the spontaneists, known as *mao-spontex*, were opposed to the Stalinists, known as *ml's*.
59 Jean Moreau, 'La nouvelle extrême-gauche', *Le Nouvel Observateur* (26 October 1970). The author, an archivist at the magazine and a friend of Gorz's, was close to the GP at the time.
60 Gorz, 'La vie, la nature, la technique', p. 29.

in the 1980s. It was Heurgon who introduced Lipietz to Gorz.[61] As an Althusserian, an economist close to Regulation Theory and subsequently an ecologist, Lipietz would find it hard to subscribe to Gorz's economic arguments, but never failed to discuss them in his writings.

During these years, Gorz gave a great deal of his energy to *Les Temps modernes*, of which he had become a cornerstone, whereas Sartre no longer wrote for it. In 1969, he pressed on the journal the—assiduous—collaboration of the very young *lycée* teacher François George (alias Daniel Verrès), for whom, to some small degree, he played the role of mentor. This budding philosopher, joyously disrespectful of any intellectual authority (to the great annoyance of Pontalis) and vehemently letting fly his anti-Stalinist shafts from a Cohn Bendit–style spontaneist position, was also able to engage in serious debate on Marxist issues.[62] With this friend, as with the Sartrean Michel Contat, whom he also began to frequent—introducing him for a time into *Temps modernes* circles—Gorz would regularly and assiduously discuss philosophical questions.

In this connection, we shall digress for a moment to recall 'the unique trust Sartre placed in very young people who were entirely—or almost entirely—unknown'.[63] However, if his enormous celebrity prevented Sartre from having relations with young or uneducated people on a completely equal footing, Gorz, being outside the university system, had no such complex.[64] Indeed, he liked to cultivate relations with young students or people far removed from the university world. He was, in fact, constantly on the lookout for possible resonances between his existential experience and his interlocutor's, and took the view that academic conventions could get in the way of that.

---

61 For an account of his relations with Gorz, see Alain Lipietz, 'André Gorz et notre jeunesse', *Multitudes* 31 (2008): 163–9.

62 He was also markedly sectarian: he had barely arrived at *Les Temps modernes* when he suggested to Gorz that any 'revisionist' having collaborated with a publication controlled by the French Communist Party should be boycotted by the magazine (Letter from François George to André Gorz, undated, GRZ). Was he aware that his interlocutor would have fallen foul of any such measure?

63 Claude Lanzmann, *Le Lièvre de Patagonie. Mémoires* (Paris: Gallimard, 2009), pp. 214–5.

64 André Gorz, 'Les adieux d'André Gorz au prolétariat', interview by Michel Contat and François George, *Le Monde* (12 October 1980).

It is quite moving, then, to read Gorz's correspondence with his Swiss friend Walter Riffel, who simply worked as a translator for Renault in Geneva; with all the students whom he would, from the outset, question about their lives—appreciating above all, where it was the case, their modest origins (Josué Pereira da Silva, Françoise Gollain); with a sympathizer who had infiltrated into the heart of the nuclear energy lobby and who described himself as a 'traitor' to society (Louis Puiseux); with an obscure admirer who empathized with the stance of *Fondements pour une morale*, published in 1977; with the brilliant students he supported emotionally (Finn Bowring) or, indeed, encouraged to undertake their own existential analysis, (Erich Hörl); or with—the tormented—Jean-Marie Vincent when they met up again at the turn of the century. Gorz was always trying to overcome his relational difficulties, which went back to his childhood and tortured him as a young man in Switzerland, and to bring out his affective side, which he regarded as a gage of authenticity. To come to terms with himself as a sensitive human subject was a constant problem, the problem of his life, which he tried never to repress. Without getting ahead of ourselves, it will be evident that Gorz the existentialist would become an enthusiastic defender of Félix Guattari, the 'ecosopher'. But let us come back to *Les Temps modernes*.

From 1968 onwards, and for two or three years, under the approving eye of Sartre, Gorz played the role of political driver of the magazine, which was increasingly turned towards politics (and ethnology of an anarchist colouration with Pierre Clastres and Marshall Sahlins). This was the period when *Les Temps modernes*, as we have been able to confirm, was 'even read and partially circulated in duplicated form, by factory committees or trade union branches.'[65] It was also the time when Gorz became one of the social theorists with the widest audience in France, from the ultra-Leftist groupings to the CFDT, alongside Marcuse, Mandel, Guattari, Gilles Deleuze or, on a different level, Michel Foucault.[66]

In late summer 1971, Gorz coordinated an important issue of *Les Temps modernes* that included a dossier on VLR's agitation at Renault, Flins and another on 'the factory and the school'. But changes were afoot that year so far as the relative influence of the magazine's plethora of writers was

---

65 André Gorz to Jacques Robin of 12–14 September 1997 (GRZ).
66 Jacques Julliard, 'Les passions d'André Gorz', *Le Nouvel Observateur* (27 September 2007). Julliard does not mention Deleuze.

concerned. With Sartre having opted to throw in his lot with the GP, more and more contributors from that group appeared in the magazine. Alain Geismar, whom Sartre had reached out to in May 1968, acted as intermediary. André Glucksmann, who had already contributed to the journal in 1967 with an article against Althusser (preceded in 1966 by a truly brilliant article in this same vein by the Hegelian Marxist and Luxemburgist Robert Paris),[67] was particularly in evidence. In May 1972, an entire issue—on the theme of the fascization of the French state—was coordinated by the editorial team of *La Cause du peuple*: taking part were Alain Geismar, Jean-Pierre Le Dantec, Jean-Pierre Barou and, with no fewer than three contributions, Glucksmann.

In the past, Gorz had been insulted by the Situationists, which was par for the course; attacked by the Althusserians at the École normale supérieure in the rue d'Ulm, which was eminently understandable; and even castigated by the students of the PSU, who criticized him for his supposed spontaneism.[68] Now Glucksmann was taking a tilt at him, at the same time as attacking the CFDT. And he was doing so not just anywhere, but in this special issue of *Les Temps modernes* with an article he had originally published pseudonymously in *La Cause du peuple*.[69] From an all-out anti-syndicalist position, Glucksmann took apart the idea defended by Bosquet in *Le Nouvel Observateur*[70] that the CFDT had a dual role: to ensure organizational continuity in a political downturn and to dissolve itself into worker's self-management in a revolutionary phase. Gorz managed, nonetheless, to have a more constructive conclusion, penned by himself, added to the article. This sparked the anger of Glucksmann, who threatened to refer the dispute to Sartre.[71] The incident would not, however, prevent him from later praising Glucksmann's staunch anti-Stalinism.

---

67 Robert Paris, 'En deçà du marxisme', *Les Temps modernes* 240 (May 1966): 1983–2002.

68 'À travers les revues', *Problèmes du socialisme* (internal publication of the students of the PSU), January 1970. This was a review of Gorz, 'Ni trade-unionistes, ni bolcheviks'.

69 Philippe Olivier [André Glucksmann], 'Syndicats, comité(s) de lutte, comités de chaîne', *Les Temps modernes* 310 bis (May 1972): 34–56 (originally published as: Philippe O., 'J'accuse', *La Cause du peuple* [February 1972]).

70 Michel Bosquet, 'Beyond Trade Unions' in *Capitalism in Crisis and Everyday Life*, pp. 115–19. Originally published in *Le Nouvel Observateur* (24 January 1972).

71 GRZ 44.2.

Generally speaking, there was little point Gorz gnashing his teeth: within the editorial board he could only share with Pouillon the bitter realization that the power structure had changed. Admittedly, the editorial secretary continued to direct all correspondence to him that contained proposals for articles or requests for translation permissions relating to the political section. From abroad, it even appeared at times that he was the sole person in charge: 'Gorz is a first rate mind, and *his* journal counts for a great deal in European circles,' explained an American to a first-time contributor.[72] He certainly had a free hand to discuss the pertinence of an argument with any particular author: with the Althusserian Maoist Jacques Rancière, for example, he was able to debate the concept of fetishism, which Rancière saw as a positive setting-aside of the subject in an analysis.[73] Similarly, Sartre was not averse to him publishing authors he liked, such as Kravetz (again), Grumbach, Antonio Lettieri, the Far Left trade unionist at the Italian CFIL (whom Gorz had known since at least 1963) and the American counterculture enthusiast Herbert Gintis, or, as a sociologist of work, the physicist Dominique Pignon.

Yet Gorz had to compromise. His relations with Sartre, to whom he submitted his editorial projects as he had always done, were sometimes tense. Unlike the older man, for example, he was reluctant to take part in the support campaign for the political prisoners in the German Federal Republic that was largely under the direction of Claude Bourdet.[74] He never saw Sartre as his spiritual father, nor did he have a truly close relationship with him.[75] However, their intellectual complicity was never in doubt. Hence, during this period, Gorz debated extensively with Sartre the literary problems posed in the writing of his Flaubert biography. It has to be said, as Gorz himself did, that Sartre, 'regarded him as one of the few people capable of understanding his works from the inside, so to speak.'[76]

---

72 Irving L. Horowitz to John Saxe-Fernandez of 19 April 1973 (Horowitz Archive, PennState University Libraries, digital collections). My emphasis (WG).

73 See Jacques Rancière's accommodating reply to André Gorz of 6 October 1973 (GRZ) with regard to the publication in the magazine (November 1973) of a new Presentation to *Lire Le Capital* [*Reading Capital*] that was left out of the new French edition.

74 Bourdet wrote in vain to Gorz on 24 January 1977 (GRZ) to invite him to sign an appeal against the limitation of freedoms in West Germany.

75 On the personal relations between Gorz and Sartre, see Michel Contat, 'André Gorz, "Morel" et Sartre' in Fourel (ed.), *André Gorz en personne*, pp. 29–38.

76 Gorz, 'La vie, la nature, la technique', p. 29.

As Gorz saw it, the situation deteriorated further after 1973 when Sartre, having lost his sight, took on a new secretary, the GP Maoist Benny Lévy (alias Pierre Victor). Despite Beauvoir's oversight, the young man's hold over Sartre spilled over into the direction taken by *Les Temps modernes*. The *Lotta Continua* issue of 1974, the preparation of which dragged on for seven months because of editorial disagreements, was the last one Gorz put together. With his decisions widely challenged—not by Sartre who barely attended meetings anymore, but by the other editors—Gorz drew his own conclusions. He did not leave the magazine, but deliberately dropped into the background. The mini-dossier on 'the nuclear swindle' which he managed to put together in January 1977, was his swansong. In March 'Pierre Victor' officially joined the management committee, together with the other former Maoists Pierre Rigoulot and Pierre Goldman: the period of Gorz's influence at *Les Temps modernes* was over.

PART THREE

The Liberation of Life
in a Time of Visceral Opposition to Work

The 1970s: Zero Growth and Ecology

'The person who pays less attention
to his desires than his work shouldn't
be surprised that they work against him.'
Raoul Vaneigem, *Nous qui désirons sans fin*, p. 164.

'We could live better producing less.'
André Gorz, 'The Tyranny of the Factory', p. 58.

CHAPTER TEN

Critique of Technology and Science

In the wake of '68, Gorz was increasingly in demand abroad. He travelled a great deal in North America and Europe, which enabled him to meet the cream of the contemporary Marxist intelligentsia and, sometimes in the same milieu, the representatives of the American counterculture who introduced him to some new questions. In terms of intellectual excitement, what he had experienced in America very much equalled the stirrings produced by May '68. Gorz wasn't an isolated case: other intellectuals who would find themselves in the ranks of ecology and anti-consumerism (not by chance) had known a similar memorable and formative stay in post-1968 California or Canada. We may think of Edgar Morin, Serge Moscovici, Alexandre Grothendieck, Pierre Samuel, Jean Baudrillard etc.

Back from America

Where Gorz was concerned, however, what came to him from a westerly direction was counterbalanced by his own contribution. From 1969 to 1971 he travelled each year to the East coast of the US, with a two-pronged reputation going before him. He was seen as a theorist who was well-informed about the transformations underway within the working class and a thinker at the cutting edge of radical critique. His major work was translated for Beacon Press of Boston—the politically progressive publisher that published Marcuse—in 1967 as *Strategy for Labour: A Radical Proposal*. Gorz added a new preface for the occasion. Like another article by Gorz,[1] this work inspired the leaders of the American student movement Greg Calvert and Carl Davidson who attempted, as leaders of Students for a Democratic Society (SDS), to apply to the student world the concepts of worker's control and 'non-reformist reforms', to use the

---

1 Gorz, 'Capitalist Relations of Production and the Socially Necessary Labour Force'.

restrained terminology that was current in the US.[2] Bob Gottlieb and David Gilbert, other SDS leaders, even made personal contact with Gorz.[3]

However, the most serious efforts to apply his ideas to the American context were made by young radical economists at Harvard (in the Union for Radical Political Economics [URPE] formed in 1968). Chief among them was Herbert Gintis, who extolled the potential of the new working class.[4] Their magazine, like its equivalent produced by the radical students at Tufts University (in Medford near Boston), ran an article by Gorz on workers' control in its first issue.[5] At this time, Gorz's reputation within the American Left exceeded the esteem in which he was held in the same circles in France, which was already substantial. As just one example of his importance, we may cite the fact that, when it came to finding Europeans to provide a brief survey of New Left political philosophy, the Americans called upon Gorz, alongside Sartre and the ubiquitous Mandel.[6] In 1973, Gorz would make the highly political texts of *Le Socialisme difficile* available to an Anglophone readership in a revised edition with the title *Socialism and Revolution*. Later Gintis, who had by then admittedly become his friend, would see him as 'the greatest of modern French social thinkers'.[7]

In November and December 1969, Gorz spent around three weeks in New York (he had already been there four years before, coming to realize how much he hated American consumerism). On 29 November, as the poster shows, he was supposed to have star billing alongside Mandel at the Town Hall to discuss revolutionary strategy in the developed countries at the invitation of the Socialist Scholars' Conference—a New Left forum—

---

2 This concept has never lost its popularity in the US. Explicitly inspired by Gorz, it is still called on by the economist Arthur MacEwan, the sociologist and social commentator Peter Dreier, the philosopher Nancy Fraser and also the former SDS member and libertarian Michael Albert (who became Gorz's publisher).

3 Author interview with Dick Howard, a member of SDS at the time, on 23 May 2014.

4 Herbert Gintis, 'The New Working Class and Revolutionary Youth', *Socialist Revolution* 3 (May 1970): 13–43.

5 See, respectively, *Upstart* (Cambridge MA) 1 (January 1971); *Collective Effort* (Medford) 1 (Sept–Oct 1971). The article 'Workers' Control' first appeared in *Socialist Revolution* (San Francisco) 6 (Nov–Dec 1970).

6 See Gorz, 'Capitalist Relations of Production and the Socially Necessary Labour Force' and 'The Way Forward'.

7 From the cover of *Ecology as Politics* (Boston, MA: South End Press, 1980).

and the Bertrand Russell Peace Foundation. Also on the platform were Goldmann, Paul Sweezy (a heavyweight of Anglo-Saxon Marxism) and James O'Connor (future theorist of ecosocialism). While Mandel, having failed to obtain a visa, did not appear, Gorz had a cold and had to have his talk read out to the 1,500 'Leftists' who had turned up.[8] During this trip, he also publicly debated the controversial theme of the 'technological society' with Marcuse.[9]

In 1970, for almost two months in October and November, he was the guest of the Cambridge Institute at Harvard University, where he gave two lectures, one on the conservatism of trade union apparatuses and the other on workers' control.[10] At the end of his stay, he stopped off in Toronto where he was one of the speakers at a conference organized by Praxis, a small research institute on social change run by Gerry Hunnius, which strove to link workers' control with participatory democracy.[11]

In November 1971 he returned to the north-eastern US for a massive conference organized at Buffalo under the patronage of the philosophical journal *Telos*, created in 1968 by the Italian-American phenomenologist Paul Piccone, which took (revolutionary) organization as its theme. Before an audience of hundreds, Gorz, who led a workshop, featured once again with Marcuse. He met up again with Gianni Sofri there, and also ran across Guido Viale, another LC activist, and Rainer Zoll, the IG Metall press officer, who had translated his *Stratégie ouvrière* into German in 1967 and became

---

8 André Gorz, 'The Working Class and Revolution in the West', *Liberation* (New York) 4 (September 1971): 31–7.

9 See the transcription of the debate at Vassar College (New York State), December 1969 in GRZ 9.24.

10 See the report of the first lecture to an audience of 200: David Landau, 'French Socialist Blasts Unionism', *The Harvard Crimson* (13 November 1970). The text of the second lecture, delivered on 20 November 1970 (published in three American journals—see above, note 5 to this chapter) is reprinted in the Union for Radical Political Economics' flagship anthology: André Gorz, 'Workers' Control: Some European Experiences' in Richard C. Edwards, Michael Reich and Thomas E. Weisskopf (eds), *The Capitalist System: A Radical Analysis of American Society* (Englewood Cliffs, NJ: Prentice-Hall, 1972), pp. 479–91.

11 The book that came out of this conference contains the above-cited text on workers' control. See Gerry Hunnius (ed.), *Participatory Democracy for Canada: Workers' Control and Community Control* (Montreal: Black Rose Books, 1971).

a friend. Increasingly tending towards Marxism and the Frankfurt School, *Telos* would often publish translations of Gorz's articles in subsequent years.

In the US, Gorz was enchanted by the interest shown by his interlocutors (the economists Gintis, Samuel Bowles, Arthur MacEwan, Michael Reich and Stephen Marglin, the sociologist Stanley Aronowitz, and engineers and doctors) in the new ideas. He was flabbergasted by what he saw:[12] a sort of counter-society made up of former executives engaging in social experimentation or organic growing, hippies living in communes, long-haired young workers alternating between work and periods of idleness or travel, militant homosexuals, feminists taking on 'phallocracy' in the radical groups (as the women of VLR did in France, not least Françoise d'Eaubonne, who coined the term), Black Panthers investing great hopes in the *Lumpenproletariat* etc. A parallel society that looked to the government for nothing but undertook to live differently in the here and now and limited the work they did purely to the satisfaction of needs. He noted admiringly that all this fine humanity was intent not so much on making revolution (except for Angela Davis's Black Panthers who wanted to see a violent one) as on living as though it had already taken place.

In a country where the authorities made out that they were fighting poverty,[13] someone spoke to him about the idea—much further refined than among the Italian operaists—of 'guaranteeing every citizen a subsistence income instead of linking income to a job'. Clearly, this must have been Gintis, author of a 1969 thesis at Harvard entitled *Alienation and Power: Towards a Radical Welfare Economics*. Gorz also heard mention of the concept of a 'post-industrial proletariat'—in France, Touraine was already expatiating on post-industrial society[14]—and met an enthusiast for reshaping production techniques—presumably Stephen Marglin, a teacher at Harvard with whom he had lengthy discussions and remained in contact.

Gorz returned home 'delighted and baffled'[15] from his stay in Cambridge, Massachussetts, which he would describe as having helped him 'understand that the classic forms and objectives of class struggle can't

---

12 Bosquet, *Critique du capitalisme quotidien*, pp. 321–39. Originally published as 'La subversion par le bonheur', *Le Nouvel Observateur* (21 December 1970).

13 Romain Huret, *The Experts' War on Poverty: Social Research and the Welfare Agenda in Postwar America* (Ithaca: Cornell University Press, 2019).

14 He published *La Société postindustrielle* (Paris: Denoël et Gonthier) in 1969 [Trans.].

15 Bosquet, *Critique du capitalisme quotidien*, p. 336 n.

change society, that the trade union struggle had to shift to new ground.'[16] In texts produced later on the occasion of meetings in Europe, he worked to develop what he had felt on the other side of the Atlantic. This took the specific form of a critique of technology and science and their overlap—the field that would later be termed 'techno-science'.

In Europe Gorz was again in demand from the media and being asked to appear at debates or conferences. He agreed to speak on alienation to the Cercle d'éducation populaire of Liège, Belgium, in February 1969. That same year, he was invited on to a Norddeutscher Rundfunk radio programme in Hamburg. On 7–9 September 1970, he accepted the invitation of Zurich bookseller Theo Pinkus to take part in a round table discussion on the New Left with Mandel, Marcuse and the young Frankfurtian Oskar Negt. Since Mandel was *persona non grata* in Switzerland, the debate was moved to the border city of Konstanz. Negt would later remember that, in the shade of the two star performers, Gorz and he had difficulty getting a word in. Immediately after this, Gorz and Mandel took part, at the invitation of the Marxist economist Wim Boerboom, in a congress on 'Capitalism in the 1970s', which ran from the 10th to the 13th of September at the Catholic University of Tilburg in Holland. Among the speakers were Gintis—whom Gorz was meeting for the first time—Jacques Valier and Maurice Dobb (another heavyweight of Anglo-Saxon Marxism). The papers of this memorable conference would reach beyond the Netherlands, being published in Germany and Italy.[17] In 1971, Gorz also took part in a television programme on the main German television channel.

Opportunities arose to produce important texts (and we shall examine their argumentation in more detail below). These included, first, a lecture delivered in English at the Philosophy faculty of the University of Heidelberg in April 1971 at the invitation of the young Swiss philosopher Peter Bieri, which dealt with the division of labour and would form the basis of a fundamental article entitled 'Technique, techniciens et lutte des classes' that was published in *Les Temps modernes* that same year.[18] Then came an

16 Gorz, *Letter to D.*, pp. 86–7.

17 See André Gorz, 'On the Relevance of Revolutionary Strategy in the Capitalist Metropoles' in Elmar Altvater et al., *Het Kapitalisme in de jaren 70* (Amsterdam: Van Gennep, 1971).

18 André Gorz, 'Technische Intelligenz und kapitalistische Arbeitsteilung' (translated from the English), *Politikon* (Göttingen) 37 (June–July 1971) (the original was published

international conference on 'the Quality of Life' organized by the IG Metall metalworkers' trade union at Oberhausen in April 1972 (with 1,200 participants): at a workshop at the event, Gorz presented a text in French entitled 'Contradictions nouvelles et nouveaux thèmes de lutte'.[19] Thirdly, there was a congress of the Dutch Scientific Workers' Union (BWA: Bond van Wetenschappelijke Arbeiders) held at Amsterdam in January 1973, at which Gorz unceremoniously dissected the class nature of science and of intellectual workers themselves.[20]

Interest in these subjects led Gorz in autumn 1973 to coordinate a work entitled *Critique de la division du travail* [Critique of the division of labour; published in English as *The Division of Labour*]. Included in the book were articles he had had published in *Les Temps modernes* (by Dominique Pignon, the Il Manifesto group, Antonio Letteri etc., as well as some of his own), together with an unpublished text by Marglin on the capitalist usage of technologies ('À quoi servent les patrons?'[21] [translated as 'What Do Bosses Do?'[22]]). This latter piece, which was submitted by Marglin to Gorz for comment in 1971, was nothing less than the origin of the new stage in Gorz's theoretical reflection.

---

in *Telos* 12 [Summer 1972]: 27–41); André Gorz, 'Technique, techniciens et lutte de classes', *Les Temps modernes* 301–02 (August–September 1971): 141–80; reprinted as 'Technology, Technicians and Class Struggle' in Gorz (ed.), *The Division of Labour*, pp. 159–89.

19 André Gorz, 'Labor and "Quality of life"' in *Ecology as politics*, pp. 130–145. Original publication: André Gorz, 'Die Zukunft der Gewerkschaften. Neue Widersprüche und neue Inhalte gewerkschaftlicher Kämpfe' (December 1971) in *Aufgabe Zukunft. Qualität des Lebens (11–14 April 1972)*, VOL. 9 (Frankfurt: Europäische Verlagsanstalt, 1974), pp. 94–116.

20 André Gorz, 'Caractères de classe de la science et des travailleurs scientifiques', *Les Temps modernes* 330 (January 1974): 1159–1177 (already published, in shorter form, in *Lotta continua* [10–11 November 1973]). Translated as 'On the Class Character of Science and Scientists' in Hilary Rose and Steven Rose (eds), *The Political Economy of Science: Ideology of/in the Natural Sciences* (London: Macmillan, 1976), pp. 59–71.

21 See Bruno Tinel, '*À quoi servent les patrons?*' *Marglin et les radicaux américains* (Lyon: ENS Éditions, 2004).

22 See Stephen Marglin, 'What Do Bosses Do?' in *The Division of Labour*, pp. 13–54.

Critique of the Division of Labour

In writing prefaces in 1969 for the new editions of their standard works—
La Nouvelle Classe ouvrière and *Strategy for Labor*—Serge Mallet took the
view that '68 had corroborated the worker self-management theses on the
new working class, while Gorz, very reserved on that point, could no longer
detect any specific mobilizing elements among the technicians. It wasn't
that their descriptions of the strike movement that had swept powerfully
across Europe and even the United States since the second half of the 1960s
diverged on matters of substance, but they drew different conclusions.

The Rejection of Work, and Factory Despotism: The New Lessons of '68.

As long as the mobilization affected all categories of workers within one
and the same factory—from the technician to the semi-skilled worker—the
rebellion took on a radical cast. That is to say, it was based on demands of
a 'qualitative' kind, very often driven by young educated workers who had
jobs at all levels of the production process. However, unlike Mallet, Gorz
focused on the fact that the strike movement in France and Italy was less
about demands couched in terms of control and more about the rejection
of work discipline. This meant opposition to 'the fragmentation of jobs,
hierarchy, the pace of work, foremen and production-related pay,' while in
the United States it found similar expression in 'silent rebellion against work
speeds and outright sabotage of the product';[23] not to mention, in all countries, the extremely high levels of annual turnover of workers (25 per cent
at Ford in Detroit, 35 per cent at Volvo in Sweden, 100 per cent in the FIAT
foundries in Italy) and of daily absenteeism (12 per cent in labour-intensive
industries in France, 15 per cent in the US car industry, 25 per cent at
FIAT).[24] Hence this significant conclusion that emerges from Gorz's analysis:
rather than aspiring to control methods of producing or to take control of
production by way of worker self-management as Mallet thought, this generation of young workers was actually manifesting a *disaffection with work*—
doing so spontaneously and without trade union mediation.

Retrospectively, Gorz would note that, as he saw it, '1968 of course was
a turning point, when resistance against the exploitation of work turned

---

23 Gorz, Preface to *The Division of Labour*, p. vii.
24 Jean Rousselet, *L'Allergie au travail* (Paris: Seuil, 1978 [1974]), pp. 41–2.

into the radical unconditional refusal of work, of having to function as "worker" in an economy in which the labour process could not be repossessed by the workers.'[25] In an unexpected but significant way, '68 also impacted on Marcuse, who would refocus his hopes for liberation on the workers—particularly the young ones—who 'are refusing to work, engage in sabotage and don't in any way identify with their jobs.'[26] The patriarch of autonomist Marxism, Mario Tronti, would draw the same lesson from '68, taking the view that it had made it possible to see 'work' in Marx's writings as 'a great misfortune.'[27] As for Cohn-Bendit, influenced by Castoriadis and Gorz, with whom he would debate in 1980 and 1983 respectively,[28] he would regard 'May' and the struggles that followed in Italy as responsible for a resurgence of the concept of proletarian autonomy, which already underlay anarcho-syndicalism.[29]

From this diffuse social situation, a whole swathe of political and existential aspirations were about to be liberated in France in the 1970s. The notion of a *galaxie 'auto'*—a cluster of tendencies bearing the prefix 'self-'—has been applied to all the disparate forms of self-organization tried out in that period.[30] Their common features were an existential concern with *autonomy*—which Gorz would go on to theorize unrelentingly—a rootedness in the social that expressed itself in *anti-statism*, a civilizational rejection of *productivism* and, lastly, a perennial basic demand for *shorter working hours*.

Though it took some time to appear clearly in the minds of the actors concerned, who hardly ever perceived it as an antagonism within this

---

25 Letter in English from André Gorz to Josué Pereira da Silva of 29 January 2006 (GRZ).

26 Herbert Marcuse, 'Socialisme ou barbarie'. This development on Marcuse's part is confirmed by Boris Frankel, *The Post-industrial Utopians* (Madison: University of Wisconsin Press, 1987), pp. 209–10.

27 Mario Tronti, *Nous opéraïstes. Le 'roman de formation' des années soixante en Italie* (Paris/Lausanne: Éditions de l'Éclat/Éditions d'en bas, 2013), p. 73.

28 Cornelius Castoriadis and Daniel Cohn-Bendit, *De l'écologie à l'autonomie* (Paris: Seuil, 1981); *Abschied vom Proletariat? Eine Diskussion mit und über André Gorz. Protokoll einer Arbeitstagung vom 30.5–3.6.1983* (Düsseldorf: DGB-Jugend, 1984 [2nd edition]).

29 *Abschied vom Proletariat?*, p. 42 (with Cohn-Bendit).

30 Pierre Rosanvallon, 'Formation et désintégration de la galaxie "auto" ' in Paul Dumouchel and Jean-Pierre Dupuy (eds), *L'Auto-organisation. De la physique au politique* (*Colloque de Cerisy, 10–17 juin 1981*) (Paris: Seuil, 1983), pp. 456–65.

'galaxy', a divide was evident from the outset (important because it heralds the distinction between two related and yet divergent future political currents: the 'Second Left'—inclining towards liberalism—and 'political ecology'—more libertarian and alternative).[31] This divide was not particularly visible at first; we have, to understand it, first and foremost, as a division between two archetypes.

On the one hand, one constellation embodies the CFDT's *worker self-management option*, approved by the 1970 Congress, reinforced in 1973 by the experience of the workers at the Lip factory in Besançon and systematized in the short work by the *CFDT Aujourd'hui* editor Pierre Rosanvallon, *L'Âge de l'autogestion* (1976). Michel Rocard also belongs to this first tendency; in 1974 he left the PSU to found his own grouping within the Socialist Party. The horizon here was the *worker's condition* and the perspective was for liberation *in* work.

On the other hand, another—diffuse—constellation, emblematized by an 'allergy to work'[32] to be found among youth and in factories,[33] proclaimed a *critique of industrialism*, at times against a 'back-to-nature' background, as expressed in the famous participatory cartoon strip by Gébé entitled *L'An 01* (1972), which was originally published in *Politique Hebdo*, and in the no less famous book by the Adret collective, *Travailler deux heures par jour* (1977). With its defence of the lived environment [*cadre de vie*], the CFDT itself was in accord with this orientation to some degree. The horizon in this case was *quality of life* and the perspective was one of liberation *from* work. This latter theme would forever remain a blind spot for Mallet (who died prematurely in 1973), Martinet, Mandel, Mothé (who, though he was in the CFDT, called himself an ecologist), Naville (even though he had read Marx through the prism of his son-in-law Paul Lafargue) and the whole of the classical Left, including the Extreme Left.[34]

---

31 On this liberal-libertarian typological aggregate, see Jacques Julliard, *Les Gauches françaises. Histoire, politique et imaginaire, 1762–2012* (Paris: Flammarion, 2012), pp. 692–5.

32 Rousselet, *L'Allergie au travail*. The author is a psychologist and, at the time, a consultant to institutions engaged in work with young people. See also the anthology compiled by Alexis Chassagne and Gaston Montracher, *La Fin du travail* (Paris: Stock, 1978).

33 See the emblematic book by Yves Le Manach, *Bye bye turbin. Suivi de Salauds! On les connaît vos usines, vos partis et vos syndicats* (Paris: Champ libre, 1973).

34 The most thoroughgoing attestation of this blindness is provided by Daniel Mothé, *L'Utopie du temps libre* (Paris: Esprit, 1977).

This second configuration also conceals another kind of refusal other than the rejection of work. Historians are silent on this and yet it runs through the experience of '68ers and comes out in what they say: this is the refusal of *social integration*, the refusal to 'succeed' in conventional terms. As Cohn-Bendit said at the time, the students were expressing 'a refusal to become the future managers of the society that exploited the working class'. Among the students at Nanterre, journalists observed, 'the idea that they will inevitably be "absorbed" by the system [. . .] is unbearable to many. "Even the most radical of us will not be able to escape absorption or rising up the social scale," said one of them.'[35] Only Gorz was writing at such an early stage of this order of things that inveigled the young rebel into the work-consumption system (we need only think of his gloomy meditation on the social inevitabilities of ageing in his 'Le vieillissement'): this put flesh on the bones of the rebellious, mocking cry of the '68 demonstrators: *Métro, boulot, dodo!*' [Metro, Work, Bed!]

Looking forward, let us say that in this decade and even the next one Gorz will position himself somewhere between these two poles—attentive both to the necessary renewal of trade unionism and to the rise of the 'new social movements'.

The revulsion at any form of authoritarianism and hierarchical spirit, which was the very driving force of the May '68 student movement, had as its counterpart in the factory the challenge to the forms of domination that were rampant there. That is why many commentators see '68 not in terms of a challenge to the political powers that be, but a—more fragmented, but more general—challenge to what Touraine dubbed 'the machinery of integration, manipulation and aggression',[36] regulating a social order defined by Marcuse as one of 'surplus repression'. Touraine argued, for example, that in 1968, 'the struggle wasn't primarily against capitalism, but against technocracy.'[37] Similarly, Castoriadis found it easy to reactivate his old Councilist analytical schemas—imbued now with arguments for worker self-management—to underscore the anti-hierarchical and anti-bureaucratic specificity of the May movement.[38] For Gorz, lastly, the form of domination in the factory, which

---

35 Frédéric Gaussen and Guy Herzlich, 'L'explosion de colère des étudiants a surpris tous les observateurs'.

36 Alain Touraine, *Le Mouvement de mai ou le communisme utopique* (Paris: Seuil, 1968), p. 14.

37 Touraine, *Le Mouvement de mai ou le communisme utopique*, p. 15.

'found itself once again at the centre of the class struggle throughout the world' was precisely 'the capitalist division of labour.'[39]

In touching on the division of labour, Gorz is touching on the quintessence of capitalism. The father of sociology Émile Durkheim (*The Division of Labour in Society* [1893]), the 'modernist' sociologist Georges Friedmann (*The Anatomy of Work* [second edition, 1964]) and, before them, even Adam Smith, the founder of political economy, had broached the subject, not without some concern. It is striking that the young Lukács, the theoretical darling of the 'Western Marxism' of the 1970s, went so far as to present this as a major cause of workers' alienation.[40]

Gorz prefers, however, to go back to the source of Marxism and reread the poignant descriptions in *Capital* (vol. 1, chapters 12–13) to convince himself there is no alienation in work more fundamental than that of the subdivision of tasks. And this is easily explicable, since it contributes to the smooth functioning of the capitalist factory, which, as Marx again notes (after Fourier), is predicated on military discipline and conditioning. As Marglin shows in his magisterial article on the manufactures of the eighteenth century,[41] the increase in the division of labour to the point of fragmentation [*parcellisation*] isn't aimed primarily at obtaining the highest level of productivity but at preventing the worker from achieving any understanding of the labour process in order the better to control him and keep his nose to the grindstone. The objective is not so much technical as disciplinary, optimal exploitation not necessarily presupposing maximum subservience:

> Capitalist technology and the capitalist division of labour were thus developed not because of their productive efficiency *in itself* but because of their efficiency in the context of alienated and forced labour: work subjugated to an alien goal. Capitalist techniques [have the] [. . .] *political* function [. . .] to perpetuate the workers' dependence, subordination and separation from the means and process of production. By making control a separate function, the

38 Edgar Morin, Claude Lefort and Jean-Marc Coudray [Cornelius Castoriadis], *Mai 1968: la brèche. Premières réflexions sur les événements* (Paris: Fayard, 1968).

39 Gorz, Preface to *The Division of Labour*, p. vii.

40 Georg Lukács, *History and Class Consciousness: Studies in Marxist Dialectics* (Boston, MA: MIT Press, 1972), p. 103.

41 Marglin, 'What do Bosses do?'

factory hierarchy is instrumental in denying the workers any possible control over the conditions and methods of machine production. Only in this way can the means and process of production be set up as an alien, autonomous power that exacts the workers' submission.[42]

As for automation, which Serge Mallet and Gorz himself had until recently seen as a possible route towards overcoming alienated labour, its 'effects [...] are entirely consistent with this process. Accompanying mechanization, which dequalifies and fragments production tasks, automation dequalifies and fragments control itself'.[43] Gorz was, at the time, beginning to realize, as he would later say, that it was an illusion to rely on technical change that would be capable of 'progressively eliminating unskilled, repetitive labour in favour of work that was increasingly intellectualized and technically advanced and hence potentially favourable to the flowering of the capacities for autonomy', since 'the choice of techniques—and hence the direction in which they developed—was always motivated by the concern to provide capital with a maximum of power and control over living labour. This concern with power played at least as determining a role as the concern with productivity'.[44]

The Exit from Fordism Has Begun

Where Gorz was concerned, there was no longer any question of appealing to the *Grundrisse* fragment on the automation of machines as foreshadowing the coming of worker self-management. He thus came to adopt the same cautious approach that Marcuse took in describing the liberating potential that an interpretation of those pages might have implied.[45] It was more in the opposing camp of the bosses that passionate supporters of automation were still to be found.

The forerunner here was American and went by the name of Peter Drucker. As early as the 1950s, this management consultant, who coined

---

42 Gorz, 'The Tyranny of the Factory', p. 56. Originally published as Michel Bosquet, 'The "Prison Factory" ', *New Left Review* 73 (May–June 1972): 23–34.

43 Gorz, 'The Tyranny of the Factory', p. 57.

44 'Entretien avec André Gorz' in Françoise Gollain, *Une Critique du travail. Entre écologie et socialisme* (Paris: La Découverte, 2000), pp. 222–3.

45 See Herbert Marcuse, *One-Dimensional Man* (London: Abacus, 1972), pp. 36–7.

the notion of 'the spirit of enterprise', had taught in his *The Practice of Management* (1954) that automation would enable the development of personality and that companies should thus require unlimited devotion to the work community from each co-worker. And it was indeed this managerial strategy which, in the early 1970s across the industrialized West, embodied capital's response to the workers' 'blues' and to youth's lack of appetite for the Fordist bait of the redistribution of the fruits of growth. 'All it [capital] needed,' as Gorz would point out, 'was to *adopt the values of the utopia of work as its own*'—a utopia based on the worker's mastery of a job and his/her total fulfilment in work.[46] With the Fordist form of regulation no longer functioning, it was now all about reducing worker resistance and getting a young, educated workforce into the workplace through 'job enlargement', 'job enrichment' (these were American notions) and the personal involvement that was supposed to ensue.

The Division of Labour: Labour Process and Class Struggle in Modern Capitalism picked up early on this capitalist counter-offensive, in which sociologists would later see a foretaste of the 'new spirit of capitalism',[47] and, in the articles by Gorz and the one written jointly by Dominique Pignon and Jean Querzola, it denounced the illusory character of the progress of the worker's condition which that counter-offensive proclaimed.

Bourgeois Uses of Science

Science and technology, inextricably linked, provide capital with a model of rationality which, by expelling choices external to itself into the sphere of subjectivity, legitimates the system. The critical spirit that fuelled the upsurge of protest in the years around 1968 locked horns with capitalism precisely over its most functional and objectivizing elements—science and technology.

In the US, the '68 movement was openly interpreted as a revolt against technocracy.[48] Among academics and students, the myth of the neutrality

---

46 André Gorz, *Critique of Economic Reason* (Gillian Handyside and Chris Turner trans) (London: Verso Books, 1989), p. 68. Italics in the original.

47 Luc Boltanski and Ève Chiapello, *The New Spirit of Capitalism* (Gregory Elliott trans.) (London: Verso Books, 2007 [1999]).

48 Theodore Roszak, *The Making of a Counter-culture: Reflections on the Technocratic Society and its Youthful Opposition* (Berkeley: University of California Press, 1969).

of science was forcefully challenged at the time. That myth, based on the positivism of the father of the sociology of the sciences Robert Merton, had begun to creak in the early 1960s with the epistemological labours of Thomas Kuhn on *The Structure of Scientific Revolutions* (1962), which showed that science was objective in what it found, but not in what it looked for. At the end of the decade, the American Lewis Mumford, who had been a critic of technology as early as the 1930s, published two volumes on *The Myth of the Machine* (1967, 1970).

In Germany, Jürgen Habermas was not to be outdone. Jumping off from (and going beyond) Marcuse's argument that, in contemporary industrial society, technology functions to instrumentalize human beings, this new torchbearer for the Frankfurt School produced his *Technology and Science as Ideology* [1968]. This critique took some time to spread widely in France. It ultimately found its place from 1970 onwards, thanks in part to what was happening in North America, through a militant group of mathematicians led by Grothendieck and Samuel under the banner 'Survivre et vivre' (Survive and Live). However, the audience for the bi-monthly magazine of the same name barely extended beyond the circles of the ecological counter-culture.[49] There followed, in 1975, the journal *Impasciences*, edited by the physicist Jean-Marc Lévy-Leblond, who took aim at scientism and the ideology of expertise.

As for the old, autochthonous reflections of the Bordeaux 'Personalist' Jacques Ellul on the enslavement of the systems of both East and West to technology (*La Technique ou l'enjeu du siècle*, 1954), these were confined to a narrow readership, as—for the same reasons—were the similar contemporary remarks by Martin Heidegger (*The Question concerning Technology* [1954]). In the technophile climate of the economic boom of the 1950s, both men's interventions were ill-timed and often fell victim to left-wing prejudice, the one on account of its Marxist heterodoxy tinged with Christianity, the other because of the reactionary cast of the argument. Kostas Axelos and Pierre Fougeyrollas from the *Arguments* group and, later, Jean-Marie Vincent were exceptions in becoming attentive readers of Heidegger.

---

49 Céline Pessis (ed.), *Survivre et vivre. Critique de la science, naissance de l'écologie* (Montreuil: L'Échappée, 2014).

It would be quite some time, therefore, before Gorz claimed a knowledge and appreciation of thinkers of this kind, who were culturally alien to him. Hannah Arendt he would read in the late 1970s, Simone Weil in the '80s at the prompting of his philosopher friend Robert Chenavier, Jacques Ellul in the '80s and Günther Anders in the late 1990s. He would reread Heidegger's lecture on technology in 1985, spurred once again by Chenavier, but he would take little from it, judging it abstruse and lacking in context.[50] Ernst Jünger and his edifying *The Worker* [1931] was a book he would never get around to.

Reading Sartre's *Critique of Dialectical Reason* in 1960 sensitized Gorz to the 'practico-inert' effect exerted by structures, apparatuses and other 'machineries'. This can be seen in his text on ageing, 'Le vieillissement'. But if we trust to his recollection of the matter and accept that his 'interest in the critique of technology owes a great deal' to that reading,[51] this was so only in the sense of producing a predisposition that would later make him receptive to some writers on this theme. In his writings of the 1960s, it was not something he lingered over. The closest he came to it perhaps was when, during the course of reporting on the Czech shoemaker Bata, where the working conditions were horrendous, he showed how upset he was by the answer he obtained from an officer of the company:

> I believe I am throwing out a lifeline when I ask:
>
> 'Do you see a difference between technical development in the capitalist and the socialist worlds?
>
> 'What, technical?' he asks in amazement. 'No, I don't see any. We study technologies from the whole world.[52]

It is by comparison with Marcuse's gloomy assessment that contemporary human beings were totally subservient to technology that we can see how far Gorz lagged behind in the importance he accorded to the phenomenon. He deemed Marcuse's clarion call excessively pessimistic, in part because of the possible social contestation of what he analysed as a *superfluity* of technical domination in the West, and in part because of the possibility of

---

50 See Gorz to Chenavier, 15 April 1985 (GRZ).

51 Gorz, *Ecologica*, p. 8.

52 Michel Bosquet, 'Reportage. L'exemple tchèque', *L'Express* (9 January 1964).

overcoming what he described as the *transitory necessity* for technical domination in the East.[53]

His critical thinking sharpened on this point later, after 1968, and even more so following his stays in the US where he discussed the theme again with Marcuse and where, most importantly, he got to know Marglin. Gorz also received input from other sources. In retrospect, he would place greatest emphasis on what he took from Ivan Illich.[54] He also became interested in the studies in the history of science pursued by the British left-wing scholars Hilary and Steven Rose and would later contribute to the book they edited: *The Political Economy of Science.*[55]

He notes that, in the capitalist system, science, which shapes technology, is the preserve of specialists and professionals, and the social monopoly of skills it produces can be explained by the fact that Western science's 'main relevance, from the outset, was to machinery that was to dominate workers, not to make them free.'[56] Hence, moreover, the ambiguous position of technicians vis-a-vis workers. This is why: '[T]here has never been anything like "free" or "independent" science' because, he explains, 'our society denies the label of "science" and of "scientific" to those skills, crafts and knowledge which are not integrated into the capitalist relations of production, are of no value and use to capitalism, and therefore are not formally taught within the institutional system of education.'[57]

And yet, Gorz stresses, 'self-acquired knowledge' may be just as effective, as is shown by the ongoing experiments in the People's Republic of China, where traditional forms of knowledge are valued and an attempt is being made to overcome the division between experts and non-experts. Can we, then, conceive of other—'vernacular'—forms of knowledge,

53 André Gorz, '*L'uomo unidimensionale* di Marcuse', *Critica marxista* 2 (1965): 231–41. This is a longer version of the review that appeared in *The Nation*, with expanded consideration of this particular point.

54 André Gorz to Josué Pereira da Silva, August 1993. This letter is mentioned by Da Silva in his *André Gorz. Trabalho e política*, p. 144.

55 André Gorz, 'On the Class Character of Science and Scientists'. Hilary and Steven Rose were the authors of *Science and Society* (1969). Gorz cites their article 'The Radicalisation of Science' (*Socialist Register* [1972]: 105–32) in *The Political Economy of Science*, p. 71.

56 Gorz, 'On the Class Character of Science and Scientists', p. 64.

57 Gorz, 'On the Class Character of Science and Scientists', pp. 63, 61.

enriched by popular experience, and of other—manageable—technologies on a human scale, to reduce the social division of labour and begin the re-appropriation by the people themselves of the means of producing life? It was in the stimulating thinking of Ivan Illich that Gorz would find a number of answers to these questions.[58]

---

58 See Gorz, Preface to *The Division of Labour*.

CHAPTER ELEVEN

Changing Life, with Ivan Illich

In November 1969, André Gorz spotted an unusual speech delivered to the students of the Catholic University of Puerto Rico and published it in *Les Temps modernes*. He introduced its author as 'a priest of Austrian origin' with a parish in 'a Puerto-Rican district of New York', who had become 'vice-president' of that university (from 1956 to 1960). The speech is a tirade against educational institutions in general, arguing that they had been engaged for two centuries in shaping minds without, for all that, producing any education.[1]

Admirable and Troublesome Thinking

Gorz found this text by Ivan Illich enticing: it clearly echoed his own attacks on the university for inhibiting individual creativity and autonomy. In June 1970 he again published an address by this anti-conformist teacher. Illich was head of the Mexican CIF (Centro Intercultural de Formación) at Cuernavaca, then of CIDOC (Centro Intercultural de Documentación), which since 1961 had been providing initiation in Latin American culture for missionary candidates and—from a Third Worldist standpoint increasingly hostile to the imperialist aims of US economic cooperation (through the Alliance for Progress)—advocating the abandonment of industrialist ideologies of development. 'We need,' said Illich, 'an alternative programme, an alternative both to development and to merely political revolution. Let me call this alternative programme either institutional or cultural revolution, because its aim is the transformation of both public and personal reality.'[2] Gorz nonetheless retained his critical sense, since in Autumn 1972 he published an article in *Les Temps modernes* by his friend Gintis (though

---

1 Ivan Illich, 'School: The Sacred Cow'. Reprinted in Ivan Illich, *Celebration of Awareness: A Call for Institutional Revolution* (Harmondsworth: Penguin Books, 1980), pp. 103–14.

2 Ivan Illich, 'A Constitution for Cultural Revolution' in *Celebration of Awareness*, p. 149.

an economist, he was also a specialist in educational and behavioural sciences), who lambasted Illich's book *Deschooling Society* (1971) for not going to the roots of the problem, namely the capitalist system itself.[3]

The importation into France of Illich's thought, remarkable for the fact that very little delay was involved, came largely through other channels, all close to Catholicism. The journal *Esprit*, whose director was Jean-Marie Domenach, one of Illich's most faithful mediators, had been carrying his texts in considerable numbers since 1967, even devoting special sections to him in March 1972 and summer 1973. This was before Les Éditions du Cerf brought out an ambivalent assessment of his work by the workers' self-management advocate Patrick Viveret, entitled *Attention Illich*, in 1976. Thanks to the efforts also of Éditions du Seuil, Illich rapidly gained a notoriety and a level of sales in France comparable to Herbert Marcuse.[4]

Le Nouvel Observateur was not quite so eager to smooth the passage of the subversive prelate. And Bosquet was not an unqualified supporter. For example, it turns out that the interview he got from Illich—which came to the editorial board to coincide with the French publication of *Deschooling Society*—was spiked because the interviewer wasn't happy with it.[5] There seemed to be a cultural barrier between the two men. Whereas the anti-capitalism of the radical Harvard economists came out of the same theoretical background as the Frenchman's Marxism, Illich's quite different approach seemed perplexing in its angle of attack, which targeted institutions (school, medicine, transport network etc.) rather than the political and economic system governing them. The two thinkers did, however, remain in contact and sent each other their writings. Reacting to an article sent to him by Illich—published by *Esprit* in March 1972 as 'Inverser les institutions' and a candidate for inclusion in *The Division of Labour*—Gorz roughed out a letter which, it seems, he never sent. In it he expressed his reservations frankly, revealing himself to be 'one of the first, and rather troublesome, of your admirers'. He showed his 'annoyance' at some features of Illich's thought and, more seriously, at his 'indifference towards the

3 Herbert Gintis, 'Critique de l'illichisme', *Les Temps modernes* 314–15 (September–October 1972): 525–57.

4 Alexei Tabet, 'La Pensée d'Ivan Illich en France. Essai d'histoire intellectuelle', MA thesis, Université de Paris 1, 2012.

5 Written interview with André Gorz by Andrea Levy, 7 January 1998, in Levy, *Reframing Socialism from the Fifties to the Fin-de-siècle*, p. 259.

material base and political reality', which ruled out all prospect of action. Summing up, he wrote, 'I am in agreement with your goals, but disagree with your ideology and your method—or absence of method.'[6]

It was during his month's holiday in summer 1972 that Bosquet translated *Retooling Society* for *Le Nouvel Observateur*, that being the first of Illich's texts to make a deep impression on him. Jean Daniel had provided him with a roneo-ed copy, which was, in fact, a first version of the book that would come to be known in French as *La Convivialité* (1973). In summarized, adapted form, this was published in the 11 September issue.[7] Though there had been an exchange of correspondence between editor-in-chief and author, the publication was unlicensed and triggered a reaction from Illich, who, in his letter to Jean Daniel, 'copied to André Gorz', deplored that the published text 'did not present the full range of ideas in the original document in a way that could withstand criticism', and asked for a declaration to that effect to be published.[8]

In an effort to head this off, Jean Daniel asked the translator to reply to Illich. Expressing great regret at the situation and presenting his excuses on behalf of the magazine, 'André Gorz (Michel Bosquet)'—this was how he signed the letter—confided that: 'I lived with your piece for about three weeks and was very much in love with it, feeling that (except for some historical differences) we were pulling in the same direction and that you should have a great impact here with lots of people.' He assured him that *Retooling Society* was, in his view, 'the most comprehensive—and subversive—of [his] writings, the one that digs furthest at the roots of alienation (or whatever we call it).' His summary, he explained, had merely removed 'the implied notions [that] were completely meaningless to the French public', since 'your propositions could be considered an exotic curiosity'.[9] Justifying his effort of filtering and mediation in this way—an effort going well beyond mere translation—Bosquet–Gorz reveals to us that his desire to render Illich's disconcerting thinking understandable to readers was also a personal effort to assimilate, in terms of more familiar categories, a line of thinking that was well off the beaten track of Marxist critique, but seemed

---

6 Deleted section of a draft letter from André Gorz to Ivan Illich, undated (SEUIL).
7 Ivan Illich, 'Pour retrouver la vie', *Le Nouvel Observateur* (11 September 1973).
8 Ivan Illich to Jean Daniel (in French), 25 September 1972 (GRZ).
9 André Gorz (Michel Bosquet) to Ivan Illich (in English), 3 October 1972 (GRZ).

to him—as it did to the readers he was reflecting—'fundamental' and something like a 'revelation'.

Limiting Heteronomy, Imagining Autonomy

The Path of Ecology

There can be no doubt that Illich had great significance for Gorz and that, from the 1970s onwards, he embraced Illichian categories that amplified and enlivened his own analytical schemas on more than one occasion.[10] 'We had a privileged and very strong relationship', the Frenchman remembered. 'I learned a lot from him but could not or would not go along with him all the way.'[11] Gorz wasn't prepared to substitute Illich for Marx. On the other hand, though he wouldn't sacrifice the Marxian critique of capitalism, insofar as it went to the heart of the mechanisms of exploitation and oppression that did human beings down, he enriched it now with the Illichian critique of a technocratic, industrial system that ravaged both life and the environment conducive to life.

What caused Marx and Illich to converge in Gorz's mind was the critique of technology. And it was that critique, as developed by Illich on the basis of the creative potential of individuals, either alone or in concert, that brought Gorz to ecology. Let us note, from the outset, that Gorz's *Marxism* and Illich's *Christianity* prompted them to understand ecology in the same way: both held to an *anthropocentric* approach that had nothing to do with the sacralization of nature. Ecology was conceived not as an attempt to recover the lost equilibrium between nature and human beings, but as the fulfilment of humans in a finite milieu, rescued from the infinite depredations of technology. For Illich, as for Gorz, 'ecology is a humanism.'[12]

The convergence of the two thinkers over the key question of the destruction wrought by technological hypertrophy expressed itself in their mutual influence on each other. On being sent *Critique de la division du travail*, Illich replied in 1974: 'You know that I really like the last article,

10 Jean-Pierre Dupuy, 'Gorz et Illich' in Alain Caillé and Christophe Fourel (eds), *Sortir du capitalisme. Le scénario Gorz* (Lormont: Le Bord de l'eau, 2013), pp. 99–103.

11 Above cited interview with Andrea Levy, p. 260.

12 Françoise Gollain, *Une critique du travail. Entre écologie et socialisme* (Paris: La Découverte, 2000), p. 47.

'Technique, techniciens et lutte des classes' ['Technology, technicians and class struggle'] because we had occasion to discuss it when it appeared in *Les Temps modernes* [in 1971]. I used it when, in *La Convivialité*, I was formulating the statements on the impact of tools.'[13] Although the introduction to the work that Gorz sent him ended with a long quotation on tools taken from *La Convivialité*, thus embedding within the book the paternity of the arguments involved, Gorz would acknowledge that he had been inspired by a later Illich text entitled 'Approach to a Radical Critique of the Industrial System'. This had appeared in *Technologie und Politik*, a Hamburg-based Illichian journal founded by Freimut Duve that had Gorz among its advisors and contributors.[14]

In his short essay *Écologie et liberté* ('Ecology and Freedom' [1977]), which is virtually his ecologist manifesto, Gorz-alias-Bosquet reminds the reader, following Marx, that technology is 'not neutral': It is 'the matrix in which the distribution of power, the social relations of production, and the hierarchical division of labour are embedded'. And he goes on to stress literally, in the spirit of Illich, that:

> Societal choices are continually being imposed upon us under the guise of technical choices. [. . .] The struggle for different technologies is essential to the struggle for a different society. [. . .] The inversion of tools is a fundamental condition of the transformation of society.[15]

Starting out from the assumption that *homo faber* relates to society through this mediation of tools—which have to be understood in the broad sense of the means of production, together with the facilities or institutions governing public space—Illich is concerned that, from the point when they passed a certain size threshold, these tools began to enslave individuals instead of serving them. Progress was thus turning against itself. Illich calls this inversion of ends 'counter-productivity'; his close collaborators Jean-Pierre Dupuy and Jean Robert, on whom Gorz also draws, condemn this as *La Trahison de l'opulence* [The betrayal of affluence] (1976).

---

13 Illich to Gorz (in French), 5 April 1974.

14 Ivan Illich, 'Ansatz zu einer radikalen Kritik am Industriesystem', *Technologie und Politik* 1 (1975): 3–11. See the letter from André Gorz to Andreas Exner of 5 July 2007 in 'Über den Horizont unserer Handlungen', p. 13.

15 André Gorz, 'Ecology and Freedom' in *Ecology as Politics*, pp. 18–19.

There was something familiar in this line of theorizing for Gorz, who had already encountered it in the work of Sartre in the form of the counter-finality secreted by the practico-inert. It was in the light of the distinction provided by the contrasting notions of individual *autonomy* and *heteronomy* that the phenomenon assumed its full meaning. Gorz, who had already made use of these categories with respect to needs (see above, p. 74), was particularly receptive to this argument. What was involved, as Illich saw it, were two very different ways of producing use-values. In the one case, individuals satisfy their needs by drawing on knowledge that derives from controlled collective practices (Gorz saw in this the principle of *autogestion* [self-management] applied to small economic units); in the other they draw on a reified knowledge in the sole possession of professionals, technocrats and specialist insitutions (Gorz dubbed this '*hétérogestion*'). This did not mean that the heteronomy inherent in the second option, which affects industry as well as services, was to be condemned in and for itself. It was legitimate insofar as it, in turn, endowed individuals with greater autonomy in their everyday life. But heteronomy should not exceed certain limits. Otherwise, the 'positive synergy' that it fostered with autonomy would be dissipated and the outcome reversed.

Appealing to the evidence of what had happened in Third World societies subject to the steamroller effect of 'development policies', Illich asserted that institutionalized schooling conveyed a standardized body of knowledge, producing qualifications that created hierarchy within populations, while devaluing and preventing practical, non-normative education for all; that professionalized medicine divested the individual of his/her curative knowledge and capacities (the decline of popular herbal medicine); and that the modernization of motorized transport supplanted modes of travel that were more archaic but capillary and accessible to all (the peasant and his pig could no longer travel as they once had done)—so many logics inherent in 'growth-centred capitalism', which Gorz himself also set about deconstructing one by one.

For Illich and for Gorz, who in his *Ecology as Politics* openly trod in his footsteps, the antidote would be for individuals to reconquer their autonomy through the establishment of *convivial tools*. Those tools, whose potential technical complexity would not in itself be an obstacle to their use (for example, telephones), were to be recognized by being on a human scale: they retained the sense of their purpose, since they were mastered by those who used them in such a way that it increased their freedom. There were, then, two families of technology, the one inhibiting autonomy, the other serving it:

> There are 'technologies of confinement' that prevent convivial usage and 'open technologies' (e.g. telecommunications, computers, photovoltaic cells) that can be used both in a convivial way and for purposes of domination. Hence the only form of technological determinism that exists is a negative one: some technologies—those requiring a subdivision of tasks, and the centralization and concentration of decision-making; those which pose an obstacle to the appropriation of the means of work, of work itself—are inevitably devices of domination, obstacles to emancipation. But there is, by contrast, no positive technological determinism: there is no technology that is good in itself and forces its emancipated or liberated use upon us.[16]

The re-appropriation of some technological tools, which promotes autonomy, also makes a new economic organization of society possible. Gorz takes up the cudgels for a dualization of sectors. One might, on the one hand, have essentials produced by planned, large-scale industry, with the necessary labour time limited to 20 hours a week,[17] and this would make room, on the other, for the rise of a non-commodity, local, relatively autarkic sector, in which production choices would be a function of predetermined consumption needs.[18] Would these ideas bring about the bucolic utopia of a 'new Monte Verità' (the famous anarcho-ecologist community in Ticino)?[19] That wasn't Gorz's aim:

> It is not a question of reverting to cottage industry, to the village economy, or the Middle Ages, but of subordinating industrial technologies to the continuing extension of individual and collective autonomy, instead of subordinating this autonomy to the continuing extension of industrial technologies.'[20]

---

16 Gorz, 'La vie, la nature, la technique', p. 52.

17 Gorz, *Ecology as Politics*, pp. 9, 48.

18 Dominique Simonnet, 'La société dualiste de Michel Bosquet' (interview), *Le Sauvage* 49 (1 January 1978): 20–1.

19 Fritz Raddatz, 'Im Nebel eines neuen Monte Verità. André Gorz über das Ende der Arbeitsgesellschaft und die Zukunft der Linken', *Die Zeit* (22 November 1991).

20 Gorz, *Ecology as Politics*, p. 40.

In this context, workers' self-management [*autogestion*] would be as much shared management as the mastery by each person of the full set of relationships with others. With these kinds of considerations, which he shared with Illich, Gorz came to swell the ranks of an alternative school of thought that asserted itself in the 1970s. Decentralizing and localist, it took aim at monolithic powers, advocating, with the American eco-anarchist Murray Bookchin (though the latter regarded Gorz's Marxist background as alien to true ecology),[21] a self-managed society made up of small communities or, with the unorthodox British economist Fritz Schumacher, a mastery of necessaries through a proliferation of small production units: 'Small is beautiful!'.

Seizing the opportunity of a special issue of the journal *Actuel Marx* on ecology to review these matters 15 years later, Gorz would link the emergence of ecological protest in the US and Europe during that decade with the range of Illichian concerns to which he had always been attentive: 'against the mega-technologies in favour of which private industries and/or public administrations deprived the citizens of their human environment', against 'what Habermas called "the colonization of the life-world" ', there had developed the struggle to preserve 'the culture of everyday life'. Gorz explains:

> [B]y 'culture of everyday life', I mean the entire range of forms of intuitive knowledge, of vernacular skills (in Ivan Illich's sense of the term), of habits, norms and commonplace behaviour through which individuals can interpret, understand and come to terms with how they fit into the world around them. [...] Resistance to this destruction of the capacity to take charge of one's own life—in other words, of the existential autonomy of individuals and groups or communities—lies at the origin of certain specific components of the ecological movement: patient self-help networks, movements for alternative therapies, the campaign for abortion rights, the campaign for the right to die 'in dignity', movements for the defence of languages, cultures and regions etc.[22]

---

21 See Murray Bookchin, 'André Gorz, *Ecology as Politics*', *Telos* 46 (21 December 1980): 177–90.

22 Gorz, *Ecologica*, pp. 49–50, 54. Originally published as 'L'écologie politique entre expertocratie et autolimitation' [Political ecology: Expertocracy versus self-limitation], *Actuel Marx* 12 ('L'écologie, ce matérialisme historique') (1992, second semester): 15–29.

And, on the nature of the ecological struggle, he concluded: 'The defence of the *environment* in the ecological sense and the reconstitution of a *life-world* condition and support each other'.[23]

When Wealth Makes You Poor

In Illich's view, the runaway progress of heteronomy also insinuates itself into another area of life, namely consumption. This happens when the synergy between productive heteronomy and the 'autonomous' needs it satisfies is interrupted: heteronomy then reaches the threshold where needs are no longer anything but artificially created and their unbridled proliferation, which obeys that heteronomous logic alone (the pursuit of profit, specifies Gorz), works counter-productively to induce dissatisfaction through saturation with possessions and simultaneous frustration at the endless desire for more. Illich speaks in this connection of the 'modernization of poverty', since the excessive and continuously renewed supply of goods gives rise to a feeling of poverty relative to this ambient affluence.

This was a paradox that *Strategy for Labor* had already identified. Gorz now argues the point at some length. Assuming that the state of poverty is never absolute, but exists relative to a particular state of wealth and attests to the social inequality of a society, 'the persistence of poverty in rich countries must be attributed to a social system which produces poverty at the same time as it produces increasing wealth. Poverty is created and maintained, that is to say produced and reproduced, at the very pace at which the level of aggregate consumption rises.'[24] And elsewhere Gorz notes that, 'endlessly recreating scarcity in order to recreate inequality and hierarchy, capitalist society gives rise to more unfulfilled needs than it satisfies.'[25] The mechanism is dissected as follows:

> As soon as a particular product is generally obtainable, inequality is reproduced by supplying a 'better' one which only the privileged can afford. This in turn will devalue the obtainable object, render it obsolete and define the 'poverty' of those who cannot afford the 'better' one. Thus the reproduction of inequality—poverty and

23 Gorz, *Ecologica*, p. 72.
24 Gorz, *Ecology as Politics*, p. 28.
25 Gorz, *Ecology as Politics*, p. 7.

privilege—at ever-higher levels is a necessary condition for the indefinite growth of demand.[26]

Though he does not cite him, Gorz is at one with Baudrillard here in the belief that, 'the system only sustains itself by producing wealth *and* poverty, by producing as many dissatisfactions as satisfactions.'[27] If poverty, as lack, drives the system, which uses it as a spur to consumption, that system also depends on the—physical or symbolic—impossibility of spreading the access to non-scalable scarce goods that have value only by dint of their scarcity (detached houses, elite tourism, trips on Concorde, luxury products etc.). The elimination of poverty in the industrialized countries cannot, therefore, be achieved by an indiscriminate increase in production, but only by a certain type of good becoming available to all: the kind of good whose use-value is not destroyed by becoming generally available, by either the counter-productiveness of the glut or the ecological damage it might cause. In this way, the obsessive, frustrating and ecologically devastating incentive to consume more and more would be inhibited and the specious equating of 'more' with 'better' would be ended:

> 'Better' may now mean doing with less. It is possible to live better by working and consuming less, provided we produce more durable things as well as things which do not destroy the environment or create insurmountable scarcities once everyone has access to them. [...] Would it not be more rational to improve the conditions and the quality of life by making more efficient use of available resources, by producing different things differently, by eliminating waste, and by refusing to produce socially those goods which are so expensive that they can never be available to all, or which are so cumbersome or polluting that their costs outweigh their benefits as soon as they become accessible to the majority?[28]

Thirty years later, ecologists without exception will be battling with a capitalism that is not changing in its fundamentals and continues to be based on an economic growth that is still being denounced as inseparable from the inequalities of wealth it causes and feeds off.[29]

---

26 André Gorz, *Paths to Paradise: On the Liberation from Work* (Malcolm Imrie trans.) (London: Pluto Press, 1985), p. 22.

27 Baudrillard, *The Consumer Society*, p. 55.

28 Gorz, *Ecology as Politics*, pp. 41, 13–14.

29 See Hervé Kempf, *Comment les riches détruisent la planète* (Paris: Seuil, 2007).

The Ideology of the Car

Belonging to a post-war generation infatuated with modernity, Gorz would never be one of those ecologists who rejected the car for the bicycle. His tirades against the 'car' were not techno-phobic but Illichian: what he was attacking were excesses and counter-productiveness. Moreover, as Claude Lanzmann would say, somewhat mischievously, Gorz 'adored cars, which he exempted from de-growth.'[30] They were a particular weakness of his! After 10 years of saving up, he managed to buy himself an old Austin, then a second-hand 'special bodywork' Renault Frégate, which he drove on holidays and for his special reports in the provinces, intoxicated by speed. It was at the wheel of this superb white convertible that he arrived in the Breton village of Landernau one day in autumn 1962 to interview the founder of the Leclerc grocery chain. Leclerc's ten-year-old son—who would later spend his student years in Paris living with Gorz, who had by then become a spiritual and emotional second father to him—was blown away by it.[31] Later on, Gorz would own a BMW, a VW Golf, a Chrysler (fitted with good suspension for his sick wife) etc., though that would not prevent him from 'considering individual car ownership to be a disastrous political choice that pits individuals against each other [...].'[32]

The author of *The Traitor* and *La Morale de l'histoire* was ahead of his time: he foresaw the Sartrean theory of 'seriality'[33] and he preceded Illich in arguing that the generalized use of the car ended up thwarting the original aim of the driver—individual autonomy.

> [T]he automobile which, incarnating the negation of Here, makes Everywhere and Nowhere gleam across its hood and affords its owner the most illusory of freedoms, the apparent liberation from the constraints and requirements of life in common.[34]

---

30 Claude Lanzmann, 'Pour Gérard Horst, André Gorz, Michel Bosquet', *Les Temps modernes* 645–6 (September 2007): 2.

31 Michel-Édouard Leclerc, 'André Gorz: la mort d'un philosophe' (2 October 2007) (available at: michel-edouard-leclerc.com; last accessed: 25 July 2022).

32 Gorz, *Letter to D.*, p. 83.

33 Developed in the *Critique of Dialectical Reason* [1960]. See Françoise Gollain, *André Gorz, une philosophie de l'émancipation* (Paris: L'Harmattan, 2018), pp. 71–2.

34 Gorz, *Traitor*, p. 267.

Traffic clutters the highways, vehicles are caught up in jams at cross-roads, and car drivers end up moving more slowly and with a greater expenditure of energy than the users of public transport.[35]

According to Bosquet–Gorz, 'automobilism' promoted consumerism and bourgeois individualism. His recriminations against this outgrowth of affluent capitalism showed up as early as his *Express* articles and would remain a constant of his work.[36] And he was not alone in his criticism. Roland Barthes saw access to the car—that 'purely magical object'—as 'the very essence of petit-bourgeois advancement' (*Mythologies* [1957]); Ralph Nader denounces the dangers of the American automobile (*Unsafe at Any Speed*, 1965); the Personalist Bernard Charbonneau was concerned at the physical and psychological hold exerted over the human being who had become an *Hommauto* ([ManCar], 1967); Ivan Illich demystified motorized transport by resorting (with the aid of Dupuy) to true calculations of its speed (*Energy and Equity*, 1973); the ecologist Philippe Saint-Marc saw the car as 'the cancer of our civilization' ('Faut-il fermer Renault?', *Le Sauvage*, 6, 1973); and in *L'Utopie ou la mort!* (1973) the Third Worldist and ecologist René Dumont summarized and condemned its ravages: waste of resources, urban pollution and a human holocaust (6,000 killed in France in 1971!).

For Gorz who, in 1973, wrote 'The Social Ideology of the Motorcar', an article he would take care to have reprinted in his later collections,[37] the car question related to an alienating individual consumption choice and, on another level, to the questionable viability of transport, but it could not in any way be reduced to these two themes: the problem was a general one and concerned land use and territorial planning as a whole. The priority granted by governments to car usage had led to people working far from their place of residence, making them dependent on forever crowded and inadequate transport, the paradox being that the development of transport, far from reducing congestion and travel times, increased them by making

35 Gorz, *La Morale de l'histoire*, p. 95.

36 See, for example, Michel Bosquet, 'Circulation. Le luxe des dimanches', *L'Express* (26 October 1962).

37 It was republished in *Ecology as Politics* and in *Ecologica*. Original publication: Michel Bosquet: 'Mettez du socialisme dans votre moteur' [Put socialism in your tank], *Le Sauvage* 6 (September–October 1973): 8–13. The title plays on an advertising slogan by an oil company [The reference is to Esso's 'Mettez un tigre dans votre moteur' / 'Put a tiger in your tank'. Trans.].

for longer 'commuter' journeys. Dormitory suburbs or dormitory villages were the result. So what was the solution? To bring people's living and working lives back to a single space:

> They will have to be able to do without transport altogether because they feel at home in their own part of town, their municipality or human-scale city, and *because they enjoy walking home from their place of work*—walking or, at a pinch, cycling. No rapid, escapist means of transport will ever make up for the misery of living in an uninhabitable city, not feeling at home anywhere, and merely *passing through* to work or, alternatively, to cut oneself off from the world and sleep.[38]

Medical Nemesis

The Cuernavaca Trip

While passing through Paris in summer 1973, to promote *La Convivialité*, Illich invited Gérard and Dorine, in addition to Dupuy, to take part in the seminar on medicine planned for Cuernavaca the following year. It was his custom at CIDOC to organize discussion groups, made up of mainly North American and European researchers. These groups, which he didn't necessarily lead personally, had the aim of gathering and comparing material and debating it (those who would pass through these groups included Paulo Freire, Paul Goodman, Fromm, Marcuse, Helder Camara, Francisco Julião, Robert—who would stay—the young Susan Sontag, the student and future *subcomandante* Marcos etc.). He would generally prepare an initial document himself, roneotyped in-house, which, after being much discussed and modified, would develop into a publishable draft. *Medical Nemesis* (1975) was the product of a year and a half of shared research, in which Gorz participated—'decisively' according to Illich—with others during his one month stay in summer 1974.

At the same time, Gorz took part in another seminar, led by Étienne Verne and Heinrich Dauber, which had continuing education as its theme—and the institutional deadlock surrounding it. In that seminar, he gave a paper which provided him with an opportunity to implement Illich's precepts:

---

38 Gorz, *Ecologica*, p. 94.

Continuing education will come not so much from specialist institutions as from the fact that individuals will be put into educational
situations on a constant basis: that is to say, into situations where
they will themselves have to determine, individually and collectively, their way of living and working, their environment and the
nature of their tools. At that point, the separation between working
and learning becomes impossible.[39]

Counterproductive Medicine and a Personal Experience of It

Coming off his hard-working, convivial stay in Mexico, where he used the
centre's library to do a great deal of reading, Bosquet, writing in *Le Nouvel
Observateur* of 21 and 28 October 1974, made a case against the illogicalities
and damaging effects of medicine that would create quite a stir. He drew
also on a book by Dupuy and Serge Karsenty, *L'Invasion pharmaceutique*
(1974) that had come to fruition in discussions with Illich. In his long
article—'Quand la médecine rend malade' [When medicine makes you
ill][40]—Bosquet noted that the most frequent illnesses, such as cardiovascular
diseases, hypertension, hypercholesterol and some cancers were sicknesses
of civilization that were social, economic and political in their causation:
they were closely linked to living conditions. However, by concentrating its
efforts on curing illnesses, medicine individualizes cases and contributes to
masking their collective, structural causes. All actions are taken in relation
to the illness, with patients regarded merely as the organic substrate. They
are not seen as persons steeped in particular social relations and a given
living environment, even though these have an effect on their condition.
Hence effects are treated without seeing the causes. As a result, medicine
plays a powerful role of social normalization:

> Whenever medicine claims to treat or even cure the diseases that
> are the hardest to pin down [. . .] [it] is in fact acting in defence of
> the status quo. It implicitly imputes the illness to the sick organism
> and not to its living and working environment, and in so doing
> throws out as a possible cause the nature of the life and work against

39 André Gorz, 'Le Programme caché de l'éducation permanente' in Heinrich Dauber
and Étienne Verne (eds), *L'École à perpétuité* (Paris: Seuil, 1977), p. 118.
40 Translated as '1. Medicine and Illness' and '2. Health and Society' in Gorz, *Ecology
as Politics*, pp. 149–80.

which the organism is rebelling or defending itself. Most illnesses, in fact, *also* mean 'I can't carry on,' an inability to adjust to or face any longer circumstances that involve physical, nervous, and psychic suffering—suffering that is unbearable in the long run for this person, or even for *any healthy person*.[41]

This inability of the medical approach to take into account the social and environmental characteristics of populations explains why the decline of certain diseases, whose occurrence—in the case of tuberculosis, for example—diminished as a result of other factors most often linked to better hygiene, hasn't always been down to the progress of medicine. However, medicine seeks to extend medicalization to the whole of existence. Its aura precedes it. Like commercial advertising, it spreads throughout society the ideology of the healthy body which states that every sign of weakness, indisposition or ageing must be treated or prevented. The cult of youth will be one of the persistent strands of this engendered mentality: learning to live with one's own medical disorders becomes something to be condemned.

As for death, as an 'accidental' outcome of sickness or old age, it is handled medically, with the result that the relations of the dying person with those around them at this special moment in life are sanitized or blocked altogether. More generally, the 'art of living'—in other words, the knowledge and practice of hygienic behaviour in daily life—is replaced by the technical interventions of medical science: 'Those in charge of this intervention have persuaded people that in order to live, survive, get well, or bear their illnesses, they need to live inside a kind of therapeutic bubble in which they are drugged, antisepticised, tranquilized, stimulated, regulated, and permanently controlled.'[42] Moreover, clinical medicine experiences a counter-productive effect, a source of excess mortality and excess hospitalization, when confronted with nosocomial pathologies, the harmful effects of certain vaccines, or biological resistance to treatments in widespread use.

Bosquet's articles in *Le Nouvel Observateur* prompted many reactions from readers—both from medical people and the 'users' of medicine. State radio invited Bosquet and Karsenty to record a programme on 'Illness and

---

41 André Gorz, 'Science and Class: The Case of Medicine' in *Ecology as Politics*, p. 187. Originally published as Michel Bosquet, 'Une médecine de classe', *Lumière et vie* 127 (April 1976): 31–43.

42 Gorz, 'Medicine and Illness', p. 160.

Society' on 22 January 1975. These debates, which made some impact in the media, contributed to raising public awareness around the need to take control of the management of one's own health, which was a way of re-appropriating one's body—as was the contemporaneous feminist battle for the right to abortion which led to the French *loi Veil* of 1975.

These debates ran alongside the emergence of a movement challenging official medicine and its ideology. Between 1972 and 1976, the scientists Dupuy, Robert, Karsenty and Philippe d'Iribarne ran the Centre de recherche sur le bien-être [Research Centre on Well-Being] (CEREBE-CNRS), which was scathing not only about consumerism but also about the obsession with perfect health. 1975 saw the birth of SMG (le Syndicat de la Médecine générale, the general medicine trade union) and its publication *Pratiques ou les cahiers de la médecine utopique*, which aimed to change the relationship with patients by involving them in the battle against the structural causes of illness and fought against the notion of profit within medicine.[43] In 1977, the activist magazine *L'Impatient* explored alternative healthcare and the return to herbal medicine. In 1980, Bosquet finally published a large dossier, entitled 'Plaidoyer pour les médecines douces' [A plea for alternative medicine] in *Le Nouvel Observateur* of 7 April. Furthermore, criticism of the dominant model of the 'body'—a model often associated with sporting ideology—a critique which since 1966 had been front and centre in the journal *Partisans*, thanks to the efforts of the Reichians and Marcusians Boris Fraenkel and Jean-Marie Brohm (and their collaborator Paul Virilio), resurfaced in the form of a new magazine, *Quel Corps?*, which first appeared in 1975 and which its founder Brohm committed to the cause of the Extreme Left.

1974 and the years that followed were dramatic ones for Gérard and Dorine. The journalist's interest in the 'critique of techno-medicine' coincided at that point with the personal preoccupations he shared with his wife. Unexplained cramps and migraines began to ruin Dorine's life, forced as she was to spend nights standing on the balcony or sitting in an armchair. She was informed that she was suffering from chronic and incurable arachnoiditis caused by the encystment—in the cranial fossae and around the cervical vertebrae—of a contrast medium that had been injected into her eight

---

43 For an update on these issues, see *Revue du MAUSS*, 41 ('Marchandiser les soins nuit gravement à la santé'), 2013. For the history of the SMG, see 'La Saga du SMG', *Pratiques* 43 (October 2008).

years before when she had been given a myelogram. And yet the radiologist had confidently reassured her: 'The medium will flush away within ten days'!

The battle against this illness would go on for the rest of her life. She explored therapeutic pathways outside official medicine, used yoga, osteopathy and homeopathy on the advice of a British acquaintance, and practised mental relaxation. In 2001 she joined the new association Aube sophrologie, which Gorz supported by speaking at its AGM the following year. Gorz would explain that, in order to surmount her recurrent pain, his companion had chosen the only route that remained open to her—namely to re-appropriate her body and her illness:

> You had nothing further to hope for from medicine. You refused to get into the habit of taking analgesics and depending on them. You decided to take control of your body, your disease, your health; to seize power over your life instead of letting medical techno-science seize power over your relationship with your body, with yourself. [. . .] Your illness took us back to the terrain of ecology and techno-criticism. [. . .] Techno-medicine appeared to me to be like a particularly aggressive form of what Foucault was later to call bio-power [. . .].[44]

44 Gorz, *Letter to D.*, pp. 94–5.

CHAPTER TWELVE

Ecological Emergency and De-growth

The protests of 1968 were directed against the alienating effects of material well-being, while accepting the pursuit of growth as a given. That optimism went out with the decade. The first signs of economic downturn presaged nothing less than a reversal of the growth trend and the undermining of a model of centuries-long development characterized by industrialization, urbanization and population growth. The physical limits to expansion were being discovered, together with the devastation expansion could bring. Industrial pollution and the ravaging of the natural environment aroused growing indignation.

The questioning of modernity came tinged with gloom. Among the ecological protesters, there was a hint of catastrophism—the French periodical *La Gueule ouverte* (founded in 1972) referred to itself sardonically in its subtitle as 'The Magazine Announcing the End of the World'—and the critique of technology assumed an anti-progressive air: the CFDT published an indictment of technology-based society with the Sorelian title *Les Dégâts du Progrès* (1977)—the harm wrought by progress. Attention shifted from triumphant Western thought. In Henry Thoreau and Mahatma Gandhi the mystically inclined American hippies found examples of a civil resistance that fuelled the ecological and peace movements, which often went hand in glove. At the philosophical level, the anti-scientism and anti-positivism of Husserl, together with Frankfurt School Critical Theory (particularly Adorno and his acidic *Minima Moralia* of 1951),[1] were a source of renewed inspiration for those attacking capitalism's tottering rationalism. Nietzsche, the man out of his time, and the misunderstood Sorel were rediscovered as subversive left-wing thinkers.

Introducing an interview with Marcuse in mid-1972, the journalist Michel Bosquet grasped this turnaround perfectly.

---

1 While available in the 1970s in German, Italian and English, it was only in France that this book remained unknown for a long time, the first translation dating from 1980.

Until recent years we had lived with a more optimistic consciousness of the march of history [. . .] inherited from Marxism, which
meant that one could—with human intervention that would accel-
erate it or slow it down—look forward optimistically to the arrival
of a classless society and, ultimately, of happiness. Suddenly all the
laws of science, progress and demography have totally called into
question this optimism and the inevitability of the march of history
towards progress.[2]

The interviewer notes that the Promethean promise, borne onward by the
Enlightenment and Marx, ran up against a sudden revelation of the physical
limits and constraints that threatened to bring down the very material process of the reproduction of life, along with capitalist accumulation. This
realization sealed his adherence to the environmentalist position. But,
before examining the specific terms in which that conversion came about,
we have to set out the theoretical innovation which environmental thinking
represented in the 1970s—and which some, soon to be imitated by our protagonist, described as 'subversive science.'[3]

What Nature?

Natural Limits

In the early 1970s, despite being something of an 'underground' publication,
a book of seminal importance revolutionized the whole approach to the
philosophy of nature. Written by Nicholas Georgescu-Roegen, *The Entropy
Law and the Economic Process* (1971) was followed, in the same vein, by
Energy and Economic Myths (1976). The author of these two works is known
today as the father of de-growth.[4]

Educated at Harvard under Joseph Schumpeter (already a fierce critic
of those who confused growth with development), the Romanian economist

2 Interview by Jean Daniel and Michel Bosquet with Herbert Marcuse, 15 June 1972,
unpublished passage (GRZ 10.3). The interview was published in *Le Nouvel Observateur*
of 8 January 1973.

3 Paul Shepard and Daniel McKinley (eds), *The Subversive Science: Essays towards an
Ecology of Man* (Boston, MA: Houghton Mifflin, 1969).

4 Jacques Grinevald, 'Nicholas Georgescu-Roegen et le "message terrestre" de la décroissance', *Entropia* 10 (Spring 2011): 135–54.

is remembered particularly for having applied the second principle of thermodynamics, known as the law of entropy, to the economic processes of extraction and transformation of resources. On the basis of that principle of physics, he established that the earth's resources in energy and materials which entered the circuit of the economy suffered a deterioration—if not, indeed, a dissipation—of their initial state when they exited that circuit. This expressed itself in ever more waste and pollution, as well as in the increased scarcity and exhaustion of the original store of resources. The effects of this phenomenon worsened over time. 'One of the most important ecological problems for mankind, therefore,' warned Georgescu-Roegen, was 'the relationship of the quality of life of one generation with another— more specifically, the distribution of mankind's dowry *among all gener- ations*.'[5] Gorz, who probably read Georgescu-Roegen in the British *Ecologist* magazine, was won over to this new concern for intergenerational fairness.[6]

However, indifference to Georgescu-Roegen's arguments remained the norm in France, as elsewhere. A collection of his writings appeared in Lausanne in 1979 thanks to Jacques Grinevald, who gave it the title *Demain la décroissance* [Tomorrow degrowth], the neologism being used for the first time by Gorz in a debate on 13 June 1972 (see below). Yet Grinevald was never to succeed in having the heterodox works of his mentor published in French. Another trailblazing book in the same bio-economic vein, *L'Économique et le Vivant* (1979) by René Passet from Bordeaux, received barely any acknowledgement. By contrast, a popularizing work, which resisted the bio-economic line of thinking but instead rode the Illich wave, was well received, including by Michel Bosquet. This was *L'Anti-économique* (1974) by Jacques Attali and Marc Guillaume, who taught at the École poly- technique in Paris, which argued that growth did more to impair life than to improve it.[7] If, on the Right, Georgescu-Roegen was granted at best a

---

5 Nicholas Georgescu-Roegen, 'Energy and Economic Myths', *The Ecologist* (June and August–September 1975) (cited here from *Southern Economic Journal* 41 (3) (Jan 1975): 374). First published in French in *La Décroissance. Entropie, écologie, économie* (Jacques Grinevald and Ivo Rens trans and intro.) (Paris: Le Sang de la terre/Ellébore, 1995 [1979]), p. 100.

6 See Gorz, *Ecology as Politics*, p. 210.

7 See André Gorz, 'Reinventing the Future', *Ecology as Politics*, pp. 55–64. Originally published as Michel Bosquet, 'Réinventer l'avenir', *Le Nouvel Observateur* (4 March 1974).

degree of esteem (from the Schumpeterian economist François Perroux), on the Left, environmental thinking centred on bio-economics seemed like a theoretical UFO in a world that was in some respects fascinated by Illich but mostly in thrall to received Marxist ideas.[8] To begin with, there was a colossal gulf between a biospheric conception of the world and an historico-social conception of humanity.

In the analysis of the capitalist system, ecologists differ from Marxists in not viewing raw materials as accounting variables that form part of the composition of capital on much the same lines as machines and labour, as though the limits on resources were merely down to economic cost. On the contrary, they look on natural resources as a finite physical entity, the pro-ductive use of which either destroys or irremediably degrades it. Moreover, ecologists evaluate the 'externalized' damage wrought by production that affects the environment and the entire planet (pollution, waste, soil depletion etc.) and require this to be included in costs. As early as 1972, Gorz—or rather Michel Bosquet, since it was through journalism that the thinker discovered ecology—observed:

> The fact is that ecology, by virtue of the new parameters it intro-duces into economic calculation, is almost by definition a subvers-ive and anti-capitalist discipline. While the only variable in capitalist bookkeeping is the growth of capital through profit, ecology introduces parameters which are extraneous to this logic: optimum husbanding of natural resources, of the environment, of biological balances; the quest for maximum durability, for use-value rather than exchange value; the optimal satisfaction and fulfilment of people in their work and outside it, rather than the maximum yield and productivity of labour from the point of view of capital.[9]

The ecologists' approach reflects a naturalistic materialism. Marx's approach too was of a materialist type but, being directed against Malthus, it confined itself to an economism that ignored the natural limits to wealth creation and capital accumulation.[10] And it did so for a reason. Marx never broke with

---

8 On the historical incomprehension of thermodynamics by Marxism, see Joan Martínez Alier, 'La confluence dans l'éco-socialisme' in Jacques Bidet and Jacques Texier (eds), *L'Idée du socialisme a-t-elle un avenir?* (Paris: PUF, 1992), pp. 181–93.

9 Bosquet, *Capitalism in Crisis and Everyday Life*, p. 184.

10 Ted Benton, 'Marxism and Natural Limits: An Ecological Critique and Reconstruc-tion', *New Left Review* 187 (Nov–Dec 1989): 51–86; Jean-Marie Harribey, 'Marxisme

the bourgeois ideological notion, formulated by Adam Smith, that the civil order rested on the rights of individuals perceived predominantly as producers, implying that the economy is independent both from nature and from the other dimensions of society.[11] As a result, if Marx drew on Hegel to denounce man's separation (*Trennung*) and alienation (*Entfremdung*), he never grasped these other than as evils specific to human action or, in other words, immanent in human economic activity, the perversion of its ends being contested, but not the primacy and potency of that economic activity.

This critical limitation is reflected in the deconstruction of the capitalist mode of production contained in *Capital*. Marx demonstrates there that the labour process in general, in the anthropological sense, which uses matter-energy and produces use-values, is simply the condition for another kind of process which engulfs it. It provides the underpinning for a historically and socially constituted process, the specific aim of which—whether we define it as supra-materialistic or, with Marx, 'mystical'—is to ensure, through the production of 'fetishistic' exchange-values 'abounding in metaphysical subtleties and theological niceties',[12] the expanded reproduction of capital, which is itself, of course, only an abstraction—in this case, the social crystallization of past labour.

This preferential attention to the circular process of capital, which operates at a level beyond its material base, in isolation and with its own specific dialectic, prevented Marx and his disciples from noticing, as Georgescu-Roegen laments, 'that nature, too, plays an important role in the economic process, as well as in the formation of economic value.'[13] The critique of political economy by way of the very logic of political economy enabled Marx to lift the veil on the internal limits to the development of the system (crises, tendency of the rate of profit to fall etc.), but not on the limits deriving from the grip the economy exerts on the ecosystem. It is not from a Marxist standpoint (modelled both on the teleology of capital driving towards its own reproduction and on the prospect of wealth that provides

écologique ou écologie politique marxienne' in Jacques Bidet and Eustache Kouvélakis (eds), *Dictionnaire Marx contemporain* (Paris: PUF, 2001), pp. 183–200.

11 Dominique Bourg, *Les Scénarios de l'écologie* (Paris: Hachette, 1996), pp. 14, 17.

12 Karl Marx, *Capital*, VOL. 1 (Ben Fowkes trans.) (Harmondsworth: Penguin Books, 1976), p. 163.

13 Nicholas Georgescu-Roegen, *The Entropy Law and the Economic Process* (Cambridge MA: Harvard University Press, 1971), p. 266.

the material basis for Communism) that the ravaging of nature by human activity becomes intelligible, but from another standpoint: the acceptance of nature's finite physical dimensions and the awareness of its entropic erosion. In 1976 Bosquet writes:

> What ecology teaches us is that the economy of human production is embedded in an economy of natural cycles, governed by the principles of thermodynamics. [...] It thus reminds us that all production is also destruction [...]. When the useful effects of an act of destruction exceed its adverse effects (its 'disutilities') and its costs, we may speak of productive destruction. But when the disutilities and costs of a productive act exceed the useful effects we derive from it, we must speak of destructive production. Now, beyond a certain point, the 'progress' of industrial growth has more destructive than useful effects. [...] The destruction of 'natural resources' (air, water, mineral resources, space, forests, ocean life) is not accounted for anywhere. This means that our industrialists (with the blessing of our technocrats) wreak ever more destruction to combat the destructive effects of their production. We never stop increasing the inputs to combat the negative effects of increasing the inputs. The growth of GNP is accompanied by a fall in the quality of life.[14]

This explanation, which foregrounds the vicious circle of 'destructive production' offset by ever more 'destructive production', leads its author to campaign for 'de-growth'. In the essay 'Ecology and Freedom' Bosquet explains:

> Science and technology have ended up making this central discovery: all productive activity depends on borrowing from the finite resources of the planet and on organizing a set of exchanges within a fragile system of multiple equilibriums. The point is not to deify nature or to 'go back' to it, but to take account of a simple fact: human activity finds in the natural world its external limits. Disregarding these limits sets off a backlash. [...] The boldest concept which modern political economy dared envisage was that of 'zero growth' in physical consumption. Only one economist, Nicholas Georgescu-Roegen, has had the common sense to point

---

14 Michel Bosquet, 'Une production destructive', *Le Nouvel Observateur* (11 October 1976).

out that, even at zero growth, the continued consumption of scarce resources will inevitably result in exhausting them completely. The point is not to refrain from consuming more and more, but to consume less and less—there is no other way of conserving the available reserves for future generations.[15]

Self-Limitation

Does this mean that André Gorz approves the environmentalist principle that the human race must live in harmony with nature? The answer is not immediately clear since he always conceived the relationship of the Human to Nature within the framework of Sartrean and Marxist humanisms that extol the power of human action [*agir*].[16] He would never abandon that philosophical framework, even though he knew the environmentalist criticism made of it by William Leiss in *The Domination of Nature* (1972).[17]

This means that his theoretical conversion to the ecological cause came about by a highly personal route, unrelated to the Copernican revolution that Serge Moscovici, as a genuine trailblazer for political ecology in France, inflicted on the infernal Nature-Culture pairing. In *La Société contre nature* (1972), that French anthropologist and sociologist—another, like Georgescu-Roegen, who was of Romanian descent—enquired into the origins of the human species to counter modern social conceptions which contended that Man was the master and possessor of Nature who had, through the invention of culture, conquered the world of things from the outside. The practical consequence being that humanity, forgetful of Nature and its laws, was today threatening to break down the ecological barriers imposed upon it, to encroach on the domain of the other species and modify the environment to the point where it became unfit to support life. Sharing the conviction with Friedrich Engels, the author of *Dialectics of Nature*, that humanity was in fact a part of Nature, because Nature shaped humanity as much as it was modified by it, Moscovici advocated the reconciliation of the human with its 'animal', 'wild' nature, so that it might recover the regulatory osmosis it

---

15 Gorz, *Ecology as Politics*, pp. 12–13. (The misspelling of Georgescu-Roegen's name has been corrected [Trans.]).

16 Françoise Gollain, 'André Gorz était-il un écologiste?', *Écologie et politique* 44 (2012): 1–15.

17 See Gorz, *Critique of Economic Reason*, p. 85.

had enjoyed in the past within the bosom of nature. Hence, as an ecological activist on the left of politics, his defence of subjectivity, ethnicity and regionalism.

For his part, Gorz would always take the view, as he noted in a one-off document of the late 1950s, that human action was transformative of nature and operative in purely human conditions:

> Because the world has up to now been the milieu of *scarcity* for human beings and because Nature, far from guaranteeing the satisfaction of Man's organic needs, has constantly to be transformed, Man is a being who has to *produce his life* and one whose condition, far from being natural, is always the historical and social condition in which that production [. . .] is carried on.[18]

His ecologism was guided by social ends or, as he would recall at the end of his life, by the 'concern for the environment, *inasmuch as* it determined the quality of life and the quality of a civilization.'[19]

It is an impressive fact that, from one end of his career to the other, Gorz never altered his way of imagining the world and humanity's struggle within it one iota. Compared with the naturalistic case made by Moscovici, Gorz's perspective turns out to be a very traditional one. It was in keeping with the 'modern' vision developed by Francis Bacon—who wished to tame nature—and the metabolism between the human and nature which it draws on greatly resembles what we find in the manuscripts of the young Marx, Communism appearing in those writings as the satisfaction of needs through mastery of the sensible world.[20] It follows that the philosophical foundations of Gorz's ecologism attest, by their similarity to the philosophy of nature of Marx (and Engels), that that philosophy is not opposed *a priori* to the environmental position—though we know that the Marxist vulgate took a different view of these matters.

Let us examine Gorz's approach. In 1967, he spoke of nature as 'quite evidently hostile to human life, from which life has to be conquered by

---

18 'Force et faiblesse du marxisme d'aujourd'hui'. Handwritten and undated (GRZ 8.26).

19 André Gorz, 'Où va l'écologie?', interview by Gilles Anquetil, *Le Nouvel Observateur* (14 December 2006). My emphasis (WG).

20 On Marx, see Reiner Grundmann, *Marxism and Ecology* (Oxford: Clarendon Press, 1991), pp. 91–106; and 'The Ecological Challenge to Marxism', *New Left Review* 187 (May–June 1991): 103–20.

constant and always threatened endeavour.'[21] This is very similar to the idea of nature he developed in *Fondements pour une morale* in 1946: 'It is the world insofar as it escapes the grasp of man and changes independently of our action. [. . .] Nature in this sense is inhuman or, better, anti-human to the precise extent that the human is anti-natural and won from Nature.' And if, contrary to this, the world is looked at in its 'utilitarian and technical dimensions', humans appear 'currently to be "killing" Nature by intervening violently in its becoming [*devenir*].'[22] Conflict and domination govern the relationship between human life and its milieu. There are, however, grounds to warn against a ruthless struggle to enslave nature, since its destruction would have dramatic consequences. Posing 'the problem of the moral relation between freedom and nature', Gorz actually writes:

> To master the nature in oneself, freedom has to take control, through work and technique, of the Nature that invests it; freedom cannot assign its own nature its place unless it has first freed itself from Nature through culture—that is to say, by a transformation of the natural world, which is never favourable in advance to the flourishing of human life and its ends. It is only by this readjustment that it will be possible for Nature to cease to be a cruel god, though it will never become man's ally; the human world has been set apart by Nature and continues to be threatened with being swallowed up by its invasive inertia. Man has subordinated Nature to himself and reversed the relation of subjugation that bound him to it, but he must be careful not to destroy it and, by that destruction, unleash the chaos of brute matter consigned once more to sterility and death. [. . .] The relationship between freedom and nature thus necessarily remains a dramatic one.[23]

In 1990, in a dialogue with the young Austrian philosopher Erich Hörl, who went so far as to charge him with being fundamentally anti-ecological, Gorz replied at length on the harmony between humanity and nature. In introductory remarks, he gave a historical basis for his reasoning:

---

21 Interview with Ilija Bojović reprinted in Bojović, *1968*, p. 122.

22 Gorz, *Fondements pour une morale*, pp. 166–7.

23 Gorz, *Fondements pour une morale*, pp. 552–3.

Nature is a self-regulating system that achieves its equilibrium and effects its reproduction by allowing countless subsystems to interact with each other, without any of them ever being able to achieve total supremacy. Humanity was part of that natural order, so long as it was made up of hunters and fishermen for whom the idea of 'work' didn't correspond to any real experience. It isn't because they wished to live in peace with nature that they didn't intervene in its cycles but because they didn't have available to them the tools that would have enabled them to make such interventions. The domination of nature began as soon as peoples became sedentary and developed effective tools.[24]

The rest of the answer postulates that 'the human is not genetically programmed to live in harmony with nature' and that what differentiates it from the rest of the living world is its ability consciously to act on nature and, in particular, to work towards its protection, which is at the same time the protection of the basis of human life. It is by deliberate action, then, that humanity preserves its living environment. This is a choice that forms part of a culture, which expresses itself through *the self-limitation of needs*—a choice that flowed spontaneously from social organization in the societies that ante-date capitalist accumulation and which should now be restored. While Hans Jonas had already laid down *The Imperative of Responsibility* [1979], which imposed a duty on humanity with regard to the preservation of the present and future conditions for life, Gorz developed the same range of issues in his own way:

> The question humanity faces is—and already was in Antiquity—that of the cultural self-limitation of its needs and its projects, which will alone enable it to avoid destroying the natural foundations of its life. In pre-capitalist societies, that self-limitation was self-evident. It was demanded by the social order. Competition, the maximization of profits and yields were prohibited by law until the beginning of the eighteenth century. [. . .] These restrictions were removed by the bourgeois-capitalist revolution in favour of the 'market society' which is, in reality, a non-society. Currently, the aim should be to restrict the rights of economic reason again by subordinating that reason to ecological and social goals, without

24 Gorz, 'La vie, la nature, la technique', pp. 41–2.

for all that giving up freedoms or people's rights to self-determination and fulfilment.[25]

Both the strength and weakness of Gorz's reasoning are worthy of note here. Since the point when the contemporary ecological crisis began to stimulate the study of pre-capitalist societies from an eco-social standpoint, we have known that the need for self-limitation—in particular in the management of the land and forests—was not always regarded as self-evident and that only the low level of demographic pressure enabled the human impact on the ecosystem to be moderated. That impact would really 'explode' in the age of fossil fuels. But the core of Gorz's argument is simply reinforced by this fact: it was indeed by social choices that humanity negotiated its place in the eco-system, in good years and bad. There remains the question of means—authoritarian or democratic—of making choices and applying them. Jonas, inclined towards decisionism, and Gorz, with a strong libertarian streak, diverge on this question, the latter having never harboured the slightest sympathy for an enlightened despotism, whatever its source.[26]

The Birth of Political Ecology

May '68 wasn't the origin of environmental campaigning, but the spirit and practices involved in the '68 movement laid the ground for what would come to be called political ecology, a new way of conceiving the defence of nature and the environment. In the past, the protection of the natural world, driven by economic, health and aesthetic arguments, then on grounds of the preservation of species, had been the business of high-ranking civil servants concerned to regulate the impact of economic activities, whistle-blowing scientists and naturalists or nature conservancy organizations.[27]

In the 1970s, with the United States leading the way, Europe saw a proliferation of environmentalist movements confronting specific problems in their *systemic* and *political* dimensions ('Act locally, think globally' was

---

25 Gorz, 'La vie, la nature, la technique', p. 43.

26 For a critique of Gorz from Jonas's anti-humanist standpoint, see Bernard Perret, 'Penser avec et contre André Gorz. Individualisme révolutionnaire *vs* éthique de la responsabilité' in Caillé and Fourel (eds), *Sortir du capitalisme*, pp. 117–26.

27 See *Vingtième siècle* 113 ('L'Invention politique de l'environnement'), (January–March 2012).

the cry)[28] and calling, against technocratic state policies, for forms of public decision-making that respected popular feeling. In France political ecology took shape during that decade as several components gradually came together.[29] Initially, there was a jumble of ill-assorted associations defending nature or the environment, alongside a number of alarmed scientists. Anarchists and feminists (including d'Eaubonne), used to the kind of grass-roots action practised in '68, then joined the ecological cause, while the break-up of the ultra-Left after 1972 made possible an influx of Maoists, now shorn of their sectarian machine politics.

A new organization would play an important political role. This was 'Les Amis de la Terre' (AT), created in July 1970 by Alain Hervé along the lines of the American 'Friends of the Earth', founded the previous year by David Brower, who had been pushed out of the Sierra Club for his anti-nuclear activism. Hervé was a PSU voter, but not a '68er. A lover of sea travel and palm trees, his own particular adventure had been to sail around on his yacht for the previous three years. A journalist by profession, he initially conceived AT as an organization for popularizing ecological themes. The priority he gave to the over-population problem meant he was close to the conservative environmentalism of Brower, the American Paul Ehrlich, the whistle-blowing author whose work *The Population Bomb: Population Control or Race to Oblivion* (1968) was translated by AT in 1971, and Edward Goldsmith, the British founder of *The Ecologist* magazine. He gathered around him both sailing friends (including Bernard Moitessier) and a large number of anthropologists (including Moscovici and Robert Jaulin, while Claude Lévi-Strauss agreed to be a patron of AT), who were inclined by their discipline to put the human at the centre of their environmentalism.

When Brower came to Paris on 21 November 1970, Hervé rushed to mount a mini-press-conference in the anti-nuclear environmentalist's hotel room, with Michel Bosquet among those invited. Bosquet, sitting on the floor, took notes, while revealing nothing of his feelings to Hervé's enquiring gaze.[30] In reality, he was already a convert. Being aware of the alarms raised in the US, he was convinced that the regeneration of the biosphere was

---

28 Willy Gianinazzi, 'Penser global, agir local. Histoire d'une idée', *EcoRev'* 46 (Summer 2018): 19–29.

29 Jean Jacob, *Histoire de l'écologie politique* (Paris: Albin Michel, 1999).

30 Alain Hervé, 'La genèse des amis de la Terre', *L'Écologiste* 21 (December–March 2007): 14.

imperilled by the intensification of pollution of all kinds.[31] He had already penned his 'J'accuse' against an economic logic that had never been inclined to take account of the costs of the external destruction it occasioned.[32] Even before developing his positive and critical conception of ecology, Gorz (alias Bosquet) was a virulent environmental protester; he can rightly be seen as one of the first architects of political ecology in France.

The Magazine Le Sauvage

Hervé knew the people at *Le Nouvel Observateur*. Claude Perdriel had already employed him in the past to write articles in one of the group's men's magazines, and Philippe Viannay had found him the premises that served as headquarters for the AT. The former was no ecologist (he was even pro-nuclear), and the latter, an enterprising lover of sun, sea and sand (he had founded the Les Glénans sailing club), was at very best an institutional environmentalist (a member of the Commission des sites, then of the Conservatoire du littoral, the French coastal protection agency). Knowing that each man saw ecology as offering a possible publishing opportunity—put crudely, a gap in the market[33]—Hervé drew on the support of his friend Goldsmith to try to convince the group's managing director to launch an environmentalist periodical. When the attempt proved unsuccessful, he resolved to join the team of *Le Nouvel Observateur* in 1972.[34]

That was a year filled with environmental scares, the year of 'dawning ecological awareness', as Jean Daniel dubbed it. Edgar Morin, having recently awakened to a planet-wide awareness, saw it as 'year 1 of the ecological era'. Two highly alarming expert reports, which Gorz scrutinized closely, appeared within a few months of each other. The first of these, *A Blueprint for Survival*, edited by Goldsmith, was published in Britain in the January issue of *The Ecologist*; the French version *Changer ou disparaître* (1972) came out immediately in book form. The second report, *The Limits to Growth*, was commissioned by the business leaders and financiers of the

31 Michel Bosquet, 'Pollution. Les asphyxiés de l'an 2000', *Le Nouvel Observateur* (12 January 1970).

32 Bosquet, *Critique du capitalisme quotidien*, pp. 280–2. Originally published as 'J'accuse', *Le Nouvel Observateur* (10 August 1970).

33 See Philippe Viannay, *Du bon usage de la France* (Paris: Ramsay, 1988), pp. 356–7 (it is necessary to read 'between the lines').

34 Author interview with Alain Hervé, 6 March 2013.

Club of Rome. It was translated into French as *Halte à la croissance?* (1972) and had a major impact worldwide (several million copies were sold). Simulating planetary development over the coming decades, the report concluded that the system would collapse if action were not taken quickly. It argued for an urgent remedy: 'zero growth' in the rich countries. The debate had begun.[35]

At Stockholm in early June 1972, the UN held the first world conference on the human environment, which adopted the concept of 'eco-development' that had been coined from a perspective of strategic economic planning by Ignacy Sachs (the free-market concept of 'sustainable development' would be a later, bastardized version). On that occasion—and with the encouragement of Viannay—Hervé prepared a special issue of *Le Nouvel Observateur* entitled *La Dernière Chance de la Terre* [Last chance for the Earth]. Working on that issue were Bosquet, who highlighted the 'Obstacles to Growth',[36] and two active supporters of the AT, Edgar Morin and the naturalist Théodore Monod. It was a sign of the times that 125,000 copies were sold. In the meantime, Bosquet–Gorz pressed his friend Marcuse not to let himself be used by participating in a conference on the Ends of Growth that was under the control of the French Minister of the Economy, Valéry Giscard d'Estaing.[37] He diverted him instead towards a great debate on ecology which, on his initiative, the magazine organized in Paris on 13 June. This was attended by 1,200 people and another 2,000 were turned away for lack of space. Another star was invited, the Dutch social democrat Sicco Mansholt, the iconoclastic president of the European Commission. Following the report to the Club of Rome, Mansholt had already attacked the policy of growth, raising an outcry at Brussels and in France. Edgar Morin and, of course, Bosquet took part in the debate, both of them warning

---

35 See the PhD thesis by Élodie Vieille-Blanchard, 'Les Limites à la croissance dans un monde global. Modélisations, prospectives, refutations', EHESS, Paris, 2011.

36 Bosquet, *Capitalism in Crisis and Everyday Life*, pp. 175–83.

37 See Gorz's well-reasoned letter (undated) and Marcuse's reply of 3 April 1972 (GRZ). Taking part in the conference, which was held from 20 to 22 June 1972, were J.K. Galbraith, Bertrand de Jouvenel, Raymond Aron, Sicco Mansholt, Peter Harper, Paul Delouvrier (EDF), Aurelio Peccei (Club of Rome) etc. Marcuse's failure to take part is regretted in the introduction to the published proceedings—*Économie et société humaine* (Paris: Denoël, 1972), p. 10.

against a technocratic takeover of the ecological imperative (Morin also spoke of the danger of Marxism taking ecology out of the equation).[38]

April 1973 saw the first issue of the monthly *Le Sauvage* as an 'ecology' supplement to *Le Nouvel Observateur* (it would subsequently be sold separately). The title was a happy one, inadvertently echoing both the pre-environmentalist *sauvagisme* of the (Émile Gravelle–style) anarchists of the turn of the century and the archetype defended by Moscovici. It was also in keeping with the primitivism beloved of Goldsmith. Reassured by the success of the June–July special issue, Perdriel, the managing director, and Viannay, the administrator, had taken the decisive step. Alain Hervé edited the publication, so in this way Les Amis de la Terre had at their disposal a semi-official mass-market publication—selling up to 40,000 copies—in which all ecological subjects were open to discussion. With the first number entitled 'L'utopie ou la mort' [Utopia or death], the ambitions for change were set very high at the outset. The following issues tackled the themes of the energy crisis, civil nuclear power, car-use reaching saturation point, solar- and wind-powered living, and the right to idleness. By regularly writing articles of substance for the magazine, which he would reprint in 1975 in the book that became, in English, *Ecology as Politics*, Bosquet–Gorz stamped a radical political line on it that combined ecology with the reconstruction of society. Other committed writers also figured in the publication: Moscovici (who argued for bicycle use and 'wilding'), Monod, Morin, Jaulin, the novelist Christiane Rochefort, the journalist Bertrand de Jouvenel (the first person to speak, as early as 1957, of 'political ecology'), and the physician and ethologist Henri Laborit.

Doing Politics Differently

In the meantime, Les Amis de la Terre had turned towards a more political activism. The arrival of the '68er Brice Lalonde was crucial in this regard. Lalonde had been active in May 1968 as a member of the PSU student organization (ESU) and a representative of the Sorbonne Fédération des Groupes d'Étudiants de Lettres of the UNEF student union, where he supported Kravetz. While rejecting the activism of small sectarian groups—he was a member of the PSU from 1969 to 1976—he had, nonetheless, learned

---

38 Herbert Marcuse et al., 'Écologie et révolution', *Le Nouvel Observateur* (19 June 1972). Also present on the stage were Goldsmith, Saint-Marc and CFDT leader Edmond Maire.

the tricks of the agitprop trade in those weeks of ferment. It was this practical experience he brought to the AT when he joined them in 1972. Hervé, who found a place for him as a copy-editor on *Le Sauvage*, quickly yielded the management of the association to him.

Following the first environmentalist candidacy for a presidential election by the agronomist René Dumont in 1974, Lalonde, who had been his campaign manager, took up the baton, putting himself forward as the ecologists' media star. Bosquet, who frequented the editorial staff of *Le Sauvage* from time to time and attended meetings of AT-Paris (with Dorine), soon developed contacts with him. According to witnesses, the two became as close as father and son. In 1977, Gorz dedicated *Écologie et liberté* to him. Before this ecological go-getter (who always had an ego problem) went astray by giving in to the lure of political careerism,[39] Bosquet shared his political and strategic vision, which was also that of Moscovici. Political ecology is, admittedly, a movement which, for Bosquet and Moscovici, stands, by its radicalism, either on the Left or on 'the left of the Left', whereas for Lalonde there are grounds for rejecting both Right and Left.[40] However, all three agree that the civilizational change called for by the ecologists, based on the rejection of productivism and gigantism, of technocracy and of blindly forging ahead with electricity generation by means of nuclear power, creates a rift with the entire political class. For Les Amis de la Terre, the point was not, for all that, to enter the political arena by adding another political party to the existing ones, since, as Bosquet said, ecology has nothing in common with political action as understood by the parties. It is 'incompatible with the traditional forms of the delegation of power and political organization.'[41]

> So the task of the environmentalist movement is to open up, starting out from the lowest level which Moscovici terms 'existential', new spaces for action and freedom in a sphere that politics neglects (this is why it is often called 'infra-political') and in which it will be

---

39 Hervé Kempf, 'Brice Lalonde. Le dandy de l'écologie', *Le Monde* (11 December 2007).

40 Michel Bosquet, 'Qu'est-ce que l'écologie politique?', *Le Sauvage* 43 (July 1977): 14–19. The article records a debate that took place at the headquarters of the AT and also involved Alain Touraine, Hervé and the anthropologist Michel Izard.

41 Michel Bosquet, 'Ce que les écologistes pensent d'eux-mêmes', *Le Nouvel Observateur* (22 March 1977).

able to be reborn in new forms: the sphere of what depends directly on people themselves, what they can carry out—or prevent—by themselves, without going through the machinery of power and institutions.[42]

Lalonde took an *autogestionnaire*, Illichian and libertarian approach.[43] Following it closely, Bosquet saw the ecological movement as a loose political and social movement that 'transcend[ed] class' by attacking precise, concrete questions of social organization or the good life. It reminded him of the American movement, of Marco Pannella's Italian Radical Party (which attracted former supporters of Lotta Continua) or even his own past conception of revolutionary reforms:

All that doesn't lead us to a social project? True enough. But it provides a set of partial objectives that are so many preliminaries for a liberated, relaxed society, a 'pacified existence' as Marcuse would say: a new policy on energy, transport, amenities, health, spatial planning etc., each of these preliminaries having to be implemented locally by the people themselves, most notably through the self-management of production units and grassroots communities. This way of tackling a general problem by way of specific partial objectives, but objectives that are popular and desirable in themselves, strangely resembles what 15 years ago we called 'the strategy of structural reforms.'[44]

The ecologists would continue to see things this way for many years. The will of the 'Greens' to act 'differently', to free themselves from the political traditions of the workers' or ultra-Leftist parties, would remain intact when the various currents organized eventually to form the French Green Party— *Les Verts*—in 1984.[45] Buttressed by a principle of autonomy, of 'Neither Left nor Right', Les Verts, led by Antoine Waechter (a fundamentalist who gained the support of most of the Lalondians once they were free of their leader) would not countenance powerless, minority participation in government; they preferred to intervene through actions or at election times with the

42 Bosquet, 'Qu'est-ce que l'écologie politique?', p. 18.
43 See Brice Lalonde, 'Court traité imagé sur les écologies', *Le Sauvage* 43 (July 1977): 51–4.
44 Michel Bosquet, 'La nébuleuse écologique', *Le Nouvel Observateur* (22 August 1977).
45 Yves Frémion, *Histoire de la révolution écologiste* (Paris: Hoëbke, 2007).

aim of popularizing their ideas and translating them into political pressure. In February 1987, Gorz would back the call, with the Left of Les Verts and alongside other signatories including Dumont, Cohn-Bendit, Lipietz, Guattari etc., for an alternative Left grouping supportive of worker self-management and political ecology, entitled 'Pour un Arc-en-ciel' [literally, For a rainbow]. This would fail the next year with the fielding of two separate candidates in the presidential election: Waechter and the red–green Juquin. In 1989 a member of the Greens offered to have Gorz write their party programme;[46] for his part, he quoted their pamphlets favourably.[47] Only the melting away of social movements in the 1990s and a desire to reposition themselves on the Left would lead Les Verts, under the leadership of Dominique Voynet, to turn themselves into a classical party with managerial aims, basing its strategy for power on an alliance with a productivist party that had a majority. However, that would not prevent leading ecologists, such as Daniel Cohn-Bendit, Dominique Voynet and Cécile Duflot from declaring allegiance to Gorz's arguments.[48]

Their Ecology and Ours

Won over by the *Blueprint for Survival* and *Limits to Growth* reports, and by the courageous stand taken by Mansholt, Bosquet–Gorz declared himself certain that 'industrial civilization' would not survive beyond the twentieth century. The plundering of resources, the pollution of the natural world and the failure to preserve the agricultural land required for coping with the demographic explosion which had at all events to be contained, ordained that the flow of production and trade be curbed. It was down to 'the developed capitalist world' to reverse a pattern of economic behaviour in which 'the industrialized world, with 16 per cent of global population, swallowed up 80 per cent of the Earth's limited and irreplaceable resources.'[49] Sharing

46 Gérard Paing to André Gorz, 19 July 1989 (GRZ).

47 See Gorz, *Ecologica*, p. 76n14.

48 See Daniel Cohn-Bendit, 'Freiheit und politische Ökologie. Ein Gespräch mit Daniel Cohn-Bendit über André Gorz', *Berliner Debatte Initial* 4 (2013): 67–72; Dominique Voynet, Afterword to Caillé and Fourel (eds), *Sortir du capitalisme*, pp. 207–09; Éric Fottorino, 'Duflot sur la planète Gorz' (24 September 2011) (available at: https://bit.ly/3RwG06a; last accessed: 25 July 2022).

49 Michel Bosquet, 'Les démons de l'expansion', *Le Nouvel Observateur* ('La Dernière Chance de la Terre') (June–July 1972).

the opinion of the American biologist and ecologist Barry Commoner, author of *The Closing Circle. Nature, Man and Technology* (1971), it was clear to Bosquet that it was the very logic of capitalist development, which had reached a paroxysm with the industrial age, that was responsible for the looming ecological disaster. As he saw it, questioning that logic presupposed 'revis[ing] or abandon[ing] a *consumption model* that is based on an artificial stimulation of needs, obsolescence, and an accelerated turnover of goods.'[50] He particularly advocated measures to avert waste and promote recycling.

In his eyes, the reduction of material affluence that was emerging as an imperative in the West had the potential virtue that it could actually make for a better life: 'While consuming and working *less* we can live *better*, though differently.'[51] This change of direction ought to be accompanied by a huge reduction in working hours and a minimum guaranteed income unconnected to employment:

> Above all we could be doing a lot less work, since the much more durable products would be made in much smaller quantities. The productivity race, brutalizing, maddening toil, the purgatory of working on high-speed assembly lines, would no longer be necessary. A twenty-hour working week would be possible and what Mansholt calls 'intellectual and cultural flowering' of the individual could and even should become a top priority when the production of superfluous fast-wearing goods is a thing of the past. [...] Sicco Mansholt speaks elsewhere of 'guaranteed subsistence for all'; and it is only logical in the context of these changes that the right to an income should cease to be tied to the holding down of a job.[52]

Should we see this passage as an outburst of utopianism prompted, in the event, by desires on Mansholt's part that were as stunning as they were unrealizable in the short term? Bosquet is aware that the prospect he is outlining is one of a '*Communist* programme' since, he writes in the same piece, 'a capitalism without the quest for maximum profit is a contradiction in terms' and 'a capitalism without growth is an economy in crisis, with its

---

50 Gorz, *Ecology as Politics*, p. 132.

51 Gorz, *Ecology as Politics*, p. 78.

52 Bosquet, *Capitalism in Crisis and Everyday Life*, pp. 174–5.

unemployed millions and chain-reaction bankruptcies.'[53] This was why, as his friend Gintis would explain in his comment on the cover of *Ecology as Politics*, his ecological realism, supported by scientifically demonstrable vital necessities, 'becomes visionary and the visionary [becomes] the rational architect of the future.'[54] In the moment of ecological crisis, moving beyond capitalism remains a pressing need.

Not that the system didn't have resources with which to react. But though it was entirely capable of incorporating ecological constraints, it would do so solely for its own profit and to maintain, if not indeed reinforce, its domination of nature and society.[55] Taking account of these constraints led to an unavoidable problem, but offered capitalism two solutions.

The inevitable effect was to inhibit growth by adversely affecting production costs and the rate of profit, with the catastrophic social consequences already referred to—the energy crisis, at its height in 1974, had this kind of impact. Authoritarian and anti-social measures aimed at enforcing austerity were to be feared at such times. But when it came to the solutions—as envisaged by The Club of Rome—this acknowledgement of crisis would give rise to what would come to be called *green capitalism*, which Bosquet analysed as monopolistic companies acquiring a stranglehold on the new activities of combatting pollution and recycling, which, as he foresaw, would lead, in an unchanged productivist orientation, to a new cycle of accumulation 'based on the capitalist takeover of Nature itself: the appropriation by capital of all the factors and conditions supporting life on the planet. Everything will be sewn up: the rule of profit will invade the last enclaves of nature [. . .].'[56]

The other 'ecological' answer to environmental constraints would consist in 'offshoring' harmful industries to Third World countries, while extending the grip of capital in the rich ones—in this case to areas of life where *intangible production* involving less pollution, was possible, such as in the fields of health, sex, culture, leisure and information, with all the

53 Bosquet, *Capitalism in Crisis and Everyday Life*, p. 175 (translation modified).

54 Herbert Gintis, back cover of *Ecology as Politics*.

55 André Gorz, 'Introduction: Two Kinds of Ecology' in *Ecology as Politics*, pp. 3–9. Originally published as Michel Bosquet, 'Partage ou crève!' [Share or die!], *Le Sauvage* 12 (April 1974): 10–12.

56 Bosquet, *Capitalism in Crisis and Everyday Life*, p. 186.

dangers of a drift into the destruction of freedom that such an extension would imply.[57] The dangers in question were that individuals would lose their autonomy and be submerged in an exclusively 'market' society.

What Nuclear Peril?

The generation of electricity by nuclear power, developed mainly by the US and France in the 1970s, was a product of political and economic decisions that had not been subject to democratic debate. Bosquet was among the ecologists who denounced the strategic choice that aimed to prevent the rise of 'alternative', clean energy sources, such as solar, geothermal or wind power. He was aware of the potentialities of solar heating as early as the 1950s, while he was also concerned at that point to enquire into the dangers of ionizing rays.[58]

With anti-nuclear protests having proliferated across France over the previous five years, Gorz marched in 1975 against a planned power station at Courceroy near Nogent-sur-Seine, 50 miles upstream from Paris. He became friends with the local opponents: Claude Aucouturier, whom he put in contact with Lalonde and helped to write documents for the press and for members of the National Assembly, and the potter Jean Tessier who was prosecuted for denouncing 'the EDF [Électricité de France] state', Gorz appearing as a witness at his trial in 1982. With the backing of les Amis de la Terre, who brought support from Paris, a 10,000 strong march was organized on 26 June 1977. At La Mutualité in Paris, Gorz spoke at a support rally. His involvement in this was personal. He and Dorine were actually in the process of having the ecological house of their dreams built at Nogent. It was completed in 1981 and they made it their weekend country home and even lived there for a while, but the building of the power station, begun in the

---

57 Gorz, *Ecology as Politics*, pp. 77–91. Originally published as Michel Bosquet, 'Le grand complot écosfasciste', *Le Sauvage* 4–5 (July–August 1973): 76–84. See also 'Le socialisme tout de suite', *Le Sauvage* 10 (February 1974): 19.

58 See Michel Bosquet, 'Le XXe siècle découvre le soleil. Au premier congrès mondial de l'héliotechnique 1,000 savants de 35 pays ont parlé d'énergie solaire', *Gazette littéraire* (supplement to the *Gazette de Lausanne*) (26 November 1955); 'Nouvelles doses de tolérance et effets biologiques des radiations ionisantes', *Industries atomiques* (Geneva) 1 (6) (May 1957): 47–50; 'Du soleil dans la maison', *Le Nouvel Observateur* (26 March 1973).

same year without any great resistance from the local population, eventually drove them away three years later. At that point they moved finally to another village in the Aube département. The failure of this battle was the more bitter for them in that the mayor of Courceroy and the local abbot, influential NIMBY–style protestors, had managed to have the local chateau made a listed building, thus shifting the site of the power station directly opposite their home!

In terms of nuclear power, Bosquet acquired a great deal of technical and political knowledge, which fed into his articles for *Le Nouvel Observateur*, *Le Sauvage* and a highly successful number of the consumer magazine *Que choisir?* (the French equivalent of *Which?* Magazine). *La Gueule ouverte*, which reviewed almost all his books, interviewed him in July 1977 on the eve of the major mobilization against the Superphénix fast-breeder reactor project at Creys-Malville. He enjoyed sustained personal contacts with scientists and trade unionists like Michel Rolant, the CFDT's officer for energy matters, Bernard Laponche, secretary of the CFDT branch at the Atomic Energy Commission, Dominique Pignon, a physicist at the CNRS whom he published in *Les Temps modernes*, and Louis Puiseux, a former economist at EDF and the author of *La Babel nucléaire* (Paris: Gallimard, 1977). This group of experts, coordinated in late 1975 by the GSIEN (Groupement des scientifiques pour l'information sur l'énergie nucléaire; Group of Scientists for Information on Nuclear Energy), which, with the aid of Amis de la Terre, published the *Gazette nucléaire*, highlighted the technical and economic problems that were covered up and left unre-solved: the reliability of nuclear installations and hence the assessment of the real risks of accident, the health effects of low doses of radiation, the storage of radioactive waste, the country's dependency on others for supplies of ura-nium and a full accounting of costs (not to mention de-commissioning costs), etc.

However, the main question, which raised the most vehement opposi-tion on the part of ecologists—and of a large part of the Extreme Left—was a *political* one. Alain Touraine, who had been critical of the ascendancy of technocracy since 1968, stressed this point in his participant-observation study *La Prophétie antinucléaire* (1980). Bosquet, the media spokesperson for this rebellion, contended that the existence of nuclear power stations, 'irrevocably prescribes a particular kind of society, to the exclusion of all others.'[59] Added to this was the denial of democratic transparency. In that regard, France and the Soviet Union were not dissimilar: 'The technocratic state in France or in the USSR is more afraid of people's fear of nuclear risk than of the risk itself. Hence it surrounds everything relating to atomic power with secrecy and reassuring lies.'[60] Moreover, being necessarily associated with draconian security measures, the technology requires an extreme centralization of energy production facilities, invested with 'extensive powers of control, surveillance and regulation.'[61]

This is the absolute opposite of solar or wind power which can be produced locally and under a self-management regime.[62] For Bosquet and the anti-nuclear campaigners, from the Amis de la Terre through the CFDT trade union federation to the Ligue Communiste Révolutionnaire, we have a choice between a centralized, technocratized surveillance society—the society of 'techno-fascist central regulation'—and a society promoting freedom through self-management at the grass roots—the society of 'convivial self-management'.[63]

The New Social Movements: Castoriadis—a Missed Encounter

Ecologists and anti-nuclear campaigners were not the only embodiments of the new social movements forming on ground deserted by the political parties and trade unions. The feminist, anti-militarist, regionalist and peasant movements (the gay movement came later) shook up the practices of machine politics and disrupted class barriers in the same way as the ecologists did. The Italian autonomists who followed Félix Guattari saw all this as a 'transversality' of struggles. Not forgetting immigrants, who were fighting to acquire rights of residence, against racism and for decent housing, to whom Gorz paid a great deal of attention. In the spring of 1971, at Matta's

---

59 André Gorz, 'From Nuclear Electricity to Electric Fascism' in *Ecology as Politics*, p. 102. Original French publication in *Le Sauvage* 20 (April 1975): 68–73.

60 André Gorz, 'Plus dangereux que Tchernobyl: La Hague', *Le Nouvel Observateur* (9 May 1986).

61 Gorz, *Ecology as Politics*, p. 109.

62 Dominique Allan Michaud, *L'Avenir de la société alternative. Les idées 1968–1990* (Paris: L'Harmattan, 1989).

63 These expressions occur in Gorz, *Ecology as Politics*, pp. 40–1.

house in Tarquinia in central Italy, he took part in an activist seminar on immigrant workers led by Charles Bettelheim.[64]

When he contributed in 1977 to a forum/debate on social experiments organized by *Le Nouvel Observateur* and the *autogestionnaire* magazine *Faire*, in which CFDT leaders (Jacques Delors and Pierre Rosanvallon), Rocardians (Michel Rocard, Alain Touraine and Patrick Viveret) and Illichian ecologists (Ivan Illich, Brice Lalonde and Freimut Duve) took part, he became convinced that the time was ripe to reject system-based thinking, ideas of political revolution and appeals to state action.[65] Societies do not unmake and remake themselves from the top down. New spaces of individual and collective freedom are possible only thanks to the abundance of autonomous initiatives with specific aims and running counter to the overarching logics of the political parties: politics—true politics—was no longer in politics.[66] 'The only way of really doing politics today is to concern oneself, as the ecologist movements do, with the *preconditions* for any true political activity.'[67]

During the 1970s, Gorz and Cornelius Castoriadis converged on several points. Both set themselves up as theorists of autonomy, backed the new social movements, supported the demands of the soldiers' movements, were fellow-travellers of the CFDT and, at the philosophical level, taunted structuralism for its hollow phrases, while detesting the so-called *nouvelle philosophie* of Bernard-Henri Lévy and friends (on this last subject, Gorz tried to elicit a contribution from Marcuse for *Le Nouvel Observateur* in late 1978,[68]

---

64 See André Gorz, 'Colloque de Tarquinia. Avant-propos', *Partisans* 61 (September–October 1971): 84–7; 'Immigrant Labour', *New Left Review* 61 (May–June 1970): 28–31; Michel Bosquet, 'À quoi servent les immigrés?', *Le Nouvel Observateur* (16 April 1973) etc.

65 Michel Bosquet, 'Les nouveaux mouvements sociaux. La stratégie de la guérilla', *Le Nouvel Observateur* (12 September 1977).

66 André Gorz, 'La politique n'est plus dans la politique', *Le Nouvel Observateur* (8 May 1978).

67 André Gorz and François Châtelet, 'Et si la politique redécouvrait la morale . . .'. See also the discussion of the German Greens: André Gorz, 'Wir können mehr machen mit weniger', *Konkret* (Hamburg) 16 (1980): 72.

68 See the letter in English of 14 December 1978 from André Gorz to Herbert Marcuse (HM) and the latter's reply in English of 20 December 1978 (GRZ), in which he declined to intervene, arguing that, 'to slaughter them (as these guys deserve) would mean that I have to read their stuff'; [. . .] this would be more than my stomach could take.'

before Pierre Vidal-Naquet and Castoriadis responded in its columns six months later).

However, because of their dissimilar political backgrounds, which separated their parallel itineraries for many years and underlay the unnecessary polemic they conducted in *Le Nouvel Observateur* over Sartre's past (see above, p. 66), the two men moved in different intellectual circles and did not associate with one another. And indeed neither made any effort to assess the other's emancipatory project against his own.[69] This is why Gorz undervalued—though he was not unaware of it—Castoriadis's brilliant contribution, which grounds social praxis and autonomy in *The Imaginary Institution of Society* [1975]). In so doing, he missed the opportunity to strengthen his own analysis of the preconditions for any 'instituted politics' by drawing on Castoriadis's analysis—ultimately not far removed from his own—of 'instituting processes'.

He preferred to save his admiration for Touraine, 'the prophet of the new social movements', who in *The Voice and the Eye: An Analysis of Social Movements* [1978]), proclaimed an end to the centrality of the workers' struggle so as to provide a better description of society 'producing itself' through the conflicts in which it is itself at stake.[70] And, having connections at Éditions Galilée, Gorz had a collection of Touraine's articles   published there under the title *Mort d'une gauche* [Death of a Left] (1979).

It was out of this particular range of issues that Gorz's next book would come.

---

69 Though this was done by Timothée Duverger, 'Écologie et autogestion dans les années 1970. Discours croisés d'André Gorz et de Cornelius Castoriadis', *Écologie et politique* 46 (2013): 139–48.

70 Michel Bosquet, 'Alain Touraine: la révolution culturelle que nous vivons', *Le Nouvel Observateur* (8 January 1979); reprinted in Fourel (ed.), *André Gorz en personne*, pp. 100–18.

PART FOUR

Freeing Up Time
in the Age of the Dual Society

1980s–1990s: Toyotism and the Precariat

'Work has always been a war waged against oneself'
Raoul Vaneigem, *Nous qui désirons sans fin*, p. 123.

'It is no longer a question of winning power as a worker,
but of winning the power no longer to function as a worker.'
André Gorz, *Farewell to the Working Class*, p. 67.

CHAPTER THIRTEEN

Farewells to the Working Class

In 1980, André Gorz made waves within Marxism and the Left with an explosive tract of an essay. The French title and subtitle sum up its provocative central ideas: *Adieux au prolétariat. Au-delà du socialisme* [Farewells to the proletariat: Beyond socialism].[1] The subtitle is intended as an allusion to the Communist prophecy of the *Grundrisse*, whereas the farewells are not meant in any way sarcastically and 'have a humorous side to them.'[2] An augmented version of the first French edition came out a year later in May 1981. It was widely read: some 20,000 copies were sold. In 1983, Gorz reiterated his arguments, substantiating them further, in his *Chemins du paradis* [Paths to paradise], subtitled *L'agonie du capital* [The death throes of capital]. The two books came at a point when the French Left was first in turmoil over its disunity, then grappling with the challenges of power. They had no immediately political aim, but claimed to offer new perspectives for the Left.

Farewell to the Working Class (as the book is known in English) marked a break with the analyses and hopes that Gorz had expressed in *La Morale de l'histoire* and *Strategy for Labor*. The Promethean myth of the revolutionary proletariat was abandoned, in a scathing *ad hoc* attack on the young Marx, who was described as assigning a historic mission to the Proletariat and investing it with Hegel's Spirit [*Geist*]. This had led to a 'Marxist religion of the proletariat', which was debunked and denounced by Gorz in terms taken from Rudolf Bahro, the Communist critic of the GDR, whose bestseller *The Alternative in Eastern Europe* [1977] Gorz (like Marcuse) had praised.[3] In doing so, Gorz was adding his own contribution to the critique of the 'religious Unconscious of Marxism', which had been begun by

---

1 The English translation is published as *Farewell to the Working Class: An Essay on Post-industrial Socialism*. On the 'provocative' aspect of the work, see Ariovaldo Santos, 'Gorz e o inquietante adeus ao proletariado' in Josué Pereira da Silva and Iram Jácome Rodrigues (eds), *André Gorz e seus críticos* (São Paulo: Annablume, 2006), pp. 127–39.

2 *Abschied vom Proletariat?*, p. 80 (Gorz).

3 See André Gorz, 'Les protestants du marxisme', *Le Nouvel Observateur* (7 May 1979).

Mathilde Niel in her pioneering *Psychanalyse du marxisme* (1967) and which would be methodically pursued by the ex-Guevarist Régis Debray in his *Critique of Political Reason* [1987].

However, as he did this, Gorz was espousing a non-determinist position he had already adopted in *La Morale de l'histoire* and which, at the time, had not prevented him from advancing the teleological idea of a socialism consciously desired and carried forward by the proletariat in struggle. That very idea was now being rejected. On the other hand, far from marking a turning point, *Farewell to the Working Class* extended and deepened the post-'68 thinking that had caused him to join the cause of the political ecology movement, to back the new social movements and to firm up his 'critique of the division of labour'. All things considered, *Farewell to the Working Class* also served as the mould for his later writings.

The Extreme Left were unhappy with the book (beginning with Gorz's former supporters Badiou and Lipietz), because it presented a de-vitalized image of the proletariat—and also because it rounded not only on dogmatic Marxism but on Marx himself. One-sided in its presentation of a Marx in Hegelian garb, the attack was aimed at his philosophy of history, not at all at his critique of capital. For Gorz, that critique remained irreplaceable:[4] he would continue to draw on it constantly. He would thus admit that his 'relationship with Marx had been ambivalent from the beginning':

> One may find in his writings—if one takes them literally—a divin-
> ization of history and the proletariat which Leninism–Stalinism–
> Maoism has turned into religious dogma. And one also finds in
> him libertarian features and stunning phenomenological analyses
> in which he uses the concepts he has teased out as instruments for
> a quasi-existentialist critique. Marx both falls short of and passes
> beyond Marxism.[5]

The Impossible Appropriation of Work

During the decade that was ending, which had seen the crisis triggered in the West by the oil shock of 1973, capitalism undertook restructurings that profoundly modified the economic and social landscape. It was on the basis of these changes, which Gorz identified as structural, that he quite naturally

---

4 André Gorz, Preface to *Adieux au proletariat* (Paris: Seuil, 1981), p. 23 n.

5 Gorz, 'La vie, la nature, la technique', p. 25.

reoriented his emancipatory project. The important developments that pre-yed on his mind were, at the technological level, *the spread of automation*, at times in the form of robotization (e.g. at Toyota), *the emergence of information technology*, and, with regard to the labour process, *a greater division of labour*. These three phenomena produced appreciable social consequences, among which Gorz counted *the de-skilling of labour* and *long-term unemployment*.

Having already raised the problem in his post-'68 writings,[6] Gorz noted that contemporary capitalism had not eliminated unskilled work and made way for technical workers capable of an overall grasp of the production process and hence of self-management. In fact, he wrote 'exactly the opposite has occurred. Automation and computerization have eliminated most skills and possibilities for initiative' and are de-skilling what remains of the 'labour force (blue and white collar).'[7] Computerization and the stultifying jobs of coding and card-punching provided a sad example of this. If we add that the production process was increasingly segmented by the division of labour, which, having once been technical and social within businesses, had become territorialized through subsidiaries and subcontracting, we can see that it had increased in 'opacity' and that we need to speak here, following Marx, of a system governed by a 'collective capitalist' wielding elusive, impersonal power.

In the beginning, as Marglin reminded us, the subdivision of tasks had domination as its chief aim. Once established, however, it led to the mechanization, automation and, irreversibly, the fragmentation of production into activities involving specialist knowledge which had value only in combination.[8] More than ever, 'workers' control' over production proved to be impossible; as happened with the Italian Council movement and with the workers at Lip, it could only degenerate into mere management of the workforce. It was necessary to come to terms with the fact that worker power collapsed as capitalism complexified through the incorporation of knowledge into (automatic and cybernetic) machines and through the division of labour (both micro- and macro-economic).

---

6 See Gorz, 'The Tyranny of the Factory', pp. 56–7. (See above, chapter 10). The English translation uses the term 'dequalification' rather than 'de-skilling'. [Trans.]

7 Gorz, *Farewell to the Working Class*, p. 28.

8 Gorz, *Critique of Economic Reason*, pp. 54–5.

In these conditions, self-criticism was required: ultimately, Gorz admitted, the hypothesis of a capitalism that had reached its highest stage, with the figure of the multi-skilled worker controlling the whole of production, was merely an 'anarcho-syndicalist' illusion cherished by Marx in the *Grundrisse* and, subsequently, by the theorists of the new working class, with whom he acknowledged aligning himself in the mid-1960s.[9] The capacities of the worker continued to be hobbled by work that was fragmented, nondescript and routine. The implications of this finding are enormous: if, in a complex system of this kind, 'the class that collectively is responsible for developing and operating the totality of the productive forces is unable to appropriate or subordinate this totality to its own ends,' if it has become 'structurally incapable of acquiring mastery of production and society',[10] then not only is worker self-management impossible, but *the working class is no longer the subject of social transformation* and there is no longer much to be hoped for from the workplace struggle. This is confirmed by actual behaviour: the technicians are caught up in managerial strategies of 'personal investment' and unskilled workers recognize themselves neither in work 'of no quality' nor as members of the working class.

> The inversion of the Marxist concept of the proletariat is thus total. Not only does the new post-industrial proletariat not find any source of power in socialized labour: all it finds there is the reality of apparatus power and its own impotence. Not only is it no longer the possible subjective agent of socialized productive labour: instead, it defines its own subjectivity through the refusal of socialized labour and the negation of work perceived itself as a negation [...].[11]

What then was this new subject that had surreptitiously replaced the vanishing figure of the proletariat?

The Non-class of Post-industrial Proletarians

The changes to the nature of work described above, combined with the economic crisis, left their mark by putting an end to full employment, which Gorz considered an irremediable situation, and producing an explosion of

9 Gorz, *Farewell to the Working Class*, pp. 27 and 71n4.
10 Gorz, 'Les adieux d'André Gorz au prolétariat', interview by Contat and George.
11 Gorz, *Farewell to the Working Class*, pp. 71–2.

unemployment which, in France, quintupled after 1974 (reaching 1.6 million in 1981, 6.9 per cent of the working population).[12] This development was part of the more general context of the decline of industry and industrial jobs. The numbers of blue-collar workers, which reached their high point in 1974, fell greatly, contrasting with the growth of the tertiary sector. Although contested by a Left in search of reassurance, the result was patent: the working class was crumbling—and its image with it.

That image had been idealized in the past. It now appeared that the aura that had surrounded 'the workers' in 1968 had been shaped by a revolutionary ideal and not in any way by the desire to remain or become workers.[13] The rejection of work, at large among the generation of '68, was at the same time a rejection of the worker's condition; the same was true of the movement out of the cities on the part of ecologists and those pursuing alternative lifestyles. The *établi* movement—in which largely middle-class militants took up industrial work for the purpose of raising political consciousness among the working class—had thus been a mere epiphenomenon running against the general trend. Much more tangible now was the disappearance of a sense of belonging to the 'working class': this affected 'all the supernumeraries of present-day social production' who were 'potentially or actually unemployed'[14] (occasional, auxiliary, temporary or agency workers and part-time employees), for whom work was losing its meaning, no longer seemed to be their chief source of identity and was simply 'becoming an expedient'.[15]

This host of individuals, the product of the break-up of an industrial society based on work and its idealization, could no longer be defined by their position in production. It formed a sociologically heteroclite 'non-class', whose members were nonetheless united by aspirations to a better life which they knew to be unachievable through employment and the income it afforded them. To the question, 'Would you prefer a wage rise or more free time?', 50 per cent of people surveyed in France who expressed

---

12 Almost 2 million unemployed—9 per cent by the way unemployment was calculated at the time.

13 See Jean-Pierre Le Goff, *Mai 68. L'héritage impossible* (Paris: La Découverte, 1998), chapter 13.

14 Gorz, *Farewell to the Working Class*, p. 68.

15 André Gorz, 'Le travail est devenu un expédient', interview by Philippe Gavi, *Libération* (28 April 1980).

an opinion opted in 1973 for 'free time', the figure rising to 57 per cent in 1977 and again in 1983 (88 per cent of German employees responded 'more free time' in 1979). The practice of job sharing in the US and Scandinavia— or the division of work within couples so as to have increased free time— ran in this same direction. The 'cultural crisis of work-based society', triggered as part of May '68, coincided with a real crisis for that society in economic and technical terms.[16]

If work was already dwindling away, then, as the state of the factories and people's feelings about it suggested, the major political issue that emerged—and that would definitively grab Gorz's attention—related to the practical impact of that dwindling which, he warned, could either be anti-social and oppressive or socially controlled and liberating.[17]

For the moment, at a theoretical level, a new horizon of expectation was emerging from the complexification of the economy and the reduction of 'necessary labour'. The very possibility of *socialism*, in the genuine sense of the control of power by the workers, became chimerical and its principle—'to each according to his work'—became iniquitous (hence the subtitle of the French original of *Farewell to the Working Class*, which trans-lates as 'Beyond Socialism'). The only thing that remained on the horizon was the goal of *Communism* which is, at bottom, the abolition of the domi-nation of work. The autonomist Negri, who dissected Marx's *Grundrisse* in *Marx Beyond Marx* [1979], and the dissident Communist Bahro (author of *The Alternative in Eastern Europe*) were invoked by Gorz to support this perspective,[18] as later the neo-Marxist Moishe Postone, who had also revisited Marx's prophetic text, would be.[19] As part of this process, incomes would come to be unhooked from work, which was in decline, and related to needs. But the word 'Communism' itself was also swept away, discredited by the disastrous experiences of the countries that had laid claim to the term. It no longer had any attraction for anyone, which was why Gorz would avoid putting it on the masthead of his programme—though he never renounced the concept.

---

16 André Gorz, 'Automation et crise de la société du travail', *Infordoc* 404 (February 1984): 17.

17 Gorz, *Farewell to the Working Class*, p. 8.

18 Gorz, *Farewell to the Working Class*, pp. 87–8.

19 Gorz, *Ecologica*, p. 19, n 10.

Among the Socialists, whether Mitterrandists (Max Gallo, Régis Debray) or Chevènementists (Jean-Pierre Chevènement himself) and among the Communists, including Eurocommunists (Christine Buci-Glucksmann), all of them favouring statist, productivist solutions, the post-industrial views of *Farewell to the Working Class* caused an outcry. By contrast, within the PSU, there were contrasting reactions. *Tribune socialiste* gave Gorz a rough ride, before Denis Clerc changed the approach and even invited him to the PSU's 'summer university' at La Roche-sur-Yon on 28 July 1980. The reaction was similar within the CFDT. Edmond Maire, the architect of the union's reformist turn towards 'responsible negotiations' (the first step on a path to the trade unions 'adapting' to capitalism, as Maire explicitly advocated), launched a scathing attack on Gorz's analyses of trade unionism's inability to reshape society.[20] Above and beyond the union's internal divergences, that position reflected a sense of rejection largely being pushed among the grassroots members. Other CFDT figures didn't see things the same way: Jacques Julliard, the co-author with Maire of a book on the CFDT in 1975, hailed Gorz's iconoclastic boldness and his sociological realism;[21] the national secretary Michel Rolant, a Marxist-inclined former agricultural worker who had followed Gorz's ideas over many years, took him along to a meeting of the union's Executive Committee even though he, with the other old crypto-Gorzians, Declercq and Descamps, were in a minority opposing Maire's line.

The Left, Power and the Place of Politics

Farewell to the Working Class was not an isolated outpouring from the margins of social thought. At that same moment, Alain Touraine, who displayed his support for Michel Rocard with a regular column in Claude Perdriel's *Le Matin*, published *L'Après-socialisme* (1980), an equally explosive book that called on the Socialist Party not to damage society's dynamism by *dirigiste* state policy. In the same heretical vein, Jacques Delors and friends promoted the idea of shorter working hours both as a way of reducing unemployment and as part of a new art of living in their *Révolution du temps choisi* of 1980.

---

20 Edmond Maire, 'Le mouvement ouvrier face aux idéologies de crise', *Le Monde* (21–22 August 1980).
21 Jacques Julliard, 'L'utopie au purgatoire?', *Le Nouvel Observateur* (10 March 1980).

After François Mitterrand's accession to power in May 1981, this Rocardian, CFDT strain of feeling provided a number of ministers (Michel Rocard, Jacques Delors, Jean Auroux) and advisers (Jacques Attali) and found its way into ministerial cabinets (Martine Aubry etc.). Ecology and anti-nuclear campaigners also got a look-in, with the appointement at the French Energy Agency (AFME) of Michel Rolant and Bernard Laponche from the CFDT. The former, an unconditional admirer of Gorz who was to become his very close friend, would invite him regularly to round table discussions on key social issues. Directing its activity towards energy saving, the AFME put a spoke in the wheels of the supply-focused policies of EDF, before the agency's funding was massively cut in 1985 during the mid-eighties oil glut.

Contrary to those who were happy to haunt the corridors of power, Gorz—like Touraine and Ellul—remained circumspect with regard to government and the role of politics. The day after their appointment, he met two ministers in the Mauroy cabinet,[22] and realized there was not much to be hoped for from the victory of the Left.[23] Less than a year afterwards, before the socialists took their free-market turn, he was writing with regret of the confiscation of the political debate by the 'best brains' of the Socialist party, who had moved into power without realizing 'that Keynesian reforms, essentially quantitative and slow to produce their effects, would have to be accompanied by qualitative reforms which, without delay, would transform life, social relations and the perception of the future in tangible areas.'[24] And he went on to list some simple measures that would be easy to apply, such as Jacques Delors's proposition on the free self-determination of working hours (though, as Delors saw it, with a reduction in pay),[25] the establishment of quality standards for common products, and energy-saving measures in the building sector.

---

22 Jacques Delors and Michel Rocard, the two ministers Gorz knew best, and the Minister of Free Time André Henry stated (in 2014) that they had no memory of such a meeting.

23 Gorz, *Letter to D.*, p. 102.

24 Michel Bosquet, 'Le PS n'existe plus', *Le Nouvel Observateur* (6 February 1982). This article appears under the heading 'Opinion'.

25 On the divergences between Gorz and Delors's supporters who advocated a voluntary, individual reduction in working hours, see Jean-Baptiste de Foucauld, 'Gorz et le temps choisi, un débat inachevé' in Fourel (ed.), *André Gorz. Un penseur pour le XXIe siècle*, pp. 147–62.

For Gorz, politics was rarely his 'main preoccupation. What comes first is the question: what is the potential for liberation contained in present developments? How does the dominant social order repress that liberation which, at the same time, it makes possible?'[26] His lack of interest in—and even his suspicion of—politics was longstanding. In his youth, he had even been inclined to think that 'each party tends demagogically towards power.'[27] He was, above all, convinced that the seizure of state power was illusory so long as the 'machinery of domination remains intact':[28] the state, like the economy, was a 'machine' of that kind, as the Americans put it,[29] conferring 'functional powers' on 'those holding positions within it, whatever the nature of their abilities or political options.'[30] If, at the economic level, power was simply 'a system of relationships, a structure'[31] without a subject, 'the same situation is true of the mechanisms of political power. They are called upon to exercise power over people without allowing anyone in particular to exercise it in a personal sense. The state might be defined as a mechanism of power to which every citizen is subordinated and which, at the same time, denies personal power to everyone.'[32]

Not that the state should be abolished, but its sway should be more limited, while recognizing that it is the guarantor of law, that is to say, of the objectified rules that keep society from dictatorship or communitarian fusion. It is at this level that the political sphere recovers a useful function which is to 'delimit, orient and codify the actions of government, to designate the ends and means they should use, and to ensure that they do not stray from their mission. Any confusion between politics and power (in the sense of the right to run the state), signifies the death of politics.'[33]

Gorz spent a long time trying to determine what the place of politics was. In that quest he was influenced first by Touraine, then by the American

---

26 André Gorz, 'La plus grande liberté possible' (debate with Peter Glotz and Tilman Fichter), *Les Temps modernes* 483 (October 1986): 66.

27 Gérard Horst, 'Opinions. Dessous de grève'.

28 Gorz, *Farewell to the Working Class*, p. 63.

29 Gorz, *Farewell to the Working Class*, pp. 56–7.

30 Gorz, *Farewell to the Working Class*, p. 63.

31 Gorz, *Farewell to the Working Class*, p. 52.

32 Gorz, *Farewell to the Working Class*, p. 57.

33 Gorz, *Farewell to the Working Class*, p. 117.

philosopher and political scientist Dick Howard, whom he had known as a student in France in 1966 and with whom he corresponded over several decades. Embodied in the institutional instruments of power, deliberation and decision-making, politics, Gorz became convinced, was 'the site of tension and always conflictual mediation between, on the one hand, the enlargement of the sphere of autonomy impelled by the demands of the movement flowing through civil society and, on the other, the state-regulated necessities arising from the workings of society as a material system.'[34] And, in a 1992 article dedicated to Howard, after he had read his recent book *Defining the Political*, 'Any approach tending to abolish the tension between these two poles is a negation of both politics and modernity.'[35] The essential thing is 'upholding the specific autonomies of civil society, political society and the state,' in order that there can be 'a sphere in which autonomous individuals may freely cooperate for their own ends.'[36] Without this, individuals would be prevented from differentiating themselves from the community and obliged to internalize the order imposed by it for the necessary social tasks to be accomplished.

As we can see, Gorz was not arguing for the Saint-Simonian, Marxian utopia that consisted in suppressing politics with an eye to creating intelligibility of relations between individuals: in his view, the reign of reason which that suppression would supposedly usher in would, on the contrary, mean the inhibition of the individual, who would be turned into a 'universal individual, stripped of all individual interests, attachments and tastes.'[37]

Freedom, Pacifism and Europe

Since the anti-imperialist struggles that spread rapidly across the world in the 1960s, Gorz had barely had a chance to focus his thinking on international political events. However, the appearance of a powerful peace movement in Europe—and especially in West Germany—in the early 1980s would prompt him to take up a position.[38]

---

34 Gorz, *Farewell to the Working Class*, pp. 116–7.

35 Gorz, *Ecologica*, p. 48.

36 Gorz, *Farewell to the Working Class*, pp. 65, 111.

37 Gorz, *Critique of Economic Reason*, p. 28.

38 See Michel Bosquet, 'Plutôt rouge que mort', *Le Nouvel Observateur* (21 November 1981).

The peace movement, which was very much bound up with *die Grünen* [the Greens], who advocated alternative ways of life to the consumerist, pro-ductivist conformism of the West, arose to counter the military build-up by the two blocs that put German security in peril, caught as the country was between the rival forces.[39] In particular, it was the American desire to base missiles on West German soil to counterbalance the renewal of the Soviet Union's arsenal that drove hundreds of thousands of protesters on to the streets. Gorz conceded that this was an expression of revolt against a military-industrial megamachine which imposed its technocratic order on society using state power (he recollected that Eisenhower, in his visionary speech of 16 April 1953, had been the first to characterize the danger of the 'military-industrial complex'). That struggle was, however, depoliticized because it was directed against American domination alone. What went with it was the 'Finlandization' of West Germany which was implied, in his view, by the *Ostpolitik* that involved going easy on the Soviet Union so as to initiate *détente*, conceived as the precondition for a reunification of the country in a remote future.[40] In an interview granted to the weekly magazine *Der Spiegel*, Gorz created a scandal in West Germany by arguing that this asymmetric behaviour, further accentuated by the lukewarm reaction of the Germans to the state of emergency declared in Poland in December 1981, could be explained by the fact that 'the cultural reference to freedom is absent from German history'.[41]

The German reaction was scathing, surprising Gorz because it came also from people with whom he was closely allied, such as Rudolf Bahro, whose book *The Alternative in Eastern Europe* he had greatly admired. Gorz had been the only French member of the International Committee, led by Miliband and Anderson, which in January 1979 had awarded the Isaac Deutscher Prize to that book (in the GDR, Bahro had been imprisoned for writing it). After being released and expatriated to West Germany, Bahro had gone to London on 3 March 1980 to receive his award. It is possible he met Gorz on that occasion. At any rate, it was not long afterwards, on 27

---

39 See *Hérodote* 28 ('Géopolitiques allemandes') (January–March 1983).

40 André Gorz, 'Quelle paix? Quelle Europe?', *Lettre internationale* 7 (September 1985): 11–16. Published in German in *Merkur. Deutsche Zeitschrift für europäisches Denken* 446 (April 1986).

41 André Gorz, 'Respekt für ein solches Verhalten?' (interview), *Der Spiegel* 4 (25 January 1982).

March, that he eagerly invited his 'dear comrade Gorz' to the May 1980 Socialist Conference at Kassel,[42] then to the second at Marburg in February 1981.[43] He took for granted their ideological affinity in ecological matters.

That was not to reckon with the divergences produced by Gorz's anti-pacifist tirade. Bahro replied in no uncertain terms in the same issue of *Der Spiegel*; he thought he saw the roots of Gorz's admonitions lying in a French chauvinism that was as eccentric as it was lamentable, since it was expressed by a 'paper Frenchman'.[44] Gorz replied in *TAZ*, the West Berlin–based alternative daily, playing down their divergences.[45] The two ecolo-Marxists managed not to fall out over this and Bahro, who continued an even-tempered correspondence with Gorz, was still able to express his opinions on these questions in *Le Nouvel Observateur*. Lastly, thanks to the interview arranged for him by his friend the political scientist Claus Leggewie (whom he had known as a student in Paris in 1973), Gorz had an opportunity to clarify his positions further, ahead of the Peace Congress that took place in Frankfurt in July 1982, assuring his interlocutor that his arguments were not based on 'any national identity'.[46]

Gorz thus made renewed contact with German culture and its intellectuals, although, for the moment, that also meant further underscoring his Germanophobia. As for his praising of the anti-totalitarian ideology cultivated in France by Glucksmann, Castoriadis and Morin (aided at *Le Nouvel Observateur* by Julliard and at *Les Temps modernes* by Pierre Rigoulot and André Granou), that stance did not involve any sort of obsession with an alleged Soviet military peril.

Endgame at Le Nouvel Observateur and Les Temps modernes

When Michel Delorme set up the Galilée publishing house in 1973, Gorz found himself entrusted with the editorship of a collection known by the

42 Rudolf Bahro to André Gorz, 27 March 1980 (GRZ). Gorz undoubtedly declined the invitation.

43 Rudolf Bahro and André Gorz, *Ökonomie, Ökologie. Zweite sozialistische Konferenz* (13–15 February 1981), (Hamburg: VSA-Verlag, 1981).

44 Rudolf Bahro, 'Rapallo. Warum eigentlich nicht?', *Der Spiegel* 6 (8 February 1982).

45 André Gorz, 'Was ist denn schon Freiheit. Antwort an Rudolf Bahro', *Die Tageszeitung* (1 March 1982) (the whole controversy was reprinted in English in *Telos* 51 [Spring 1982]).

46 Gorz, 'Friedensbewegung'.

mysterious initials 'R/C', which stood for 'Révolution culturelle'. Over the next decade, Gorz would happily publish François George, DellaVolpian and Kantian–Marxist philosopher Lucio Colletti, Jean-Marie Vincent, Marcuse, Louis Puiseux, Guy Aznar, Jean-Paul Lambert of *La Gueule ouverte*, Alain Touraine and many others. Between 1973 and 1976, Dorine Horst was to manage the publishing house's foreign rights and Gorz would publish all his future books there. This self-publishing no doubt explains why those books did not always have the benefit of editorial work to correct an aspect that disconcerted quite a number of readers: the whimsical disorder evident in almost every table of contents.

In the 1970s, with his reputation bolstered by writings that had often had an international impact, Bosquet–Gorz further established himself as an intellectual at *Le Nouvel Observateur*. In 1973, he took the view that 49 of his articles were of sufficient political significance to be included in the anthology *Critique du capitalisme quotidien*, which was the first book in his own collection at Galilée.[47] At the magazine, the Illichian, environmentalist utopianism that flowed unfailingly from his pen (and his books, which were regularly reviewed by the likes of François George, Jacques Attali, Pierre Rosanvallon and Jacques Julliard) attested to the professional independence that he now enjoyed as a seasoned journalist. However, that independence troubled his employer and editor, who would take it upon themselves to contain it. Hence, Bosquet's last decade at *Le Nouvel Observateur* was one of gradual marginalization within a magazine that was growing more moderate (as it lined up behind the Parti socialiste), taking a 'boho' turn and becoming simultaneously deluged with advertising.

Late in 1973 (26 November, 10 and 24 December), Bosquet announced the economic crisis ahead of time and also pointed out the dead-end represented by affluence, while pounding away on the themes of frugality, shorter working hours and more creative free time. At that point, Jean Daniel removed him from the economics desk, replacing him with a non-specialist, but more conformist new arrival, François-Henri de Virieu. Later, Bosquet received a further snub when his first opinion piece on alternative medicines was published, against his will, in the Readers' Letters section. His dossier on the subject (7 April 1980) was no better appreciated, being

---

47 The abridged English translation of this volume *Capitalism in Crisis and Everyday Life* contains slightly fewer articles [Trans.]

followed the next week by a polemical response from the magazine's accredited doctor, Norbert Bensaïd (cousin of Jean Daniel).

It was over the campaign he had been carrying on since 1975 against civilian nuclear power that discord proved most strident. Jean Daniel's refusal to grant him a special supplement on energy forced him to turn to the consumer magazine *Que choisir?*, which produced it in a print-run of 130,000 copies (February 1978). After his outpourings over the Three Mile Island accident of 28 March 1979, Daniel's open opposition to his campaign—together with the publication of a reader's letter on his 'crude antinuclear attitude' (29 October 1979)—led him to suspend Bosquet's vitriolic articles, which then appeared in *Le Sauvage*. Some months later, Bosquet–Gorz had it out with his editor on this matter:

> You told me you had made up your mind on this thanks to reading and contacts. Don't you think it would have been a fair and friendly thing to do also to check by speaking to me about it whether the positions you ascribe to me are actually the ones I hold, and whether the questions you've considered are the only ones that might be asked?[48]

There was no lack of effort to persuade the anti-nuclear activist to yield in his intransigence, to the point where Perdriel took him out for a meal with EDF managers who were graduates of the élite École Polytechnique.[49] But to no avail.

Mitterrand's accession to power in 1981 ratcheted up the tension another notch. So as not to damage his electoral chances, Perdriel had already scuppered *Le Sauvage*, which was preparing to support the campaign of the ecologist Lalonde. From this point onwards, Bosquet's inconvenient articles attacking the pro-nuclear U-turn of the Socialist government that had approved the expansion of the nuclear reprocessing plant at La Hague, appeared under the heading 'Opinion' (8 August 1981) or 'Debate' (3 and 17 October 1981)! The distance the magazine put between itself and its troublesome writer no doubt also helped to maintain the flow of advertising revenue that came in from EDF. The conclusion to the letter of complaint Bosquet sent to his boss in 1980 expressed both the contradictoriness in his

---

48 André Gorz to Jean Daniel, 24 July 1980 (GRZ).
49 Author interview with Alain Hervé, 6 March 2013.

professional position and the difficulties he was grappling with at the level of human relations, deprived as he was of his measure of independence:

> How difficult everything is, my dear Jean. You would like me to treat you simply as a friend and privileged interlocutor, not as the holder of decision-making power. Yet at the same time, you alone hold that power and use it, even towards me, in a way that isn't always friendly. I don't blame you for that. Your situation is a contradictory one, as is mine, and we each contribute to our respective misfortunes. But we remain bound by something that is both less and more than friendship. Affectionately yours, […].[50]

The last article by Michel Bosquet bears the date 11 December 1982. The penultimate one is dated 11 September. Family concerns had made his work on the magazine less frequent and had precipitated his departure. However, to a *Nouvel Observateur* subscriber who wrote in to enquire why Bosquet's articles had disappeared, he replied, declaring himself very much 'affected' by this question which no one had yet addressed to him in writing:

> I left *Le Nouvel Obs* last December to take 'early retirement' after finding myself almost alone in my views (though I am telling you nothing new) on a certain number of questions (policy on employ-ment, time, energy and industry etc.) that are important, as I see it, for the success or failure of a government of the Left.[51]

Gorz's last years at *Les Temps modernes* were no happier. As a counter to Pierre Victor joining the editorial board in March 1977, Gorz managed to have François George co-opted on to it the following month. In January 1980 he brought in another ally, Dominique Pignon. Since the beginning of the '70s, he had managed to get an increasing number of Marxist articles on economics published in the journal (Mario Cogoy, Paul Sweezy, André Granou, Bowles-Gintis etc.), but his power remained limited to that field. In 1978 he was unable to stop a planned issue on autonomist Marxism proposed by Yann Moulier-Boutang being vetoed by Victor[52] (that movement had had

---

50 Letter to Jean Daniel cited previously.

51 Letter from 'Gorz (aka Michel Bosquet)' to Gilles Monod, 9 April 1983 (private archives). Gilles Monod, a young environmentalist and anti-nuclear campaigner, influenced by reading *Ecology as Politics*, cancelled his subscription when he received this reply.

52 See the account by Yann Moulier-Boutang, 'André Gorz, pour mémoire', *Multitudes* 31 (Winter 2007): 159–60.

its moment of glory in Italy the year before in the form of the youth riots of the *Indiani Metropolitani* [Metropolitan Indians] and other 'autonomists').[53]

After the death of Sartre in 1980, Lanzmann took over but there was increasing conflict within the journal, which lost readers. For example, in commenting on the reactions to the rue des Rosiers anti-Semitic attack, Lanzmann perfidiously equated anti-Zionism with anti-Semitism (October 1980), forcing Pignon, Rigoulot and Gorz to distance themselves from him (December 1980). The attitude to Mitterrand's victory (May 1981) proved no less divisive among the editors (George left as early as April). Then the clampdown on the Solidarity movement in Poland set Rigoulot and Pignon against the majority of the editorial board, including Gorz, who wished to retain the reference to socialism in the realm of ideas (January 1982).

Israel's war in Lebanon in summer 1982 further exacerbated dissensions. The defence of Israel mounted by Beauvoir, Lanzmann and Pouillon—the most Sartrean thinkers at *Les Temps modernes*—now separated them from the other editors, Élisabeth de Fontenay, Pignon and Gorz. The latter did, however, express a view that was distinct from the others. Arguing that 'Jewish humanism, by the eminently dialectical character of its relation to the universal, was like no other', he deplored its negation by the Israeli leaders and by the 'diaspora' that supported them.[54] He was thus implying a philosophical conception of Judaism that he had not previously been known to hold, but one that was in tune with the controversial final positions adopted by Sartre. Influenced by Lévy (Victor), these had been published in *Le Nouvel Observateur*, causing Jean Daniel some embarrassment though apparently Gorz was not put out by them.[55]

Fontenay and Pignon left *Les Temps modernes* in January 1983. Gorz, 'having become a *minority of one*',[56] left not long afterwards but didn't officially announce his withdrawal until October, citing his move away from Paris. He would write only very rarely in the journal thereafter. In May, in

---

53 The organized autonomist movement (Autonomia Operaia) was formed in 1973 following the dissolution of Potere Operaio.

54 André Gorz, 'Sur deux fronts', *Les Temps modernes* 435 (October 1982): 646–50.

55 See Jean-Paul Sartre and Benny Lévy, *L'Espoir maintenant. Les entretiens de 1980* (Paris: Verdier, 1991).

56 André Gorz to Robert Chenavier, 10 April 1983 (GRZ). (Phrase in italics in English in the original [Trans.].)

a letter to Alain Lipietz, who contributed to *Les Temps modernes* from time to time, he revealed the circumstances of his resignation:

> One shouldn't support with one's presence an undertaking that one cannot influence. Since the last two resignations, the acceptance and rejection of articles, together with the choice of themes, have been based on criteria—incoherent ones, as it happens—that my opinions cannot affect. It was, in particular, the rejection of a 'Tourainian' analysis of the peace movement [in Europe] (an analysis I had had revised after it was accepted on a first occasion—something no one remembered) that made my mind up for me. But I had always said that if Pignon left, I would do the same. As it happens, he was pushed out. That said, I haven't fallen out or got angry with my old companions: I simply don't agree with their way of running (and not running) a magazine.[57]

Gorz concluded his letter with the hope that *Alternatives économiques* 'might perhaps, in a way, take over' from *Les Temps modernes*. This new magazine had been created by a colleague of Rolant's at the AFME, the economist Denis Clerc, whose empathy for the author of *Farewell to the Working Class* we have already mentioned. Despite its realism about 'market constraints', which counterbalanced its desire not to reduce everything to economic logic, *Alternatives* [...] would find itself out of step with the pro-market turn taken by the Socialist government. Gorz, who encouraged his friends to read the publication, gave regular interviews to it between 1982 and 1984. He did, however, decline its director's invitation to join the editorial board in 1984 on account of his move to the provinces. When they met and corresponded, Gorz and Clerc engaged in a frank exchange of views, which brought out the differences in their positions, particularly with regard to the basic income issue.

Retirement or Full-Time Living

In summer 1983 Gérard and Dorine left their Parisian flat at 176, rue de Tolbiac and moved into their ecological house, with its trapezoidal spaces, at Nogent-sur-Seine. In March 1984, they moved again to a spacious eighteenth-century country house in the small village of Vosnon (population:

---

57 André Gorz to Alain Lipietz, 20 May 1983 (GRZ).

120) on the borders of Champagne and Burgundy. Though there was no lack of space at Vosnon, Gorz disposed of part of his library in the autumn to sell the flat (which he would end up keeping for quite a while before letting it go to Michel Rolant for his daughter, a flight attendant), a sign that his 'farewell to the working class' left him looking towards other sets of issues.

If Gorz had quit *Le Nouvel Observateur* late in 1982 and decided to take retirement as early as possible—at 60 (he was a beneficiary of the lowering of the retirement age approved in the previous year by the Mauroy government)—he had his reasons for doing so. Dorine, already suffering from her chronic illness (which she was now constantly reminded of by the sound of blood pulsing through an area between her ear and neck), had just been operated on for endometrial cancer, the prognosis giving cause for considerable concern. It was therefore time for him to ask himself what was 'the inessential I needed to give up so I could concentrate on the essential'[58]—by which he meant being with his partner.

Since it put an end to the bitterness of recent years, his departure from *Le Nouvel Observateur* was not painful: he was giving up professional camaraderie and restrictions on his time to take up full-time living again. He would confide to a journalist: 'I've always dreamt of being able to do what I want. And to be free of economic pressures. I've dreamt of becoming a retired writer.'[59] He would then have the necessary thinking time to produce no fewer than six books and some two hundred articles or interviews. And that did not prevent this son of a timber factory owner, who had accompanied his father to view the forests that were to be thinned, from also planting, in the two and a half acres of garden around the property, a grove (*Horst* in German) of two hundred trees, which he described to a friend as his life's great work (a Lacanian might have plenty to say about this childless man), setting up an orchard and a kitchen garden, and producing his own compost, while Dorine tended her garden of shrubs and hedges. He knew what he was talking about when he showed his fellow-feeling towards Françoise Gollain (a French intellectual who had moved to the Welsh hills) over her 'vocation as a market-gardener that combines so well with rumination-meditation-reflection.'[60] Strangers to the fashionable Parisian

58 Gorz, *Letter to D.*, p. 102.
59 Cited by Jürg Altwegg, 'Gegen Entfremdung. André Gorz zum siebzigsten Geburtstag' (Interview), *Frankfurter Allgemeine Zeitung* (9 February 1993).
60 André Gorz to Françoise Gollain, 20–26 April 2007 (GRZ).

world they had always avoided, in the countryside they rediscovered the intensity of daily life as a couple.

In May 1983, Horst's mother informed him that he was the owner of around a million Austrian schillings' worth of shares (the then equivalent of 56,000 dollars) which came to him, no doubt, from his father's will. She concluded that Gérard and Dorine could be 'very satisfied??!!'[61] Money didn't much interest the couple who already had enough and gave a lot away. What was significant rather was Gérard's reconciliation with his mother, which had come about some months earlier. Her son managed fully to express feelings of affection for her that he had been incapable of admitting up to that point. A letter addressed to this 88-year-old lady in April 1983 begins with these words: 'Once again: I love you very much, it has always been that way. You have always been a good mother and always will be.'[62] Two and a half years later, his mother made a present to him of the diary that covered the first seven years of her son's life, in which he discovered, at the age of 62, the infinite love that had surrounded him.

It takes an hour and a half of motorway driving and half an hour of backroads to get to Vosnon from Paris—and even more than that for the 'de-growther' Françoise Gollain who, after the train, took a bus and completed the journey on her folding bicycle. But the couple was in no way isolated in the countryside of the Aube département: a stream of friends, students and journalists visited. In 1999 a visiting interviewer wrote:

> André Gorz and his wife Dorine receive us in the downstairs library of a spartanly-furnished residence: two nondescript armchairs, a round table and four straight-backed chairs, a television [they did not have one in 1990] and then books, newspapers and magazines. The walls are colourless and have no paintings on them. There is just a black-and-white photo of a Mediterranean landscape.[63]

To the journalists who visited, Gorz laid out his vision didactically. With his other interlocutors, discussions were always serious and intellectual, if not indeed theoretical: he gave the impression they were being made to sit an exam, though this was done without an ounce of arrogance. But when Dorine, armed with her very British sense of humour and an inner vitality

61 Maria Horst-Starka to Gérard Horst (in German), 5 May 1983 (GRZ).

62 Gérard Horst to Maria Horst-Starka (in German), 25 April 1983 (GRZ).

63 Michel Zlotowski, Presentation of the interview 'Oficios del saber y del trabajo'.

that counteracted her illness, intervened with her deadpan comments, the discussion eased and lightened on contact with the everydayness of life. Between Gérard and Dorine, it had eventually become a game: he would say he 'needed theory to structure [his] thinking', while she would reply that 'theory is always threatening to become a straitjacket that prevents us from seeing the shifting complexity of the real world.'[64] When questioned about the readability of Gorz's work by the wife (Éliane Carr) of the English villager with whom she took tea, Dorine (who in the past had not been averse to attending Lévi-Strauss's lectures at the Collège de France) declared, laughing, 'I don't understand much of it!'[65]

The couple provided their various visitors with an organic meal or afternoon tea. Their vegetarianism was political in character and hence not systematic—even poorly observed. They were not averse to meat, as in the Turkish restaurant in London where 'their favourite dish was lamb shank'.[66] A student who spent time with Gorz in the 1970s recalls, nonetheless, that, on the pretext of eating vegetarian, Gorz had introduced him to vegetable croquettes and organic couscous in 'alternative' restaurants he wouldn't recommend to anyone.[67] Gérard and Dorine, being aware very early on that the production of (red) meat had a large environmental footprint,[68] chose 'foods that were relatively rich in organically cultivated wholegrains.'[69] Rather than shopping locally, the couple preferred to do a 44 mile round trip every Friday to 'buy organic' at Troyes, taking in a visit to a restaurant and a trip around the bookshops. Their Epicureanism is not to be confused with the hedonism of the affluent: there is nothing surprising about the surprise colleagues Lanzmann and Pouillon felt one day when they saw our two ascetics take the caviar they had brought to Nogent and put it aside for later.[70]

The visitors to Vosnon were somewhat fewer in number than the cohort of extraordinary acquaintances and friends that had passed through

---

64 Gorz, *Letter to D.*, p. 58 (translation modified).

65 Author interview with Éliane Carr, 10 November 2015.

66 André Gorz to Robert Chenavier, 9 September 1985 (GRZ).

67 Michel-Édouard Leclerc, 'André Gorz: la mort d'un philosophe'.

68 See Gorz, *Paths to Paradise*, p. 96.

69 Draft of a letter from Gorz to Dorine's doctor, undated (GRZ 7.35).

70 The story is told by Claude Lanzmann in 'Pour Gérard Horst, André Gorz, Michel Bosquet', p. 2.

their successive Paris apartments in earlier years, where Dorine sometimes received guests several times a week: the Marcuses, Illich, Marglin, Touraine, Morin, Vincent, Trentin, Jotterand, Favrod, Kravetz, Grumbach, Rolant, Laponche, Rosanvallon, Rossanda, Howard, Leggewie, Contat, George and Lévi-Strauss, not to mention the urbanist Paul Virilio, the Maoist Maria Antonietta Macciocchi, the anti-psychiatrist David Cooper, the former council Communist Paul Mattick, the economist Suzanne de Brunhoff, the PSU student Michel-Édouard Leclerc, the photographer William Klein and the political ecologists of *La Gueule ouverte* (Lambert) and *Le Sauvage* (Lalonde), activists from the Italian Far Left, doctors and women from Bobigny being prosecuted for abortion, employees of Lip and their PSU managing director Claude Neuschwander, whom Gorz also met at AFME debates etc.

Visits to Vosnon reflected the natural renewal of Gorz and Dorine's relationships. This was true of Jacques Robin and Roger Sue of the GRIT and of Alain Caillé and Ahmet Insel of MAUSS, of which more below. Relations were now more intense with the bordering countries, such as Belgium and Germany: on the Belgian side, we may cite Philippe van Parijs, and from the Rhineland and Saarland Martin Jander, Otto Kallscheuer, Claus Leggewie, Hans Leo Krämer and Hans Horch. Young researchers captivated by Gorz's work also came to the Aube, among them Jeremy Tatman from Britain in 1993 to record an interview, out of which he would develop a book in 1997, in collaboration with sociology professor Conrad Lodziak (*André Gorz: A Critical Introduction*).

Among PhD students writing on Gorz (these included Michael Mundhenk and Andrea Levy in Canada, and Joaquin Valdivielso in Spain), three gained particularly from their visits to Vosnon and this led to the publication of important works. The Brazilian Josué Pereira da Silva worked up his PhD thesis (New York, 1993) into a book entitled *André Gorz. Trabalho e política* (2002). Privately, Gorz wrote of him: 'Teacher at the University of Campinas. Adorable. The son of an illiterate landless peasant in the Northeast, he started out as a miner, took his equivalent of A-levels at 32 while working, won a scholarship, discovered *Farewell to the Working Class* in 1983 and has never quite got over it.'[71] The Englishman Finn Bowring, author of *André Gorz and the Sartrean Legacy* (2000), and the

---

71 André Gorz to Françoise Gollain, 1 August 2001 (GRZ).

Franco-Welsh Françoise Gollain, author of *Une Critique du travail* (2000), were both young philosophers who won Gorz over by their deeply rooted concern to unite their philosophical approaches with their own existential quests.

Once settled in the countryside, Gorz gave himself over, between articles, to writing long—handwritten or typed—letters in which he struck up passionate, scholarly debates with distant, but intellectually close, interlocutors. His correspondence is of this order (sometimes running over several decades) with François George, the Savoyard philosopher and schoolteacher Robert Chenavier, the political scientist Dick Howard, his publisher Otto Kallscheuer, his disciple Françoise Gollain, the theorist of open-source software Stefan Meretz and the politically committed journalist Franz Schandl, not to mention a number of less sustained but very detailed exchanges with Edgar Morin, Denis Clerc, the sociologists Alain Caillé, Claus Offe, Michael Opielka and Oskar Negt, the social forecaster Guy Aznar (the only one, with Riffel, to be addressed as 'dear brother') or Jean-Marie Vincent.

In the 1980s Gorz was constantly in demand from foreign television stations, or to lecture, or to debate with trade unionists and other activists. He received invitations from Germany, Belgium and Switzerland, where he had a remarkably large readership. He was also called on to visit Finland, Denmark and Italy. In France, he took part in debates under the most diverse banners, from the Culture et liberté popular education movement—where he debated with Lipietz—to the French Friends of the Earth's Club de Réflexion; from the Movement for a Non-Violent Alternative—where he debated with Serge July—to the Movement of Christian Managerial Staff; from the Jesuit magazine *Projet* (with its CFDT connections) to the Cercle Condorcet, which was an offshoot of the Ligue de l'enseignement, both organizations being chaired by Claude Julien who, as director of *Le Monde diplomatique*, had published important articles by Gorz and would continue to do so. At the request of Bernard Thoreau, he also played a role in a CFDT training course in Paris in 1988. We may note, lastly, that Barry Jones, the advocate for reduced working hours who became Australia's Minister of Science, also met up with him to record a programme for ABC Radio during a trip to Paris in 1986.

In the 1990s, though still just as much in demand, Gorz accepted fewer invitations on account of his age and the increasingly frail health of his partner. There is nothing, for example, to suggest that he accepted the prestigious invitation from the government of Sweden—a country where his books were immediately translated—to take part in a four-day debate with Günter Grass, Oskar Lafontaine, Amartya Sen, Jacques Attali, Alain Touraine and others. That same year he declined an invitation from Inácio Neutzling, of the Jesuit University of Rio Grande do Sul to go to Brazil, though he assured Neutzling of his admiration for Helder Camara, the red archbishop of the Northeast region.

As we shall see, however, Gorz would continue to be centrally involved in fundamental social debates around work.

CHAPTER FOURTEEN

Autonomy and the Dangers of the Dual Society

Translations of *Écologie et liberté* [Ecology and freedom] (1977) and *The Traitor* [1958] appeared in Germany in 1980. *Farewell to the Working Class* and *Paths to Paradise* appeared in German translation immediately after they were published in France. They made a substantial impact, to the point where we may say that Gorz was one of the intellectuals who contributed most to turning Germany's 'Reds' into 'Greens'. In this he was at least the equal of Rudolf Bahro, who himself strove, after 1980, to find him a platform in the Federal Republic for his views on the subject of the ecological crisis. Early in 1983, on the initiative of the publisher Hinrich Oetjen, the youth training school of the main German trade union federation (DGB), which had close affinities to the SPD, organized four days of discussion in the Paris suburbs (Gorz being unable to travel to Germany) on *Farewell to the Working Class* with Gorz present and former members of the German Socialist Student Union (SDS) Tilman Fichter and Bernd Rabehl also participating, together with ecologist Daniel Cohn-Bendit, then living in exile in Frankfurt.[1] A coach carrying some 40 young trade union officials and activists made the trip. At the end of the year, Gorz learned that *Wege ins Paradies* had become a bestseller and the philosopher Jürgen Habermas devoted the whole of his winter seminar to it in Frankfurt.[2] Hans Leo Krämer, professor of sociology at Saarbrucken, also devoted a seminar to Gorz's writings and managed to take his students to Vosnon in summer 1984 for discussions with the author.[3]

The Renewal of Ties with Germany

In acknowledging the interest the German intellectual sphere and the German Left were taking in his ideas, Gorz was making his peace with a German culture he had long rejected and ignored. Back in 1980 he had

---

1 *Abschied vom Proletariat?*
2 Jean Ziegler to André Gorz, 14 December 1983.
3 Personal communication, Hans Leo Krämer, 10 September 2014.

granted an interview on the Greens to the Hamburg political monthly *Konkret*. With approaches coming from academics and journalists, he now intensified his intellectual relations with Germany, Austria and German-speaking Switzerland.[4]

From 1983 onwards, he was in touch again with the German sociologist Claus Offe, a man he had known since 1970 (a period when that former assistant to Habermas was at Harvard) and someone who, from a position close to the Greens, wrote on themes close to Gorz's heart, such as the redistribution of work and the decline of its normativity. After speaking on German–Swiss television alongside the socialist Jean Ziegler in April 1984, Gorz gave a talk in the November on the theme of 'freeing up time' at the Congress of the Swiss Socialist Party (PSS) in Sankt-Gallen.[5] This was not a surprising invitation, given the ecosocialist sensibilities of the PSS. The party's Central Secretary Rudolf Strahm, who declared himself explicitly 'Gorzian', wrote: 'Your presence at the congress and the discussions and conversations between comrades that followed have, as it were, strengthened the argument for "Gorz instead of Keynes". In that sense, you have lent important impetus to the studies and reading of the party's members.'[6] (In terms of ecosocialism and particularly with regard to the '68 leitmotif of 'changing life', we should note that Gorz played a role early on with another Social Democratic party; as early as 1976, the Austrian Social Democrats had invited him to debate the party's programme in its theoretical journal and subsequently, in 1978, to give a talk at Graz.)

When invited by the students of Mainz University in 1985, Gorz was heartbroken not to be able to make the trip (family matters, recurrent as we know, prevented him from doing so); the intention had been that he should

---

4 Original writings by—and interviews with—Gorz appeared in the 1980s not only in *Konkret*, but also in *Aesthetik und Kommunikation* (Berlin), *Sozialismus* (Hamburg), *Tagesanzeiger Magazin* (Zurich), *Der Spiegel* (Hamburg), *Die Tageszeitung* (Berlin), *Frankfurter Rundschau* (Frankfurt), *Links* (Offenbach), *Bilanz* (Zurich), *Oberösterreichisches Tagblatt* (Linz), *Gewerkschaftliche Monatshefte* (Cologne), *Basler Magazin* (Basel), *Prokla* (Berlin), *Stadtrevue* (Cologne), *Rote Revue* (Berne), *Neue Gesellschaft*. *Frankfurter Hefte* (Bonn), *Ran* (Berlin), *Widerspruch* (Zurich) and *Die Zeit* (Hamburg).

5 André Gorz, 'Socialisme: thèmes pour demain', *Les Temps modernes* 471 (October 1985): 431–45. The article later appeared in German translation in the PSS's magazine (see *Rote Revue* 2 (February 1985): 2–7).

6 Rudolf H. Strahm to André Gorz (in German), 5 December 1984 (GRZ). See also Rudolf H. Strahm, 'Gorz statt Keynes', *Rote Revue* 2 (February 1985): 8–9.

debate the prospects for an emancipated society with one of the heirs to Frankfurt School Critical Theory, sociologist Oskar Negt, whose book in favour of the 35-hour week he greatly admired (*Lebendige Arbeit, enteignete Zeit*, 1984). When he asked the organizers to pass on his letter, which contained a long discussion of Negt's book, he was very much reckoning on getting back in touch with the man he had known at Konstanz in 1970.[7] German intellectuals close to the political ecology movement contacted him in 1985, either to interview him[8] or to ask him for contributions to collective works (on the welfare state and basic income), one such person being the young academic and parliamentary adviser to *die Grünen* Michael Opielka,[9] who sent him his own writings for discussion and recruited him—together with Gorz's alter ego, the Swede Gunnar Adler-Karlsson—into his ephemeral, low-key Institute for Social Ecology (1987–91).

Without ever having really abandoned it, Gorz went back to the German language, though he said—somewhat playfully, it would seem—that he no longer had complete command of it[10] (he did, admittedly, continue to use English in his correspondence with Claus Offe). He also made up for lost time by reading German authors. In the 1980s he acquired a more thorough knowledge of Hannah Arendt, delved into Husserl again and read Max Weber for the first time. He also studied the Frankfurt School and their successors, in the form of Horkheimer–Adorno, Habermas, Axel Honneth and, as we have already seen, Oskar Negt. His letters to Robert Chenavier between 1985 and 1988 contain long discussions on Husserl, Habermas and the crisis of meaning. These investigations and meditations bore fruit in a book of great importance that had been in preparation since

---

7 Letter in German from Gorz to ASTA (the organizing association), 27 July 1985 (GRZ). Gorz said he did not have an address for Negt, with whom he had already been hoping to correspond.

8 André Gorz, 'Die Zukunft der Arbeit', interview by Thomas Kluge and Thomas Jahn in Winfried Hammann and Thomas Kluge (eds), *In Zukunft. Berichte über den Wandel des Fortschritts* (Hamburg: Rowohlt, 1985), pp. 213–39.

9 André Gorz, 'Richtziele für eine Neugestaltung des Wohlfahrtsstaates' in Michael Opielka and Ilona Ostner (eds), *Umbau des Sozialstaates* (Essen: Klartext Verlag, 1986), pp. 137–48; André Gorz, 'Garantierte Grundversorgung aus rechter und linker Sicht' in Michael Opielka and Georg Vobruba (eds), *Das garantierte Grundeinkommen. Entwicklung und Perspektiven einer Forderung* (Frankfurt: Fischer Taschenbuch Verlag, 1986), pp. 53–62.

10 André Gorz to Hans Leo Krämer, 2 June 1984 (private archives).

1985 and was published in 1988 with a title combining multiple angles of attack: *Métamorphoses du travail. Quête du sens. Critique de la raison économique* [Metamorphoses of Work. Quest for Meaning. Critique of Economic Reason].[11] Within two years, the book was translated into the three languages that had long been the main international medium for Gorzian thinking: German, English and Swedish.

Functional Integration

By stressing its impersonal character, Gorz had already shown in *Farewell to the Working Class* that 'contemporary technocratic power [had] an essentially *functional* legitimacy'.[12] In *Paths to Paradise* he saw it, as did Touraine, as 'domination by a technical system', in which the means become their own ends and 'managers are its servants not its masters'.[13] In *Critique of Economic Reason*, he refined his analysis. As that power becomes more complex, functions come to be organized by a formalization of the procedures that maintain the rational stability of the system. Guided on this question by Max Weber, who attributed purposive rationality (*Zweckrationalität*)—as opposed to 'value-rationality' (*Wertrationalität*)—to economic and bureaucratic apparatuses, he defined as 'functional any conduct which is rationally programmed to attain results beyond the agents' comprehension, irrespective of their intentions'.[14] The reader will recognize here 'the sphere of heteronomy', conceptualized long before by Gorz, or 'the cogs of a huge machine' that includes 'the totality of specialized activities which individuals have to accomplish as functions co-ordinated from outside by a pre-established organization'.[15] In purely existentialist terms that Gorz had never set aside, this translates as:

> If the being of the individual in his/her practical reality is no more
> than the sum of its social determinations (which are also cultural

---

11 Published in English as *Critique of Economic Reason*.

12 Gorz, *Farewell to the Working Class*, p. 53.

13 Gorz, *Paths to Paradise*, p. 39.

14 Gorz, *Critique of Economic Reason*, p. 32. It should perhaps be noted that minor changes were made to the text by the author during the preparation of the English translation. Where these make no substantial difference to the argument, I shall disregard them and use the published English text. [Trans.]

15 Gorz, *Critique of Economic Reason*, p. 32.

etc.), then individuals are at every moment what society makes them and needs them to be. The subject of actions is society; and as every modern society is, at bottom, a great material system with inert operational demands reminiscent of a great machine, the subject of actions is a machine and the only moral criterion is the conformity of individual actions to the systemic necessities (in German: *Sachzwänge*) of the social totality.[16]

Studying Habermas's major work *Theory of Communicative Action* [1981], Gorz stresses the important affinity between what he calls the 'functional integration' of individuals or heteronomy and what Habermas calls 'systemic integration'. Whatever one calls it, this hetero-regulated sphere of the state industrial megamachine stands over against the auto-regulated sphere of civil society, which operates by the rationality of 'individuals pursuing ends which, even if they motivate functional patterns of conduct, are irrational in regard to the ultimate objectives of the organizations in which they work.' It follows that: 'This splitting of the social system and this divorce between different rationalities produces a split within the lives of individuals themselves: their professional and private lives are dominated by norms and values that are radically different from one another, if not indeed contradictory.'[17] And socialist attempts to replace spontaneous hetero-regulation by the market by the programmed hetero-regulation of the plan have changed nothing. This has always led to the same outcome: 'Social disintegration, that is, [...] individuals' loss of motivation vis-à-vis their functionalized work,' for, on the scale of large systems, 'the Marxian utopia by which functional work and personal activity could be made to coincide is ontologically unrealizable.'[18]

The megamachine has its intrinsic reasons and its circular logic: within it, 'the techniques of domination and the imperatives of rationalization are inextricably linked, to the extent that one may consider rational organization to be the goal of domination or, conversely, domination to be the goal of rational organization.'[19]

---

16 André Gorz to Alain Lipietz, 20 May 1983 (GRZ).

17 Gorz, *Critique of Economic Reason*, p. 36.

18 Gorz, *Critique of Economic Reason*, p. 42.

19 Gorz, *Critique of Economic Reason*, p. 43.

For Gorz there are, however, two types of hetero-regulation, between which Habermas fails to differentiate: on the one hand, *prescriptive regulators* which force individuals, on pain of penalty, to adopt functional forms of behaviour and, on the other, *incentive regulators* which induce individuals to accept them of their own free will. Among the former are rules and regulations, timetables, procedures etc., while among the second are remuneration and also security, social recognition etc. Only this latter type of regulator produces a genuine functional integration of individuals. By offering them compensations that make them exist as consumers (and socialized beings), it actually induces them to accept work as the obvious way of satisfying their needs. We shall see that, in the history of capitalism, this outcome has not been easy to achieve, because it has assumed that the worker spontaneously prefers to earn more rather than to work less, and in the age of Fordism one cannot be completely sure of that, because 'compensatory consumption' (as Bahro says) never completely reconciles the workers with their condition.

The consequence of all this has, nonetheless, been social atomization—that is to say, the isolation of individuals in their role as selfish consumers, a role which advertising extols and sustains.

The Subject of Autonomy

Gilles Lipovetsky's view of contemporary hedonism and narcissism, in which he observes that the trend towards uniformity of behaviour, denounced by Marcuse, has been succeeded by an explosion of styles of consumption that has consolidated heightened individualism amid a general dearth of meaning, does not contradict with Gorz's findings.[20] As Gorz sees it, however, individuals are equipped with other resources that ontologically precede their integration: they always have the possibility of escaping their confinement in individualism, which isn't the blissful enjoyment of the person who is free to make choices, but the passively experienced distillation of behaviours functional to the reproduction of capital. And they can do so by creating networks of mutual assistance, exchange, self-creation, common interests etc. which form bonds that extend beyond the isolation of the consumer/individual.

---

20 Gilles Lipovetsky, *L'Ère du vide. Essais sur l'individualisme contemporain* (Paris: Gallimard, 1983).

This is shown by the writings of the French sociologist Michel Maffesoli, an observer, after the fashion of the Situationists, of the re-appropriation and subversion of everyday practices that individuals perform to maintain their continuing life-force, and by Rainer Zoll, a German sociologist much appreciated in France by Gorz and Vincent, who recorded the new forms of solidarity at work in the daily lives of the young.[21] Gorz was convinced that the resistance to individualism would come from *individuals*. It was no use capitalism trying to buy its own political stability among the individuals it forced to work by contriving a private sphere for them outside work, in which they would believe they could find sovereignty, '[t]he sphere of individual sovereignty is *not based upon a mere desire to consume*, nor solely upon entertainment and leisure activities.'[22]

> It [that sphere of individual sovereignty] is based, more profoundly, upon activities unrelated to any economic goal which are an end in themselves: communication, gift giving, aesthetic creation and enjoyment, the production and reproduction of life, affection, the realization of physical, sensuous and intellectual capacities, the creation of non-commodity use-values (shared goods or services) that could not be produced as commodities because of their unprofitability.[23]

The opening-up to multiple deployments of the individual's modes of being, which we may define with Gorz as his/her 'individualization' or 'subjectivation' is definitely not the sort of closure upon oneself that characterizes individualism. This methodological distinction has since become generally accepted within value sociology.[24] Though the question has been raised,[25] we must therefore conclude that there was no 'socialist individualism' in the

21 Michel Maffesoli, *The Time of the Tribes. The Decline of Individualism in Mass Society* (London: SAGE Publications, 1995); Rainer Zoll, *Nouvel individualisme et solidarité quotidienne* (Paris: Kimé, 1992).

22 Gorz, *Farewell to the Working Class*, p. 80 (translation modified).

23 Gorz, *Farewell to the Working Class*, pp. 80–1 (translation modified).

24 'Talk of individualization should not be confused with individualism. Individualization corresponds to a choice-based culture, in which each person asserts his/her autonomy, his/her capacity to direct their action without control or constraint' (Pierre Bréchon, 'L'individualisation progresse, mais pas l'individualisme', *Le Monde* [25 April 2009]).

25 Adrian Little, *The Political Thought of André Gorz* (New York: Routledge, 1996). See especially chapter 6, 'Towards Socialist Individualism?', pp. 140–61.

Gorzian approach. It remains for us to understand the meaning and place of the individual in the emancipatory scheme Gorz strove to mobilize in opposition to—and as a replacement for—proletarian Prometheanism.

The Return of the Individual Subject

It was in the 1980s, if not indeed from 1975 onwards, that the political question of the individual came most firmly to the fore, on account of the crisis of the great totalizing systems of interpretation and action, such as Marxism. The idea of collective autonomy or workers' autonomy grew tired and worn, and the idea of *individual autonomy* took over.[26]

Thus, for example, as part of a philosophical project that aimed, by drawing on the theories of Freud, to re-found the 'subject', Castoriadis (in 1975, precisely) gave meaning to autonomy as a mode of human *being* that was the foundation of social praxis.[27] Alain Touraine, always on the look-out for the formative forces in society, saw in the incipient ebbing of social movements a 'return of the actor' or, in other words, of the subject. 'Today,' he explained, 'we are tired of the historical prophecies that have led to nothing but authoritarian regimes and doctrinaire interpretations; hence the new stress on the notion of subject, which successfully conveys the distance that individuals and collectives have put between themselves and institutions, practices and ideologies.'[28]

A remarkable conference hosted by the Centre de recherche et de documentation sur Hegel et Marx, founded by Jacques d'Hondt at the University of Poitiers, is emblematic of that refocussing, which explored Marx from the angle of the individual and freedom.[29] For his part, Jean-Marie Vincent, who had already cast off his Trotskyism with an exposé of the aporias of Marxism, produced a short but effective clarification, at the end of the decade, of the notion of freedom. Linking freedom indissociably with the individual, he

---

26 See Pascal Ory (ed.), *Nouvelle histoire des idées politiques* (Paris: Hachette, 1989), pp. 715, 755.

27 Cornelius Castoriadis, *The Imaginary Institution of Society* (Kathleen Blamey trans.) (Cambridge: Polity Press, 1997 [1975]), pp. 101–07.

28 Alain Touraine, *Return of the Actor: Social Theory in Postindustrial Society* (Minneapolis: University of Minnesota Press, 1988 [1984]).

29 Present were Bernard Bourgeois, Jacques D'Hondt, Lucien Sève, Jean-Yves Calvez and Jean-Claude Bourdin. The proceedings are available in Guy Planty-Bonjour (ed.), *Droit et liberté selon Marx* (Paris: PUF, 1986).

described it as creative and as productive of the constantly reinvented relationship between individuals and their society, whereas Marxists had too often thought they could transcend the fragmentation of bourgeois society through an appeal to the outdated, mythic schema of community—the result being that workers within the socialist movement had too often believed they could find their identity in both class and work, the latter conceived as social production and, hence, as the foundation of society.[30]

By placing the individual and his/her autonomy at the centre of his philosophy,[31] André Gorz was also in tune with the *Zeitgeist*. However, his choice to do so was also unusual for being part of a long-standing position, since his adherence to Marxism had never meant rejecting the existentialist principle which placed the individual subject at the heart of stratagems for liberation.[32] *Farewell to the Working Class* nonetheless represented a novel departure in that it precisely cast light on the limitations hobbling Marxism in that area. The book criticized the labour movement for having 'generally opposed the yearning for individual autonomy, and dismissed it as a residual sign of petty-bourgeois individualism.' And if 'autonomy is not a proletarian value', it was because the illusion that a proletarian could escape the general condition by individual means undermined the proletarians' capacity to unite in a single class capable of seeing off the bourgeoisie: 'The political imperatives of the class struggle have thus prevented the labour movement from examining the desire for autonomy as a *specifically existential* demand.'[33]

In this way, the exemplary political activist repressed 'his or her subjectivity' to 'become the objective mouthpiece of the class thinking through him or her. Rigidity, dogmatism, cant and authoritarianism are inherent qualities of such impersonal thinking devoid of objectivity.'[34] The proletariat thereby finds itself hypostatized. It then becomes comparable to other transcendent categories of the economic machine in which it plays a role: just

---

30 Jean-Marie Vincent, 'Liberté et socialité', *Futur antérieur* 2 (Summer 1990): 22–37.

31 Finn Bowring, *André Gorz and the Sartrean Legacy: Arguments for a Person-Centred Social Theory* (London: MacMillan, 2000).

32 Françoise Gollain, 'André Gorz, affects et philosophie' in Fourel (ed.), *André Gorz en personne*, pp. 63–74; Dick Howard, 'André Gorz & the Philosophical Foundation of the Political', *Logos* 12 (3) (2013).

33 Gorz, *Farewell to the Working Class*, pp. 35–6.

34 Gorz, *Farewell to the Working Class*, p. 37 (translation modified).

as Capital dispossesses the worker of his labour, so the Proletariat dispossesses the proletarian of his/her subjectivity. There is a symmetry here based on the common destruction of 'all autonomous capacities and possibilities among proletarians'[35] and, at the same time, an identical underlying assumption: the fetishization of work that produces value or wealth and through which the proletarian class acquires objectivity and substance. Labour value, which was initially economic, also becomes an ethical matter.

This gives rise to a 'socialist morality' which demands that workers invest their whole being in their work and conflate it with their personal goals. It is a morality 'which mirrors the morality of the bourgeoisie in the heroic age of capitalism. It equates morality with love of work, while at the same time depersonalizing work through the process of industrialization and socialization. In other words, it calls for love of depersonalization—or self-sacrifice.'[36] From that standpoint, Right and Left seem the same.

It is clear that, for Gorz, the defence of 'the free development of the individual', to use Marx's expression, involves a critique of the centrality of work that is part and parcel of both proletarian and bourgeois ideology. The whole of his later work adds depth to that critique.

Lifeworld and Subject: Habermas versus Touraine

Contrary to the postmodernists, whether functionalist or structuralist, Habermas and Touraine understand modernity as a movement of emancipation, notes Gorz, thereby making clear his interest in the two authors. It is their ways of conceiving forms of resistance to oppressive socialization that lead him to prefer one of them to the other.[37] As he sees it, that particular problematic is crucial for grasping the nature and potentialities of the new emerging subject. He confronts this in *Critique of Economic Reason*[38] and returns to it on the occasion of a study he first publishes in a collective work in English devoted to the writings of Touraine.[39]

---

35 Gorz, *Farewell to the Working Class*, p. 37.

36 Gorz, *Farewell to the Working Class*, p. 10.

37 Gollain, *Une Critique du travail*, pp. 69–76.

38 Gorz, *Critique of Economic Reason*, pp. 173–90.

39 André Gorz, *Reclaiming Work* (Chris Turner trans.) (Cambridge: Polity Press, 1999), pp. 127–47. Originally published as 'A Sociology of the Subject' in Jon Clark and Marco Diani (eds), *Alain Touraine: Consensus and Controversy* (London: Falmer Press, 1996).

For Habermas, the site of dissidence is the 'lifeworld' (*Lebenswelt*), which has to be reclaimed from the state and commercial apparatuses that have colonized it. In Gorz's opinion, however, the appreciation of this lifeworld poses a problem, since the concept remains 'abstractly insubstantial' in Habermas's writings. In a long letter of 1987 to Robert Chenavier, who was always ready to lend a theoretical ear, Gorz explained:

> For the concept of lifeworld to have a critical potential with respect to the system, it obviously has at least to be lived experience of the world. Impossible, then, on the basis of the socially constituted, hetero-determined individual. The question is: how does a subject live out his functional determination—particularly computer-assisted work and other 'advanced' occupations which we are merrily told have re-professionalizing virtues? But, for the question to be asked, there first has to be a subject and that subject has to not be a product of the functioning of society and of the machinery of socialization. Now, there is no autonomous subject in Habermas. So, to have some idea of what the lifeworld is, we have to go back again to Husserl, who invented the concept, to Merleau, who refined it, and to Horkheimer/Adorno who applied it properly since, just like Merleau-Ponty, *they* were aware that the individual *has a body*, that the lived experience of the world comes through the body, that the world (the system of industrialized apparatuses) does violence to the body and that that violence is only tolerated if a more powerful repressive violence channels its violent rejection on to scapegoats and the phantasms that the culture industry obligingly provides (and racism too).[40]

The concept takes on another meaning in Habermas than the one Husserl originally gave it. The lived experience that gives meaning to life is emptied out and replaced by a set of intangible elements that the notion of lifeworld reduces to. Gorz explains his view of all this particularly incisively in a letter written to sociologist Alain Caillé in 1992:

> In Husserl, 'lifeworld' referred to the world inasmuch as it reveals itself to our intuitive experience and provides 'the ground of our

---

40 André Gorz to Robert Chenavier, 21 December 1987 (GRZ).

evident truths.' That definition has been deflected in a sociological direction in Habermas. Whereas Husserl understood the lifeworld as the correlate of lived experience—an experience [whose incompleteness] makes evident truths and certainties fragile in principle and open to doubt—in Habermas the lifeworld becomes the set of familiar realities in which are rooted our intuitive understanding, our habits, knowledge and skills, acquired and transmitted by education, tradition and shared interpretative schemas. In this conception, the lifeworld tends to become conflated with the behaviour, conceptions, relations and beliefs which, in a given society, 'are self-evident' and are socially conformist. It's impossible, from that standpoint, to say anything about the quality and savour of the lived experience of that lifeworld (for example, about the difference between the lived experience of a repressive, integrist society and a society of free citizens). It is its inaccessibility to critique on the basis of the actual lived experience of it that I objected to in Habermas.

In a second shift in meaning, lifeworld has come to signify, above and beyond the world accessible to intuitive understanding, the familiar social space in which one is 'at home' and in which one orients oneself, communicates and makes oneself understood by others on the basis of complicity and *spontaneous* behaviour: pretty much what the Germans call *Heimat*.[41]

With such assumptions, the reaction to the system emanating from the lifeworld is likely to be based in tradition and neophobia and it encourages recourse to identitary and communal allegiances that are clearly politically ambiguous—it is to such senses of belonging that Alain de Benoist, the ideologue of the New Right, appeals.[42] For Gorz, however—drawing in this connection on Habermas's successor at Frankfurt Axel Honneth—subjects do not have pre-given identities.[43] 'An original rift prevents the individual

---

41 André Gorz to Alain Caillé, 21 January 1992 (GRZ).

42 Gorz, *Reclaiming Work*, pp. 117–26.

43 On this subject and this convergence, which the author traces back to the philosophical couple of Sartre and Adorno, see Silvio Camargo, 'Experiência social e crítica em André Gorz e Axel Honneth', *Revista brasileira de ciências sociais* 74 (October 2010): 107–93.

subject from coinciding with the "identity" its social belonging confers upon it.'[44] Now, he tells us, 'it is only by dint of this original gap that the individual can make an autonomous judgement of social reality and refuse to conform to its norms.'[45] 'As I see it,' he later writes to Vincent, 'subjectivity [the subject] isn't the interiorization/acceptance of these norms and self-censorships, but lies in the gap felt, experienced and suffered between what one has to be in order to function and what one feels diffusely. And criticism must begin with a hermeneutics of this non-identity with self.'[46]

Touraine writes about this Gorzian problematic in his contribution to a *Festschrift* published for Gorz's 65th birthday.[47] It was taken up by Touraine himself, with Gorz detecting its presence in Touraine's *Critique of Modernity* [1992], which opposes 'subjectivation' to 'socialization' to assert the primacy of the subject 'who rebels against rules and integration.'[48] Gorz even believed the sociologist had drawn unconscious inspiration from *The Traitor* to differentiate between the Self-Other and the I-Subject; this conviction is revealed in a letter Gorz wrote in September 1977 which also has the virtue of responding to the question of his own convergence with a politically moderate sociologist. To an acquaintance who enquired about his political itinerary:

> I found in Touraine the imprint left by my writings, without realizing that it came from me (and he probably isn't conscious of this himself). The happy discovery that he thinks as I do on an absolutely fundamental question is the reason for an affinity between him and me that transcends our political divergences. The political use he makes of his intellectual tools (his Social-Democratic reformism) isn't the only one possible.[49]

---

44 Gorz, *Critique of Economic Reason*, pp. 175–6.

45 Gorz, *Critique of Economic Reason*, p. 89n7.

46 André Gorz to Jean-Marie Vincent, 7 August 2000, in André Gorz and Jean-Marie Vincent, 'Correspondance' (Willy Gianinazzi ed.), *Variations* 17 (2012) (available at: variations.revues.org/348; last accessed: 27 July 2022).

47 Alain Touraine, 'Die Verweigerung der Integration' in Hans Leo Krämer and Claus Leggewie (eds), *Wege ins Reich der Freiheit* (Berlin: Rotbuch Verlag, 1989), pp. 166–73.

48 Cited by Gorz in *Reclaiming Work*, pp. 142, 140.

49 André Gorz to Jacques Robin, 12–14 September 1997 (GRZ).

Since the days when they made a similar analysis of the new social movements, if not before, Touraine had felt an unshakeable esteem for Gorz.[50] In 1993, he described it as follows:

> André Gorz is the most truly Marxist of the European thinkers and also—should one say: but also?—the most imaginative and the most actively anti-doctrinaire. With him, Marxism has the liberating force it had in . . . Marx, when the latter criticized French Jacobinism or the Hegelian Right. If he no longer believes in the proletariat or its avant-garde, if he is wary of recourse to the state to solve society's problems, that isn't so that he can withdraw into a lukewarm reformist pragmatism, but to rediscover the force of protest that drove the labour movement in the past and which today remains almost entirely unutilized politically.[51]

Reacting to Gorz sending him his latest book *Misères du présent, richesse du possible* [published in English as *Reclaiming Work: Beyond the Wage-Based Society*], Touraine told him in October 1997 that he agreed with his 'resistance to the idea of *Lebenswelt*'. He thanked him for the study of his thinking, which 'provided a good explanation for [himself] of what differentiated [his] position from that of Habermas'. He believed he could share with Gorz the idea that one has to keep one foot in instrumentality and another in what he called the sphere of 'identities'. However, he located his divergence in his own preference for the broadening of work to include sustainable development activities rather than to build 'voluntary microsocieties', which he was wary of because they 'brought down the weight of the small group very heavily on the individual.'[52]

This very much raised the question of self-determined activity as opposed to necessary work. It is clear here too that, since the point when Gorz first opened himself to Illichian themes, that question had nagged away at him: it is nothing less than the central idea around which his critique of work revolves.

---

50 He was among the few dozen people who attended the public opening of the Promenade André Gorz on the banks of the Seine in Paris, 21 September 2013.

51 Alain Touraine, 'Le plus imaginatif des penseurs', *Globe Hebdo* 12 (28 April 1993): 36. Touraine's piece is published in a text box inserted into Gorz's interview with Maurice Najman entitled 'Comment en finir avec le capitalisme'.

52 Alain Touraine to André Gorz, 15 October 1997 (GRZ).

The Sphere of Autonomy and Beyond

During the 1980s, a process of dualization of the economy occurred in the industrialized countries of the West. It made the arrival of post-Fordism complete, that phase also being referred to, by another automobile-related reference, as Toyotism. The large production units, affected by worker resistance and by market fluctuations, increased in flexibility by reducing their workforces through outsourcing, adjustable at any moment, and employing non-unionized—and often exploited—workers. Moreover, alongside industry and the modern tertiary sector (research, IT, communications, biotechnologies) where most jobs for highly qualified workers were created, service activities expanded (distribution, catering, surveillance, cleaning, the care sector, etc.), employing low-skilled, poorly paid workers.

In France, this dualization was underpinned in law by the legalization of fixed-term contracts (1979) and could be seen particularly in the rise of temporary work (legal since 1972) or part-time working (from 9.2 per cent of the workforce in 1982, that would go on rising till it reached a record level of 17.9 per cent in 1999). It therefore assumed a social dimension, which the demographer Emmanuel Todd would later sum up in the term *la fracture sociale*—the working population becoming split between protected, stably-employed workers, on the one hand and, on the other, a mass of unemployed and insecure workers on a part-time basis, confined to casual jobs and with no trade-union protection. This new social reality was what underlay the tumultuous autonomist movement of students and insecure workers that shook Italy in 1977. Though that movement was seen by Asor Rosa through the outdated filter of proto-*operaismo* and the PCI, in which the traditional working class was regarded as central, that observer was the first to condemn the establishment of a dual economy that divided workers into the 'secure' and the 'insecure' (*Le due società*, 1977).

André Gorz was just as clear-sighted on this, but instead of regarding precarious employment as a peripheral phenomenon of current capitalist restructuring, he stressed the potentialities for struggle concealed in this discrimination. While bemoaning the persistence of work-based ideology among those employees in a privileged position, he took the view that the others, forming a 'mass of disaffected non-workers', were a '*possible* social subject' for a leftward exit from capitalism.[53] At the end of his life, Gorz

---

53 Gorz, *Paths to Paradise*, p. 35.

would return with more precision to the question of the characteristics of this new proletariat:

> The young and the less young who manage the discontinuity of waged work as best they can, surfing from one job to another without committing themselves totally to seeking stable employment; all those people who pursue a freer, more frugal way of life in which money and commodities aren't the supreme value—they are all part of the post-industrial, post-Fordist proletariat.
>
> It is they who populate the radical alter-globalist and anti-capitalist movements, the unemployed unions, the movements for open-source software. It is through them that a culture of rebellion, derision, imagination and liberated language is gaining ground.[54]

The fact remains that while he argued in *Farewell to the Working Class* for 'a dual society' (a chapter of the book is titled 'Towards a Dual Society'), his arguments often seemed ambiguous. The expression 'dual society' was probably unfortunate (Gorz would later refer to it as a foolish blunder).[55] It is clear, however, that in outlining the two spheres, the one dominated by autonomy the other by heteronomy, it was not his intention to endorse the current two-speed economy which generates social segregation, nor did he wish to sanction its positive theorization by certain technocrats (the senior civil servants Jean Amado and Christian Stoffaës and the *énarque* Alain Minc) or American neo-liberals (Milton Friedman), against whom he frequently inveighed. As he saw it, the whole of the economy based on wage-earning was, in its essence, steeped in heteronomy.

Heteronomy and Autonomy as Moments of Life

In *Farewell to the Working Class*, Gorz defines heteronomy as the set of working relations that deprive the worker of the free choice of intrinsic ends for which he is working (working to make a living is an extrinsic, unfree end). It rests on the division of labour required by the great technological complexity of modern production, which prevents the worker from having an overall view of the process. Also belonging to heteronomy is the work that has to be carried out, like it or not, for a society to function and

---

54 André Gorz, 'Vers la multiactivité', interview by Vladimir Safatle (2005) in *Le Fil rouge de l'écologie*, pp. 96–7.

55 Gorz, *Ecologica*, p. 11.

reproduce itself. It is for these reasons that heteronomy cannot be wholly eliminated, but simply reduced. Even if it will never be a general source of fulfilling work—except, perhaps, for a privileged minority of creative workers—we have to welcome the positive element it contains since, thanks to technical improvements bringing constant productivity gains, the time devoted to socially necessary labour is diminishing. Heteronomy works against itself. Far from preventing autonomy, it subserves it, since, as Gorz would argue 10 years later, 'the chief consequence of our drive towards effi-ciency and economic rationalization is that it frees us from work, frees up our time and releases us from the rule of economic rationality itself.'[56]

But it is only like that in a set-up where the time released does not equate to enforced part-time working or unemployment, but is used to people's advantage. With the satisfaction of basic needs achieved elsewhere, auton-omy would then correspond to the activities in which desire, fantasy and the free choice of ends can flourish and, so far as productive goals are con-cerned, to those involving the 'autoproduction of all that is optional, gratu-itous, superfluous, of all, in short, which is not necessary, which gives life its spice and value: as *useless* as life itself, yet exalting life as the one end which gives all others their meaning.'[57] As Gorz explained better to Guy Aznar, a social forecasting specialist (close to les Amis de la Terre and soon to be their chairperson), who for his part was more inclined to equate auton-omy with a sense of 'personal involvement' in one's work (though modern management had that same goal!), 'the optional is everything you can do or not do, as you like, without your continuing existence depending on it'; it was, he said, 'living time'—i.e. time that one does not count.[58]

Gorz sums up the 'cultural mutation announcing the transition to post-industrial society' in the following formula: ' "Real life" begins outside of work.'[59] So the time was ripe for him to linger over those pages of volume 3 of *Capital*,[60] in which Marx made plain that the realm of freedom began on

---

56 André Gorz, *Capitalism, Socialism, Ecology* (Chris Turner trans.) (London: Verso Books, 1994), p. 45.

57 Gorz, *Paths to Paradise*, p. 57.

58 André Gorz to Guy Aznar, 21 April 1983, answering a letter from Aznar of 11 April (GRZ).

59 Gorz, *Farewell to the Working Class*, p. 81.

60 Karl Marx, *Capital*, VOL. 3 (Ben Fowkes trans.) (London: Penguin Books, 1991), pp. 957–9.

the other side of work, insofar as work was a matter of necessity, and the reduction of working hours was therefore its basic prerequisite.[61] It was also the appropriate moment to point out that the famous 'Fragment on Machines' in the *Grundrisse*[62] contained 'the idea that economically oriented social labour should serve to extend the sphere of individual autonomy—meaning free-time activity.'[63]

In keeping with Marx's conception, Gorz did not regard the spheres of heteronomy and autonomy as impermeable. It was precisely from their separation that the current segregation came about, consigning part of the population to unemployment, material insecurity and social deprivation. From *Farewell to the Working Class* onwards, Gorz was aware of this. Against this *spatial* dualization of social life, he followed the inventive Aznar (author of *Non aux loisirs, non à la retraite* in 1978 and *Tous à mi-temps!* in 1981) and conceived a *temporal* dualization that would run through individuals themselves, all of them belonging simultaneously to each sphere and being able to find fulfilment precisely by dint of that dual belonging.[64] This ideal of 'multi-activity', as a philosopher who followed in Gorz's footsteps explains, 'means that everyone has access simultaneously to political, productive, cultural—as well as private—activities.'[65] Instead of trying to bring down joblessness by illusory attempts to return to full employment, this is about promoting alternation between the two spheres by the only means possible: *a massive reduction in working hours*, which can then be shared out among everyone. This is the precondition for all individuals having the leisure to apportion their time as they see fit, while taking part in producing those things that are necessary.

Gorz explains that this rebalancing of the relation between working time and disposable time changes and, indeed, reverses the very meaning of these two moments: 'work itself [. . .] [becomes] a means towards the extension of the sphere of non-work, a temporary occupation by which individuals acquire the possibility of pursuing their main activities.'[66]

---

61 Gorz, *Farewell to the Working Class*, p. 95.

62 Marx, *Grundrisse*, pp. 690–720.

63 Gorz, *Farewell to the Working Class*, p. 81.

64 Gorz, *Farewell to the Working Class*, p. 102.

65 Dominique Méda, 'La fin de la valeur "travail" ' in *Le Travail, quel avenir?* (Paris: Gallimard, 1997), p. 239.

66 Gorz, *Farewell to the Working Class*, p. 81.

[A]s the periods of disposable time become longer, non-working time can become something other than the obverse of working time: something other than time for rest, relaxation and recuperation; or for activities secondary and complementary to working life; or idleness—which is but the obverse of compulsory, hetero-determined wage slavery; or entertainment—the counterpart of work which, by its monotony, is anaesthetizing and exhausting. [. . .] It is then possible for our jobs and workplaces to cease to be our only sources of identity and the only spaces in which socialization is possible; and for the sphere of non-work to cease to be the sphere of private life and consumerism. It becomes possible for new relations of cooperation, communication and exchange to be forged in this free time and for a new societal and cultural space, composed of autonomous activities with freely chosen aims, to be opened up. There is, then, a possible evolution towards a new relation between working time and disposable time finally reversing the present situation: it allows for autonomous activities to become more important than working life, the sphere of freedom more important than the sphere of necessity. The way we organize the time we spend living need no longer be dictated by the time we spend working; on the contrary, work must come to occupy a subordinate place within the life plan of the individual.[67]

In this way free (finally freed-up) time cannot just be the obverse of work, as it was in the days when Gorz refused to join with those worshipping the alleged leisure civilization. From now on, it would be free time that would assign work its place.

An Alternative Economy and Working for Oneself

Farewell to the Working Class and *Paths to Paradise* may seem excessively rigid or radical in their way of normatively pitting heteronomy against autonomy. If heteronomy means an absence of control over the ends of work, autonomy, as Gorz sees it, is not simply its opposite. It is more than that because it corresponds to the work that is itself *its own end*. Strictly speaking, it is autotelic: it was on this basis that Aristotle in his *Nicomachean Ethics* distinguished instrumental work (*poiesis*) from action in public space

---

67 Gorz, *Critique of Economic Reason*, pp. 92–3.

(*praxis*). What, then, are we to think of work that corresponds to neither definition because we have control of its ends and yet is necessitated by its—personal or social—usefulness? Restricting autonomy to *work as end in itself* by leaving aside the criterion of *the ends—or purposes—of work* amounts to confining autonomy to extra-economic activities, such as those engaged in by the artist, the poet, the priest, the activist, the volunteer etc. But how are we to categorize those activities that are economic in nature—that is to say, socially useful—but not performed for commercial ends? This is the whole range of problems raised by the *alternative economy* that was emerging in the 1970s and would, in various different forms, come to be termed the third sector, or the social or collaborative economy.[68]

It isn't certain that Gorz immediately grasped the full implications of this.

In October 1984, he was contacted by Erik Van den Abbeele, leader of the Mouvement pour une alternative de base (MAB), headquartered in Belgium, to contribute to a collection on the theme of the alternative economy. MAB, founded 10 years earlier, had equivalents in France in the form of the Agence de liaison pour le développement d'une économie alternative (ALDEA), created by Patrice Sauvage in 1981, and the Réseau de l'économie alternative et solidaire (REAS), formed by Aline and Jacques Archimbaud in 1985. MAB regarded this different way of producing as one pole of a 'dual economy' based on autonomy, self-management, self-sufficiency and localism. Gorz responded by warning against the very idea of an alternative or informal sphere of the economy, since economies are only ever preserves of capitalist logic. It was not, then, for some alleged alternative 'economy'—subservient, by definition, to what Aristotle identified as the labour of reproduction—to be given the task of reducing the scope of the economy; that role should go to 'free activities' located outside the *oikos* (the domestic economy) by Aristotle.[69]

These words show that Gorz feared non-commercial activities claiming to be 'alternative' would inevitably fall back into the lap of economic and managerial logic—later, fair trade and NGOs would be beset by similar

---

68 Dominique Allan Michaud, *L'Avenir de la société alternative*.

69 André Gorz, 'Voorbij de economie. Een kritiek op dual-economische opvattingen', interview by Erik Van den Abbeele in Erik Van den Abbeele (ed.), *Ontmanteling van de groei. Leesboek over een andere economie* (Nijmegen: Markant, 1985), pp. 89 ff. (French manuscript dated December 1984, GRZ 10.13).

dangers.[70] He did, however, acknowledge that there was a median role for that sphere. With micro-social and local activities of a cooperative, community-based or associative type in mind, he made reference to an 'intermediary level connecting socially necessary, heteronomous work and autonomous activity entirely determined by individual choice', arguing that such a level 'constitutes the social fabric of civil society'.[71] In *Critique of Economic Reason*, he revisited this controversial point, implicitly linking this sphere that has no economic rationality or goals with what he termed 'work-for-oneself'[72] or, in other words, a personal activity (such as housework, cooking, DIY) which is necessary or useful but not done for financial gain. The point is that work-for-oneself—corresponding to German *Eigenarbeit*, as investigated by Claus Offe[73]—can mutate into co-operative activity (community crèches, DIY workshops, urban vegetable gardens etc.) within a grassroots community: such a community then becomes 'the intermediate micro-social space between the private and the public, macro-social spheres'; it opens up 'the private sphere [. . .] to a space of *common sovereignty*, shielded from commodity relations, where individuals *together* determine for themselves their common needs, and decide the most appropriate actions for satisfying them'.[74]

The Commodification of Domestic Tasks, a New Servitude

Examining the structure of the labour market that was emerging in the US—and subsequently in France—in the 1980s, Gorz observed that, apart from the jobs of secretary, shop assistant and checkout clerk, the insecure, low-paid jobs newly created in the service sector concerned tasks that had previously been performed within households or, in other words, the work of reproduction, which in general fell in our societies on the *femina*

---

70 For an account of how such an unfortunate turn might come about, see Dominique Dambert and Didier Adès, 'Vive le "social business"!', *Le Monde* (12 January 2010).

71 Gorz, *Paths to Paradise*, p. 63.

72 Gorz, *Critique of Economic Reason*, pp. 154–64.

73 Rolf G. Heinze and Claus Offe (eds), *Formen der Eigenarbeit. Theorie, Empirie, Vorschläge* (Opladen: Westdeutscher Verlag, 1990). On the French situation, see also Florence Weber, *Le Travail à-côté. Une ethnographie des perceptions* (Paris: Éditions de l'EHESS, 2009 [1989]).

74 Gorz, *Critique of Economic Reason*, p. 159.

domestica (child rearing, education, cleaning, cooking etc.).[75] As he saw it, it was not about bemoaning the loss of autonomy that women could be said to have lost, as Illich did in *Gender* [1982], wanting to keep them in the home. Gorz took issue with that position in *Critique of Economic Reason*,[76] while at the same time engaging in serious discussion about it in his correspondence with his friend.

Gorz formulated another type of question in this regard, one directly addressed to feminists. While not receiving remuneration for the work of reproduction that they provide within family life—something called for by the German feminist Claudia von Werlhof and other feminists who attacked Gorz[77]—did women actually find themselves compensated for this by the current socialization of domestic labour that released them from the (surplus) labour they had up to that point provided free of charge? Gorz gave his view on this in an interview with Belgian feminists from the GRIF group (Groupe de recherche et d'information feminists), Françoise Collin and Marie-Victoire Louis. He argued that the liberation of part of womankind from their domestic tasks was being achieved at the expense of the intensified exploitation of other women (and men), who were being forced into inferior jobs and thus personally suffering the consequences of society's segmentation into an economic elite and a class of servants.[78]

> The emancipation of women will not be achieved by making them the same as men, who have only their labour power to sell and are made incapable of investing themselves in their work. It will be achieved when women have emancipated men by teaching them that no wage can make up for doing a job you detest and that extra-economic values take precedence over the others and are alone capable of conveying meaning.[79]

Rather than by access to work, then, which a massive reduction in working hours would in any case make possible, it was through the distribution of

---

75 André Gorz, 'The American Model and the Future of the Left', *Telos* 64 (Summer 1985): 117–21.

76 Gorz, *Critique of Economic Reason*, pp. 161–4.

77 See La Tapeuse, 'Les noeuds gorziens ou là où il y a de la gêne, il n'y a pas de plaisir', *Cash* 5 (April 1987): 24–6.

78 'Questions à André Gorz', *Les Cahiers du Grif* 30 (Spring 1985): 25–34.

79 André Gorz to Ivan Illich, 24 April [1979] (GRZ).

domestic tasks within the couple that women—and, hence, also men—would arrange time in such a way as to afford each of them existential fulfilment.

Similarly, Gorz took issue with the ideology of jobs for jobs' sake that the new-style CFDT was espousing when it argued for the professionalization of personal services (including care for the sick, the disabled or the dependent) with the aim of expanding 'sources of employment'. Having agreed to preface a book by the national union leader Pierre Héritier,[80] with whom he in fact disagreed, he wrote to him: 'Isn't there a contradiction between the desire to free up time' by the reduction of working hours—one of the union's traditional demands—'and the desire to have activities turned into professional, waged work which, if there were no lack of time, would be able to develop on a basis of voluntary cooperation and, in part, become part of time for living?' And he went on to point out the divergence, 'in relation to the expansion the economic field may or must undergo, over the limits beyond which that field perverts or destroys the meaningfulness of activities, which is preserved only when those activities are pursued because we enjoy pursuing them.'[81]

Instead of asking, then, what 'form must a society take in which full-time work on the part of all its citizens is no longer either necessary or economically useful', and how it should 'proceed so that productivity gains and savings in working time redound to everyone's advantage?', the question was being posed the wrong way round: 'how can we proceed so that, in spite of productivity gains, the economy still consumes as much work as it did in the past' and 'to what new fields of activity can commodity exchange be extended so as to somehow replace other jobs lost elsewhere in industry and industrialized services?'[82] And this was so because the model implicitly envisaged was of an economy that was constantly taking in new fields of activity to ensure 'new growth'.

80 Pierre Héritier, *Nouvelle croissance et emploi* (Paris: Syros, 1988).

81 André Gorz to Pierre Héritier, 20 August 1988 (GRZ).

82 Gorz, *Capitalism, Socialism, Ecology*, p. 47.

CHAPTER FIFTEEN

The Invention and End of Work

In France, as across the whole of Europe, unemployment shot up during the 1980s (from 5 to 9 per cent of the working-age population), reaching a record level in the following decade (10.9 per cent in 1977—2.8 million unemployed).[1] The political debate on remedies was enlivened as a result, and studies on the employment situation proliferated in France and throughout the world. It was within this two-decade-long context that doubts about the place of work in society emerged, not only practically among young insecure workers and the unemployed, who experimented with other ways of thinking about life, but also at the theoretical level in sociological or philosophical writings. These latter were absolutely new, as they broke with an intellectual tradition that had gone unchallenged since the eighteenth century.[2]

By basing political economy on labour as a source of wealth, Adam Smith gave rise to the tradition that sees contemporary civilization as a 'work-based society'. Hegel followed firmly in his footsteps, grasping work as the *praxis* through which human beings realize themselves. Marx didn't contest this view. His materialism even caused him to view work as a *natural* condition of human existence. However, among the Moderns who glorified work in general, Marx stood out by showing that in bourgeois society work acquires an alienated, commodity character that reifies human *praxis*.[3] It has been deduced from this that it is by transforming it that work can be liberated. Within this critical undercurrent, which often acknowledges its debt to Marx's anthropology, we find authors from many different horizons: from Lukács to Arendt,[4] Fromm to Galbraith, and Friedmann to Liepitz,

---

1 In terms of the way the figures were calculated at the time, 12.6 per cent of the working-age population and 3.3 million were unemployed .

2 Daniel Mercure and Jan Spurk (eds), *Le Travail dans l'histoire de la pensée occidentale* (Quebec: Presses de l'université Laval, 2003).

3 Manfred Bischoff, 'L'humanité a-t-elle toujours "travaillé"?', *Théologiques* 3 (2) (1995): 45–69.

4 Though Arendt criticizes Marx for wishing to 'abolish' work. He had in fact written in *The German Ideology*: 'The point is not to liberate work, but to eliminate it'.

not forgetting sociologists of work emblematic of this standpoint, such as Robert Castel and Oskar Negt.

Turning its back on this *doxa* of doing/making, whether apologetic or anthropological, a new approach emerged in the 1980s. It no longer sought to rescue work. It could be seen initially among German writers, particularly in the article by the LSE sociologist Ralf Dahrendorf—a former Liberal minister in Willy Brandt's government and a one–time European commissioner—on the 'disappearance of work-based society' and in Claus Offe's sociological analysis of the fading of work as a normative category of individual behaviour.[5] In France, Gorz wrote as early as 1983 in *Paths to Paradise* about 'the era of the abolition of work' and the 'end of the work-based society'. He was followed by Jean-Marie Vincent, who produced a striking *Critique du travail* in 1987, in which he made the distinction, following Aristotle, between making and acting (this was the book's subtitle). Reinterpreting the work of Marx through the lens of Ernst Bloch and Martin Heidegger, he concluded that 'resuscitating the subject' required his decentring from work.

It was in the middle of the next decade, when European unemployment was at its height, that books arising from this same heretical current of thought would meet with great success. American economist Jeremy Rifkin's *The End of Work* (1995) became an international bestseller. Studied and reviewed by Gorz as soon as it appeared in English, the book contended that increased productivity gains meant that in the future there would be less and less work, which would free up time to develop the social economy. In France, Dominique Méda's philosophical work *Le Travail* (1995), subtitled *Une valeur en voie de disparition* [An endangered value], argued for the de-sacralization of work. Lastly, Viviane Forrester's *The Economic Horror* [1996] conveyed these arguments to the general public with an attack on

---

5 Ralf Dahrendorf, 'Im Entschwinden der Arbeitsgesellschaft', *Merkur* 8 (1980): 749–60. In the epigraph to *Paths to Paradise*, Gorz refers to Dahrendorf, 'Die Arbeitsgesellschaft ist am Ende', *Die Zeit* (26 November 1982). Claus Offe, 'Arbeit als soziologische Schlüsselkategorie?' in Joachim Matthes (ed.), *Krise der Arbeitsgesellschaft?* (Frankfurt/New York: Campus Verlag, 1983), pp. 38–65. This paper, presented to the Bamberg conference of 17 October 1982, was translated, no doubt through Gorz's good offices, as 'Le travail comme catégorie de la sociologie' in *Les Temps modernes* 466 (1985). Gorz, who had been sent it by Offe before it was published, refers to it in *Critique of Economic Reason* (p. 103 n).

the stubborn stratagems that sought to represent the taboo of work as indestructible and the unemployment statistics as remediable. With a more limited audience, on the other hand, but unearthed by Gorz, who sensed that it went to the heart of the subject, the clear and straightforward *Qu'il n'y a pas de problème de l'emploi* (1994) by the anti-conformist Rightist Renaud Camus, asserted that the lack of work wasn't a problem, the only problem was one of income and the use of time.

What Is Work the Name Of?

'The "work" capitalism is abolishing on a massive scale in its final phase is a social construction. It is for this very reason that it can be abolished.'[6] If work does not, then, have an anthropological character that cuts across time, if it is historically shaped by social relations, what is it the name of? Gorz doesn't beat about the bush: 'The notion of work [*travail*] is an invention of modernity or, more exactly, of industrial capitalism.'[7] The first chapter of *Critique of Economic Reason*, entitled 'The Invention of Work', illustrates this assertion by showing that work hasn't always had the same meaning or the same place or importance in society.

Ponos, Poiesis and Praxis

There are fundamental differences between the activities of times past and the modern 'work' that the cheerleaders for capital believe they can celebrate as permanent and natural. Drawing freely on the analyses developed by Hannah Arendt in her famous work *The Human Condition* (1958)—though he pays scant regard to the trans-historical distinction Arendt makes between work and labour (believing, in fact, that Arendt 'never understood Marx at all')[8]—Gorz notes that, strictly speaking, there was no work before capitalism, insofar as it had no social existence at that point.

In ancient Greece, where one could divide human activities into three mutually exclusive categories (*ponos, poiesis, praxis*), it was confined to *the private sphere*. As practised by slaves, work existed as forced labour, by women as drudgery, and in every case it was associated with *ponos*, hardship—hence

---

6 Gorz, *Reclaiming Work*, p. 3.
7 Gorz, *Capitalism, Socialism, Ecology*, p. 53.
8 André Gorz to Robert Chenavier, 9 October 1999 (GRZ).

the French noun *travail,* deriving from *tripalium*, an instrument of torture used on recalcitrants in the Early Middle Ages. The second category corresponds to *poiesis*, that is to say, to the 'creative' activity of the farmers who render the earth fertile and the artisans who do not labour, but 'work' combining the useful with the beautiful, which is in itself a way of raising oneself above necessity. *Ponos* and *poiesis* were looked down on because they were carried on outside the only sphere that counted, *the public sphere*, where *praxis* flourished, that is to say, where free men carried on the business of the *polis* and had time to devote themselves to *skhole* (Latin *otium*)—study, leisure and contemplation. Transposing the Peripatetics' categories, we have, on the one hand, instrumental *making*—in thrall to material necessity—and, on the other, autonomous *acting*, which is a free pursuit. That is why, in this society where politics and culture have precedence, '[t]he free man refuses to submit to necessity. He controls his body so that he will not be a slave to his needs.'[9] Plato, like Marx later, cleaves to 'the idea that liberty, that is, the human realm, only begins "beyond the realm of necessity", that Man is only capable of moral conduct when his actions cease to express his pressing bodily needs and dependence on the environment, and are solely the result of his sovereign determination.'[10] Setting itself apart from work-based societies, the Athenian *polis* is the Western prototype of the 'culture-based society' to which Gorz aspires for the whole of humanity.[11]

In medieval times, work, which was performed only by the common people, was embedded in material and spiritual life, the aims of which dictated its pace. Only such work was done as was needed to meet settled, established needs. Limits were set on it that were not to be transgressed—as witness the corporate prohibitions of all kinds or the patronal and religious feasts (as many as one in three days of the working year were non-working days).

This all changed in the eighteenth and nineteenth centuries with the rapid spread of textile manufacture. Gorz draws here on Max Weber's *The Protestant Ethic and the Spirit of Capitalism* [1905] to show how entrepreneurs *socialized*[12] *work* in order to prevent the workers' control of the means

---

9 Gorz, *Critique of Economic Reason*, p. 14.

10 Gorz, *Critique of Economic Reason*.

11 Gorz, *Reclaiming Work*, p. 78.

12 Gorz specifies that he means this in the sense of *Vergesellschaftung*, not *Sozialisierung* [Trans.]

of production and to subject them to entirely novel criteria of economic profitability. Workers were forced to work more by reducing their wages, increasing their pace of work, and lengthening their working hours. This subjection to work was accompanied by the corresponding ideology specific to Protestantism, but not invented out of thin air: in the Middle Ages, Christianity had already begun to re-evaluate work under the influence of certain monastic rules. The result was as follows:

> Productive activity was cut off from its meaning, its motivations and its object and became simply a means of earning a wage. It ceased to be part of life and became the means of "earning a living". Time for working and time for living became disjoined; labour, its tools, its products acquired a reality distinct from that of the worker and were governed by decisions taken by someone else.[13]

The economic rationalization of work thus won out over 'the ancient idea of freedom and existential autonomy'.[14] That economic revolution, which established the modern form of work, ultimately presents an ambivalence from which Marx only freed himself in some brilliant passages in his mature writings:

> [A]s a result of capitalist rationalization, work ceases to be an individual activity and a submission to basic necessities; but at the precise point at which it is stripped of its limitations and servility to become *poiesis*, the affirmation of universal potency, it dehumanizes those who perform it.[15]

The Impossible Reconciliation of Life and Work

The work-based utopia in Marx's writings consists in wishing to reconcile what industrial capitalism has separated: life and work. But not doing so by a return to closed, traditional life-communities, since modern work, by virtue of its generality, facilitates access to universality. It was, rather, by the control and intelligibility of productive processes that the workers would supposedly achieve the unity of Reason.[16] From *Farewell to the Working Class*

---

13 Gorz, *Critique of Economic Reason*, pp. 21–2 (a typographical error in the English translation has been corrected here, Trans.).

14 Gorz, *Critique of Economic Reason*, p. 22.

15 Gorz, *Critique of Economic Reason*, p. 20 (translation modified).

16 Gorz, *Critique of Economic Reason*, pp. 25–30.

onwards, Gorz consistently pointed out that this Communist utopia was unrealizable, now that capitalism had achieved a stage of irreversible complexity.[17] Nor was it desirable in political terms on account of its totalizing character, which crushes individual liberty: 'All attempts to do away with alienation in complex societies by striving for the unity of system and life-world—of functional, heteronomous tasks and personal activity—have produced disastrous results.'[18] Moreover, Marx himself, who mainly entertained that utopianism in his youthful writings, seemed to turn away from it in *Capital*, when he located liberty not in some union with necessary labour, but outside of such labour—Marcuse too had noted this and shifted his appeal more towards the utopianism of Fourier and that of the Surrealists.[19]

Economic Rationality

Capitalism prides itself on a logic that possesses rationality, but it has pushed that rationality to extremes, to the detriment of other logics that pre-existed it. Exclusive and expansionist, economic rationality eventually turned into capitalist irrationality.

Its Capitalist Irrationality

The invention of modern work marks the full advent of capitalist rationality. This latter is fashioned on the basis of accounting calculation, to the exclusion of any other non-monetary consideration, since calculation serves to maximize the yield of factors of production and, hence, profit, which is the only goal the capitalist has in mind. As Max Weber sensed, capitalist rationality produces an initial inversion: 'it at the same time expresses what is, seen from the viewpoint of personal happiness, so *irrational* about this sort of life, where a man exists for the sake of his business, instead of the reverse.'[20] The 'spirit of capitalism' also severed, then inverted the relationship between work and need: 'The goal of work was no longer the satisfaction of felt needs,

---

17 Richard Sobel, 'Travail, liberté et nécessité dans l'utopie communiste. André Gorz, lecteur de Marx', *Actuel Marx* 46 (2009): 163–76.

18 Gorz, *Capitalism, Socialism, Ecology*, p. 11.

19 See Herbert Marcuse, *An Essay on Liberation* (Harmondsworth: Penguin Books, 1973), pp. 29–30.

20 Quoted by Gorz, *Critique of Economic Reason*, p. 18.

and effort was no longer matched to the level of satisfaction to be attained.'[21] By keeping wages low, capitalist rationality prevented workers from deciding between working hours and levels of consumption: it required of them daily, full-time working, which became a norm.[22] With difficulty, but ineluctably, that norm eventually became established in people's lives as self-evident— even at the end of the Second Empire, the so-called 'sublimes' celebrated Holy Monday and the most skilled of them limited their work to three-and-a-half days per week[23] (subsequently, intermittent working and a high turnover of labour characterized the revolutionary syndicalist workers, who revived the principle of 'self-limitation in terms of the norm of sufficiency').[24]

Consumption itself became subject to this spiral of the 'ever more', driven by the pursuit of maximum profit. With the need 'to make it worth investing increasing amounts of capital' requiring 'that increasing production should find purchasers', consumption necessarily had to 'continue to expand well beyond the satisfaction of actually *felt* needs'. Consumption had necessarily 'to be in the service of production.'[25] As Gorz had already stressed in *La Morale de l'histoire* and in *Strategy for Labor*, here again the order of things was turned upside down: 'Production would no longer have the function of satisfying existing needs in the most efficient way possible; on the contrary, it was needs, which would increasingly have the function of enabling production to keep growing.'[26]

Capitalism does not, therefore, sever all relations between work and need: the axiom accepted as self-evident remains that of 'working to earn one's living', though not as a function of a *chosen* level of need, but as a function of an *ever-increasing* level of need that has to be met through full-time work. Just as production takes precedence over consumption, which is there only to make it function, work takes precedence over needs which, assisted by the inevitable advertising, are there only to make it necessary. This is

---

21 Gorz, *Critique of Economic Reason*, p. 113.

22 Christian Topalov, *Naissance du chômeur. 1880–1910* (Paris: Albin Michel, 1994).

23 Robert Beck, 'Apogée et déclin de la Saint Lundi dans la France du XIXe siècle', *Revue d'histoire du XIXe siècle* 29 (2004): 153–71; Denis Poulot, *Le Sublime ou le travailleur comme il est en 1870, et ce qu'il peut être* (Paris: Maspero, 1980 [1870]).

24 Gorz, *Ecologica*, p. 67.

25 Gorz, *Critique of Economic Reason*, p. 114.

26 Gorz, *Critique of Economic Reason*, p. 114.

how it is with individuals under capitalism: alienated and subjugated, first as producers and a second time as consumers.

Extending Its Scope

Built on the principle of 'ever more'—the obsession with 'growth'—capitalist rationality operates on two fronts. It involves the permanent pursuit of greater productivity, though the intensification of that productivity, which entails greater output, is not indefinite, on account of social resistance and the limits of the market. That is why it also tends towards an extension of its application to ever more and ever wider new areas.[27] For example, the commodification of activities belonging to the sphere of private life through the extension of personal services (or the disguising of those activities as jobs) knows no barriers, something which, as we have seen, Gorz condemns. These services cover such diverse areas as education, health and maternity, as seen in the practice of surrogacy.[28] The same goes for 'common goods', such as plant, human and animal genomes that are being privatized.[29]

Its Rational Kernel

Capitalist rationality, which takes forms that stand the world on its head, contains within it the *economic rationality* to which it gave entirely free rein. That economic rationality is, as it were, its truly rational kernel: its aim is to optimize the factors of production deployed, which implies economizing on work, materials and time per unit of output. It reaches its most fully accomplished form when it is necessitated by market competition. It is the only viable way of conceiving the economy. Gorz came to this conclusion in his new book *Capitalism, Sociology, Ecology*. Published in October 1991 and comprising texts written since 1988, it marked a turn in Gorzian thought towards greater reformism and pragmatism, which we shall now have to pin down more precisely.

---

27 Adeline Barbin, *André Gorz. Travail, économie et liberté* (Chasseneuil-du-Poitou: CNDP, 2013). See especially the first section: 'L'extension du domaine de la rationalité économique'.

28 Gorz, *Critique of Economic Reason*, pp. 150–2.

29 Gorz, 'Le savoir, la valeur, le capital', interview by Thomas Schaffroth (2003) in *Le Fil rouge de l'écologie*, p. 87.

Questioned in 1988 by the Australian political scientist John Keane, who pressed him to say precisely how he would conceive a socialist society that would counter the free play of the market, Gorz conceded that trade in goods and markets was indispensable in a complex society that could no longer forgo the technical and spatial division of labour.[30] On that point he was at one with the post-Marxist Jacques Bidet, author of *Théorie de la modernité* (1990). Reworking this interview for his book, Gorz concluded that: 'we have to distinguish between capitalism and the logic of capital:' the former 'is a social system in which life, activities, the scale of values, and the aims of individuals and society are all dominated by relations subordinated to economic rationality and directed towards the valorization of capital'; the latter 'is the only form of pure economic rationality' and the only 'economically rational way to run an enterprise.'[31]

Ecosocialism

Might capitalism be the only possible economic system? The collapse of the Communist regimes in Eastern Europe, which came with the fall of the Berlin Wall on 9 November 1989, might suggest that the answer was yes. The main—paradoxical—consequence of that collapse was that it swept away any attempt to imagine the alternative in authentically Communist terms. At the end of the 1980s, Gorz would devote himself, rather, to redefining socialism, which he conceived as osmotic with the postulates of political ecology and, hence, as an 'eco-socialism'.

Redefining Socialism

If 'the economy will never know any other than capitalist rationality,'[32] as he explained to a journalist, how was socialism to be conceived? The question seemed to come down to the extent to which 'the criteria of economic rationality should be subordinated to other types of rationality'[33]—that is to say, to 'democratically determined goals.'[34] What was needed was to win

---

30 André Gorz, 'A Land of Cockayne?' (interview), *New Statesman and Society* (12 May 1989), pp. 25–31.

31 Gorz, *Capitalism, Socialism, Ecology*, p. 100.

32 Jürg Altwegg, 'Gegen Entfremdung'.

33 Gorz, *Capitalism, Socialism, Ecology*, p. 76.

34 Gorz, *Capitalism, Socialism, Ecology*, p. 77.

back from the megamachine 'broader and broader spaces in which a "logic of life" can unfold freely'.[35]

This strategy corresponds to the one Gorz discovered, when writing *Critique of Economic Reason*, in Karl Polanyi's *Great Transformation* (1944), which defines 'socialism as the subordination of the economy to society and of economic goals to the societal goals which encompass them and assign them their subordinate place as means to an end'.[36] In *Capitalism, Socialism, Ecology*, Gorz went further. He drew on the ideas of the East German philosopher and economist Rainer Land, a productivist, who wished chiefly to democratize economic decisions. Land reciprocated by devoting his autumn 1990 seminar at the Humboldt University in Berlin to *Critique of Economic Reason*. If, Gorz argued, emancipation could no longer be equated, as in the Marxian utopia, with the suppression of the relative autonomy of the state and cultural apparatuses etc., if it was no longer the re-establishment of a unity between life and economic functionality, and if the abolition of commodity relations was no longer on the agenda, then socialism had to be conceived very modestly as an 'orienting', a 'shaping' of the development of the economy that asserted its own extra-economic rationality, but also preserved the 'economy's relative autonomy and its capacity to evolve'.[37]

Capitalism, Socialism, Ecology was a book written under certain pressures. Published initially in German by Rotbuch of Berlin in 1991, it was the brainchild of publisher Otto Kallscheuer, right down to the organization of its contents, and supervised by him throughout the writing. Kallscheuer was also professor of philosophy at Frankfurt and had already engaged in fulsome intellectual exchanges with the author of *Critique of Economic Reason* as Gorz was writing it. From 1986 onwards, he had fed him writings by Charles Taylor, Karl-Otto Apel, Habermas etc. which he thought ought to interest him.

He wanted to give Gorz's new book the title 'Subversion and Solidarity',[38] but its content wasn't really in keeping with that rather combative title. The one eventually settled on was *Und jetzt wohin*? [And now

---

35 Gorz, *Capitalism, Socialism, Ecology*, p. 11.

36 Gorz, *Critique of Economic Reason*, p. 130.

37 Gorz, *Capitalism, Socialism, Ecology*, p. 9.

38 Draft plan of the book attached to Otto Kallscheuer's letter to Gorz of 18 July 1990 (GRZ).

where to?], with the subtitle *Zur Zukunft der Linken* [On the future of the Left], which gave a better idea of the book's aims: to provide perspectives for Social Democracy in Germany—and also in Europe, as advocated in Kallscheuer's afterword.

Reducing Working Hours

The labour movement set itself the goal of controlling the means of production, but it had always fought for reducing the burden of labour on workers through shorter working hours too. In the 1970s, shorter working hours were a constant demand of the French trade unions (of the CFDT in particular) and the Left. That is why, as soon as he came to power, François Mitterrand reduced the working week from 40 to 39 hours.

For Gorz, the feasibility and aptness of this reform, which he envisaged on a grand scale, ensued from the reduction in the general quantity of necessary work implied by constant advances in productivity, further accelerated by information technology, which eliminated more jobs than it created. That reform was rooted in the history of capitalism: in 1900, 3,000 hours of work per year were needed in France. By 1990, the figure was down to 1,800. It was also a social justice measure, since it could be expected to reduce social dualization and unemployment by distributing work more evenly.

However, the first grounds leading Gorz to campaign for reduced working hours (RWH) weren't socio-economic, but were in line with an existential and an ecologist principle that was entirely in the spirit of '68: 'The only way to live better is [. . .] to work less', he railed in *Le Sauvage* in 1973.[39] Five years later, it was while wondering 'what it is that we need to be happy' that he spelled out in *Le Nouvel Observateur* some points of a programme of social transformation for the next two decades, including the reduction of the working week to 20 hours.[40] He also makes reference to an immediate reduction to 32 and even 30 hours per week.[41]

---

39 Gorz, *Ecology as Politics*, p. 68. Originally published as Michel Bosquet, 'Combien vaut un rayon de soleil?' [What is a ray of sunlight worth?], *Le Sauvage* 2 (March 1973): 7–9.

40 Michel Bosquet, 'Ce qui nous manque pour être heureux', *Le Nouvel Observateur* (11 September 1978).

41 In *Farewell to the Working Class* (p. 9) and *Capitalism, Socialism, Ecology* (p. 114) respectively.

Having made a first outline of RWH in *Critique of Economic Reason*,[42] Gorz launched into a technical feasibility study that broached the vexed question of maintaining or lowering current wage levels. The CFDT, Jacques Delors and his friends in the *Échanges et projets* club and the Greens, spurred on by Alain Lipietz, were all inclined to accept a partial reduction in income. As Gorz saw it, this was barely necessary: if the increase in productivity and production continued, it ought to be possible to maintain present wage levels. However, since payment of the full wage was likely to increase costs and depress recruitment in those sectors employing large quantities of labour and achieving low productivity gains, a two-part income had to be envisaged—as advocated by Guy Aznar in *Le Travail c'est fini et c'est une bonne nouvelle* (1990)—including a 'second cheque' that complemented the main wage, which continued to reflect hours worked. Gorz proposed that that 'cheque' should be paid for not by a tax on robots, which would inhibit innovation, but by a tax on consumption.[43]

At the end of his life, Gorz would regret this framework for achieving RWH, partially indexed to assumptions about growth, commenting that it was already outdated when he devised it. He would refuse to allow extracts from *Capitalism, Socialism, Ecology* to be reproduced in a journal (taking the view that it was 'the worst thing I wrote').[44]

In Gorz's view, RWH served to increase the individual's autonomy by restricting the space governed by economic rationality. The aim was that the free time it created could enable everyone, depending on their desires and 'situation in life', to study or return to education, change job and 'experiment with other lifestyles or a second life outside work'.[45] As he saw it, it was possible to give free rein to one's projects and to other activities that were not mere passive leisure only if one had sufficient stretches of time available: RWH was not, therefore confined to a mere shortening of working hours at the daily level. It was from this perspective, at least from his 1978 *Nouvel*

---

42 Gorz, *Critique of Economic Reason*, pp. 199–202.

43 Gorz, *Capitalism, Socialism, Ecology*, pp. 102–17. Originally published as 'Une politique pour réduire la durée du travail et résorber le chômage', *Partage* 54 (October 1989). An updated German version appeared in *Neue Gesellschaft. Frankfurter Hefte* 11 (November 1990): 986–93.

44 André Gorz to Françoise Gollain, acting as intermediary for the nascent journal *Entropia* (20 July 2006) (GRZ).

45 Gorz, *Capitalism, Socialism, Ecology*, p. 76.

Observateur article on happiness onwards, that he came to favour another form of RWH. This consisted in freeing up time on the basis of a lifetime calculation of working hours, which everyone could distribute throughout their life as they saw fit, in exchange for a lifetime income. The volume of work required could be set at 20,000 hours over a lifetime (as against the current 40,000) or 1,100 hours annually (as against the current 1,600).[46]

The idea of a social income distributed on the basis of wealth produced rather than work directly performed was borrowed from the Distributist theory devised by Jacques Duboin in the 1930s and disseminated and developed by his daughter Marie-Louise in the journal *La Grande Relève*. Gorz saw this as a way of moving beyond commodity relations.[47] While recognizing its faults, which stemmed from the idea that the socioeconomic system could be changed through a reform of money, he defended it tooth and nail against the scepticism of Denis Clerc, since, as he wrote, 'the Distributists are the heirs of a Proudhonian anarcho-federalism in which the state is reduced to a minimal 'clearing-house' function, and this makes them more sympathetic than the statists.'[48]

The alternative idea of defining working hours on a lifetime basis came to him from the Swedish Trade Union Confederation's economist Gösta Rehn, who had spent many years working on a formula for *à la carte* retirement; this was also in line with original proposals made by another Swedish economist, Gunnar Adler-Karlsson, yet another of Gorz's correspondents. It was this proposal of a lifelong social income, enabling a person to alternate between periods of work and periods devoted to life projects that Gorz would explore during the 1990s.

Counsellor to the Powerful

The majority of Gorz's contributions in *Capitalism, Socialism, Ecology* attest to his concern at that point to exert a positive influence on the policy of reforms in Germany and France. Where the former country was concerned,

---

46 Gorz, *Paths to Paradise*, pp. 40–2 and *Critique of Economic Reason*, pp. 195–9. The contemporary data Gorz provides count the working hours of all 'active' employees, which includes part-time workers and the unemployed. If, more properly, we deduct the unemployed, we get a figure of more than 60,000 hours for a working life and 1,800 hours annually (1,573 in 2013).

47 Gorz, *Paths to Paradise*, p. 117n7.

48 André Gorz to Denis Clerc, 19 May 1983 (GRZ).

this was true of his commentary on the programme of the SPD, which under the aegis of Oskar Lafontaine had been opening up to political ecology,[49] his article 'Redefining Socialism',[50] the above-mentioned plan for a reduction in working hours, the preamble to which he co-wrote with the German trade unionist Martin Jander, with whom he had discussions at the DGB seminar in 1983[51] (all of these having appeared in the SPD publication *Neue Gesellschaft*) and his article for the *Festschrift* offered to Willy Brandt on his seventieth birthday.[52]

In Germany, his writings were taken seriously by mainstream politicians of the Left. The intellectual Peter Glotz, secretary of the SPD, interviewed him in 1986 (and again in 1997) and provided a home for his articles in the party's theoretical magazine, which he edited. Glotz's ideas on freeing up time (*Manifesto for a New Left*, 1985) which Gorz often quoted, were so close to his own that it would be difficult to say who influenced whom. As for Lafontaine, the leader of the SPD Left, Gorz warmly dedicated one of his books to him. Erring by a year, on account of the usual concealments of his actual birthdate (see p. 63n35), his friends Krämer and Leggewie presented him with a *Festschrift* for his 65th birthday by goading into action a group of German writers with close affinities to his positions: Kallscheuer, Glotz, Zoll, Offe, Negt, Honneth, Hans Horch and Detlev Claussen, together with the French intellectual Alain Touraine.[53] This was also the period when German, Austrian and Belgian television stations came calling, together with those of the three Swiss language areas.

Gorz's arguments also found an echo within European institutions: he was invited to Strasbourg on 1 February 1990 by the Council of Europe for the Grand Debates organized, under the aegis of Morin, Passet, Moscovici

---

49 Gorz, *Capitalism, Socialism, Ecology*, pp. 27–37. Originally published as 'Sozialismus, Ökologie und kultureller Umbruch', *Neue Gesellschaft. Frankfurter Hefte* 8 (August 1989): 732–8.

50 Gorz, *Capitalism, Socialism, Ecology*, pp. 38–43. Originally published as 'Eine neue Definition des Sozialismus', *Neue Gesellschaft. Frankfurter Hefte* 6 (June 1990): 519–23.

51 Gorz, *Capitalism, Socialism, Ecology*, pp. 102–17.

52 Gorz, *Capitalism, Socialism, Ecology*, pp. 67–77. Originally published as 'Des zentralen Konfliktes alte und neue Akteure' in Helga Grebing et al. (eds), *Sozialismus in Europa. Bilanz und Perspektiven. Festschrift für Willy Brandt* (Essen: Klartext Verlag, 1989), pp. 67–76.

53 Krämer and Leggewie (eds), *Wege ins Reich der Freiheit*.

and Robin, by the Director of Culture, the Spanish sociologist José Vidal-Beneyto, and in May he gave an interview to the Observatoire européen de la protection sociale. While he had less of an audience in France than in Germany, his thinking did generate some interest in the corridors of—Socialist—power and around the party. On the initiative of Guy Roustang, Gorz agreed, for example, to take part in a meeting of the national Economic Planning Committee in 1989. Around that same time, the ex-Trotskyist Henri Weber, now adviser to the President of the National Assembly Laurent Fabius, organized a brainstorming session with a number of consultants to assess the possibility of the Socialist Party adopting Gorz's proposals for a massive reduction in working hours, though most of the participants did not see those proposals as indicating a way forward.[54] A Rocardian student magazine interviewed him.[55] Gorz was also questioned in 1990 by Jean-François Alessandrini, soon to be adviser to Martine Aubry, on flexible working, the reduction of working hours and the *revenu minimum d'insertion* (RMI), introduced by Rocard in December 1988, for a magazine published by the French Ministry of Labour.[56]

However, Martine Aubry, appointed Minister of Labour the following year, was not yet convinced of the usefulness of reduced working hours when it came to redistributing employment. In these early '90s, the path ahead was still a long one and social mobilization to that end embryonic. Gorz's appearance on television on the theme of the 'End of Work' in the France3/La Sept programme *Océaniques* of October 1991 still had a utopian air about it.

Ecological Rationality

Green Capitalism

The rise of 'ecobusiness' simply confirmed for Gorz that, though they forced some constraints and reorientations on the economy, ecological policies—soon to be described in terms of 'sustainable development'—did not stem

54 Jérôme Vidal, 'André Gorz sur la ligne de crête du présent', *Revue internationale des livres et des idées* (9 July 2010).

55 André Gorz, 'Vers une civilisation du temps libéré', interview by Frédéric Audren, *Pantagruel* 4 (Summer 1992): 6–17.

56 André Gorz, 'Une redistribution plus équitable du travail est nécessaire', *Partenaires* 7 (September 1990): 26–8.

the system's underlying trend to increase output and continue the destruction of the biosphere and of the spaces of liberty where its rationality was not yet operative. The principle of maximization that underlay capitalism and ordained *growth* in all areas was still intact. In that context, the expertocracy that drew on scientific ecology merely provided lubricants to the production/destruction engine as it threatened to seize up from the ecological catastrophe it bore within it. Gorz could have pointed out—having seen this as early as 1954 (see above, p. 49n6)—that already, with the enormous mass of victims it implied, global warming could not be halted.

Political ecology was something different for Gorz. The aim being the reconciliation of human beings with a milieu they had every interest in preserving, it required the economy to loosen its grip both on nature and on human beings. It implied the *de-growth* of that economy, 'and an accompanying expansion of those activities not governed by monetary evaluation and the pursuit of maximum efficiency and profit'.[57]

The Norm of the Sufficient, and the Good Life

Confident in his ecological awareness, Gorz was very soon in a position to criticize Lipietz for the element of his Marxism that was not properly thought-out: 'How', he wrote in 1983, 'can one be a socialist or a Communist and incapable of imagining an economy that isn't based on the indefinite growth of GNP?'[58] Against productivist logic, or 'growth-ist' logic as would later become the term, could one not erect another logic centred on life and another vision of the production of wealth?[59]

In *Capitalism, Socialism, Ecology*, Gorz took aim at the economic imperative of productivity and pitted against it 'ecological rationality', which 'consists in satisfying material needs in the best way possible with as small a quantity as possible of goods with a high use-value and durability, and thus doing so with a minimum of work, capital and natural resources'.[60] It met the behavioural norm of *sufficiency*. Writing in 1992 in an issue of the journal *Actuel Marx* devoted to ecology (this was the philosophical journal

---

57 Gorz, *Capitalism, Socialism, Ecology*, p. 95.

58 André Gorz to Alain Lipietz, 18 August 1983 (GRZ).

59 See also Dominique Méda, *La Mystique de la croissance. Comment s'en libérer* (Paris: Flammarion, 2013).

60 Gorz, *Capitalism, Socialism, Ecology*, p. 32.

co-edited by Jacques Bidet), Gorz noted that this norm antedated capitalism and that it was against it that capitalism had fought to impose its logic of 'ever more'.[61] By way of various forms of dispossession, nascent manufacturing capitalism had done all it could to enable production to 'free itself from the decisional power of the direct producers or, in other words, become independent of the relation between the needs and desires they feel, the extent of the effort they are prepared to expend to satisfy those needs and desires, and the intensity, duration and quality of that effort.'[62] The extraction of a surplus could not have been achieved otherwise.

Looking now to move beyond capitalism, one might envisage the restoration of the relation—and hence the trade-off—between the extent of the needs one wished to satisfy and the quantity of effort it was deemed acceptable to deploy as a result. That would be a two-way relation, since the decision to be made would also lead to 'limiting needs and desires so as to be able to limit the effort that has to be expended.'[63] This norm of 'the sufficient', reminiscent of the precepts of Epicurus, was the basis of the eco-socialist utopia Gorz was working towards: the utopia of a 'good life', as he put it, in which the temperate character of this synergy between need and expenditure went hand in hand with a wealth of social bonds.

The Holism of Life Systems: From Edgar Morin to Félix Guattari

When it came to grasping the global nature and complexity of life systems, Gorz paid attention to two authors in particular: Edgar Morin and Félix Guattari. After Morin had sent him a copy of one of the volumes of his major work *La Méthode* (*La Vie de la vie*, 1980), Gorz published a highly positive review in *Le Nouvel Observateur* in 1981, laying out the bio-anthropo-ethics undergirding the book.[64] On that occasion, he exchanged a number of scholarly letters with Morin. Gorz became acquainted with the thought of Guattari in the latter half of the 1990s at a time when they were collaborating closely on *Transversales*, a journal with affinities to the

---

61 André Gorz, 'Political Ecology between Expertocracy and Self-Limitation' in *Ecologica*, pp. 43–76.

62 Gorz, *Ecologica*, p. 63.

63 Gorz, *Ecologica*, p. 59.

64 Michel Bosquet, 'La dynamite d'Edgar Morin', *Le Nouvel Observateur* (5 January 1981). This was reprinted as a fourth appendix to the French original of *Paths to Paradise* (*Les Chemins du paradis*) but was not included in the English translation. [Trans.]

pioneers of systems theory.[65] A psychoanalyst, Guattari indirectly brought to Morin's vital holism a threefold dimension based on the psychological, sociopolitical and ecological well-being of the individual immersed in the 'molecular revolutions' of his subjectivity.

In conclusion, though the ecological movement 'did not arise out of a concern for the "defence of nature" but out of a resistance to the private appropriation and the destruction of that common good par excellence that is the lifeworld',[66] the fact is that ecology originates, as its ethico-political extensions (described as 'ecosophical' by Guattari in his *The Three Ecologies* [1989]) attest, 'from a holistic approach to complex systems':

> It is alone in attempting to understand life not in order to dominate it but to treat it considerately. It is alone, in this concern, in seeing itself as a component of culture, integrated and assimilated into experiential knowledge, illuminating the quest for wisdom and the good life.[67]

65 On Gorz's collaboration on that magazine, see chapter 16.
66 Gorz, *Immaterial*, p. 147.
67 Gorz, *Immaterial*, pp. 150–1.

CHAPTER SIXTEEN

Beyond the Wage-Based Society

By the time Gorz wrote *Critique of Economic Reason*, Fordism was already dead and buried. The constant falling of the rate of profit that characterized the late Fordist period had been arrested thanks to two major transformations, one relating to the labour process, the other to economic relations. The former was brought about by the methods of Toyotism (just-in-time delivery, robotization, outsourcing) which, when accompanied by new working relations (involvement, flexibility), overcame trade-union and labour resistance; the latter involved states, which dashed to the help of businesses rocked by the economic crisis, drastically diminishing their tax burden, privatizing profitable state-owned businesses and opening up the public sector to competition.

These neo-liberal practices, whose corollary was the asphyxiation of the welfare state, systemically increased inequalities of wealth and, from the mid-1980s onwards, generated the so-called new poverty (that affected the newly vulnerable lower-middle classes). While they also produced structural unemployment, Gorz reflected on the accompanying discourses around the rehabilitation of work, which ran counter to what was happening in reality.

The Ideology of Work

Automation, robotization and production geared to just-in-time delivery required increased capacities of control, organization, planning and adaptation that would be exercized by a new generation of technicians, who would be called upon to show unfailing personal involvement in their work. The enhancement and intellectualization of jobs, the value now attached to initiative and communication skills, the profit sharing and the team working that masked hierarchical relations and encouraged emulation gave the impression that workers' autonomy and sense of fulfilment—they had become 'co-workers' in the enterprise—were increasing. Might the ideal of the theorists of the new working class and the worker-self-management advocates actually be coming about?

Gorz didn't think so. First, because 'it [was] not the working class which [was] achieving these possibilities of self-organization and increasing technological power', but just 'a small core of privileged workers' who found themselves on the right side of the social divide.[1] Second, because the constraint on them, far from disappearing, was merely being better internalized and the degree of autonomy that elite experienced in their work in no way eliminated the 'heteronomy' of 'functions coordinated from outside, by an external organization, aiming at a pre-established goal'.[2] That 'autonomy within heteronomy' was, then, 'a dominated, enslaved, subaltern, instrumentalized autonomy, which from the outset had not the means to will itself as a demand for total emancipation'.[3]

It would only be a few years before the labour sociologists reached a definitive judgement: the individual's unconditional devotion to his 'mission'—thinking about work even when he isn't working—leads to a rise in cases of stress, exhaustion, depression and suicide; ultimately, it weakens the private and family identities of the person and his identity as a citizen while rendering his self-esteem fragile since it is dependent on the vagaries of his career.[4] Thus, while calling for the initiative, creativity and autonomy of 'colleagues', who are expected to commit themselves passionately to their work to the point of identifying wholly with the company, that company denies the divergence of interests between living labour and capital that had previously been recognized by Fordism through the institution of collective bargaining: it restores a pre-capitalist relation of personal submission (a 'quasi-vassalage'), in which the whole personality finds itself under subjection.[5] This latter analysis, taken from the Italian philosopher Paolo Virno, was broached by Gorz in his new book *Reclaiming Work*, first published in French in 1997. After going back extensively over the human damage engendered by post-Fordism, Gorz now denounced the illusions of other autonomists like Negri (exiled in France) who overestimated the liberatory reality of contemporary processes of 'subjectivation in work', much as he

1 Gorz, *Critique of Economic Reason*, pp. 70–1.

2 Gorz, *Critique of Economic Reason*, p. 79.

3 'Entretien avec André Gorz' in Gollain, *Une Critique du travail*, p. 226.

4 Christophe Dejours, *Souffrance en France. La banalisation de l'injustice sociale* (Paris: Seuil, 1998); Vincent de Gaulejac, *La Société malade de la gestion. Idéologie gestionnaire, pouvoir managérial et harcèlement social* (Paris: Seuil, 2005).

5 Gorz, *Reclaiming Work*, pp. 27–39.

himself had done in the 1960s when he believed that it would not be possible to halt increased autonomy once it was introduced into companies.[6]

This post-Fordist *New Spirit of Capitalism* [1999], described by Boltanski and Chiapello in their major study of that name, went together with a revival of the work ethic. This was not only promoted by Thatcherism (and later by its French variant under Nicolas Sarkozy, who extolled the 'value of work' as an ideological theme), but also defended implicitly by the trade unions and Left parties and intellectuals who lost their way trying to find conventional solutions to unemployment. As Gorz saw it, that ideology ran counter to 'the meaning of the current technological revolution', which could not be 'to rehabilitate the work ethic and identification with one's work', since 'a job whose effect and aim are to save work [in the sense of reducing the need for work] cannot, at the same time, glorify work as the essential source of personal identity and fulfilment.'[7]

And he lamented, as he already had in *Farewell to the Working Class*, the harmful political consequences of this underlying vision which the labour movement came to share with the employers: 'The ideology of effort and individual merit, the defence of employment and the identification with work thus became right-wing themes that enabled swathes of the working class to be won over to a new national-productivist alliance in support of liberal-capitalist modernization.'[8]

Overturning a Paradigm

Reclaiming Work is Gorz's most accomplished and mature book, both for its dismantling of the poverty-ridden workings of post-Fordism and its highlighting of the *possibilities* for its transcendence to be found in the interstices of that system. The representation of work, an essential strand in the liberal management of populations, is subject to this critical regime. With blackmail by unemployment at its height, work, which had become a scarce 'good', was now no longer seen by the mass of the population in its

---

6 Gorz, *Reclaiming Work*, pp. 39–41.

7 Gorz, *Critique of Economic Reason*, p. 88. Cf. Karl Marx: 'Capital itself is the moving contradiction: [in] that it presses to reduce labour time to a minimum, while it posits labour time, on the other side, as sole measure and source of wealth. Hence it diminishes labour time in the necessary form, so as to increase it in the superfluous form.' (*Grundrisse*, p. 706).

8 André Gorz, 'Droite/gauche. Essai de rédéfinition', *Revue du MAUSS* 14 (1991): 20.

anthropological dimension but solely from a utilitarian perspective: the question of the *occupation* one follows (with its set of skills) or the *work* one does (by acting in some way on tangible reality) was less important than the 'employment' one *has* or *doesn't have*, because it is employment—in its general sense of work of some kind or another—that provides one with an indispensable 'source of income'.

Casting a veil over the *economic* and *existential* questions of work (What is the purpose of production? What place should work have in life?), this ideology of employment for employment's sake spreads the belief that the key problem of our 'unemployment-sick' societies is employment, whereas the problem is actually our fixation on employment. That ideology is all the more hypocritical and cynical for the fact that, by pushing for the masses to be put to work and to accept any 'offer' of a job whatever—masses who are precisely excluded from work because of its growing scarcity—it plunges them into depression and guilt at their persistent exclusion. The norm of work imposes itself as something self-evident, relegating those who do not meet it to marginality—the worst of all this not being to *be* unemployed but to *feel* unemployed through the reproving attitude society has towards you. Behind an assumption shared by the majority, this—overwhelming—ideology prevents us from reflecting on another kind of society that would no longer be so obsessively attached to employment. Yet it is possible to think differently, to 'invert one's values'—in short, to change paradigm and to see, as one does so, that whole swathes of society are already questioning the axiom that work is the value by which life must be ordered.

Surveys conducted by sociologists and journalists in the Western countries in the 1980s and 90s are eloquent. They show that for many people, particularly young people, precarious employment over long periods was not something they merely accepted passively, but was seen rather as an opportunity to take responsibility themselves for the production of sociality outside of work and to invent a regime of daily life based on freedom of action.[9]

---

9 Gorz mentions, among others: Rainer Zoll (ed.), *Nicht so wie unsere Eltern. Ein neues kulturelles Modell?* (Frankfurt: Suhrkamp, 1989); Paul Grell and Anne Wéry, *Héros obscurs de la précarité. Récits de pratiques et stratégies de connaissance* (Paris: L'Harmattan, 1993); and the surveys of the journalist Alain Lebaube published in *Le Monde*. Later he would provide a preface to a study tending in this same direction: Sébastien Scherer, *La Vie quotidienne des jeunes chômeurs* (Paris: PUF, 1999).

The emergence of unemployment among managerial staff and longer life-expectancy, combined with the frequent recourse to early retirement, also contributed to a downplaying of the importance of work. Opinion polls reflect a similar mind set. In Germany, only 10 per cent of the active population regarded their work as the most important thing in their lives; in the US 18 per cent (as against 38 per cent in 1955). In Western Europe, only nine per cent of the young people questioned cited work as the 'main factor for success in life'.[10]

Criticism of Oskar Negt

Oskar Negt, a student of Adorno and subsequently assistant to Habermas, forged a reputation for himself by combining Critical Theory and Marxism. His sociology is based on an anthropology of work. Negt and Gorz liked each other and in an open letter in the *Festschrift* of 1989, Negt recognized Gorz, 10 years his senior, as one of his 'hidden mentors'. He recalled the importance his work on the strategy of 'revolutionary reforms' had had for him, then went on forcefully to express his incomprehension at the 'critical individualism' that underlay his *Farewell to the Working Class*.[11] Reacting to this 'friendly and devastating criticism',[12] Gorz declined to follow Negt's reasoning on one crucial point—though, as with Marcuse, Lipietz or Bahro, this did not damage the good relations between them.

Analysing the nature of contemporary work, Negt saw no presence of the 'iron cage' Weber spoke of (in other words, the 'systemic integration' denounced by Habermas), but saw work rather as the privileged site of social recognition and the possible personal fulfilment of the worker.[13] The Hegelian conception of work underlying this vision became fully apparent to Gorz when he saw Negt conceiving 'work as a *historico-fundamental* category'[14] tending to free itself progressively from capital and assert itself as an autonomous activity of transformation of matter. Gorz remarked that

---

10 Gorz, *Reclaiming Work*, pp. 63–4.

11 Oskar Negt, 'Aus produktiver Phantasie. Ein revolutionärer Realist unserer Zeit' in Krämer and Leggewie (eds), *Wege ins Reich der Freiheit*, pp. 54–73.

12 Gorz to Oskar Negt (in English), 23 May 1990 (GRZ).

13 Oskar Negt, *Lebendige Arbeit, enteignete Zeit. Politische und kulturelle Dimensionen des Kampfes um die Arbeitszeit* (Frankfurt: Campus Verlag, 1984), pp. 43–4.

14 Negt, 'Aus produktiver Phantasie', p. 69.

this ideal of creative work (*poiesis*) by which the worker realized himself, was in reality a legacy of the artisan workers of the nineteenth century who still had mastery of matter and that to seek to apply it to—largely dematerialized, specialized—contemporary work was to run the risk of inviting (both blue- and white-collar) workers to see tasks that precisely exclude personal self-realization as a means for achieving just that; this was merely to reinforce the ideology of work, which played the employers' game.[15]

In fact, that ideal is exclusive today to an elite group of workers who regard the reduced working week as incompatible with their ethic of involvement and productivity: Mothé, in his opposition to the idea of reduced working hours, made himself the reactionary representative of that group in a polemic with Gorz.[16] In current conditions, work cannot be creative and involving. As field studies show, it is outside of wage-labour that individuals—particularly, young people—acquire the capacities and desire to commit themselves to self-directed activities, thanks to the opportunities offered, initially, by late entry into working life and subsequently by unstable and irregular employment. 'The aspiration to all-round personal development in autonomous activities does not, therefore, presuppose a prior transformation of work.'[17] It is, rather, the de facto reduction of working hours across a lifetime that is the mechanism for that. Contributing to a *Festschrift* for Negt in 2004, Gorz would welcome his—always stimulating—writings, but would reiterate his criticism, noting that Negt's idea of 'real work' and his insistence on the current form of paid work, with its connection to the provision of means of subsistence and social recognition, ultimately prevented him from producing a critique of actually existing work.[18]

Guaranteed Social Income

It is quite clear that when the production process requires less and less work and distributes less and less in terms of wages, it is no longer possible to

15 Gorz, *Capitalism, Socialism, Ecology*, pp. 58–60.

16 Daniel Mothé, 'Faut-il réduire le temps du travail?', *Autogestions* 19 (1985): 15–17; André Gorz, 'Ne pas confondre activité autonome et travail salarié', *Autogestions* 19 (1985): 17–19.

17 Gorz, *Capitalism, Socialism, Ecology*, p. 59.

18 André Gorz, 'Wa(h)re Arbeit' in Tatjana Freytag and Marcus Hawel (eds), *Arbeit und Utopie. Oskar Negt zum 70. Geburtstag* (Frankfurt: Humanities Online, 2004), pp. 29–37.

restrict the right to an income only to those with a job or, most importantly, to have the level of income depend on the quantity of work performed by each individual.[19] Hence the idea of *guaranteeing a minimum income*. In a general way, this is not a new idea. It was applied in Great Britain in the late eighteenth century in the wake of the pauperization that followed the enclosures. It had a supporter in that defender of the Rights of Man Thomas Paine, who submitted his plan of 'a dividend for all' to the members of the French Directory. The humanist, anarchist visionary Bertrand Russell followed him in this regard, announcing his proposal at the end of the First World War. In France, Jacques Duboin incorporated the idea into his scheme for a Distributist economy in the 1930s. In the United States, the principle came close to being implemented in the 1960s campaign to defeat poverty in the form of a 'negative income tax'. This particular version of the idea was picked up by the Giscardian economist Lionel Stoléru in his book *Vaincre la pauvreté dans les pays riches* (1974).

Since the idea has had numerous advocates over the years, often separated widely in time, we may reasonably assume a range of differing motivations and a wide range of detailed proposals, each different in purpose and scope.[20] The idea seems to have been proposed at times as a measure of public assistance, at others as a variable regulating labour and its cost, and at yet others as a subversive, emancipatory move. That is why it has found support in varied quarters, Conservative, Christian, 'progressive' and 'green'. In the 1980s, as poverty worsened, it was eventually applied at a minimal level in a number of European countries in a form comparable to the future French *revenu minimum d'insertion*. In the countries where it didn't find concrete embodiment, it became the subject of frequent debates, coming to be seen primarily as a way of increasing the autonomy of individuals vis-à-vis the economic system. In this particular perspective, ecologists were generally first in line—with the exception of Les Verts in France who shared Lipietz's (initial) reservations about the idea. Opielka and Offe spring to mind in the Federal Republic—Gorz debated with them by correspondence in 1985 and 1986—but it was in Belgium that an admirer of Gorz's, won

---

19 Gorz, *Critique of Economic Reason*, p. 203.

20 See Yannick Vanderborght and Philippe Van Parijs, *L'Allocation universelle* (Paris: La Découverte, 2005); *Multitudes* 27 ('Revenu garanti: questions ouvertes') (Winter 2006); *Le Monde Diplomatique* 710 ('Une utopie à portée de main') (May 2013); *Mouvements*, 73 ('Un revenu pour exister') (Spring 2013).

over by his *Paths to Paradise*, would spearhead a substantial, radical version of the guaranteed social income.

Right- and Left-Wing Versions

As we have seen, Gorz subscribed to the principle of the guaranteed social income,[21] which he describes at length in *Paths to Paradise* as a lifetime income paid in exchange for a quantity of work, which productivity gains will have reduced to a minimum.[22] The aim was to increase individuals' autonomy by reducing their working hours and increasing their—temporal and material—capability to engage in activities for themselves. Reiterating this scheme in 1984 in an alternative Belgian magazine, Gorz attracted a first series of objections in the form of a response from Philippe van Parijs, a left-wing libertarian and ecologist, who was both inspired and frustrated by Gorz's arguments.[23] In an exchange of letters that preceded the publication of their positions, this young teacher at the Catholic University of Louvain, very much a stickler for the Gorzian principle of autonomy, raised in particular the delicate question of the *oversight*, implied in Gorz's model, of the obligatory working hours to be performed in return for the social income. Gorz played down the issue:

> The objection that the accomplishment of certain quotas (for example, at least 2,000 hours of work over five years) can only be achieved by heavy totalitarian-bureaucratic oversight is incomprehensible to me: does the current entitlement to a pension or to unemployment insurance require an oppressive machinery of oversight?[24]

So began a friendly intellectual relationship between Gorz and Van Parijs.[25] However, Van Parijs opened up a different path—which Gorz himself would

---

21 Françoise Gollain, 'André Gorz, vers l'inconditionnalité du revenu', *L'Économie politique* 67 (July 2015): 52–64.

22 Gorz, *Paths to Paradise*, pp. 40–7.

23 André Gorz, 'Au-delà de la société du travail', *Virages* (Brussels) 2 (April 1984): 8–12; Philippe Van Parijs, 'La porte étroite. Dialogue avec André Gorz', *Virages* (Brussels) 2 (April 1984): 13–15.

24 André Gorz to Philippe van Parijs, 5 March 1984, in response to a letter from van Parijs of 24 February (GRZ).

25 Philippe Van Parijs, 'De la sphère autonome à l'allocation universelle' in Fourel (ed.), *André Gorz, un penseur pour le XXIe siècle*, pp. 163–77.

not take for years—since he was becoming the foremost advocate of the idea of a guaranteed basic income free of any conditions: the universal allowance (*allocation universelle*). With that title—and in the name of the Collectif Charles Fourier which consisted of researchers from his university—Van Parijs wrote a short manifesto text in March 1984 which appeared to some fanfare in a number of countries—Belgium, Switzerland, Germany, Italy and, later, France. He invited Gorz to respond in a Brussels periodical of Left Christian origins called *La Revue nouvelle*, where the manifesto made its first appearance in a magazine in April 1985.

In his reply, 'Allocation universelle: version de droite et version de gauche',[26] Gorz stressed the conditions in which—and only in which—guaranteed income was a left-wing solution.[27] The criterion he specified was that of the social divide: did the payment of a basic income reinforce that divide or reduce it?

The point is that there is a right-wing version of the universal allowance, advocated for example by Milton Friedman in *Capitalism and Freedom* (1962), which deepens social division by stimulating the creation of jobs of an occasional, precarious, thankless or seasonal type etc.: this consists in indirectly subsidizing the employers for these—otherwise economically unviable—low-grade activities by allowing them to pay low wages by granting a social assistance payment at a rate so low that people are forced into work.

It is clear where the Left alternative lies: the basic allowance must be set as an acceptable (Gorz calls it a 'normal') living wage, so as to prevent people being forced to work for a pittance. And not only that. It must be conceived not as the 'wages for unemployment and exclusion', but as the assurance that we are part of society, that we can participate in the production of what is necessary on the scale available to us in our particular lives. The work performed in exchange for this allowance is thus an expression of our right to work. For that right to be respected, it is essential that the claim to a basic allowance be inextricably linked to the demand for a generalized reduction of working hours that would allow working time to be shared: 'The Left alternative to the fragmented, 'dual' society is one in which everyone can

---

26 André Gorz, 'Allocation universelle: version de droite et version de gauche', *La Revue nouvelle* 81 (April 1985): 419–28 (apart from the hook paragraph, which refers to the Collectif Fourier, the article was actually written in November 1984 and is not a direct response to the manifesto).

27 See also *Critique of Economic Reason*, pp. 203–12.

work, but work very little.'[28] If Gorz harboured some suspicion with regard to the universal allowance, it was that it also ran the risk of maintaining 'the split within society'[29] by severing, through its unconditionality, any link between income and work.

The idea nonetheless made headway in France. A left-wing Gaullist, the economist Yoland Bresson, championed it in his book *L'Après-salariat* (1984), though he set it at a very low level. If the Distributists of *La Grande Relève*, led by Marie-Louise Duboin, were natural supporters, it is the anti-utilitarians of the *Bulletin du MAUSS* group—and in particular its director Alain Caillé—we have to thank for launching discussion in favour of the measure in their September 1987 issue. Under the title 'Du revenu social: au-delà de l'aide, la citoyenneté?' [On the social income: beyond assistance, citizenship?], that issue reprinted the articles by the Collectif Fourier and Gorz that had appeared in *La Revue nouvelle*.

For Gorz, Marie-Louise Duboin, whom he would engage in dialogue both face to face and by correspondence, remained an important figure in the theoretical debate that would occupy him in the following years.[30] The same was true of the sociologist and founder of the anti-utilitarian social science movement MAUSS (Mouvement antiutilitariste dans les sciences sociales) Alain Caillé, who drew on Marcel Mauss's theory of the gift to combat the prevailing utilitarianism and economism and who, when MAUSS was created in 1981, would call on Gorz to speak at the association's meetings.

In France, the basic income wasn't a theme solely debated by committed intellectuals. It was also a concrete demand of 'the social movement', and particularly of a fringe of it which seemed to embody, after the category of the 'proletariat' had been hollowed out, the greatly sought-after 'social subject': the unemployed and insecure workers organized into associations.

---

28 Gorz, 'Allocation universelle': 423.

29 Gorz, *Capitalism, Socialism, Ecology*, p. 96. See also, André Gorz, 'Emploi et revenu, un divorce nécessaire?', interview by Denis Clerc, *Alternatives économiques* 23 (July–September 1984): 15–17 (Van Parijs's arguments, presented at the Marx conference of the École des hautes études en sciences sociales in December 1983, are explicitly criticized in this interview).

30 On the relationship between Gorz and Duboin, see the dossier 'Trente ans de dialogue avec André Gorz', *La Grande Relève* 1981 (November 2007).

With the Movement of the Unemployed and the Insecure Workers

There was one question on the lips of all Gorz's doubting or confused inter-locutors: on what 'real movement' was he relying to lend credibility to his prophecy of a new civilization of free time? The non-class of post-industrial proletarians that he had begun to sketch out in *Farewell to the Working Class* formed no homogeneous grouping of individuals, except abstractly in the sense that they were all out of phase with secure, full-time employment. For that reason, dissidence and opposition could only spring, in the first instance, from an individual act of will: 'from the ashes of the historical subject—Party, State, Class—arises the individual subject who cries "no" to all the old garbage,' rages Gorz.[31] Far removed from the processes of sociali-zation inherent in the stable work that had made workers' organization possible, these individual situations reflected a loose social grouping, shaped by unemployment or the new forms of insecure—part-time or intermit-tent—employment. Though it was to be found on the fringes of the world of work, this loose agglomeration of people nonetheless represented a massive number of individuals who, though not able to combine through traditional trade union channels, found ways of creating networks, coordi-nation and places to communicate.[32]

The French trade union of the unemployed—Association syndicale des chômeurs (ASC)—took off in February 1982 under the leadership of Maurice Pagat, a strong personality who knew how to exploit his political contacts and win support in Catholic circles. As the first unemployed dem-onstration was taking place in Paris on 30 May 1985—at which Pagat com-pared the movement 'to the heroic beginnings of Fernand Pelloutier's *Bourses du travail*'—unemployed centres and local associations were already up and running in a number of French towns and cities. The *Manifeste pour la garantie des moyens d'existence pour tous* [Manifesto for Guaranteed Means of Existence for All], launched in February 1987 by Cash (Asso-ciation des chômeurs et des précaires [ACP]), a Parisian grouping including a large number of people in insecure employment, expressed a shared demand: the introduction of a social income equivalent to the SMIC (*salaire*

---

31 *Abschied vom Proletariat?*, p. 123 (Gorz).

32 Guy Standing, *The Precariat: The New Dangerous Class* (London: Bloomsbury Publishing, 2011); Patrick Cingolani, *Révolutions précaires. Essai sur l'avenir de l'éman-cipation* (Paris: La Découverte, 2014).

minimum interprofessionnel de croissance)—the ASC, for its part, proposed a level of two-thirds of the SMIC—or up to the level of the SMIC if it was in addition to other forms of partial income, with recipients being available for any kind of work in return.

It was with his journalist's hat on that Gorz came to know Pagat and supported him in his struggle.[33] The trade unionist, in turn, steeped himself in Gorz's political analyses and proposals, inviting him on several occasions to the union's study days and national convention ('even though', as he wrote to him in 1992, 'I know how much you dislike taking part in this type of meeting').[34] Between 1983 and 2003 some 30 articles by Gorz appeared in *Partage*, the trade union's magazine, some of them written expressly for it. The high point of Gorz's trade union engagement came with the lecture he gave at the ASC's study day at the Maison des chômeurs, Saint-Ouen on 13 December 1986, with some 50 activists and researchers present, on the theme 'The technical revolution, employment and the guaranteed social income'. On that occasion, he met the autonomists of *Cash* who, reporting the event, spotted a contradiction in his talk: 'Why criticize the ideology of work and simultaneously take the view that an egalitarian society can be achieved only through a right to employment for all?'[35]

The introduction of the *revenu minimum d'insertion* (RMI: equivalent to the UK's income support) by Michel Rocard's government in December 1988 put an end to this first upsurge of the unemployed and insecure workers' movement: the members of ASC, who had actively exerted pressure on Rocard, were satisfied; those of *Cash* were disappointed and saw the ground cut from under them since the insecure workers, whom they represented in greater numbers, were excluded from a benefit that prohibited the simultaneous receipt of other forms of income.

---

33 See Michel Bosquet, 'La grève de Maurice Pagat', *Le Nouvel Observateur* (11 December 1982). The strike in question was a hunger strike to protest, in part, at the suicide of two unemployed workers.

34 Maurice Pagat to André Gorz, 13 June 1992 (GRZ).

35 Anonymous, 'Gorz, technocrate ou utopiste?', *Cash* 5 (January 1987): 2. Gorz takes up the arguments of the 'Cash' group in *Capitalism, Socialism, Ecology*, p. 91.

Unconditionality of the Universal Allowance

The conference on the Universal Allowance, organized by Van Parijs at Louvain in 1986 with the participation of Yoland Bresson and Marie-Louise Duboin from France, Guy Standing from Britain, Adler-Karlsson from Sweden and the Germans Opielka and Offe, saw the creation of the Basic Income European Network (BIEN). At a conference on the same theme, which followed at Louvain in September 1989, Gorz was viewed as the black sheep of the family, contributing a critical article in which he expressed his fear that the universal allowance might lead to a de-socialization of the individuals who remained outside the world of work.[36] In the first half of the 1990s, Gorz spent a lot of time explaining his conception of the social income, which was to be understood as 'a continuous income for discontinuous work'[37] and therefore had to remain linked to work, if not to working hours. He stated clearly that the right to work was part of the contract the individual struck with society, in exchange for the right to an income:

> One cannot wish to ground either citizenship or a sense of true belonging to society in society giving *you* something without you having the opportunity to give anything back. For, all in all, the establishment of a universal allowance does not by itself open up a societal space for non-economic activities. It merely *dispenses* from work and in fact, in current conditions, tends to make the exclusion from any participation in the process of production less visible or even invisible—that exclusion by which one finds oneself in a situation of having nothing to give, no socially recognized capability.[38]

Gorz came to think, then, of this right to work, which he admitted to regarding as a duty, as a source of citizenship. It was so also for another reason, since it was socialization through work that enabled us to accord primacy to society (*Gesellschaft*) over community (*Gemeinschaft*), to cite the classic

---

36 André Gorz, 'On the difference between society and community, and why basic income cannot by itself confer full membership of either' in Philippe Van Parijs (ed.), *Arguing for Basic Income: Ethical Foundations for a Radical Reform* (London: Verso Books, 1992), pp. 178–84.

37 Gorz, 'Sortir de la société salariale', *Transversales Science Culture* 25 (January–February 1994): 16.

38 André Gorz to Alain Caillé, 21 January 1992 (GRZ).

distinction made by Ferdinand Tönnies, and hence to counterbalance the influence of the group:

> Wage labour, restrictive and unpleasant as it may be in other respects, liberates us from our imprisonment in a narrow community. [...] Work and micro-social activities or—and this amounts to the same—functional integration and belonging to a community are complementary to one another, each containing the critique of the other and freeing us from the other.[39]

New Convergences

With unemployment and poverty reaching new heights, it was during the 1990s that the basic income debate rapidly gained momentum in France. The Habermasian philosopher Jean-Marc Ferry argued for a universal allowance at the European level (*L'Allocation universelle*, 1995). The remarkable Centre des jeunes dirigeants d'entreprise (CJD) could not conceive of the twenty-first century company without a system of 'flexicurity', based on a basic or subsistence income [*revenu d'existence*].[40] Magazines, mostly politically committed ones, published dossiers on the issue: *Transversales* (edited by Jacques Robin) in May 1992, *Futuribles* (Hugues de Jouvenel) in February 1994, *La Revue du MAUSS* (Alain Caillé) in January–June 1996, *Futur antérieur* (Vincent and Negri) in September 1996. It was by reflecting on these publications and moving closer to the intellectual networks that animated them that Gorz would develop his thinking. If he would now 'rather keep on writing rather than meet politicians',[41] his new allegiances would involve him in taking public stances that required a response from them.

His most prolific exchanges were with Jacques Robin, a man four years his senior. Robin, who had trained as a doctor, had spent many years attempting to describe the multi-dimensional implications of the changes in technology and information/communications. After '68, he managed the informal Groupe des Dix [Group of Ten] that was engaged in a 'systemist'

---

39 André Gorz, 'Revenu minimum et citoyenneté', *Futuribles* 184 (February 1994): 59.

40 A book with the title *L'Entreprise au XXIe siècle* [The company in the twenty-first century] was published by the CJD in 1996.

41 Marie-Béatrice Baudet, 'Les réflexions d'André Gorz et de Guy Aznar ont ouvert le débat', *Le Monde* (10 November 1993) (Dossier 'Le Retour de la réduction du temps de travail').

effort to bring together culture and science (with Edgar Morin, Henri Laborit, René Passet, Jacques Attali, Henri Atlan and Joël de Rosnay as members, among others). From the 1980s onwards, he led what was to become the Groupe de réflexions inter-et trans-disciplinaires (GRIT: Group of Inter- and Transdisciplinary Thinking). This comprised Jean-Pierre Dupuy from the outset, with, as before, Atlan, Morin, Passet and de Rosnay. Patrick Viveret would join them later.

After they first made contact in 1992, the acquaintanceship between the solitary Gorz and the heavily networked Robin led, early in 1994, to the first of the many articles Gorz published in *Transversales*, the journal of GRIT, and to a co-authored declaration that appeared in *Libération* on 24 February.[42] In that declaration, which was part of the—once again topical—debate on a shorter working week, the Socialists were encouraged (after the example of Michel Rocard, who was preaching a tax policy based on a negotiated 32-hour week) to work for a clear reduction of working hours, which the two writers set at 32–33 hours with, as an economic feasibility measure (conceptualized by Guy Aznar), the payment to employees of a 'second cheque' raised from targeted indirect taxes. After his article in the February issue of *Futuribles* on the universal allowance,[43] Gorz took part in a seminar on the subject on 30 March in Paris, where he met Robin and the other contributors to that issue: Van Parijs, Aznar, Clerc etc. In April, at his house at Vosnon, with the cameras of the Arte TV channel present, he debated the question of the decline and meaning of work with Jean-Baptiste de Foucauld, an associate of Delors. Lastly, Robin and Gorz revived their double-act to give *Le Monde* a long declaration, published on 8 October 1996, in which they observed that 'another economy and another society are now asking to be born, in which the work of production will occupy only a subordinate place, while the time for producing society, producing oneself and producing meaning will come to predominate'.[44]

Alain Caillé, the driving force behind MAUSS, was another important contact for Gorz. They kept up a sustained correspondence from the early 1990s onwards, discussing the Right–Left divide, which Gorz saw as lying

---

42 Gorz, 'Sortir de la société salariale'; André Gorz and Jacques Robin, 'Pour l'emploi autrement', *Libération* (24 February 1994).

43 André Gorz, 'Revenu minimum et citoyenneté'.

44 André Gorz and Jacques Robin, 'Forger un autre avenir', *Le Monde* (8 October 1996).

between productivism and anti-productivism; the concepts of Habermas, which left him dissatisfied; and lastly, the vexed question of the unconditionality of the universal allowance. Passing over their divergences, particularly where the universal allowance was concerned, Caillé of MAUSS and, after him, Robin of GRIT gathered 35 signatures for a statement *Le Monde* published on 28 June 1995 entitled 'Chômage: appel au débat' [Unemployment: Call for a debate]. The signatories included Gorz, Aznar, Bresson, Ferry, Lipietz, Negri, Pagat, Passet, Roustang, Viveret, together with Aline and Jacques Archimbaud, Annie Dreuille, Serge Latouche, Jean-Louis Laville, Roger Sue, Bernard Perret and even Mothé. The statement advocated three sets of *interdependent* measures (Lipietz called them 'the indivisible triptych') which seemed necessary for the emergence of new forms of solidarity: reduced working hours; the promotion of the associative activities making up the solidarity economy; and the establishment of a minimum income that could be received concurrently with other resources without any obligation for job-seeking.

A year later, in June 1996, on the back of this statement, the AECEP association (Appel européen pour une citoyenneté et une économie plurielles [European Appeal for a Plural Citizenship and Economy]) was created. At one of its later meetings, with the principal signatories (Caillé, Robin, Laville, Negri, Sue, Viveret etc.) present at the maison Grenelle in Paris, headquarters of both the AECEP and GRIT, Gorz argued for a radical position that was entirely new for him: he went over to supporting an *unconditional* universal allowance, arguing at the same time that it should be set at a relatively high level. Caillé, who had long advocated a guaranteed income (with nothing demanded in exchange, though it would be set at a moderate level and restricted to the destitute), actually felt troubled by the radical nature of the proposal. When Gorz sent him *Reclaiming Work*, he responded with a letter:

> You write in your dedication that you like my move towards radicalism. I'm rather tempted to return the compliment and tell you that I like your move—quite clear, I believe—towards an anti-utilitarian style of argument. Despite my disagreement, at least for the foreseeable future, over your idea of a radically unconditional income set at a high level (though the cautious formulations in your book trouble me less than when you spoke at AECEP), I greatly

liked your book. It is truly inspired and many of its statements go to the very heart of the matter.[45]

Why Unconditionality?

Gorz's conversion to an *unconditional* universal allowance can be seen as implicit in his article 'Revenu de citoyenneté et pluralité des fins légitimes', which *Transversales* published in summer 1996. Gorz takes over Caillé's idea that the activity of human beings is driven by a plurality of legitimate ends that exceed the frame of commodity logic and that the granting of an unconditional citizenship income has the precise function of cultivating that plurality. He asks himself on what condition one may still speak of citizenship when nothing is required in return any longer. The condition, as he sees it, is that one and the same person should be given the opportunity 'to participate, simultaneously or alternately, in work and in "activities outside of work".[46]

In *Reclaiming Work*, published in September 1997, Gorz laid out the four reasons for his conversion, which were all rooted in the perspectives opened up by the changes wrought by post-Fordism.

1. When intelligence and imagination become the main productive force, then hours worked cease to be the measure of work: it then becomes 'difficult to define an irreducible quantity of work to be performed by each person' in exchange for the guaranteed income.[47]

2. Unconditionality and the granting of a guaranteed income at a sufficient level make it possible to escape the stigmatization of the unemployed that ensues from the various forms of workfare, including the incitement to part-time working that is implied in Bresson's writings by the idea of a minimal basic income.[48] These two criteria combined encourage the blossoming and non-commodification of voluntary, artistic, cultural, family or mutual-aid activities, 'which are only meaningful when done for their own sake'.[49] From

---

45 Alain Caillé to André Gorz, 1 November 1997 (GRZ).

46 André Gorz, 'Revenu de citoyenneté et pluralité des fins légitimes', *Transversales Science Culture* 40 (July–August 1996): 6–8.

47 Gorz, *Reclaiming Work*, p. 85.

48 Gorz, *Reclaiming Work*, pp. 80–82.

49 Gorz, *Reclaiming Work*, p. 87.

this same standpoint, the granting of what some call a citizen income should not be justified by the performance of voluntary or charitable activities, as proposed by Jeremy Rifkin and Claus Offe, or by everyone's participation in the collective intelligence that underlies living capital, as Antonio Negri and his autonomist Marxist friends argue—they who see this 'invisible' work extending right into our general behaviour in life. Unconditionality must be understood as the guarantee of complete freedom in our ways of acting outside of economic circuits. Instead of remunerating work performed, the universal allowance 'should make activities possible which in themselves *are* wealth and are an end in themselves. It should withdraw these activities from the market and from any economic evaluation and pre-definition.'[50]

3. The 'general intellect', as Marx had foreseen in the *Grundrisse*, is a productive force that reduces the contribution of immediate work to very little. But the autonomy of individuals that ensues is limited in such a way that it can be controlled and subjugated. The universal allowance serves, rather, to unshackle it:

> [I]t is one of the functions of an unconditional basic income to make the right to develop one's capacities an unconditional right to an autonomy which transcends its productive function; an autonomy experienced and valued for its own sake on a variety of planes: moral (autonomy of value-judgement), political (autonomy of decision-making regarding the common good), cultural (invention of life-styles, consumption models and arts of living) and existential (the capacity to take care of oneself, rather than leave the experts and authorities to decide what is good for us).'[51]

4. The universal allowance corresponds best to the economy that is emerging, as it is meant to be taken from the socially produced volume of wealth, not from the volume of incomes from work, which is tending to contract (the funding of pensions runs up against the same set of problems) or revenues from capital, which are rising today only because of the inflation of speculative bubbles that are doomed to implode. The distribution of means

---

50 André Gorz, 'Valeur et richesse: le divorce', *Transversales Science Culture* 3 (July–September 2002): 47; see also Gorz, *Immaterial*, pp. 26–9.

51 Gorz, *Reclaiming Work*, p. 88.

of payment becomes, as Jacques Duboin foresaw, a 'social income':[52] it supposes the creation of another form of money, corresponding to the value of commodities produced and hence not capable of being hoarded, which Passet, following Duboin, calls 'consumption money'.[53] What we are speaking about at this point is a 'primary income':

> When fully thought through, the universal grant of a basic income can be seen as equivalent to a *pooling* of socially produced wealth. [. . .] It cannot be achieved immediately, but we must begin to conceptualize it and prepare the way for it as of now. *It has heuristic value: it reflects the most basic and advanced meaning of present developments.*[54]

Unsurprisingly, on 15 October 1997 Gorz informed Van Parijs that he had joined BIEN.

The Central Figure of the Insecure Worker

The accession of the 'plural' Left (Socialists, Communists, Radicals and Greens) to power in 1997 provided a heaven-sent opportunity to move on the reforms called for by the AECEP, as well as by the movement of the unemployed and insecurely employed that was reborn from its ashes. That movement made the headlines in the winter of 1997–98 with huge protests and the occupation of administrative buildings and other public or private places in order to call primarily for an increase in the levels of basic welfare benefits.[55] At this juncture, Gorz hailed the emergence of a 'shared public awareness' that 'the main pattern and normal condition' of employment (at

---

52 For Gorz's relationship to Jacques Duboin, see Marie-Louise Duboin, 'André Gorz et l'économie distributive' in Fourel (ed.), *André Gorz, un penseur pour le XXIe siècle*, pp. 125–46.

53 Gorz, *Reclaiming Work*, p. 90.

54 Gorz, *Reclaiming Work*, pp. 90–1 (The text here was slightly remodelled by Gorz for the 1999 English version, but the changes do not significantly affect the overall presentation of the argument and I have retained the published translation [Trans.]). See Carlo Vercellone, 'Capitalisme cognitive et revenu social garanti comme revenu primaire' in Caillé and Fourel (eds), *Sortir du capitalisme*, pp. 137–48.

55 Marie Agnès Combesque, *Ça suffit! Histoire du mouvement des chômeurs* (Paris: Plon, 1998).

the point of recruitment) 'is now one of insecurity for workers'[56] (in 1997, 73 per cent of new employment was on fixed-term contracts).

The group *Agir ensemble contre le chômage* (AC!), formed in 1994 following demonstrations against the CIP Youth Employment Contract (also known as the *SMIC jeunes*), campaigned for an optimal guaranteed income. Gorz, who took part in its meetings in Paris, was delighted to see that AC! wasn't calling for an illusory return to full employment, but 'inventing and testing out full-employment of life.'[57] The guaranteed income was conceived not so much as a right to participate actually or virtually in the production of social wealth, but as a means of developing far more enriching activities than people were limited to by the system—activities 'which create intrinsic wealth that is neither measurable nor exchangeable' by the yardstick of a market.[58] The agitation was also carried on by the MNCP, which had succeeded the ASC. The MNCP was one of the movements heeding Gorz's proposals (and those of the AECEP), particularly thanks to Annie Dreuille, an official at the Toulouse Maison des chômeurs, who strove heroically to promote autonomous spaces and initiatives for the purpose of achieving 'social citizenship' for the unemployed. This Catholic activist was steeped in Gorz's writings and retained very close ties to him, as is attested by the three visits she paid to Vosnon.

The Jospin Socialist government chose to put down the movement by force. And the reforms it undertook seemed to offer no solution to the problems faced. Instead of the four-day week (32 hours) and arrangements to support optional part-time working that would have been accompanied by appropriate tax reforms, the employment minister Martine Aubry passed the 35-hour laws in 1998 and 2000, which had some success in increasing new job numbers but the costs of which, borne by businesses, would lead to the intensification of work and a deterioration of working conditions. Instead of boosting activities outside the market economy, a later social law focused on the return to work by establishing the 'employment bonus' (PPE).

A cycle of struggles and hope came to an end. Particularly as the economic upturn from 1998 onwards, which reconnected growth with

---

56 André Gorz, 'Misères du présent, richesse du possible', interview by Carlo Vercellone, Patrick Dieuaide and Pierre Peronnet, *Alice* 1 (Autumn 1998): 31–5.

57 Gorz, *Immaterial*, p. 132.

58 Gorz, *Immaterial*, pp. 130–1.

employment by temporarily reducing the numbers of unemployed (until 2001), eased the social pressure and indefinitely postponed the attendant demands.

Multi-activity and a Plural Economy

'It isn't the job of the economy to provide work, to create employment.'[59] On the contrary, it saves work and 'therefore produces massively that crucial resource which, for the founders of modern economic theory,[60] should be "the true measure of wealth": time freed from economic necessities and constraints.'[61] Everything is tending, then, towards the emergence of 'a society in which wealth will be measured by the time freed up from work, by the time available for the activities that have their meaning and end in themselves and equate with the flourishing of life.'[62]

Admittedly, capital and the state that serves it carefully maintain people's incapacity to use free time, which is harnessed and monetized to become a commodity. It must, above all, not be 'a time for oneself, for thinking, for contemplation, for disinterested, objectless enjoyment, in which people take time out, regenerate themselves and recreate themselves as subjects'.[63] With regard to this 'time for oneself', Gorz refers his readers to the joyous *Art de la sieste* (1998) by the urbanist Thierry Paquot, though the happy writings of another poet of the city and of life necessarily come to mind in this context: Pierre Sansot, author of *Les Gens de peu* (1991), *Du bon usage de la lenteur* (1998) etc.

The need for a sufficient income is one thing, the need to act, to make things, to pit oneself against others and be appreciated by them is another: capitalism systematically links the two and bases its hold over society on this confusion. But the right to an income is no longer based on

---

59 André Gorz, 'Bâtir la civilisation du temps libéré' (1993) in *Bâtir la civilisation du temps libéré* (Paris: Les liens qui libèrent/Le Monde diplomatique, 2013), p. 47.

60 An allusion to Leontief, to Keynes and to an anonymous Ricardian cited by Marx in the *Grundrisse*. See *Ecologica*, pp. 72–3.

61 André Gorz, 'Bâtir la civilisation du temps libéré', p. 49.

62 Gorz, Preface to *Shihonshugi, shakaishugi, ekoroji* (Tokyo, 1993). This is the Japanese version of *Capitalism, Socialism, Ecology* (manuscript in French, GRZ 8.43).

63 Gorz, 'De l'aptitude au temps libre', *Transversales Science Culture* 50 (March–April 1998), p. 24.

employment; nor should these other vital needs we speak of depend on paid work, done to order. This latter will consequently occupy a decreasing place in society and in everyone's lives. '*Working time will cease to be the dominant social time*'.[64] This perspective, which corresponds to ongoing cultural changes, helps to back up 'the aspiration for a multi-active life, within which each person can give work its limited place, instead of relegating "life" to the limited time allowed for it by the constraints of "work".'[65] Summing this up in a play on words, Gorz says, *L'emploi du temps n'est plus le temps de l'emploi*—one's timetable is no longer just the time spent doing one's job.[66]

But multi-activity isn't just the form in which people's aspiration to autonomy seeks its fulfilment. It is also the subjectivation of a capacity for autonomy which the post-Fordist economy demands from 'human capital'. There is the source of a conflict between the company and the workers here, and it bears on the status of that autonomy, its scope, its 'rights over itself'.[67] Thus the report by Jean Boissonnat, commissioned by the French General Planning Commission in 1995, advocated that, where there was a drop in the need for labour, contracts for staff activity outside of companies should be issued solely on the employer's terms. The electoral agreement of the 'pink-green' alliance that came to power in 1997 did, however, make provision for boosting multi-activity in a 'third sector'. Did this mean autonomy could still be preserved?

In 1999, Alain Lipietz drafted a report for the Minister of Employment Martine Aubry as a basis for a framework law. By stressing the *societal* (social, cultural and ecological) *usefulness* of the third sector, which positions itself outside the private and the public sectors, this report also stressed the need to clarify and define its status, with a view to enacting public measures to promote it (tax breaks and subsidies). It was not unanimously welcomed.

The backers of the 'social economy', like the sociologist Jean-Louis Laville, the Green Jacques Archimbaud or the economist Christophe Fourel (in the orbit of the *Alternatives économiques* group) approved the perspective

---

64 Gorz, *Reclaiming Work*, p. 73.

65 Gorz, *Reclaiming Work*.

66 André Gorz, 'Gorz, bourreau du travail', interview by Robert Maggiori and Jean-Baptiste Marongiu, *Libération* 25 (September 1997).

67 Gorz, *Reclaiming Work*, p. 74.

it outlined, insofar as it promoted the rise of a protected economic sector that was both a market and non-market entity.[68] The social economy was not aiming, as they saw it, to be a sector of non-monetized mutual aid but, by combining paid work with diverse types of voluntary activity, it was rejecting the marketization of services and promoting a common good.[69]

By contrast, those who preferred to speak of a 'plural economy' and whom we might now call 'convivialists', like Gorz and Caillé, or the 'anti-economists' like Latouche, who was also a member of MAUSS, feared that framing the third sector's aims officially (validating that sector socially) might curb the autonomy of initiatives and exclude activities of no obvious utility that could nonetheless play a part in creating social bonds and offering individual fulfilment.[70] As Gorz saw it, this 'plural economy' should refuse to function as an auxiliary, salve or safety-valve for the dominant economic system and should be 'the lever for setting the whole of society in movement and challenging [. . .] the domination of society and culture by the logic of capitalist valorization. If the supporters and theorists of the "social economy" were approaching this in the same spirit. [. . .] I would be less reticent about them,' he wrote to Jacques Robin.[71]

If we come back now to the principle of multi-activity, then as Gorz saw it the basic social income, linked to the expansion of free time, was not so much a reducer as a multiplier of activity. Instead of being forced to work at a job to have an income, it enabled a person to have an income to do and make things in an unfettered way—in other words, to engage in all sorts

---

68 See Christophe Fourel (ed.), *La Nouvelle Économie sociale. Efficacité, solidarité et démocratie* (Paris: Syros, 2001). For an overall view, see Timothée Duverger, *L'Économie sociale et solidaire. Une histoire de la société civile en France et en Europe de 1968 à nos jours* (Lormont: Le Bord de l'eau, 2016).

69 Jean-Louis Laville, 'Penser le changement social' in Caillé and Fourel (eds), *Sortir du capitalisme*, pp. 92–3.

70 See *Transversales Science Culture*, 57 ('Le Tiers Secteur en débat'), May–June 1999, including André Gorz, 'Le tiers secteur au-delà de la société salariale', pp. 26–8. On the case for the social validation of all activity, including the autonomous, see Jean-Marie Harribey, 'Le revenu d'existence ou l'impensé sur le travail', *Le Monde* (20 October 2014) (available at: lemonde.fr; last accessed: 27 July 2022). In response, see Jean-Éric Hyafil, 'Le revenu universel, rémunération du bien commun', *Le Monde* (7 November 2014) (available at: lemonde.fr; last accessed: 27 July 2022).

71 André Gorz to Jacques Robin, 23–25 March 2001 (GRZ).

of 'self-organized, self-managed, voluntary' activities that were 'open to everyone'.[72] He had in mind workshops, clubs, cooperatives, voluntary associations, and networks of an artistic, political, scientific, ecosophic, sporting, craft-related or relational type; and activities of self-producing, repair, restoration of the natural and cultural heritage, enhancement of the environment, energy-saving and the exchange of services.

Inspired by the Swedish essayist Nordal Akerman,[73] whom he contacted back in 1986 and met in 1990, and also by Jean Zin, a radical environmentalist philosopher living in the fastnesses of the Lot département, with whom he carried on a correspondence,[74] he reactivated Murray Bookchin's idea of municipal cooperatives producing for themselves, which he now envisaged as high-tech, globally interconnected forms of organization.[75] He was, moreover, particularly sensitive to what was represented by the cooperative circles or Local Exchange Trading Systems (LETS) that had been developing in North America and Europe since the late 1980s.[76] These forms of exchange actually escaped commodity fetishism. Regulated by a time-based currency, they eliminated exchange-value and the hoarding of money, met authentic needs, and promoted the specific skills everyone had within themselves.

Where Gorz is concerned, it would be going too far to say, as Jean Zin does, that 'he actually harbours an ideal of autarky, rejecting the specialization of work and the division of labour (as though that were possible, as though one could do everything oneself!). Yet,' he rightly adds, 'the aim is not so much the independence afforded by autarky, but rather self-production in the sense of a conscious production of oneself and a re-appropriation of one's life, a projected re-appropriation of one's lifeworld.'[77] This is because Gorz knows very well that a 'residual problem' remains, 'relating to types of production requiring a technical level and resources that cannot be commanded on the scale of a local community and require skills which it

---

72 Gorz, *Reclaiming Work*, p. 100.

73 Gorz, *Reclaiming Work*, pp. 105–06.

74 Jean Zin sent him his article, 'La coopérative municipale' (4 November 2003). This would appear in *EcoRev'* 15 (Winter 2003–04).

75 Gorz, *Wissen, Wert und Kapital*, p. 102.

76 Gorz, *Reclaiming Work*, p. 102–06.

77 Jean Zin, 'André Gorz, pionnier de l'écologie politique' in Fourel (ed.), *André Gorz. Un penseur pour le XXIe siècle*, pp. 76–7.

is difficult to imagine being pooled (transmitted and made accessible to everyone)', such as microsurgery technology or the design of high-tech equipment.[78]

What Is Wealth?

In the previous chapter we were able to see that the economic and the ecological logics are antithetical. This is confirmed when we look at them from the key angle of the assessment of wealth:

> [W]hat appears, from the ecological point of view, as a waste and destruction of resources is perceived from the economic point of view as a source of growth: competition between enterprises speeds up innovation, and the volume of sales and velocity of capital circulation increase as a result of obsolescence and the more rapid renewal of products. And what, from the ecological point of view, seems a saving (product durability, prevention of illness and accidents, lower energy and resource consumption) reduces the production of economically measurable wealth in the form of GNP, and appears on the macro-economic level as a source of loss.[79]

In 2000–01, at the request of the French Secretary of State for the Solidarity Economy Guy Hascoët of the Green party, Patrick Viveret drafted a report aimed at reconsidering wealth (*Reconsidérer la richesse*, 2003), in order to take account of those elements that lie beyond the realm of national accounting. The author, a councillor at the Court of Auditors (*Cour des comptes*) was a close associate of Jacques Robin and succeeded him at the head of *Transversales*. As a student at Nanterre in 1968, he had striven to make Gorz's arguments in *Le Socialisme difficile* known among the 22 March Movement.[80] His report was both a challenge to the classical representations of wealth ('thermometers that make people ill') and a highlighting of everything at the social and ecological level that promotes human development and calls for other criteria for calculating wealth.[81]

---

78 André Gorz to Françoise Gollain, 7 July 2005 (GRZ).

79 Gorz, *Capitalism, Socialism, Ecology*, pp. 32–3.

80 Personal communication from Patrick Viveret to the author of 18 October 2013.

81 On this issue, see Jean Gadrey and Florence Jany-Catrice, *Les Nouveaux Indicateurs de richesse* (Paris: La Découverte, 2012 [3rd edition]).

Just like the Lipietz Report, Patrick Viveret's proposals on these new indicators of wealth were refined through public debate. Receiving the preliminary draft of the report from Robin, Gorz took part in the discussion with a very long letter which he sent to Robin in March 2001 and which was, in large part, turned into an article for *Transversales*. He praised the author of the report,

> [. . .] who not only accepted his own subjectivity but gave it to be understood almost throughout his text that wealth neither can nor should be defined in terms of an objective, abstract or quantitative standard of measure, which is universally applicable, irrespective of all that is felt and experienced. [. . .] The fundamentally political dimension of what at first seems a technico-economic undertaking is thus clearly asserted.[82]

The economy's independence from politics and ethics, which rests on the fetishism of money, has its source in the technique of calculation that disqualifies everything that is not measurable and quantifiable. That is why the plurality of values in which the lifeworld is steeped demands other criteria and a plurality of indicators or standards of measurement that transcend the order of the economy.

> Their function is to lay down priorities, ends and forms of wealth that are neither monetizable nor measurable by a common yardstick, nor consequently exchangeable for one another. They designate 'the other of the economy', the limits or prohibitions to which it must yield, the goals it must be made to serve—in short, the model or project of development or society which the economy must serve and which it is incapable of defining purely on its own terms. I am taking pleasure here in reformulating in my own way what is clearly said in Patrick's text (though more cautiously).[83]

Wealth is not reducible, then, to the increasing valorization of production. Marx had already argued this in imagining the final stage of capitalism when it had reached maturity. In 1993, in a work of Marxist exegesis that Gorz

---

82 Aforementioned letter from Gorz to Jacques Robin, 23–25 March 2001.

83 Letter from Gorz to Jacques Robin, 23–25 March 2001. Everything but the last sentence also appears in Gorz, 'Richesse, travail et revenu garanti', *Transversales Science Culture* 68 (April 2001): 12.

would discover almost 10 years later, when he would describe it as 'magisterial', Moishe Postone had observed that the famous 'Machine Fragment' in the *Grundrisse* described the process that enabled real wealth to be extracted from the narrow base of value: as industry develops, the creation of true wealth depends less on value, based on time and quantity of work employed, and more on the high level of productivity of the science and technology deployed.[84] Referring to a 'not very well-known' paragraph in the *Grundrisse* on 'bourgeois wealth', Gorz went even further, taking up a question Marx had asked: namely, what is wealth, 'when the limited bourgeois form is stripped away'? Marx replies that it is nothing but the development, within universal exchange, of the totality of human faculties and capacities as such, as ends in themselves, and not as something "measured on a *pre-determined yardstick*".'[85] And Gorz comments: 'What interests and pleases me above all in this passage is that the "faculties of enjoyment, production, creation, cognition" etc. are not understood as "productive forces" that enable wealth to be created, but as ends in themselves, as wealth itself.'[86]

Here we are then, at last, beyond productivism—and, indeed, beyond economics as we know it:

> To consider the development of human faculties as the creation of wealth is, in fact, already to abandon a utilitarian market-economistic conception of wealth. To take human development as an end in itself is to say that it has value in and for itself, irrespective of its immediate economic utility. It is by not being functional to the immediate production process that it will enrich the orientation, purpose and nature of production and economic exchanges and 'put them in their place'.[87]

There is a difference between what is commonly referred to as wealth, which, 'as it is measured in economics, is only ever an increase in value-based exchange', and 'the production of substantive wealth', which may be

---

84 Moishe Postone, *Time, Labor and Social Domination* (Cambridge: Cambridge University Press, 2003 [1993]), pp. 196–7. See also Marx, *Grundrisse*, p. 701.

85 Marx, *Grundrisse*, p. 488.

86 André Gorz, 'Richesse, travail et revenu garanti', pp. 12–13. The passage from Marx is provided in full and with a commentary in *The Immaterial*, p. 112.

87 Gorz, 'Richesse, travail et revenu garanti', p. 13.

independent of that.[88] There is, therefore, another economy. It is the source of intrinsic wealth or values, 'which represent the end goal of, and condition for, human activities: knowledge, skills, the art of living, culture etc.' This wealth and these values express 'the density and multilateralism of relations, both personal and social'; they indicate 'the degree of flourishing of the human faculties and capacities' of a society.[89]

---

88 André Gorz to Françoise Gollain, 15 and 25–27 December 2004 (GRZ).

89 Gorz, 'Valeur et richesse: le divorce', pp. 45–6.

PART FIVE

Towards the Civilization of Free Time in the Era of the Immaterial

The 2000s: Financialization and Circulation of Knowledge

'Creation constrained goes back to being work.'
Raoul Vaneigem, *Nous qui désirons sans fin*, p. 152.

'The trend towards self-providing is gaining ground again as a result of the increasing proportion of immaterial contents in the nature of commodities.'
André Gorz, *Ecologica*, p. 33.

CHAPTER SEVENTEEN

Towards the Intelligent Society?

As the twentieth century was drawing to a close, André Gorz made a serious appraisal of the latest developments within capitalism, which had forsaken industry for services and was shifting its nerve centre from real production to finance. This process of the 'dematerialization' of capitalist flows was accompanied by their globalization. Material work (still Taylorized) was 'off-shored' to the emerging countries. The capitalist company was becoming a 'transnational network of telematically interconnected semi-autonomous units'.[1] None of this would have been possible without the 'third industrial revolution' (following those of machines and energy): the enormous advance of information technology and cybernetics, wrought by constant, rapid progress in computer technology since the 1980s (while the expression 'third industrial revolution' has passed into common usage, for exactitude we should speak rather of a 'post-industrial revolution').

Though he never traded in his typewriter for a computer, Gorz kept a constant eye on the prospects opened up by the digitization of knowledge.

The Third Industrial Revolution

As early as the late 1970s, a book by Jacques Attali (*La Nouvelle économie française*, 1977) and a report by Simon Nora and Alain Minc (*L'Informatisation de la société*, 1978) sensed the extraordinary upheavals presaged by the rise of the microprocessor. Bosquet drew the lesson that micro-computing could assist in the decentralization of small productive units—their movement away from cities.[2] By 1984, Gorz was predicting the electronic money, mail, stock management and a 'proliferation of "intelligent tools" that would enable everyone to manufacture a thousand things.'[3] In *Farewell to the*

---

1 André Gorz and Jacques Robin, 'Forger un autre avenir'.

2 Michel Bosquet, 'Une pastille contre le travail', *Le Nouvel Observateur* (23 April 1978).

3 André Gorz, 'Emploi et revenu, un divorce nécessaire?', interview by Denis Clerc, p. 17.

308 | WILLY GIANINAZZI

Working Class, he focused primarily on the social consequences of information technology: the deskilling of occupations and the rise of unemployment. The latter would last for almost 20 years, with (low) growth no longer creating jobs.

Gorz came across Alvin Toffler's *The Third Wave* (1980) shortly after he published *Farewell to the Working Class* and the global bestseller opened up new lines of thinking for him. According to the American futurologist, the succeeding 'waves' of agriculture and industry were now being followed by a wave of—individualized and democratized—knowledge, made possible by personal computers, and this ought to lead to an age of self-providing. In more nuanced fashion, Gorz assigned an ambivalent social significance to information technology: it was a 'crossroads technology' that could as easily lead to hyper-centralization and surveillance as to the greater circulation of knowledge promoting worker self-management.[4] Drawing on the studies of Jacques Robin (*Changer d'ère*, 1989), corroborated by a key work by the American foresight theorist Jeremy Rifkin (*The Age of Access*, 2000), Gorz observed that information technology, a genuine breakthrough phenomenon, went so far as to transform the nature of fixed and variable capital, which became de-materialized: 'The most important form of fixed capital is now the knowledge stored in, and instantly available from, information technologies, and the most important form of labour power is brainpower.'[5]

The Immaterial

In January 2003, Gorz brought out *L'Immatériel. Connaissance, valeur et capital*, which would be the last theoretical work published in his lifetime.[6] Over the preceding years, he had undertaken a long labour of preparation that required him to familiarize himself with the vast literature (including managerial works) on the *immateriality* that was overtaking contemporary capitalism (Pierre Lévy, Enzo Rullani, Hervé Sérieyx, etc.). Besides the *Transversales* group (Robin, Viveret, Passet etc.), he followed with interest

---

4 Gorz, *Paths to Paradise*, pp. 29, 84.

5 Gorz, *Reclaiming Work*, p. 6. See also Gorz, 'Vom totalitären Vorhaben des Kapitals. Notizen zu Jeremy Rifkins *The Age of Access*', *Widerspruch* (Zurich) (40) (2001): 33–40.

6 The English translation was published, at the prompting of its translator, as *The Immaterial: Knowledge, Value and Capital*.

the many authors in the sphere of autonomist Marxism who either wrote books,[7] or articles in the journal *Futur antérieur* (Antonio Negri, Maurizio Lazzarato, Paolo Virno, Carlo Vercellone etc.) or, later, *Multitudes* (Yann Moulier-Boutang, Antonella Corsani etc.). He also followed the Foucauldians of the short-lived journal *Alice* (Muriel Combes, Bernard Aspe). Many of these writers repaid the compliment, either by reviewing (Negri, Moulier-Boutang) or interviewing him.[8] They engaged critically with his thinking and his writings because, as Negri observed, writing with Vincent, these 'have always situated themselves coherently in a revolutionary perspective and because they exert a wide influence' and 'also, no doubt, because they are particularly close to our political positions.'[9]

Cognitive Capitalism

On the vexed and difficult subject of cognitive capitalism or the knowledge economy, Gorz produced a host of articles and interviews. They were published partly in Germany, but also in *Transversales*, *Partage*, *Variations* (Vincent's new journal), *Alternatives économiques*, *Multitudes* and *EcoRev'*. This last-named journal was created on the initiative of critical Greens in spring of 2000. Thanks to the intervention of its co-founder Jean Zin, who was also active in GRIT, it enjoyed Gorz's backing from the outset. With the economist Jérôme Gleizes as its main driving force, it would always maintain its allegiance to his heritage.

---

7 Paolo Virno, *Mondanità. L'idea di 'Mondo' tra esperienza sensibile e sfera pubblica* (Rome: Manifestolibri, 1994); Christian Marazzi, *Capital and Affects: The Politics of the Language Economy* (Semiotext(e)/Foreign Agents, 2011 [1994]); Christian Azaïs, Antonella Corsani and Patrick Dieuaide (eds), *Vers un capitalisme cognitif. Entre mutations du travail et territoires* (Paris: L'Harmattan, 2001); Carlo Vercellone (ed.), *Sommes-nous sortis du capitalisme industriel?* (Paris: La Dispute, 2003). See also the later, but crucial, work by Yann Moulier-Boutang, *Cognitive Capitalism* (Chichester: Polity Press, 2012 [2007]).

8 Gorz, 'Misères du présent, richesse du possible', interview by Carlo Vercellone, Patrick Dieuaide and Pierre Peronnet, pp. 31–5; André Gorz, 'Économie de la connaissance, exploitation des savoirs', interview by Carlo Vercellone and Yann Moulier-Boutang, *Multitudes* 15 (Winter 2004): 205–16.

9 Antonio Negri and Jean-Marie Vincent, 'Paradoxes autour du travail', *Futur antérieur* 10 (April 1992): 5. On their theoretical disagreements, see Françoise Gollain, 'L'apport d'André Gorz au débat sur le capitalisme cognitif', *Revue du MAUSS* 35 (2010): 541–58.

The first article by Gorz that succinctly established a lucid diagnosis of the present state of affairs (co-written with Jacques Robin) appeared in *Le Monde* in 1996, but the most elaborate was the report presented to the conference on *Die Wissensgesellschaft* [the knowledge society] at the Heinrich-Böll-Stiftung in Bonn in May 2001.[10] It was by expanding upon that contribution that Gorz produced *The Immaterial*. The interview he gave to *Multitudes* in 2004 after the book came out, which he planned to include as an appendix to a potential second edition, is also instructive.[11]

The Immaterial opens with a rereading of the 'superb passage'[12] in the *Grundrisse* that Marx devoted to the apotheosis of capitalist machinery. In the 1960s Gorz had seen this as a justification for worker self-management (see p. 98n11); in the 1980s he took it to justify the de-centring from work of individuals' capacities for fulfilment (see p. 253); now, from the precise mid-point of the 1990s onwards, he found in it a process of 'intellectualization' of capital that would see the material base of its reproduction shrink away:[13] the Communism that might arise out of this process would then provide the basis for an 'intelligent society'.

In the age of automatic machines, as Marx saw it, knowledge became 'the principal productive force'. Work in its immediate form ceased to be the measure of social wealth, which now depended on 'the general state of science and on the progress of technology'. Strictly speaking, the 'production process' could no longer be confused with the 'labour process'.[14] 'Techno-scientific knowledge [was] therefore, from the outset, not only *on the side of* capital as domination and subsumption of living labour by machinery but it even form[ed] part of fixed capital as a means of extorting surplus labour.'[15]

However, Gorz perceived a certain 'wavering' on Marx's part. He grew convinced, reading neo-*operaismo* writings (the early, enlightening works of Paolo Virno and of the Italian Swiss economist Christian Marazzi, but

10 André Gorz and Jacques Robin, 'Forger un autre avenir'; 'Welches Wissen? Welche Gesellschaft?' in Andreas Poltermann (ed.), *Gut zu wissen. Links zur Wissensgesellschaft* (Münster: Westphälisches Dampfboot, 2002), pp. 15–35.

11 André Gorz, 'Économie de la connaissance, exploitation des savoirs'.

12 André Gorz to Robert Chenavier, 9 October 1999 (GRZ).

13 On this last avatar, see Carlo Vercellone, 'André Gorz et la dynamique du capitalisme', *Sens public* (11–12) (October 2009): 159–75.

14 Gorz, *Immaterial*, pp. 2–3. The quotations are from Marx's *Grundrisse*, pp. 704–05.

15 Gorz, *Immaterial*, p. 48.

also of Yann Moulier-Boutang), that it was necessary to go further. The author of the *Grundrisse* neglected the fact that the 'general intellect'—or 'general social knowledge', as he also termed it—was not limited to the *dead labour* 'fixed' in the machine: it was also a living labour delivered by the human brain.[16] For, though the capitalist production process is out to capture scientific knowledge as formalized, objectivized information, there is another disposition of the intellect that gains the upper hand in the era of cognitive capitalism, making this something absolutely new. It is not so much scientific as cultural, and linked less to information than to communication: to language, says Marazzi, who sees a 'linguistic turn' in the economy in operation here.

Gorz, who greatly stresses this distinction, gives a name to this second disposition. He calls it *savoir* or 'experiential knowledge' and defines it primarily as 'a practical ability, an expertise that does not necessarily involve formalizable, codifiable knowledge.'[17] The mobilization, involvement and motivation which, as we saw in the previous chapter, characterize the managerial methods of post-Fordism, make the powers of cooperation, adaptation, discernment, anticipation, reactiveness to the unforeseen, imagination, creativity etc. highly productive. These are all informal attitudes that have to do with spontaneous intelligence and experiential knowledge which are acquired subjectively in everyday life (including outside of work) and cannot really be taught. These *skills*—or this *virtuosity*, as Virno puts it—provide an 'immaterial labour that is impossible to quantify, store, certify, formalize or even objectify' and 'cannot be legitimately equated with fixed capital'.[18] As Gorz sees it, it is at the point where the followers of Foucault refer to this subsumption of life by capital as a 'bio-economy'[19] that one part of the problem faced by capitalism lies.

---

16 Paolo Virno, 'Quelques notes à propos du "general intellect" ', *Futur antérieur* 10 ([April] 1992): 51. In a sentence no one quotes, Marx does, however, stress 'to what degree [. . .] the powers of social production have been produced, not only in the form of knowledge, but also as immediate organs of social practice, of the real life process' (*Grundrisse*, p. 706).

17 Gorz, *Immaterial*, p. 41.

18 Gorz, *Immaterial*, pp. 7, 45.

19 Andrea Fumagalli, 'Bioeconomics and the valorisation process' in Vladimir Cvijanović, Andrea Fumagalli and Carlo Vercellone (eds), *Cognitive Capitalism and Its Reflections in South-Eastern Europe* (Frankfurt: Peter Lang, 2010), pp. 41–59.

This means that what he chooses to call 'human capital' is not measurable and the assessment of the immaterial assets of a firm could scarcely be more random—and yet it is an essential requirement of shareholders and credit institutions. Moreover, by consigning immediate labour as a factor of production to a secondary role, then immaterial labour, as Marx had foreseen, robs labour time of its classic function as measure of wealth created. Capital, which always needs a yardstick for its valorization in the marketplace, seems no longer to be based on anything. As Gorz saw it, the categories of value and surplus labour lost their meaning; for Vincent (with whom he debated)[20] or Negri and his associates, they simply acquired another meaning, in keeping with the 'cognitive' turn assumed by valorization. However, beyond these different assessments, all were agreed that *domination* was now total. With the regulative function of value withering away, it gave way to personalized wage relations in which cynicism could only vie with voluntary servility.

For Gorz, however, this was not all. The proliferation and immeasurability of collective intelligence—in Virno's terms, 'mass intellectuality'—drove capital to appropriate this for itself by formalizing it as knowledge which it could not privatize directly, but to which it could assign a market value by privatizing access through technical (access codes etc.) or legal (copyright, patents) artifices, as Rifkin had also clearly seen. Gorz equated this with the establishment of a 'monopoly rent',[21] while the economist Moulier-Boutang described it figuratively as the creation of new enclosures. As he sees it, this is never complete or satisfactory, not just because (experiential) knowledge always extends beyond the confines of work, but also because the market value of these products is constantly decreasing, in keeping with their infinite reproducibility at a tiny marginal cost (this is the case with pharmaceutical products or digital products—software, music and films).[22] To combat this tendency of the products of intelligence to become virtually 'cost-free', capital strives fiercely to contrive their 'scarcity'.

20 Jean-Marie Vincent and André Gorz, 'Dialogue avec André Gorz', *Variations* 1 (2001): 9–18; Willy Gianinazzi, ' "Vivre une vie qui ne se vit pas". Quand Jean-Marie Vincent et André Gorz débattaient de valeur et subjectivité', *Variations* 17 (2012) (available at: variations.revues.org/354; last accessed: 27 July 2022).

21 Gorz, *Immaterial*, pp. 68–76.

22 See also Jeremy Rifkin, *The Zero Marginal Cost Society* (London: Palgrave Macmillan, 2014).

But we shall see that, in the highly strategic field of the digital, capitalists by no means have free rein to achieve their ends.

All these difficulties encountered by the valorization process, which the financialization of the economy attempts to circumvent (see the following chapter), explain why Gorz can state flatly that 'so-called cognitive capitalism is itself the crisis of capitalism'.[23]

The Production of the Consumer

The scarcity of immaterial products, which preserves their value, may thus be obtained through their monopolization. Another trick is to append to these products, as with any other commodity, new symbolic, affective, aesthetic qualities that make them unique for the duration of a marketing campaign. Or else, as Naomi Klein 'excellently described' in her resoundingly successful book *No Logo* (2000), to tend to the *brand image*, which then becomes the essence of the product's value.

This all assumes that one has aroused 'wishes, desires, self-images and lifestyles' in individuals that will 'transform them into that new species of buyers "who have no need of what they desire and no desire for what they need"',[24] to cite the chilling definition of the consumer by Freud's nephew Edward Bernays, for decades a master manipulator within the US advertising industry. This 'production of the consumer' matches the consumer's subjectivity to the symbolism of the commodities which that subjectivity in its turn contributes to shaping, through an invisible labour of *self-production*. We should be quite clear on the matter: this is nothing less than 'a seizure of power by immaterial fixed capital over public space, the culture of everyday life and the social imaginary'.[25]

Self-Production

'Self-production' is a concept developed by Gorz. It is based on the identical expression Alain Touraine employs in his *Critique of Modernity* [1992] to refer to the human subject as it makes itself and is enriched by contact with

---

23 Gorz, *Immaterial*, p. 55.
24 Gorz, *Immaterial*, p. 77.
25 Gorz, *Immaterial*, p. 81.

writers at *Transversales* like Félix Guattari,[26] or Roger Sue, who stressed 'the transition from the productive individual to the production of the individual, in which the individual is not so much the instrument of its production as its raw material.'[27] Gorz was pointing to the singular subjectivation of a common cultural core—the collective intelligence—consisting 'essentially in acquiring, developing and enriching capacities for enjoyment, action, communication, creation, cognition etc. as ends in themselves.'[28]

Now, it is true that, 'in becoming the foundation of a value-production based on continual innovation, communication and improvisation, immaterial labour tends, in the end, to become indistinguishable from a labour of self-production.'[29] Would work, then, in the sense that it has in political economy, be eliminated and replaced by the free development of personal activity?

> Fixed capital no longer has a separate existence; it's subsumed and internalized by men and women who concretely and practically experience that the main productive force is neither machine-capital nor money-capital, but the living passion with which they imagine and invent and increase their own cognitive capacities at the same time as their production of knowledge and wealth. Here the production of oneself is the production of wealth [. . .].[30]

However, this 'proto-Communism' is only virtual,[31] as self-production represents a sort of 'primitive accumulation' which companies enjoy almost free of charge. The managers in big firms take care to see to it that the 'autonomy' of self-production, the guarantee of all its productive powers, is preserved by giving the illusion of transforming collaborators, service providers, consultants and other 'co-workers' into autonomous small entrepreneurs, whether salaried or freelance. One of their neoliberal cheerleaders,

---

26 In Guattari we find expressions like 'singular production of existence', 'production of human existence', 'production of self as subject', 'production of subjectivity' etc.

27 Roger Sue, *Renouer le lien social. Liberté, égalité, association* (Paris: Odile Jacob, 2001), p. 182.

28 André Gorz, 'La personne devient une entreprise. Note sur le travail de production de soi', *EcoRev'* 7 (Winter 2001): 8.

29 Gorz, *Immaterial*, p. 13.

30 Gorz, *Ecologica*, p. 14. Originally published as 'L'écologie politique, une éthique de la libération', interview by Marc Robert, *EcoRev'* 21 (Autumn–Winter 2005).

31 Gorz, *Ecologica*.

Pierre Lévy, is thus able proudly to declare that 'the person is becoming an enterprise'.[32]

And yet the subjective essence of self-production harbours within it genuine potentialities for autonomy which put this question at the heart of a 'central conflict'. Potentialities that are not the same as 'self-valorization' or 'self-entrepreneurship'—that is to say, the selling of oneself as a commodity (Negri's ambiguous notion of self-valorization is not a very felicitous one, containing as it does the main driving principle of capitalism but being, as he sees it, an anti-economic category).[33] The 'coinciding of worker and business' may in fact be viewed from another angle:

> One may see it as a sign that the capacities constitutive of labour-power are no longer subsumable by capital as a distinct entity, and that the nature of production now requires a mode of self-organized social cooperation likely to lead, sooner or later, to the individual and collective emancipation of the workers. It will seem, then, that capitalism engenders, in its most advanced sector, the germs of its effective negation. That, at least, is what the dissidents of digital capitalism are showing.[34]

Digital Dissidence

In *Reclaiming Work*, André Gorz evinces some scepticism regarding the capacities of subjects to escape the managerial grip of the post-Fordist company. By contrast, *The Immaterial* is optimistic about the emancipatory potentialities concealed within the knowledge economy. This is because, between the two, Gorz has sized up how much the digital change affecting the whole of society has accelerated, particularly thanks to the rise of the internet: 'The computer emerges here as the universal and universally accessible tool through which all forms of knowledge and all activities can theoretically be pooled. And it is, indeed, this right to free access and to shared

---

32 Gorz, 'La personne devient une entreprise', pp. 7–10. On domination through autonomization in work, see the book Gorz drew on in this connection: Manfred Moldaschl and Günter Voss (eds), *Subjektivierung von Arbeit* (Munich: Hampp, 2002).

33 André Gorz, 'Penser l'exode de la société du travail et de la marchandise', *Mouvements* 50 (June–August 2007): 104.

34 André Gorz, 'Économie de la connaissance, exploitation des savoirs'.

use that are called for by the anarcho-communist Free Software and Free Network communities.'[35]

Based on an ethic of cooperation and giving, the practice of these 'hacker' communities ('hackers' in the original sense of computer enthusiasts) consists in making knowledge available to all (making it 'open source') outside of any commercial relationship. It ranges free against proprietary software and mockingly responds to copyright with its own 'copyleft'. This leads to a 'really existing anarcho-communism', to borrow British writer Richard Barbrook's phrase, Barbrook being known for his attacks on the liberal/libertarian ideology that hovers over Silicon Valley. Gorz also takes inspiration from the Finnish philosopher Pekka Himanen, who gives 'the hacker ethic' a boost with his book of that same name.[36] These 'dissident communities of the digital' (a phrase taken from Peter Glotz, then professor of media at Sankt-Gallen in Switzerland) are rising up against 'the privatization of the means of access to that "common good of humanity" that is knowledge in all its forms.'[37] Their struggles have a 'strategic import' because they are tilting against capitalism, but doing so within capitalism and at the very heart of capital's mechanisms of power. And capital cannot do without the workers in the immaterial sphere at the point when the new information and communications technologies (ICT) are exploding.

However, though the free software movement made stunning progress from the last years of the twentieth century onwards, playing into Gorz's most utopian (if not, indeed, unfounded) hopes, it was still not clear which way things would go. In 1999, Gorz wrote to the Simone Weil specialist Robert Chenavier, with whom he was engaged in detailed theoretical discussion on the meaning of contemporary 'work': 'The issue over—and for— the Net is whether this will be a site of convivial cooperation (in Illich's sense, where a convivial tool = a tool that neither programmes nor predetermines the use people make of it) or, conversely, a place of monetization and commercialization of communication and exchange.'[38]

---

35 Gorz, *Immaterial*, p. 14.

36 Pekka Himanen, *The Hacker Ethic and the Spirit of the Information Age* (London: Martin Secker & Warburg, 2001).

37 Gorz, *Immaterial*, p. 115.

38 André Gorz to Robert Chenavier, 9 October 1999 (GRZ).

Wissenskommunismus **or Knowledge Communism**

The German translation of *The Immaterial* was brought out in September 2004 by the Zurich-based left-wing publisher Rotpunkt with the title *Wissen, Wert und Kapital. Zur Kritik der Wissensökonomie*. [Knowledge, value and capital: A contribution to the critique of the knowledge economy]. Gorz asserted that he had rewritten 'a good third'[39] of the book in German. Basing himself on that rewriting, he would subsequently prepare an updated second edition in French. It would never see the light of day, though his archives preserve the re-translations into French and the unpublished preface. In the latter, Gorz explains that this new edition of *The Immaterial*, taken directly from the German version, differs from the first edition by 'a number of modifications and additions', mainly to Chapters 3 and 4, made 'over the eighteen months that followed the publication of the [French original] by Galilée.' He adds that 'they originate in further reading and in exchanges of ideas with two people',[40] the persons in question being Stefan Meretz and Erich Hörl.

Meretz is a Berlin computer scientist who came across an interview with Gorz in the newspaper *TAZ* on the subject of *The Immaterial* and wrote him a long letter on 18 August 2003. An intense correspondence followed, continuing until August 2007.[41] 'Chapter 3 of the new edition, which relates to the digital sphere,' explains Gorz in the preface, 'has been enhanced with many references to the thoughts and writings of Meretz, the philosophical dimension of which enchanted me. The exchange of letters that has developed between us has been one of the most fertile and illuminating I have ever known.' What he liked in Meretz was that he 'explore[d] by theory and practice the possibilities of extending the principle of free software and the hacker ethic to other fields of the economy and, ultimately, to the whole of society.'[42]

39 André Gorz to Stefan Meretz, May–June 2004 (GRZ).

40 GRZ 9.5.

41 See Stefan Meretz, 'André Gorz und der Wissenskommunismus' in Hans Leo Krämer (ed.), *Der Horizont unserer Handlungen: den Zusammenbruch des Kapitalismus denken* (Saarbrücken: Kooperationsstelle Wissenschaft und Arbeitswelt, 2013), pp. 111–9.

42 GRZ 9.5.

Meretz was a member of Oekonux.[43] Oekonux.de was a discussion forum and a site for registering projects under Linux licence, founded by the German computer scientist Stefan Merten in 1999, who was himself exploring paths from free software to a form of production transcending capitalism. Meretz introduced Gorz to this network, inviting him in his first letter to take part in the third Oekonux Conference at Vienna in May 2004. He elicited some supportive words from him: 'With a number of you, I have discovered that the joy and pleasure of giving and receiving are contagious and liberating. You are the group I would really like to have belonged to. I am, unfortunately, a doddery old man who can only look on at your project from a distance.'[44]

The French edition of *The Immaterial* already reflected Himanen's 'greenhorn' wonderment; the Swiss edition included the very radical analyses and testimonies that Gorz had picked up in the interim from the German proponents of 'free software', some of whom, like Merten, Meretz and the mathematician Wolf Göhring, were steeped in Marxist culture.

> [These individuals] are asking themselves [. . .] how 'work' could be eliminated in favour of a communicational concertation that would take place with the involvement of all participants and the outcome of which would not actually belong to anyone. The question of *what* should be produced, and *how* and *to what end* ought to be able to be resolved without the mediation of the market by the interconnected producer-consumers.[45]

In this way, one would attain the emancipation of human capital from the valorization process. What would an 'authentic knowledge economy' be, then, but a *Wissenskommunismus*—that is to say, a 'Communism treating knowledge as a common good, where the pooling of that knowledge would abolish the exchange relation, the money relation'?[46] And Gorz points out, indeed, the remarkable productive superiority of free over patented software:

---

43 Stefan Meretz, born 1962 and a teacher of *kritische Psychologie*, would subsequently be behind many sites hosting digital criticism. See meretz.de.

44 André Gorz, 'Jenseits von Arbeit, Ware und Wert' (April 2004) in Stefan Meretz, 'André Gorz über Oekonux', email of 26 April 2004 (available at: oekonux.de; last accessed: 27 July 2022).

45 Gorz, *Wissen, Wert und Kapital*, pp. 92–3. The translation here is from Gorz's own unpublished translations into French (GRZ 9.5).

46 Gorz, *Wissen, Wert und Kapital*, p. 11.

[It] shows that the greatest creativity flourishes when the creators, freed from the imperatives of profitability and 'competitiveness', can set their capabilities and practical knowledge to work freely and cooperatively. Emerging in their practice we see the conditions that would allow the social relations of the production of knowledge to become the foundation of an authentic knowledge society. Contrary to the general view, among them knowledge does not assume the form of a chunk of formalized information detachable from its possessors, but of a social activity that develops communicational, egalitarian relations, free of domination.[47]

The felt superiority of *cooperation* over *competition* is an inducement for the latter to wither away. 'Cognitive capitalism engenders, in and of itself, the prospect of its possible elimination. In its deepest reaches a Communist core begins to form', argues Gorz; 'this is not about a pure "vision", but about a practice developed at the highest level by people whose creative Communism is indispensable to capitalism.'[48]

Gorz no doubt underestimates the difficulty of the question he himself raises here: namely whether and how the collaborative model that applies in the world of 'copyleft' can become a mode of production, to the exclusion of any other and 'extended to all social activities'.[49] On the other hand, he quite straightforwardly grasps the ambivalence and dilemmas of the contemporary situation:

The pioneers of the free software movement always have one foot in the opposing camp. They are exposed to the greed of the producers of copyrighted software and are themselves subject to the need to sell their products, since they cannot live outside of all market and monetary relations. [. . .] In their situation, they feel permanently torn and the need to sell their 'work' is experienced as an unbearable limitation of their potential.[50]

He makes the same observation elsewhere in more elevated language:

---

47 Gorz, *Wissen, Wert und Kapital*, p. 13.

48 Gorz, *Wissen, Wert und Kapital*, p. 93.

49 André Gorz, 'Jenseits von Arbeit, Ware und Wert'. On this theme, see Sébastien Broca, 'Du logiciel libre aux théories de l'intelligence collective', *Revue TIC&Société* 2 (2) 2008: 81–101 (available at: ticetsociete.revues.org/451; last accessed: 27 July 2022).

50 Gorz, *Wissen, Wert und Kapital*, p. 92.

In current conditions, digital dissidence [. . .] permits only the symbolic emancipation of immaterial work from the social relations of capital, not its real emancipation. It erupts as a challenge in a context in which firms are perfectly aware that they will only achieve the total mobilization of all their *co-workers'* energies if they manage totally to subsume their most intimate psychical motivations. [. . .] The total control of the minds of their co-workers and their time becomes a central issue. [. . .] The practice of free productive cooperation, a source of fulfilment and pleasure in work ('work is fun'), which, among hackers, is self-organized on a global scale, is confined here within the limits of a capitalist company and subjected to the ethic of productivity by a clever system of symbolic and material rewards.[51]

The contradiction between 'fulfilment of self' and 'commercialization of self' ('self-valorization') is far from being resolved, while, on the other hand, the establishment of a universal basic income would be the beginning of a solution, insofar as it nullifies the imperative to sell oneself.[52] And yet the battle for freedom on the Net and free creation on social networks still goes on in our own day and political groupings (e.g. the Pirate Party) form against intellectual property, while, conversely, firms make use of the open source collaborative model to tap into unpaid labour (crowdsourcing) or massively appropriate for themselves technical designs made under Linux licence (most notably in telephone technology).[53]

Progressions of the Inhuman

The Immaterial has a fourth and last chapter which is certainly the most original of all. Gorz attached great importance to it. He would, consequently, be disappointed that few reviewers of the work discussed its arguments.[54] Others found them overblown.[55] In that chapter, with its troubling

---

51 Gorz, 'Économie de la connaissance, exploitation des savoirs', pp. 207–08.

52 Gorz, *Immaterial*, pp. 129–36.

53 *EcoRev'* 37 ('Réseau(x) et société de l'intelligence. Le numérique sème-t-il la révolution?'), Summer 2011; *Mouvements*, 79 ('(Contre-)pouvoirs du numérique'), 2014.

54 A counter-example was Marie-Louise Duboin, 'Revenu d'existence ou revenu social?', *La Grande Relève* (March 2003).

55 For example, Ladislas Dowbor in his review of November 2005 (available at: dowbor.org/2005/11; last accessed: 27 July 2022).

perspectives, Gorz wondered whether the direction taken by cybernetics prefigured not an 'intelligent society', but a 'post-human civilization'. The former could only be conceived through a synergistic balance between science and lifeworld, formalized and living knowledge, the machine and the body. In fact, contemporary developments in artificial intelligence and life were constantly driving these further apart. By relegating every expression of life to the background, they were closing down enquiry into the meaning, aims and needs related to sentient human beings.

The obsolescence of Man, which Günther Anders had begun to detect in the 1960s (in a book of the same name that Gorz read and deemed 'fundamental') was now programmed in. Actively deployed knowledge was leaving the human brain and taking on the appearance of a substance that could be transferred to machines, preserved and transformed into a patentable, valorizable factor of production.

> It is now nothing but a complex of formalized information, a dead means of production, uprooted from any living base or social context, and it is destined, like all the dead labour embodied in machines, to function as fixed capital and to be valorized. In order to be productive, dead knowledge no longer needs to be known and understood by anyone. Its industrial production is aimed, so far as possible, at making human faculties *substitutable*, up to and including life and intelligence.[56]

Techno-science serves the forward march of capitalism because it obeys a single mathematizing rationality. There is, in fact, a close affinity between the domination exerted by objectivized scientific knowledge and the domination exerted by capital through a process of valorization detached from any substantial, concrete content: 'Both methodically leave out of account what is not formalizable and calculable.'[57] As Gorz had already written in *Critique of Economic Reason*, 'The self-denial of the subject proper to calculation techniques becomes the paradigm of all thought'.[58] In *The Immaterial*, Gorz identified and studied a *subjectless thought* that had formed historically in the language of mathematical calculation and, after having shaped capitalist logic, was now triumphant in the sphere of cybernetics.

---

56 Gorz, *Wissen, Wert und Kapital*, p. 106.
57 Gorz, *Wissen, Wert und Kapital*, p. 106.
58 Gorz, *Critique of Economic Reason*, p. 123.

He gathered material from his friend Finn Bowring's books on the appropriation of life by the biotechnologies (*Science, Seeds and Cyborgs*, 2003), from the practitioners of artificial intelligence, such as the computer scientist Ray Kurzweil and the robotics researcher Hans Moravec and then, for the German edition, from the as yet unpublished thesis of Erich Hörl, another friend and a specialist in digital media, on the history of the mathematization of the sciences (*Die heiligen Kanäle* [2005]). Drawing also on Husserl, who, in *The Crisis of European Sciences*, had demonstrated that, in the history of thought, setting aside the experience of the sensible world had its source in the 'mathematization of nature', Gorz retraced the path of that exclusion. He referred to Kepler, Galileo, Descartes and Leibniz as having discovered that the laws of the intellect, freed from the subjectivity of the body, were also the laws that governed the universe.

This epistemic revolution reached a decisive turning point with George Boole in the middle of the nineteenth century. In Boole's view, all the operations of the mind could in theory be transcribed into the universal language of symbolic algebra, so that it was possible to conceive of *thinking machines*. That would come to pass a hundred years later with the first computers. Artificial intelligence came, then, to be conceived as the reduction of the human mind to a programmed machine. Thought, literally disembodied and reduced to mathematical logic, became capable of a knowledge that reached beyond what the experience of the tangible world reveals to us. But in that way, it 'would pursue knowledge for its own sake and regard indifference to contents, interests and passions as the condition of access to truth.'[59]

Escaping determinate existence is also the distinctive feature of science when it rejects the contingency of the body, finitude and death: 'the techno-scientific rationalization of human reproduction' invents new fields for itself with *in vitro* fertilization, surrogate motherhood and, ultimately, human cloning. As for the artificial life for which genetic engineering, nanotechnologies applied to the body and cyborgs (that is to say, human beings endowed with machinic elements) clear a path, it is vested with a eugenic mission that is desired by science and underwritten by politics, in total disregard of the will of the 'remodelled' human beings who will not have chosen to be so (the children that are the outcome of these practices).

---

59 Gorz, *Immaterial*, p. 155.

There is, then, an enormous difference between 'biological embodiment' and 'machinic embodiment': 'through the first native form, we are given to ourselves; it is the natural contingency of the chance occurrence of our birth. The second is manufactured by others for a determinate goal.'[60] To the point where, 'as cyborgs we handle machines forming extensions of our bodies without understanding either their operation or their design.'[61] Though technologies, which have up to this point been auxiliary, have always enabled human beings to produce themselves, it could now be the case that 'we [would] have ourselves produced by them.'[62] We would then have entered a post-biological, post-human era . . .

---

60 Gorz, *Immaterial*, p. 187.

61 Gorz, *Immaterial*, p. 187.

62 Gorz, *Immaterial*, p. 188. On this issue, see a work to which Gorz also refers: Peter Sloterdijk, 'Domestikation des Seins' in *Nicht gerettet. Versuche nach Heidegger* (Frankfurt: Suhrkamp, 2001).

CHAPTER EIGHTEEN

Another World Is Possible

After turning 80, Gorz abandoned any further intentions of writing works of theory. In 2004, he agreed to Gallimard re-issuing *Critique of Economic Reason* as a paperback, thereby admitting that it was definitely his most ambitious, most fully developed book and also one of the most penetrating and relevant at the theoretical level that he had written. Though it dated from 1988, and his thought had markedly evolved in the intervening period, he still regarded the second part of the work as valid, the section which dissected economic reason and separated market from non-market activities.

In the three years left to him (2005–07), he published around a dozen new texts. In France he gave three interviews—to *Libération*, *EcoRev'* and the *Nouvel Observateur*—and as many articles to *Entropia*, a new journal advocating de-growth, *Mouvements*, a journal for radical social transformation founded in 1998, and *EcoRev'*.

Abroad, he made his voice heard in Brazil in particular, a country singularly receptive to his themes, since cooperatives, participatory democracy and local currencies all thrived there. Within the Workers' Party of Brazil, guaranteed minimum income was supported by Senator Eduardo Suplicy, a member of BIEN (which owed the change of its name to Basic Income Earth Network[1] to his action) and the prime mover behind Brazil's Conditional Minimum Income (*bolsa familia*) which was introduced in 2004. Two books on Gorz's thought are available from the São Paulo–based publisher Annablume: the first, published in 2002, developed out of Josué Pereira da Silva's PhD thesis; the second, published in 2006, is a collection of studies jointly edited by the same da Silva. The Rio de Janeiro–based alter-globalist periodical *Glob(al)* reprinted an interview with Gorz in 2003.[2] After opening its columns to a condensed version of André Langer's well-crafted MA thesis on Gorz's thinking, the journal of the Instituto Humanitas Unisinos at the Jesuit University of São Leopoldo (Rio Grande do Sul) also

---

1 Until 2004 it was known as the Basic Income European Network [Trans.].
2 André Gorz, 'Le savoir, la valeur, le capital', interview by Thomas Schaffroth (2003).

sought an interview with Gorz in 2005.[3] The website of that institute, directed by Inácio Neutzling, which had invited Gorz to Brazil in 1991, would continue to promote his thinking, as would Langer.[4] Also in 2005, the cultural supplement of the *Folha de São Paulo* published an interview with the author of *Reclaiming Work* and *The Immaterial*, both of which had just appeared in translation in Brazil.[5]

In 2006, the Copenhagen journal *Social Kritik* in turn published an interview with Gorz.[6] He was approached by the student Niels Fastrup who, beguiled by *The Immaterial*, cherished the ambition of inserting Gorz into the political and social debate in Denmark. This was somewhat to Gorz's astonishment, since he felt his principles were already being applied there— such as a guaranteed income set at 1,500 euros per person (for those with a child; 1,134 euros for those without) or the withdrawal from work, which affected 25 per cent of people of working age and even more if one includes those involved in job-sharing.[7]

Gorz was put in contact with the Utopia group by Marie-Louise Duboin and in August 2007 completed a long, powerful preface to the movement's manifesto which he entitled 'The Exit from Capitalism has Already Begun.'[8] Utopia saw itself as a pro-alterglobalist and pro-ecology force present within the Socialists, the Greens and Jean-Luc Mélanchon's Parti de gauche; its priority issues were the reduction of the working week to 32 hours and basic income. Lastly, in late spring of 2007, while giving up on the idea of reissuing some of his out-of-print books, which 'alongside what is still valid, contain much (too much) that is obsolete',[9] Gorz prepared a collection of his articles which he saw as the most significant and topical.

---

3 Gorz, *Ecologica*, pp. 139–83. Originally published as 'A crise e o êxodo da sociedade salarial', interview by Sonia Montaño, *Cadernos IHU Idéas* 31 (2005).

4 See ihu.unisinos.br (last accessed on 18 February 2022).

5 Gorz, 'Vers la multiactivité', interview by Vladimir Safatle (2005).

6 André Gorz 'Vidensøkonomi & kapitalismens krise?', interview by Niels Fastrup, *Social Kritik* 107 (December 2006).

7 See Gorz to Françoise Gollain, 5–6 September 2005 (GRZ).

8 André Gorz, 'La sortie du capitalisme a déjà commencé' in *Manifeste Utopia* (Lyon: Parangon, 2008), pp. 5–14. Gorz, *Ecologica*, pp. 21-42.

9 Letter from Gorz to Franz Schandl (in German), 7 November 2006, in 'Über den Horizont unserer Handlungen', p. 13.

Entitled *Ecologica*, in keeping with his wishes the book would be published posthumously in 2008. Though sadly lacking the preface he didn't have the time to write, the collection shows that he continued to locate his thinking within political ecology and that he had been a precursor of that movement. Apart from four recent texts produced between 2005 and 2007, it contains the article on 'the car' that was published in *Le Sauvage* in 1973, an adaptation of extracts from *Farewell to the Working Class* advocating de-growth, and the substantial article on ecology 'Political ecology: Expertocracy versus self-limitation' that had appeared in *Actuel Marx* in 1992 and in *New Left Review* the following year (though shorn of its conclusion, which Gorz in his last years no doubt viewed as too 'reformist'!).[10]

The Exit from Capitalism Has Begun

The sudden halt to the US property and finance boom in July 2007 and the international banking crisis that followed in Autumn 2008 had dramatic consequences for the affected populations. They brought it home to those people—and public opinion in general—that, with globalization, the economy had entered the era of all-out financialization. This had, however, occurred earlier, since it had already produced the Internet Bubble (the proliferation of over-valued start-ups) that had caused the gigantic stock market crash of 2001–02. For years then, Gorz had been trying to describe this new path that post-Fordist capitalism had embarked upon. Well-informed, he foreshadowed capitalism's crises and even hinted at the systemic collapse to which that path seemed inevitably to be leading.

The Financialization of the Immaterial

It wasn't enough for capital to break worker solidarity in the second half of the 1970s to restore the rate of profit by drastically reducing the cost of labour. Once robotization had been achieved, it had to press forward with the rational use of computers through a re-engineering of jobs in all sectors, which enabled the workforce to be further reduced in the 1990s.

---

10 André Gorz, 'L'écologie politique entre expertocratie et autolimitation', *Actuel Marx* 12 (1992): 15-29. Published as 'Political Ecology between Expertocracy and Self-Limitation' in Gorz, *Ecologica* (Chris Turner trans.). We are grateful to Françoise Gollain for having drawn our attention to this significant cut.

The outcome was paradoxical. To understand it, we have to go back to the Marxist labour theory of value. Since 'the average quantity of abstract labour embodied in commodities is, in the last analysis, what determines the relation of equivalence—the exchange-value—of commodities,'[11] then inevitably, 'with the contraction in the volume of material labour, the exchange value of products has tended to fall, as well as the volume of profits.'[12] As for the expansion of personal services, on which economists and trade unionists had been counting to boost the economy and employment once again, that had monetized activities which produced no value: 'The pay of these service workers comes from the income their clients have derived from productive labour; it is a *secondary income* [. . .].'[13]

The answer to this problem was found by valorizing the immaterial products of intelligence, this latter having become a decisive factor of production. But since these products were not ordinary commodities with a determinate exchange-value, this, as we have seen, was possible only by employing technical artifices or marketing tricks that yielded *monopoly rents* unrelated to the value of the labour embodied in them, which was now more than ever an obsolete consideration. As Gorz said, with the economists Vercellone and Marazzi following him on this, profit had turned into rent. It was that rent, based on values which, not being measurable, were virtual and volatile, that would make it possible to rescue the profitability of capital. It was that rent too which made contemporary capitalism extremely unstable and vulnerable and saw it run up against its own limits.

The market price of the stocks that came out of this 'immaterial economy'—that is to say, the forecasts of their profitability—would become their 'true' value. This is why Gorz could declare that 'the value of immaterial capital is essentially a stock-market fiction.'[14] From that point on, financialization was on the march.[15] Profits were directed towards financial dealings and, deserting productive investment, fed less and less into the accumulation of fixed (equipment) and variable (wages) capital. 'The left-wing ideologues'

11 Gorz, *Wissen, Wert und Kapital*, p. 79.

12 André Gorz, 'La valeur du capital immatériel est une fiction boursière', interview by Denis Clerc and Christophe Fourel, *Alternatives économiques* 212 (March 2003): 68.

13 Gorz, *Ecologica*, p. 168.

14 Gorz, 'La valeur du capital immatériel est une fiction boursière', p. 69.

15 For an analysis of these mechanisms, see Christian Marazzi, *The Violence of Financial Capitalism* (Los Angeles: Semiotext(e), 2010).

who claim to see financialization as 'a parasitic activity preying upon the real economy, are ignoring the reality of the facts': 'the sale and purchase of fictive capital on the stock markets brings in more than the productive valorization of real capital.'[16] As early as 1998, Gorz declared, 'The moment capital becomes financialized, it no longer knows what to do with the surplus value produced! Today, money is trying to produce money without involving labour at all.'[17]

It follows from this, he writes 10 years later, at the point when the property bubble is bursting,[18] that 'the real economy is becoming an appendage of the speculative bubbles sustained by the finance industry,' which only generates money 'by operations on the financial market that are more and more risky and less and less controllable.'[19] With the production of commodities valorizing less and less labour and putting ever fewer means of payment in circulation, the maintenance of consumption levels becomes possible only through the *credit* granted to households, which is now the principal engine of 'growth'. As the US mortgage bubble shows, 'growth is obtained by monetary creation, guaranteed by fictive assets and directed towards American consumption, not accumulation'; echoing the announcement two years earlier by the chairman of the Federal Reserve (the 'Fed') that that bubble might possibly burst,[20] he predicted in late summer of 2005 that, 'We are moving towards a slump and a crisis of the entire credit system.'[21] This was not the first such sagacious warning. In 1983, he issued the following gloomy prediction:

> As far as the world economic crisis is concerned, we are still in the
> first stages of a lengthy process which will last for another few
> decades. The worst may still be to come, the collapse of various

---

16 Gorz, 'Penser l'exode de la société du travail et de la marchandise', p. 98.

17 Gorz, 'Gorz, bourreau du travail', interview by Robert Maggiori and Jean-Baptiste Marongiu.

18 Gorz, *Ecologica*, pp. 21–42. Originally published as 'Le travail dans la sortie du capitalisme', *EcoRev*' 28 (Autumn 2007): 8–15.

19 Gorz, *Ecologica*, pp. 25, 24.

20 See Alan Greenspan, 'Risk transfer and financial stability' (5 May 2005) (available at: federalreserve.gov/newsevents/speech/2005speech.htm; last accessed on 18 February 2022).

21 André Gorz to Françoise Gollain, 5–6 September 2005.

large banks, possibly even states. Such collapses, or the means by which they might be prevented, will deepen still further the current crisis in society [. . .].[22]

Value Criticism and Crisis Theory

Gorz had travelled a long way since *Critique of Economic Reason*. In that verbose tome, he strove to trace the contours of autonomy, the better to cope with the inevitability—and even the justifiability—of economic heteronomy. In *Capitalism, Socialism, Ecology*, he signed up to the Polanyian argument of a re-embedding of the economy in politics and society, there again with a concern to rescue properly understood economic reason. Lastly, in *Reclaiming Work*, creative autonomy remained dependent on commodity circulation through the distribution of means of payment in the form of a universal basic income. This raft of solutions, incompatible with the domination of capital, but not with its survival, was now swept away: insofar as the capitalist economy was dying, it was in the depths of the crisis of value that the danger of barbarism lurked, but that was also where the germs of another economy lay, one without commodities and based on immeasurable wealth—an economy that had to be enabled to exist and grow.

This manifest radicalization of his thinking, still nascent as he was writing *The Immaterial*, but already strikingly in evidence in the months following the French edition when he rewrote the German version, followed new reading that Gorz undertook from 2002 onwards. The main sources here were works by Moishe Postone and Robert Kurz, who brought to his attention the arguments of the Value Criticism (*Wertkritik*) school of Marxism.

Kurz, a prolific essayist and freelance journalist, was the founder at Nuremberg of the journal of that current of thinking, which in 1990 took the name *Krisis*. Merten, whom we have already encountered, was a member of the Krisis group, but, meeting incomprehension over his battle for free software, left to found Oekonux. Though Gorz already knew Kurz's voluminous 'black book of capitalism' (*Schwarzbuch des Kapitalismus*, 1999) and the original English edition of Postone's *Time, Labor and Social Domination* (1993), it was through Meretz, also a member of Krisis, that he

---

22 Gorz, 'Afterword: A Discussion with André Gorz on Alienation, Freedom, Utopia and Himself' in *Traitor*, p. 304.

330 | WILLY GIANINAZZI

received—shortly after that man's first letter to him in 2003—several issues of a periodical published in Vienna, *Streifzüge*, which, apart from his own contributions, contained articles by members of the Krisis group.

Streifzüge was another journal from within this same school of Marxism. It was founded by the journalist Franz Schandl in 1996. Whereas Kurz in 2004 based his position on the primacy of critical theory, broke away and created the journal *Exit*, Schandl's magazine stressed, as the continuing *Krisis* writers did, concrete experiences that could contribute to the critique of work and the commodity form. Gorz subscribed to *Streifzüge* in December 2003. From that point on, he corresponded at length with Schandl until just before he died in September 2007.[23] He was also in contact with another *Streifzüge* writer, the ecologist Andreas Exner (already a member of the Austrian ATTAC group), who asked him in summer 2006 for a contribution to a collective work on basic income.[24] That was the most Kurzian of all the articles written by Gorz. Completed in January 2007, it was anticipated in the summer in *Streifzüge* and, translated and augmented, in *Mouvements*, where it was published as 'Penser l'exode de la société du travail et de la marchandise' [Conceiving the exodus from the work- and commodity-based society]. In July, however, Gorz confided regretfully to Exner: 'I discovered the value-criticism school much too late.'[25]

Alluding to Postone and Kurz, Gorz believed he had taken over in his recent articles 'the key elements of the orientations of these original Kurzians, recognizing in them a theoretical development of [his] own orientations.'[26] And in June 2007, on being sent the article intended for publication in *Mouvements*, a French representative of that school, Gérard Briche, replied to him in the following terms:

---

23 'Uber den Horizont unserer Handlungen. Aus den nachgelassenen Briefen des André Gorz' (letters in German from André Gorz to Franz Schandl and Andreas Exner), *Streifzüge* 41 (2007): 9–13.

24 André Gorz, 'Seid realistisch—verlangt das Unmögliche' in Andreas Exner, Werner Rätz and Birgit Zenker (eds), *Grundeinkommen. Soziale Sicherheit ohne Arbeit* (Vienna: Deuticke Verlag, 2007), pp. 70–8.

25 André Gorz to Andreas Exner, 5 July 2007, in 'Uber den Horizont unserer Handlungen', p. 13. For information on *Wertkritik*, see Gruppe Krisis, *Manifest gegen die Arbeit* (1999) and the websites palimpsaó.fr, krisis.org, exit-online.org and streif-zuege.org.

26 Preface for a projected second French edition of *The Immaterial* (GRZ 9.5)

The convergence of your analyses with those of the *Wertkritik* school is increasingly evident [. . .] and the fact that, having thought about these things quite independently, we arrive at similar conclusions is a powerful confirmation of the analyses we are presenting, which run largely counter to the dominant current of so-called 'left-wing' thought.[27]

The convergences were striking in several respects.[28] Gorz had great respect for the reinterpretation of Marx's critical theory by Postone, a Canadian historian teaching at Chicago who was one of the sources for the value-criticism school. In his book, Postone, basing himself on the *Grundrisse*, presents labour as the principle of social organization specific to capitalism alone. Like the Gorz of *Farewell to the Working Class* onwards, he is critical of traditional Marxism, which criticizes capitalism from the standpoint of labour—that is to say, by challenging relations of ownership, not the productive forces shaped by industrial capitalism, to which labour belongs as much as capital. Defending work, as the labour movement has done (Postone), or defending the ideology of work, as the Left does (Gorz), is reactionary.

The relationship to money throws light on the matter. As the vehicle of valorization, money is a *fetish* which apparently ranges labour against capital (with opposing pecuniary interests), but in reality brings the two together in the same abstract logic of capitalism. In this Postonian vein—which is not dissimilar to the analysis Horst made of the fetishism of money in 1947 (see above, p. 39)—Gorz explains:

> Labour and capital are fundamentally complicit in their antagonism, inasmuch as 'earning money' is their determining goal. In the eyes of capital, the nature of production is of less importance than its profitability; in the eyes of the worker, it is of less importance than the jobs it creates and the wages it distributes. For each, *what* is produced is of little significance, provided it brings a return. Both are consciously or otherwise in the service of the valorization of capital.[29]

As we have already seen in an earlier chapter, Postone's interpretation also interests Gorz on another level, which confirms his thinking on the possible

---

27 Gérard Briche to André Gorz, 19 June 2007 (GRZ).

28 See also Anselm Jappe, 'André Gorz et la critique de la valeur' in Caillé and Fourel (eds), *Sortir du capitalisme*, pp. 161–9.

29 Gorz, *Ecologica*, p. 151.

creation of wealth outside the value form. Referring to an economist resistant to his own arguments, Gorz suggests to a correspondent:

> Advise him to read Postone. He will learn that the difference between wealth and value isn't what he thinks it is, that there is wealth created by human activity that is without value (in the sense of political economy), because it can neither be accumulated, exchanged nor monetized (and is thus, in its initial objective, not productive of capital) and that 'intrinsic values' have nothing to do with neo-classical economics but go back to Kant's *The Metaphysics of Morals*, where we read: 'That which has a price has only a relative value, not a dignity, since it is exchangeable against anything else. But what has no price and hence is not exchangeable has a dignity, an absolute value.'[30]

Gorz was unstinting in his praise for Robert Kurz, whose latest books he would have liked to see translated in France, as indeed he would have liked to see Postone's. Expressing this wish to Hugues Jallon who was vainly offering, in the name of the La Découverte publishing house, to have him bring out an anthology of his own writings, Gorz called Kurz 'a first-rank theorist of the metamorphosis of capitalism and the scale of its crisis,' adding that he was 'the main rival and antagonist of Toni Negri (who doesn't come anywhere near him in terms of erudition and theoretical capability).'[31] Around November 2005, he became acquainted with Kurz's 'masterwork', *Das Weltkapital* [Global capital] (2005)—and later, also, Anselm Jappe's *Les Aventures de la marchandise. Pour une critique de la valeur* [Adventures of the commodity: For a criticism of value] (2003) which belongs to the same school of thinking. Thanks to Kurz, Gorz recognized the vital function of financial bubbles for the survival of the system[32] and found confirmation of his idea that the crisis was not due to the excesses of finance but to 'capitalism's incapacity to reproduce itself'[33] (Kurz was critical of ATTAC for not understanding this point). Capitalism was, thus, reaching its internal limits, with the nub of the problem lying, as Gorz had been saying at least since *Paths to Paradise*, in the so-called third industrial revolution:

---

30 André Gorz to Françoise Gollain, 15 and 25–27 December 2004 (GRZ). Gorz found the quotation from Kant in Oskar Negt.

31 André Gorz to Hugues Jallon, 19 January 2006 (GRZ).

32 Gorz, *Ecologica*, pp. 123–4.

33 Gorz, *Ecologica*, p. 26.

The micro-electronics revolution makes it possible to produce increasing quantities of commodities with a declining volume of work, so that sooner or later the system must run up against its internal limits. This capitalism, which is automating itself to death, will have to try to survive by distributing purchasing power that does not correspond to the value of work performed.[34]

Outlines of Another Economy

Gorz's last texts talk up more than ever the utopian potential for a Communist, ecological society overturning the hellish capitalist logic of the destruction of nature and humanity. They are tinged with Marxist catastrophism, technological optimism and utopian enthusiasm. These writings are torn between a gloomy, uncompromising picture of the tentacular grip of capitalism living on while locked into its insoluble contradictions and running up against its own limits, and an almost intoxicating attraction for the openings the capitalist behemoth nonetheless offers—particularly through technological advances that might be appropriated and subverted by those concretely trying to find civilized paths out of capitalism.

Not that technology has demiurgic powers: 'The realm of freedom', Gorz had written in *Farewell to the Working Class*, 'can never arise out of material processes.' Moreover, though 'The logic of capital has brought us to the threshold of liberation [. . .], it can only be crossed at the cost of a radical break [. . .]. This rupture can only come from individuals themselves.'[35] This 'radical' break (the Kurzians would now call it '*kategorisch*') 'cannot be spontaneous, cannot be brought about by great collective movements, but must be both "mental" and practical (Guattari puts that very well in his way), without any systematic goal or any reference to a "new order" '; it 'cannot be rapid or violent without giving birth to a totalitarian order.'[36] Gorz also explicitly returns to the positions expressed in *Farewell to the Working Class* 'on the crisis/decadence/corruption/impotence of politics and parties' by indicating his agreement with the Kurzians that 'there is nothing to be hoped for from states/governments'[37] (for the Kurzians, 'actually existing

---

34 Gorz, 'Penser l'exode de la société du travail et de la marchandise', pp. 95–6.
35 Gorz, *Farewell to the Working Class*, p. 74.
36 Gorz to Françoise Gollain, 26 July 2007 (GRZ).
37 Gorz to Françoise Gollain, 26 July 2007 (GRZ).

socialism' was a state capitalism and the Socialists—with their fitting slogan 'to each according to his work'—have never been anything other than the left wing of capital).

What Sort of De-growth?

While it did not inspire a vast movement, the notion of de-growth found an astonishing audience among the French public in the 2000s. The bi-weekly publication *La Décroissance* [De-growth], first published in 2004, achieved sales of 25,000 copies. Yet the concept, which is often equated, when transposed to the individual level, with 'voluntary simplicity', remains vague in its anti-productivist, anti-industrial, anti-consumerist and even anti-economic assumptions, with which it shares the failing of defining itself negatively. It is only really in the agro-pastoral world, which has seen a large influx of neo-rurals advocating the 'simple life' so beloved of Diogenes, that we find extensive practices, such as permaculture or biodynamic agri-culture—developed by Pierre Rabhi—showing evidence of de-growth.

The birth in November 2006 of a journal of de-growth studies, *Entropia*, was aimed at filling a theoretical void. Edited by the painter Jean-Claude Besson-Girard, the main driving force behind the publication was the econ-omist Serge Latouche, a merciless critic of development, progress and economism (he is the author of *L'Invention de l'économie*, 2005) and hence particularly appreciated by Gorz. (Though they did not know each other, they held each other in mutual esteem). Thanks to the intermediation of the de-growther Françoise Gollain, who was in regular contact with Gorz by mail, Latouche asked him to contribute to the second issue of the journal on the theme of 'De-growth and Work'. With the participation of the 'Gorzians' Bernard Guibert—an old Sartrean friend of Gorz's who had joined the AT—and Gollain (she contributed an excellent overview of her mentor's thinking),[38] the issue was conceived as 'a gentle but heartfelt homage' to the author of *Ecology as Politics*.

We know that since 1972, an *annus mirabilis* for bringing ecological issues to the fore, Gorz had been arguing that the race to ever more growth

---

38 Françoise Gollain, 'André Gorz ou le refus de la domination du travail', *Entropia* 2 (Spring 2007): 63–79. Translated as 'André Gorz: Wage Labour, Free Time and Ecological Reconstruction', *Green Letters* 20 (2) (2016): 127–39 (available at: https://bit.ly/3KK7sLB; last accessed: 27 July 2022).

had to stop, as it was laying waste to the planet and the environment. To Gollain, won over in her youth to Gorz's reasoning in *Ecology as Politics*, he was 'undoubtedly to be numbered among the founders of the de-growth movement'.[39] However, Gorz also thought, as he wrote to her on several occasions, that the concept of de-growth was 'unfortunate'[40] and that 'de-growth couldn't be a policy'.[41] This was because, as he explained in the article he sent to Latouche on 24 September 2006, while de-growth was, admittedly, a 'good idea', because it prompted thinking on how to live better and differently, it couldn't be applied within the framework of capitalism without leading to a depression: capital needed growth by any and every means—that was its problem! It wasn't enough then to level *external* criticism at the economic system on the grounds of protecting the biosphere, we also needed an understanding of the *internal* limits that growth itself imposed on capitalism. This objection on Gorz's part is in line with the objections made by theorists of the value-criticism school, Robert Kurz and Anselm Jappe.

And, in actual fact, the de-growth of the economy based on exchange-value was already a reality. Since it could no longer be fuelled by the expansion of productive labour, the valorization of capital increasingly rested on monetary fictions with unstable and unpredictable outcomes. Unlike Moulier-Boutang, who saw in *Cognitive Capitalism* [2007] not the death throes of capital but 'a new Great Transformation', Gorz had little belief in the capacities of the existing economic system to adapt and stabilize itself (it was the case in the past that the system had been able to recover only by resorting to war). Chiming with Kurz's school of thought, he simply wondered whether the outcome of this capitalist development would take the form of 'a passively experienced catastrophic crisis' or an active 'choice of society', freed from 'the domination by capital of our mode of life, our needs and the way of satisfying them.'[42] The idea of de-growth obviously presupposed an exit from that domination; it could not, then, be any other than anti-capitalist—and the movement that argued for it would gain in strength

---

39 Gollain, 'André Gorz ou le refus de la domination du travail', p. 127. See also Françoise Gollain's introduction to Gollain (ed.), *André Gorz. Pour une pensée de l'éco-socialisme* (Neuvy-en-Champagne: Le Passager clandestin, 2014), pp. 9–56.

40 André Gorz to Françoise Gollain, 5–6 September 2005.

41 André Gorz to Françoise Gollain, 20 July 2006 (GRZ).

42 Gorz, *Ecologica*, p. 126.

and coherence by being aware of that. And, indeed, was it not based on 'the idea of the *sufficient*', which is alien to the dominant economic universe?[43]

So far as the 'external' critique that the de-growth movement preferred to level against the system went, it was not without the necessary radicalism. Its hostility to ecological management policies—so-called 'sustainable development' or 'ecological transition'—proved this and Gorz did not contest the point. But this 'ecological restructuring', as he explained in *EcoRev'* in 2007, brings no solution to the damage wrought by growth, since 'it is impossible to avoid climate catastrophe without a radical break with the economic logic and methods that have been taking us in that direction for 150 years':[44]

> De-growth is therefore imperative for our survival. But it presupposes a different economy, a different lifestyle, a different civilization and different social relations. In the absence of these, collapse could be avoided only through restrictions, rationing and the kind of authoritarian resource-allocation typical of a war economy. The exit from capitalism will happen, then, one way or another, in either a civilized or a barbarous fashion.[45]

Interconnected Self-Providing and High-Tech Craft Production

Capitalism has pulled off the trick of decoupling the worker from the consumer: we no longer consume anything we produce, and we no longer produce anything we consume. The—schizophrenic—subject is losing his integrity and his power of determination (for Postone, as a reader of Gorz, this is how the socially mediating role of labour comes to be imposed at the heart of the capitalist mode of functioning, since 'no one consumes what one produces, but one's own labor or labor products, nevertheless, function as the necessary means of obtaining the products of others').[46]

The harnessing of positive externalities, which takes the form of obtaining free work from the consumer who is invited to contribute to improving a product or to perform a service himself, changes nothing: this 'contributive economy', which is tending to expand from the immaterial sector to

---

43 Gorz, *Ecologica*, p. 126.

44 Gorz, *Ecologica*, p. 26.

45 Gorz, *Ecologica*, p. 27.

46 Postone, *Time, Labor, and Social Domination*, p. 150. The book includes several references to Gorz's work.

the whole economy, in no way advances the freedom of choice of the 'pro-sumer' that is produced in this way. The 'unification of the subject of production and the subject of consumption' is achieved in a different way— through 'self-providing outside the market', which alone 'offers a way out from the determination by capital of the content of needs and the mode of their satisfaction.'[47] This reunification must not be conceived purely on an individual or private scale:

> 'Prosumption' (a contraction of production and consumption) may currently extend to entire populations and be coordinated at a planetary level by the interconnection of communal high-tech self-providing workshops, self-organized in cooperative networks of mutual assistance, and the permanent dissemination of innovations and ideas.[48]

The internet and free software make that cooperation possible. But a giant step forward was taken with the development of 3D printers (also known as 'fabbers'), which make it possible to expand the range of what one manu-factures on one's own. Initially used in industry for the rapid creation of prototypes, they made their appearance in the 'free software' world at the dawn of the twenty-first century. We are speaking here of small-scale machine tools that carry out plans sent by computer and use materials in particle form (sand, glue, resin, metals etc.) by the addition of layers to pro-duce unique parts in small quantities.

As soon as he discovered their existence in the scientific and political literature, Gorz became an enthusiast. He was very impressed by the prac-tical observations of the visionary Austro-American philosopher Frithjof Bergmann, an emulator of Thoreau in the forests of New Hampshire, then a university professor in a Michigan ravaged by the crisis of the car industry and unemployment. Gorz read his book *Neue Arbeit, neue Kultur* (2004; not available in English), in which 'fabbers' were presented as an excellent tool for boosting the collaborative self-providing efforts of groups excluded from waged work. Later, while staying at a hotel in Bad Ragaz in Sankt-Gallen canton, guided in the use of the establishment's computer by visiting friend Erich Hörl, he feverishly printed off dozens of pages from the internet on the subject, including writings by Merten and Meretz.

---

47 Gorz, 'Penser l'exode de la société du travail et de la marchandise', p. 105.
48 Gorz, 'Penser l'exode de la société du travail et de la marchandise', p. 105.

This cutting-edge craft production, he argued, would 'enable groups that are excluded or doomed to inactivity or underemployment by the "development" of capitalism to come together in communal workshops to produce everything they and their communities need.'[49] 'Transport, warehousing, marketing and factory assembly, which represent two thirds or more of current costs, would be eliminated.'[50] An economy 'beyond "employment", money and commodities' would come into being.[51]

The populations of the global South might also be interested in the introduction of these networked, local workshops, since those people had nothing to gain from capitalist development, whether Keynesian or free-market: sooner or later, digitization and robotization would bring about the collapse of full-time employment. It wasn't by chance, Gorz went on, that a prophetic work like Robert Kurz's *Der Kollaps der Modernisierung* (1991; Portuguese translation in 1992) became a bestseller in Brazil or that Mandela's South Africa had welcomed the introduction of 3D printers which Bergmann foresaw. He concluded with the words: 'I do not say that these radical transformations will come about. I am simply saying that, for the first time, we can wish them to come about. The means exist, as well as the people who are methodically working towards their realization.'[52]

From Universal Basic Income to an Economy based on Free Goods and Services

The advocates of Value Criticism regard the universal grant as a 'good idea' that collapses on closer scrutiny. By allocating money to consume, the measure merely sustains the fetishism of money and commodities and, as a consequence, keeps its recipients under the capitalist yoke; and it does so by way of a transfer of incomes, the sum total of which just goes on declining. Challenged by Franz Schandl, Gorz asserts, not unreasonably: 'I have always been clear that commodity relations cannot be eliminated without at the same time eliminating money relations, and also that an unconditional basic income cannot be an income transfer and that it presupposes

---

49 Gorz, *Ecologica*, p. 129.
50 Gorz, *Ecologica*, p. 130.
51 Gorz, *Ecologica*.
52 Gorz, *Ecologica*, p. 41.

an alternative money and an alternative form of economic activity [*alternatives Wirtschaften*].'[53]

However, after reworking the section of *The Immaterial* on 'The Arguments for a Basic Income' for the German edition, he wrote to Schandl: 'I have thought about your objections (justified in principle) to the subsistence income [*Existenzgeld*] and have taken account of them, without entirely abandoning the idea.'[54] In that paragraph, now re-titled 'The Ambiguity of the Basic Income', he admits, first of all, that 'it may seem paradoxical that I should continue to support this demand after welcoming the prospect of a society beyond markets, money and exchange relations.'[55] But the subsistence income cannot be 'ordinary money' from the economic circuit:[56]

> It can only be financed by tax levied on the profits made by businesses. An economy that produces more and more commodities with less and less capital-productive work; an economy, then, which, thanks to productivity gains, distributes less and less in terms of means of payment even as production is rising, cannot finance increasing income transfers by raising taxes on wages and profits.[57]

The subsistence income makes sense only if it is combined with the creation of self-providing local activities:

> It will serve, then, not to perpetuate the consumption of commodities and a life dependent on 'alienated' production decisions, but solely to distribute goods which, *for the moment*, can only be produced on the basis of a transregional division of labour and

---

53 Gorz to Franz Schandl, 3 December 2003, 'Über den Horizont unserer Handlungen', p. 9.

54 Gorz to Franz Schandl, 5 August 2004, 'Über den Horizont unserer Handlungen', p. 9.

55 Gorz, *Wissen, Wert und Kapital*, p. 9.

56 On this issue, see the section 'Comment financer un revenu pour tous' *Mouvements* 73 (Spring 2013); Laurent Baronian and Carlo Vercellone, 'Monnaie du commun et revenu social garanti', *Terrains Théories* 1 (2015); Christian Arnsperger, 'Revenu de base, économie soutenable et alternatives monétaires', *L'Économie politique* 67 (July 2015): 34–49.

57 Gorz, *Wissen, Wert und Kapital*, p. 97.

without which local self-providing would not be possible (e.g. semi-conductors).[58]

Even when confined to a transient objective, the call for a subsistence income nonetheless reveals 'the need for another economy, an end to the fetishism of money and market society. It announces the obsolescence of an economy based on commodity labour and prepares for its collapse.'[59]

Gorz makes clear, then, in a 2005 interview aimed at a Brazilian audience that, 'the subsistence income will be a different money from the kind we use today. It won't have the same functions. [...] It will be created "from below", the product of a general groundswell [...] in response to a combination of the different forms of crisis we sense looming.'[60] Gorz does not 'think that the subsistence income can be introduced gradually and peacefully through top-down reform': its introduction 'depends largely on groups and movements whose practices are limning out the possibilities of another world and preparing the ground for it.'[61] As Gorz sees it, however, one problem remains unsolved: 'that of the currency in which the basic income is delivered and the system of prices on the basis of which it is set. [...] Duboin's idea of issuing a money that is cancelled when it is spent doesn't solve the problem, since it explicitly postulates that the goods bought with the guaranteed income have a market *price*.'[62]

Gorz returned to Duboin's Distributist model in the article he was writing for Exner, with whose 'criticisms of most conceptions [*Vorstellungen*] of basic income' he says he fully agrees.[63] 'By formally preserving the commodity form for the wealth produced and the need for money to have access to that wealth,' this model 'preserves an essential aspect of capitalist relations of domination'. In calling for a universal income, it is not about pursuing, 'the illusory goal of a reorganization of capitalism which, by its dynamic, would lead to its transformation or even its extinction,' since, admittedly, 'the guaranteed social income remains of itself immanent to capitalism, but

58 Gorz, *Wissen, Wert und Kapital*, p. 103.
59 Gorz, *Wissen, Wert und Kapital*, p. 97.
60 Gorz, *Ecologica*, pp. 174–5.
61 Gorz, *Ecologica*.
62 André Gorz to Jean Zin, 11 July 2006 (GRZ).
63 André Gorz to Andreas Exner, 10 August 2006, in 'Über den Horizont', p. 13.

we must nonetheless call for it *in a perspective which transcends the system.*[64] This was his last word on the subject.

As Gorz explained to Marie-Louise Duboin, if he had 'difficulties with the notions of distribution and basic income', that was because he was 'increasingly coming to accept the hypothesis that we are moving (potentially) towards an "economy" of free goods and services.'[65] The fact was that, with the knowledge economy and the possibilities for hi-tech self-providing, 'an economy beyond "employment", money and commodities, based on the pooling of the products of an activity originally conceived as shared—a zero-cost economy—[was beginning] to seem possible.'[66]

'This is, of course, a utopia,' he wrote. 'But it is a concrete utopia. It represents an extension of the free software movement, which sees itself as a germinal form of economy of zero cost and pooled resources or, in other words, of a communism.'[67]

The Possibility of Barbarism

Unlike those whom age mellowed or deflected from the cause, Gorz never deviated in his search for paths to a radically better potential future beyond the democratic capitalist order. For him, human existence simply consisted in relentlessly making choices among possibilities afforded at life's crossroads. For Kierkegaard, a forerunner of existentialism, that possibility was frightening and paralysing because it contained within itself the avoidance of that which is possible. Gorz had been marked in his youth by this despairing impediment to free choice. Sartre had reproached him for it in 1946. He had overcome it through an interpretation of Sartre and Marx which led to a two-pronged theory of social transformation—based on both the will of the subject and the possibilities of the situation. From that point on, socialism seemed to him an optional necessity, then Communism a desirable possibility, placed within our grasp by the very evolution of capitalism. But he always weighed up the choice between good and evil, between the good and bad directions potentially available within the state of things.

64 André Gorz, 'Penser l'exode', pp. 96, 97, 100.

65 André Gorz to Marie-Louise Duboin, 25 September 2006. Reprinted in *Trente ans de dialogue avec André Gorz*, p. 14.

66 Gorz, *Ecologica*, p. 130.

67 Gorz, *Ecologica*, p. 131. On this subject, see the seminal work by Jean-Louis Sagot-Duvauroux, *De la gratuité* (Paris/Tel Aviv: L'Éclat, 2006 [1995]).

Gorz did not regard autonomy as an innate aspiration that would be proof against potential 'fundamentalist/totalitarian regressions'.[68] At the end of his life, his theoretical optimism did not prevent him from detecting the signs of a potential barbarism. When he wrote of this in his correspondence, it was clear that a book by Robert Kurz, *Weltordnungskrieg* [War for the world order, 2003], written in the wake of 9/11, had made a deep impression on him. Starting out from the fact that human beings had become increasingly unnecessary in the reproduction of the system and had, to a very large extent, been excluded from the forms of social integration and recognition that Fordist-type work used to represent, Kurz argued that we were seeing a process of 'de-civilization'.

> That is to say, the domination of armed gangs, criminal gangs of exterminatory, suicidal predators and looters, whose destructive rage expresses what Hannah Arendt called *Weltverlorenheit* (a state of world-loss), which turns into *Selbstverlorenheit* (a state of self-loss). We are far from the violence that gives birth to history and/or to the affirmation of the dignity a people has been robbed of. [...] In that light, the self-destructive violence of the 'revolt of the *banlieues*' of November [2005] assumes another dimension and another meaning.[69]

Since then, we have seen manifestations of religious fanaticism and regression, retreats into identity and community, nationalist fixations, the rise of racist and xenophobic hatreds, the rejection of the elites and the political class, and explosions of urban violence with no declared objective. It is no mistake to see these phenomena as disjointed, impotent reactions—adding only further to social disintegration—to the anti-social consequences of the grip on the world of the finance-based economy, aided and abetted by states and managerial-style politicians of all stripes.

68 André Gorz to Jean-Louis Laville, 29 December 1994 (GRZ).
69 André Gorz to Robert Chenavier, 22 February 2006 (GRZ).

CHAPTER NINETEEN

The Final Freedom

In 2005 André Gorz prepared a new edition of *The Traitor* for Gallimard to issue in 'pocket' format. As he did when he had revised the book for the new English edition in 1989, he took out a dozen or so pages of long-winded or dated digression on Romain Rolland's 'above-the-fray' attitude and why intellectuals should be commited to Communism. He supplemented the book with his text on ageing ('Le vieillissement') that had originally been published in the early 1960s.

We Are Less Old Today

This dive into his autobiographical writings prompted him to follow up on this account of ageing with a new preface, though it remained unpublished during his lifetime.[1] After pointing out that his description of ageing, proffered when in the prime of life, veered towards 'an undertaking of identifying the alienations the adult is called upon to internalize' and that it was 'both a personal and an intellectual experience',[2] Gorz, now deep into the 'third age', pondered what old age was and what he had himself become.

Knowingly or not, he said, old age is a break with the past. It is an exit from what Max Weber called the 'cage of servitude' created by the world of work: it is not, therefore, necessarily the ordeal of being 'set aside' that it seemed to Simone de Beauvoir to be. At retirement age, 'a second life and second youth' begin. It is possible once again to break free of the conditioning of the 'practico-inert', to try out richer regimes of life and take a freer look at the paths of emancipation entwined within the potentiality of things. Thanks to the fact that the digital revolution was occurring at this same time, a revolution that opened new horizons for the collective appropriation of production, he felt fired with the optimism of youth, with the conviction that 'another world is possible'. 'We are less old than we were 20 years ago,

---

1 André Gorz, 'Nous sommes moins vieux qu'il y a vingt ans' (title ascribed by the editors) in Fourel (ed.), *André Gorz. Un penseur pour le XXIe siècle*, pp. 268–74.
2 Gorz, 'Nous sommes moins vieux qu'il y a vingt ans', p. 270.

individually and socially,' he declared, going on to conclude that, 'I did not foresee this when I was 36. I did not foresee that, past the age of 60, I would begin a second life with the partner I had united with for life.'[3]

The Story of a Love

Between March and June 2006, Gorz took up his pen again to compose an account of his life, the life he had spent with his partner. *Letter to D.* is the powerfully emotive story of their love and intellectual closeness and complementarity. A story studded with the details of their resistance to the canons of consumption and fashion, their refusal to let advertising and marketing impose on them needs they didn't have, their spontaneous proclivity for the simple life, their scorn for money: 'Ecology became a way of life and a daily practice for us, although that didn't stop us from feeling a completely different civilization was needed.'[4]

Love, when experienced in this way, escapes social conformism; it is irreducible to a social function; it rejects the third-party interposition that is the institution of marriage—hence Gorz's indignant response when a religious believer (the ecologist Dominique Bourg, who had come to visit him) defended that practice in 1996. Love is a secession in the purest existential tradition, but also in terms of Touraine's schemas, which Gorz admitted he had followed: '[L]ove is the mutual fascination of two human subjects based precisely on what is most indefinable about them, least socializable, most resistant to the roles and images of themselves that society imposes on them and to cultural allegiances.'[5] That being the case, the author wishes to show that, 'instead of being a withdrawal into oneself, a love can renew itself and flourish throughout a lifetime by inscribing itself in the successive transformations of the period in which the couple concerned have also been actors.'[6]

This brief narrative (106 short pages in English) begins with a poignant declaration: 'We've lived together now for 58 years and I love you more than ever. I once more feel a gnawing emptiness in the hollow of my chest that

---

3 Gorz, 'Nous sommes moins vieux qu'il y a vingt ans', p. 274.

4 Gorz, *Letter to D.*, p. 101.

5 Gorz, *Letter to D.*, p. 25. Translation modified, partly to include the last phrase—*aux appartenances culturelles*—which is omitted from the English translation [Trans.]

6 André Gorz to a correspondent known only as Jean-Luc, undated [2006], (GRZ 1.11).

is only filled when your body is pressed next to mine.'[7] But, from the outset, Gorz sets himself a question that he addresses to his beloved: 'Why is there so little of you in what I've written when our union has been the most important thing in our life?'[8] *Letter to D.* is an act of reparation. Rereading *The Traitor* in winter 2005–06 was a source of consternation to him (this was why he added a 'complement' to it for the new French reprint which would appear after his death in 2008).[9] The book was supposed to show that his commitment to Dorine had been the decisive turning point that had enabled him to find the will to live. That plan had not been fulfilled. It was thwarted throughout the novel by an obsessional need to theorize, to intellectualize, to be 'pure, transparent mind'. And yet it was thanks to his partner that the author of *The Traitor* had been able to overcome his suicidal nihilism. It then took Dorine's illness—and his decision to retire to take care of her—for Gorz at last to resolve to 'live fully in the present, mindful above all of the richness of [their] shared life'.[10] And to announce, solemnly, as the narrative was drawing to its end:

> I'm now reliving the moments when I made that resolution with a sense of urgency. I don't have any major work in the pipeline. I don't want to 'put off living till later' any longer, to use Georges Bataille's phrase. You've given me all of your life and all of you; I'd like to be able to give you all of me in the time we have left.[11]

Gérard Horst's exceptional love for his partner was a plain fact recognized by all who had spent any length of time around him. When Serge Lafaurie of *Le Nouvel Observateur*, amazed one day that he wouldn't make a foreign reporting trip on account of his sick wife, told him, 'You could leave her for a couple of days, it wouldn't kill her,' he retorted, 'Yes it would!'[12] When Jean Daniel, attempting to describe this 'character from a Russian novel', one of the most 'fascinating', but also most 'mysterious' people he had ever happened to be around, asked himself what he could be sure of, he concluded: 'First, that he and his partner Doreen form one of the most intimately

---

7 Gorz, *Letter to D.*, p. 1.

8 Gorz, *Letter to D.*, p. 2.

9 See Gorz, *Le Traître* suivi *de Le Vieillissement*, pp. 412–13.

10 Gorz, *Le Traître*, p. 104 (translation modified).

11 Gorz, *Le Traître*, pp. 104–05.

12 Author interview with Serge Lafaurie, 18 November 2011.

bonded, most obsessionally attentive and most thoroughly complementary couples he had ever seen.'[13]

When Gorz wrote his 'letter' to Dorine, he wasn't sure he was going to publish it, out of discretion towards her. He thought he might give it to her as a birthday present and keep it for only a few friends or close acquaintances to read. Michel Delorme, his editor at Galilée, to whom he nonetheless submitted an outline of the manuscript, persuaded him to publish, convinced as he was that it was a fine, major book and one that could reach a large audience. Dorine did not recognize herself entirely in the picture that was painted of her, even if Gorz was telling the truth—his truth.[14] She respected the decision to see it delivered to the public, even though she was uncomfortable with it; but 'loving a writer involves loving what he writes', she told a journalist.[15] She merely requested that this Letter to Dorine should become, more anonymously, *Letter to D.* and not appear in English in her lifetime.

Upon reading *Letter to D.*, a number of Gorz's old friends, who had fallen out of touch, dropped him affectionate notes. These included Paul Virilio, Freddy Buache from Lausanne and, among others, Tiennot Grumbach who, since he first knew Gorz, had spent his life as a 'lawyer-comrade (*avocamarade*)'[16] passionately defending workers' rights. When the book was published in October, Michel Contat took advantage of a visit to Vosnon to speak warmly of it in *Le Monde*. Lafaurie and his wife, who hadn't been back there for more than 20 years, visited in July 2007. The little book was a stunning commercial success: in two months, it sold 21,000 copies. 'We're becoming famous!' Gorz remarked sardonically to a friend.[17] If we include foreign language editions in the two countries where Gorz had his main audience, Germany and Brazil, sales of 120,000 were reached in 2011. *Le Figaro* had its word to say on the subject: 'One can admire this figure of an independent, intelligent woman, who is nonetheless entirely devoted to her husband. It seems that men have been buying *Letter to D.* in large numbers: let's hazard a guess that they are buying it to give to their

13 Daniel, *L'Ère des ruptures*, p. 50.

14 Michel Contat, 'André Gorz. Le philosophe et sa femme', *Le Monde* (27 October 2006).

15 Elisabeth von Thadden, 'Von Luft und Liebe', *Die Zeit* (20 September 2007).

16 A portmanteau term that combines the word *avocat* with *camarade* [Trans.].

17 Finn Bowring, 'The Writer's Malady. André Gorz, 1923–2007', *Radical Philosophy* 148 (March–April 2008): 52.

wives as a way of expressing the gratitude to them that they aren't necessarily capable of showing outwardly [. . .]'.[18] Since 2016, the story has been staged as a play in France.

The Choice of an Ending

Things began to go wrong in the first half of 2007. In March–April, Gérard gave Dorine bronchitis, which she treated for 10 days before her condition deteriorated. She complained of unexplained pains and was rushed into hospital with a bowel obstruction. This was operated on on 14 May. On 2 April, Gorz had hurriedly seen a solicitor and made a will. As executor, he thought first of Dominique Bourg from Troyes, a close friend of the environmental activist Nicolas Hulot, whom he had known 10 years before but who had since been appointed professor at the University of Lausanne. In July, he approached his friend Christophe Fourel, whom he had met in 1987 at a debate held by the journal *Projet* on the minimum income, but, rather than accept, Fourel would become one of the main advocates of his thinking by organizing conferences on his work and publishing related essay collections. Dominique Bourg therefore became Gorz's executor.

Gorz's publisher Michel Delorme was sounded out on the possibility of managing his literary estate, but in the end it was with Olivier Corpet, who had published several of his articles in the journal *Autogestions* in the 1980s, that Gorz struck an agreement: this gave over the management of Gorz's literary legacy to the Institut Mémoires de l'édition contemporaine (IMEC), of which Corpet was director. IMEC is an archive centre near Caen which holds the personal papers of, among others, Althusser, Derrida, Foucault, Guattari, Morin and Touraine. La Cimade was chosen as the couple's 'universal legatee'. Created in 1939, it is an ecumenical aid association for migrants and refugees and Gorz had followed its activities for many years.

In 1989, the couple had approached a co-founder of la Cimade, Madeleine Barot, who had just been awarded the title 'Righteous among the Nations', with an offer to set up a fund, financed by themselves, to grant scholarships to students from Eastern Europe. Gorz had himself received generous aid from a couple of benefactors when he had been a student at Lausanne. He and Dorine went to Paris to discuss their idea with the

---

18 Astrid de Larminat, 'L'amour se bonifie avec l'âge', *Le Figaro* (14 December 2006).

association's chair Jacques Maury and subsequently submitted a written plan to him, but the fall of the Berlin Wall rendered their project obsolete. Much later, they made a second approach, this time with the aim of bequeathing their estate to la Cimade. Hence, over the remaining four years of their lives, Maury kept them informed of the association's activities, bringing various chairpersons, secretaries and communications chiefs to see them at Vosnon.

The journalists who travelled to their home in the Aube département to meet the two protagonists of *Letter to D.* occasionally questioned them about their lack of progeny. Gorz referred to their financial and job insecurity at the time—and alluded to his immaturity: 'It was a sacrifice D. made. Because she sensed very clearly that I wasn't mature enough to be a father.'[19] In 1949 Gérard had confided to Riffel that he had turned to a doctor, the husband of the woman who kept the Waschmuth boarding house, to obtain an abortion for his partner.[20] Gérard and Dorine explained that, at all events, 'they had given up on having children because they had nothing to hand on, and also they had no family feelings.'[21] 'In my opinion,' mused Gorz, 'good fathers are those who needed a father in their childhood. I didn't want to have a father because I didn't like my father. [. . .] We didn't have to start a family to hand anything on, since we'd never had families ourselves.'[22]

Michel-Édouard Leclerc, to whom we owe the most striking, affectionate memories of Gorz in the immediate aftermath of his death, had come to a different conclusion. He tells how he had for many years been shocked by Gorz's explanations about the absence of children: 'Rather than saying that Dorine wasn't able to have one, he ventured into political arguments which seemed to me quite unacceptable, unless all hope were to be snuffed out.'[23] Might the unconscious have been at work in a reply Gorz gave in an interview filmed in 1990 when, in speaking about 'looking after the upbringing and education of your children', he added 'if you are able to

---

19 Jean-Baptiste Marongiu and Frédérique Roussel, 'Aux noms de l'amour', *Libération* (5 October 2006) (reportage at Vosnon).

20 Told to the author by Walter Riffel on 23 September 2016. Riffel does not recall either the date of the event or whether the partner in question was Dorine.

21 Elisabeth von Thadden, 'Von Luft und Liebe'.

22 Frédérique Roussel, 'André Gorz, dernière lettre à D.', *Libération* (25 September 2007) (a reference to the audio recording of the above mentioned reportage at Vosnon).

23 Leclerc, 'André Gorz, la mort d'un philosophe'.

have any'?[24] At Vosnon, Dorine developed an affection for Katheline, the neighbouring family's young child (and, subsequently, teenager), whom she cared for as though she were her own grandchild.

Summer dispelled the gloom. Gorz began to write again and carefully sorted his archives into cardboard boxes to be sent to IMEC. The documentary maker Henning Burk, who had been captivated by *The Immaterial*, came back to Vosnon to make a programme on *Letter to D.* for the German-speaking TV channel 3Sat. Friends visited the couple. Finn Bowring spent four days with them, from 6 to 9 September. 'Dorine is coming back to life— such a long way back!' Gorz confided, somewhat relieved, to Françoise Gollain.[25] For that reason he agreed to Gollain's idea of a debate with Latouche that Besson-Girard was keen on mounting amid great fanfare at the Sorbonne on 17 September. Gorz, however, proposed that they hold it at Vosnon ('It's much better at our place. Ask them to come'). In late August, a journalist from the German mass circulation weekly *Die Zeit*, who wanted to interview him about *Letter to D.*, also obtained an appointment at his home for 10 September, though she was warned that this would take place only 'if nothing happens between now and then,' and if she would also listen to Dorine's angle on the story.[26] The interview took place. 'But how does one speak to this couple about death?' She did essay a question: 'Would breaking-up [*Trennung*] have felt like a failure? Now the two of them laugh. Breaking-up—unthinkable!'[27]

Two days later, the telephone rang at Françoise Gollain's house. In a small, tired, defeated voice, Gorz apologized for having to cancel the meeting with the de-growthers of *Entropia*. Dorine had been in terrible pain for several days. During this same period, Gorz asked Christophe Fourel, to whom he spoke by telephone, to put off his visit until after the couple's trip. What trip was he referring to? For some years, Gérard and Dorine had been in the habit of going off to the spa resort of Bad Ragaz in the autumn and his Parisian friend took Gorz to be referring to that. There was still a sliver of hope perhaps. The cases had been brought down from the attic, but this time they would remain empty.

---

24 Marian Handwerker (director), *André Gorz* (film) (Belgium: La Confédération des syndicats chrétiens, September 1990).

25 André Gorz to Françoise Gollain, 26 July 2007 (GRZ).

26 See the fax in French from Elisabeth von Thadden to Gorz of 28 August 2007 (GRZ).

27 Elisabeth von Thadden, 'Von Luft und Liebe'.

Gorz also told Meretz and Jean Zin that he was sorry he hadn't seen them earlier. He advised his lifelong friend Walter Riffel from Eastern Switzerland (Ostschweiz), with whom he enjoyed walking at Bad Ragaz, not to come to Vosnon because he didn't know if he would be there (Riffel would nonetheless make the trip and would be staggered to find a note on the door that stopped him in his tracks). The last text Gorz wrote was a final draft of his demanding preface to the Utopia manifesto that he was putting together for *EcoRev*.[28] He finished it in handwritten form on 17 September, then, annoyed that the fax machine wasn't working properly (he had had one for some years), became panicky on the phone to *EcoRev*, explaining that time was pressing: he had to 'go away'.

Gérard and Dorine's minds were made up: they would 'leave' together. They had discussed the matter often and had come to a joint decision long before. *Letter to D.*—Gorz confessed that he wept as he wrote it—foreshadowed the epilogue in an emotionally charged dream scene of the kind only literature can provide. A sublime declaration of love, it ended on a denial of the very possibility of living without the other partner:

> At night I sometimes see the figure of a man, on an empty road in a deserted landscape, walking behind a hearse. I am that man. It's you the hearse is taking away. I don't want to be there for your cremation; I don't want to be given an urn with your ashes in it. [. . .] Neither of us wants to outlive the other. We've often said to ourselves that if, by some miracle, we were to have a second life, we'd like to spend it together.[29]

Already in 1975, when Dorine's chronic illness was becoming unbearable, Gorz had composed a literary fragment, astonishingly similar for its serene and tender tone, in which he was, however, more explicit:

> This thing I'm writing will be the last. I may perhaps not reach the end of it.
>
> When you can't go on, I'll parcel it up and take it to the post with some letters. Then I'll lie down beside you and you'll lie down beside me, as we have for 28 years. But this time we shan't wake up again. It's better this way. I love you.

---

28 Gorz, *Ecologica*, pp. 21–42.

29 Gorz, *Letter to D.*, p. 106.

As soon as I had that idea, I felt at peace. I knew it was the only right solution. Once again we'll view things the same way, once again we'll have the same future. You'll stop looking at me as someone who is going to outlive you and find a replacement for you. You weren't a guest in my life. You were at home there. I shan't bring anyone else to this house. I shan't leave you alone at the last moment. That too we'll go through together.[30]

On Monday morning 24 September, Lucette, the loyal neighbour who took care of the housework, entered by the back door of their house. She missed a simple message stuck to the door which read 'Contact the gendarmerie', but did find a note pinned up in the living room with the warning: 'Don't go upstairs'. Gérard and Dorine were lying there side by side. The plastic bags over their heads were merely a supplementary precaution. Syringes had done the work. We should remember that Gorz had a knowledge of chemistry; he had also researched suicide techniques, using the book *Suicide mode d'emploi*,[31] and also the human right to end one's life (relying here on the book, *La Mort opportune*).[32] The gendarmes established that the couple had died on the evening of Saturday 22 September.

In full view on the table were a brown paper envelope containing a copy of the will, a letter for Lucette ('my guardian angel'), signed in Dorine's shaky hand ('For many long years you have helped me greatly. And now I ask you to understand that we have come serenely to the end of the road'), some jewels for Katheline, a letter for the mayor of Vosnon, who was a friend ('Dear Éliane, we have always known that we wanted to end our lives together. Forgive us for the unpleasant tasks we are leaving you') and 41 stamped, addressed envelopes containing the announcement of their death for that same Éliane to post.[33] The announcement read as follows: 'Gérard

---

30 Handwritten note, GRZ 50.4, reproduced by Christophe Fourel, *Lettre à G. André Gorz en héritage* (Lormont: Le Bord de l'eau, 2017), pp. 127–8.

31 Claude Guillon and Yves Le Bonniec, *Suicide, mode d'emploi. Histoire, technique, actualité* (Paris: Éditions Alain Moreau, 1982).

32 Jacques Pohier, *La Mort opportune. Les Droits des vivants sur leur fin de vie* (Paris: Seuil, 1998).

33 Attached was the list of the addressees of that announcement: 1. Cimade; 2. Finn Bowring; 3. Françoise Gollain; 4. Walter Riffel; 5. M. and Mme Dominique Bourg; 6. Michel Delorme; 7. Chris Turner [translator]; 8. Franz Schandl; 9. Stefan Meretz; 10. M. and Mme Michel Contat; 11. M. and Mme Robert Chenavier; 12. Solicitor;

Horst, known as André Gorz, and his wife Dorine have united in death as they had been united for life.' Michel Delorme, his publisher, received a letter from Gorz written that same Saturday: 'My dear Michel, my last thought is for you. We have enjoyed an exemplary friendship. A beautiful professional journey together has come to an end [. . .].'[34] Appended to the letter was the laudatory article that had just appeared in *Die Zeit*: Gorz had been looking forward to its publication as confirmation of the success of his *Letter to D.* in Germany.

The couple were joining the club of those joint suicides who were too attached to life to allow decline to get the better of their exhausted bodies and who refused to believe that life without the other could have the slightest meaning: Paul Lafargue and his partner Laura, Karl Marx's daughter; Stefan Zweig and his sick spouse; Arthur Koestler and his last wife. In 1983 Gérard and Dorine had spoken about the then-topical Koestler case, but it could not have had much relevance to them then, particularly as Dorine was battling successfully against her cancer at the time. Though the suicide of the Lafargues had met with silent reproof from their Guesdist comrades in 1911, the action of the Horsts, 'as fine as ancient Stoicism', left the Catholic Jacques Julliard indignant, but in an unexpected way: 'How can the Church condemn such an act of dignity?'[35]

The funeral was held at the crematorium of Rosières-près-Troyes on 1 October 2007. A good 30 people were present: three representatives of la Cimade including Jacques Maury, villagers from Vosnon including the mayor, Denis Clerc, Michel Contat, Olivier Corpet, Mme Delorme, Christophe Fourel, Jérôme Gleizes and Emmanuel Dessendier of *EcoRev'*, Erich Hörl, Serge Lafaurie, Rossana Rossanda and Jean Zin. Erika Angerer-Horst paid tribute to her brother in Vienna on 29 September with a

---

13. Thomas Schaffroth; 14. Erich Hörl; 15. Heinrich Dauber; 16. Otto Kallscheuer; 17. Hans Leo Krämer; 18. Rainer Zoll; 19. Jean Zin; 20. Pierre Franzen [*Widerspruch*]; 21. Andreas Simmen [Rotpunkt Verlag]; 22. Tiennot Grumbach; 23. Jeremy Tatman; 24. Serge and Ida Ravanel; 25. Josué Pereira da Silva; 26. Olivier Corpet; 27. Ronald Fraser; 28. Lazare Rozensztroch; 29. Conrad Lodziak; 30. Jacques Maury; 31. Christophe Fourel; 32. Jean Moreau; 33. Annie Dreuille; 34. Marie-Louise Duboin; 35. Dick Howard; 36. François Noudelmann; 37. Niels Fastrup; 38. Serge Lafaurie and 39. Henning Burk. And to be informed after the funeral: 40. Erika Angerer [Gérard's sister] and 41. Alan Stace [Dorine's half-brother] (private archives).

34 Ben Macintyre, 'In life, in Death, in Love', *The Times* (18 October 2007).

35 Julliard, 'Les passions d'André Gorz'.

commemorative soirée, in which Franz Schandl and Erich Kitzmüller (who had interviewed Gorz in 1992) took part, alongside Gorz's Swiss publisher Andreas Simmen and his German translator Eva Moldenhauer.

At Rosières, Patrick Peugeot, the incumbent chairperson of la Cimade, opened the ceremony, making it clear that it was in no way a religious occasion. Pastor Jacques Maury read the elegy by Jean Daniel, published in *Le Nouvel Observateur*, with its lyrical closing words: 'There is no end more overwhelming in its beauty nor more devastating in its purity than this communion in suicide, death and love.' Serge Lafaurie, one of the couple's oldest friends, then addressed the gathering, quoting the poet Paul Valéry, whom Gorz had always held dear. Finally, the mayor of Vosnon Mme Éliane Carr recited some moving passages from *Letter to D*. After calling in at the solicitor's, the representatives of la Cimade took the two urns back to Vosnon.

In the presence of a few devotees, the ashes were mingled and scattered beneath the lime tree where Dorine liked to take her tea and beneath the trees proudly planted by Gérard. She was 83 years old and Gérard 84. They would not live to see the persimmon trees take on their bright winter colours. The chestnuts and apples lay on the ground, the plants in the flowerbeds were withered. The time for working and living was past.

In recent times, Gorz had repeatedly recited the following line from the poem 'Corona' by Paul Celan, the Jewish poet from Bukovina who survived the concentration camps, acquired French nationality, and ended his own life by drowning in the Seine: *Es ist Zeit, dass es Zeit wird* ('It is time that it were time').[36]

In *Being and Nothingness*, Sartre wrote, 'To be dead is to be a prey for the living' and this is true also of the work of André Gorz which ended with his demise. Present and future generations may now begin to appropriate it. Not for purposes of adulation, but to criticize it in the light of the perspectives, potentialities and possibilities the present offers for the advent of a desirable post-capitalist and post-growth civilization that will keep us from the paths of barbarism.[37]

---

36 See Paul Celan, *Die Gedichte* (Frankfurt: Suhrkamp, 2003), p. 39. Information supplied by Walter Riffel in conversation with the author, 17 March 2016.

37 In completing this biography, we would like to thank Élisabeth Lau, Sandrine Samson, Françoise Gollain and Christophe Fourel for their precious advice and assistance. And also the translator Chris Turner, whose skills combine with a one-time close relationship with André Gorz, whom we, by contrast, never met.

Abbreviations and Acronyms

AC!   Agir ensemble contre le chômage! [Act together against unemployment!], a French campaigning organization launched in November 1993

ACP   Association des chômeurs et des précaires (or Cash) [(French) Association of the Unemployed and Insecurely Employed]

AECEP   Appel européen pour une citoyenneté et une économie plurielles [European Appeal for a Plural Citizenship and Economy]. The Association that emerged out of the appeal published in *Le Monde* on 28 June 1995.

AFME   Agence française pour la maîtrise de l'énergie [French Agency for Energy Management], founded in 1982 and replaced in 1991 by the ADEME

ASC   Association syndicale des chômeurs [The (French) Unemployed Trades Union]

AT   Les Amis de la Terre (France) [The French branch of Friends of the Earth]

ATTAC   Association pour la taxation des transactions financières et pour l'action citoyenne [Association for the Taxation of Financial Transactions and for Citizens' Action]

BIEN   Basic Income European Network, which became the Basic Income Earth Network

CDM   Citoyens du monde [World Citizens], founded in 1948

CFDT   Confédération française démocratique du travail [French Democratic Confederation of Labour]

CFTC   Confédération française des travailleurs chrétiens [French Confederation of Christian Workers]

CGIL   Confédération générale italienne du travail [Italian General Confederation of Labour]

CGT   Confédération générale des travailleurs [(French) General Confederation of Labour]

CIDOC   Centro Intercultural de Documentación, founded by Ivan Illich in 1966 at Cuernavaca, Mexico

CIP   Contrat d'insertion professionnelle ['Integration into Employment' Contract]

CISL   Confederazione Italiana Sindacati Lavoratori [Italian Confederation of Workers' Trade Unions]

CPSU   Communist Party of the Soviet Union

CVN   Comité Vietnam national [National Vietnam Committee]

DGB   Deutscher Gewerkschaftsbund [German Trade Union Confederation]

ESU   Étudiants socialistes unifiés [Unified Socialist Students] (the youth organ-
        ization of the PSU)

FIOM   The Italian Metalworkers Federation (a member of the CGIL)

GP   Gauche prolétarienne [Proletarian Left], a French Maoist party founded in
        1968 and dissolved in 1974

GRIF   Groupe de recherche et d'information féministes [Feminist Research and
        Information Group] (Belgium)

GRIT   Groupe de réflexions inter- et transdisciplinaires [Inter- and
        Transdisciplinary Study Group]

IG Metall Industriegewerkschaft Metall [(German) Metalworkers' Union] (a member
        of the DGB)

JCR   Jeunesse communiste révolutionnaire [Revolutionary Communist Youth], a
        French Trotskyist organization, 1966–68

LC   Lotta continua [Continuous Struggle], Italian extra-parliamentary political
        movement

LCR   Ligue communiste révolutionnaire [Revolutionary Communist League],
        a French Trotskyist party, 1974–2009

LETS   Local Exchange Trading System

MAUSS   Mouvement anti-utilitariste dans les sciences sociales [(French) Anti-
        Utilitarian Movement in the Social Sciences]

MNCP   Mouvement national des chômeurs et précaires (ex-ASC) [National
        Movement of the Unemployed and the Insecurely Employed (formerly
        ASC)]

MNEF   Mutuelle nationale des étudiants de France [French Students' National
        Mutual Society]

PCF   Parti communiste français [French Communist Party]

PCI   Parti communiste italien [Italian Communist Party]

PO   Potere operaio (Italy) [Workers' Power], Italian Left-wing political group,
        active between 1967 and 1973

POP   Parti ouvrier et populaire [Workers' and People's Party] (Canton of Vaud,
        Switzerland)

PPE   Prime pour l'emploi ['Employment bonus']

PSIUP   Partito Socialista Italiano di Unità Proletaria [Italian Proletarian Unity
        Socialist Party]

PSU   Parti socialiste unifié [(French) Unified Socialist Party]

RDR   Rassemblement démocratique révolutionnaire, a short-lived French party backed by Sartre, advocating a socialism independent of either the USSR or the USA, 1947–48

RMI   Revenu minimum d'insertion [(French) minimum income benefit]

RWH   Reduced Working Hours

SDS   Sozialistischer Deutscher Studentenbund [(West) German Socialist Student Union]

SDS   Students for a Democratic Society, USA

SGEN   Syndicat général de l'enseignement national [(French) National Education Trade Union (CFDT affiliated)]

SMIC   Salaire minimum interprofessionnel de croissance [Guaranteed minimum wage]

SPD   Sozialdemokratische Partei Deutschlands [Social Democratic Party of Germany]

UJC (ml)   Union des jeunesses communistes marxistes-léninistes [Union of (Marxist-Leninist) Communist Youth]. French Maoist party, 1966–68.

UMGC   Universal Movement for a Global Confederation

UNEF   Union Nationale des Étudiants de France

URPE   Union for Radical Political Economics, USA

VLR   Vive la Révolution. A French Maoist libertarian group founded in July 1969.

Bibliography

WORKS BY GÉRARD HORST / G. H. / MICHEL BOSQUET / ANDRÉ GORZ
(Arranged by Date of Publication)

HORST, Gérard. 'Kafka et le problème de la transcendance' (1945) in Christophe Fourel (ed.), *André Gorz. Un penseur pour le XXIe siècle*. Paris: La Découverte, 2012 [1945].

——. 'Le problème juif'. *Servir*, 29 May 1947.

——. 'La littérature américaine industrialisée'. *Servir*, 19 June 1947.

——. 'Opinions. Dessous de grève'. *Gazette de Lausanne*, 28 June 1947.

——. 'Le paradoxe soviétique'. *Servir*, 10 July 1947.

——. '*La Peste* d'Albert Camus'. *Servir*, 17 July 1947.

——. 'Qui est Sartre?' *Servir*, 31 July 1947.

——. 'Du libéralisme au communisme. Faire et avoir'. *Servir*, 14 August 1947.

——. 'Pour une Europe fédéraliste, mais comment ?' *Servir*, 4 September 1947.

G. H. 'Que veut l'Amérique?' *Servir*, 2 October 1947.

——. 'Les nouvelles maladies de la démocratie'. *Servir*, 6 November 1947.

HORST, Gérard. 'Vienne. Février 1948'. *Servir*, 19 February 1948.

——. 'Problèmes autrichiens, problèmes universels'. *Servir*, 25 March 1948.

G. H. 'Sartre contre le chrétien?' *Servir*, 29 April 1948.

HORST, Gérard. 'L'enjeu palestinien'. *Servir*, 13 May 1948.

——. 'Une nouvelle face de la guerre palestinienne'. *Servir*, 20 May 1948.

G. H. 'Arrière-plan Marshall'. *Servir*, 10 June 1948.

——. 'Le Doigt. Un manifeste des étudiants lausannois'. *Servir*, 8 July 1948.

HORST, Gérard. 'Y a-t-il un communisme yougoslave?' *Servir*, 5 August 1948.

G. H. '*Gagner son temps* par Roger Philippe'. *Servir*, 26 August 1948.

——. 'Vaincre la Russie par la persuasion?' *Servir*, 30 September 1948.

——. 'La défense de l'Europe se passe de canons'. *Servir*, 14 October 1948.

——. 'Préparatifs d'invasion'. *Servir*, 21 October 1948.

——. 'Une première de Sartre à Lausanne'. *Servir*, 25 November 1948.

HORST, Gérard. 'L'action de Garry Davis a-t-elle une couleur politique?' *Servir*, 20 January 1949.

G. H. 'Un Citoyen du Monde en prison: Jean-Bernard Moreau'. *Peuple du monde*, 21 May 1949.

BOSQUET, Michel. 'Le XXe siècle découvre le soleil. Au premier congrès mondial de l'héliotechnique 1,000 savants de 35 pays ont parlé d'énergie solaire'. *Gazette littéraire* (supplement to the *Gazette de Lausanne*), 26 November 1955.

———. 'Nouvelles doses de tolérance et effets biologiques des radiations ionisantes'. *Industries atomiques* (Geneva) 1(6) (May 1957): 47–50.

GORZ, André. *Le Traître*. Paris: Seuil, 1958.

———. 'Le point de vue d'André Gorz, auteur du *Traître*'. *Gazette littéraire* (supplement to *La Gazette de Lausanne*), 18 October 1958.

———. *La Morale de l'histoire*. Paris: Seuil, 1959.

BOSQUET, Michel. 'Vie quotidienne. L'aventure de Grenoble'. *L'Express*, 2 April 1959.

———. 'Reportage. La perspective à l'Est'. *L'Express*, 11 June 1959.

———. 'Est-Ouest. La tentative yougoslave'. *L'Express*, 20 August 1959.

———. 'Économie. Le "circuit du pauvre" '. *L'Express*, 3 March 1960.

———. 'Socialisme. Le laboratoire italien'. *L'Express*, 4 January 1962.

———. 'Italie. Le grand pari'. *L'Express*, 1 February 1962.

GORZ, André. 'Avant-propos'. *Les Temps modernes* 196–7 ('Données et problèmes de la lutte ouvrière') (September–October 1962): 392.

BOSQUET, Michel. 'Reportage. Grève à l'italienne'. *L'Express*, 27 September 1962.

———. 'Reportage. Leclerc et la liberté'. *L'Express*, 11 October 1962.

———. 'Circulation. Le luxe des dimanches'. *L'Express*, 26 October 1962.

———. 'Communistes. Les premiers pas'. *L'Express*, 20 December 1962.

GORZ, André. *Stratégie ouvrière et néocapitalisme*. Paris: Seuil, 1964.

———. *Historia y Enajenación*. México: Fondo de Cultura Económica, 1964.

BOSQUET, Michel. 'Reportage. L'exemple tchèque'. *L'Express*, 9 January 1964.

GORZ, André. 'Call for Intellectual Subversion'. *The Nation*, 25 May 1964.

———. 'Civilisation opulente et massification'. *Démocratie nouvelle* 9 (September 1964).

BOSQUET, Michel. 'Aspects of Italian Communism'. *The Socialist Register* (October 1964): 82–91.

———. 'L'automobile en crise'. *Le Nouvel Observateur*, 19 November 1964.

GORZ, André. '*L'uomo unidimensionale* di Marcuse'. *Critica marxista* 2 (1965): 231–41.

BOSQUET, Michel, and Claude Krief. 'Que faire avec la "fédération"'. *Le Nouvel Observateur*, 10 June 1965.

GORZ, André. 'Capitalist Relations of Production and the Socially Necessary Labour Force'. *International Socialist Journal* (Milan) 10 (August 1965): 463–80. Reprinted in Arthur Lothstein (ed.), *All We Are Saying: The Philosophy of the New Left*. New York: Putnam, 1970, pp. 155–71.

——. 'Loisirs et sociétés industrielles'. *Démocratie nouvelle* 5 (May 1966).

——. 'Sartre and Marx'. *New Left Review* 37 (May–June 1966): 33–52.

Bosquet, Michel. 'Les chômeurs de la relance'. *Le Nouvel Observateur*, 17 August 1966.

——. 'Et si on nationalisait la Bourse [...]'. *Le Nouvel Observateur*, 12 October 1966.

Gorz, André. *Strategy for Labor: A Radical Proposal* (Martin Nicolaus and Victoria Ortiz, trans.). Boston, MA: Beacon Press, 1967.

——. *Le Socialisme difficile*. Paris: Seuil, 1967.

——. 'L'auto-gestion n'est pas une panacée' in *Le Socialisme difficile*. Paris: Seuil, 1967, pp. 137–42.

——. 'State of Mind'. *The New York Review of Books*, 14 September 1967.

Bosquet, Michel. 'L'assassin de "Che" Guevara'. *Le Nouvel Observateur*, 1 November 1967.

——. 'Réponse à Laurent Schwartz'. *Le Nouvel Observateur*, 8 November 1967.

——. 'Fidel Castro est-il fou?'. *Le Nouvel Observateur*, 28 February 1968.

Gorz, André. 'The Way Forward'. *New Left Review* 52 (November–December 1968): 47–66. First published in French as: 'Limites et potentialités du mouvement de mai', *Les Temps modernes* 266–7 (August–September 1968): 260–1.

——. *Réforme et révolution*. Paris: Seuil, 1969.

——. 'Quattro domande ad André Gorz'. *Giovane critica* 20 (Spring 1969): 50–6.

——. Présentation to *Les Temps modernes* 279 ('Italie') (October 1969): 332.

Bosquet, Michel. 'Pollution. Les asphyxiés de l'an 2000'. *Le Nouvel Observateur*, 12 January 1970.

Gorz, André. 'Immigrant Labour'. *New Left Review* 61 (May–June 1970): 28–31.

Bosquet, Michel. 'J'accuse'. *Le Nouvel Observateur*, 10 August 1970.

——. 'La subversion par le bonheur'. *Le Nouvel Observateur*, 21 December 1970.

——. '1970: L'année des otages'. *Le Nouvel Observateur*, 28 December 1970.

Gorz, André. 'On the Relevance of Revolutionary Strategy in the Capitalist Metropoles' in Elmar Altvater et al., *Het Kapitalisme in de jaren 70*. Amsterdam: Van Gennep, 1971.

——. Introduction to *I Protagonisti della Storia universale, Volume 14: Il Mondo contemporaneo. La pace e la rivoluzione*. Milan: CEI, 1971, pp. xi–xxx.

——. 'Destroy the University'. *Partisan Review* 38(3) (Summer 1971): 314–18. First published in French as: 'Détruire l'Université', *Les Temps modernes* 285 (April 1970): 1553–8.

——. 'The Working Class and Revolution in the West'. *Liberation* (New York) 4 (September 1971): 31–7.

——. 'Colloque de Tarquinia. Avant-propos'. *Partisans* 61 (September–October 1971): 84–7.

——. 'Workers' Control: Some European Experiences' in Richard C. Edwards, Michael Reich and Thomas E. Weisskopf (eds), *The Capitalist System: A Radical Analysis of American Society*. Englewood Cliffs, NJ: Prentice-Hall, 1972, pp. 479–91.

Bosquet, Michel. 'Les démons de l'expansion'. *Le Nouvel Observateur* ('La Dernière Chance de la Terre'), June–July 1972.

Gorz, André. *Socialism and Revolution* (Norman Denny trans.). New York: Anchor Books, 1973.

——. 'Unions and Politics' in *Socialism and Revolution* (Norman Denny trans.). New York: Anchor Books, 1973, pp. 71–107.

——. 'Reform and Revolution' in *Socialism and Revolution* (Norman Denny trans.). New York: Anchor Books, 1973, pp. 133–77.

——. 'Arduous Socialism' in *Socialism and Revolution* (Norman Denny trans.). New York: Anchor Books, 1973, 179–214.

Bosquet, Michel. *Critique du capitalisme quotidien*. Paris: Galilée, 1973.

——. 'Combien vaut un rayon de soleil?' *Le Sauvage* 2 (March 1973): 7–9.

——. 'Du soleil dans la maison'. *Le Nouvel Observateur*, 26 March 1973.

——. 'A quoi servent les immigrés?'. *Le Nouvel Observateur*, 16 April 1973.

——. 'Mettez du socialisme dans votre moteur' [Put socialism in your tank]. *Le Sauvage* 6 (September–October 1973): 8–13.

Gorz, André. 'Sul carattere di classe della scienza e dei lavoratori scientifici', *Lotta Continua* (10–11 November 1973).

——. 'Die Zukunft der Gewerkschaften. Neue Widersprüche und neue Inhalte gewerkschaftlicher Kämpfe' (December 1971) in *Aufgabe Zukunft. Qualität des Lebens* (*11–14 April 1972*), VOL. 9. Frankfurt: Europäische Verlagsanstalt, 1974, pp. 94–116.

——. 'Partage ou crève!'. *Le Sauvage*, 12 April 1974, pp. 10–12

——. 'On the Class Character of Science and Scientists' in Hilary Rose and Steven Rose (eds), *The Political Economy of Science: Ideology of/in the Natural Sciences*. London: Macmillan, 1976, pp. 59–71. First published in French as: 'Caractères de classe de la science et des travailleurs scientifiques', *Les Temps modernes* 330 (January 1974): 1159–77.

Bosquet, Michel. 'Une production destructive'. *Le Nouvel Observateur*, 11 October 1976.

Gorz, André. 'Sartre malgré lui?' *Le Nouvel Observateur*, 6 December 1976.

——. 'Le Programme caché de l'éducation permanente' in Heinrich Dauber and Étienne Verne (eds), *L'École à perpétuité*. Paris: Seuil, 1977.

——. *Fondements pour une morale*. Paris: Galilée, 1977.

BOSQUET, Michel. *Capitalism in Crisis and Everyday Life* (John Howe trans.). Hassocks: Harvester Press, 1977.

——. ' "Socialism" and the Motor Car' in *Capitalism in Crisis and Everyday Life* (John Howe trans.). Hassocks: Harvester Press, 1977, pp. 27–8. First published in French as: 'Le "socialisme" et la bagnole', *Le Nouvel Observateur* (11 May 1966).

——. 'Small Tradesmen: The End of the Line' in *Capitalism in Crisis and Everyday Life* (John Howe trans.). Hassocks: Harvester Press, 1977, pp. 57–63. First published in French as: 'La mort des "petits" ', *Le Nouvel Observateur* (4 May 1970).

——. 'Beyond Trade Unions' in *Capitalism in Crisis and Everyday Life* (John Howe trans.). Hassocks: Harvester Press, 1977, pp. 115–19.

——. 'Other People's Hunger' in *Capitalism in Crisis and Everyday Life* (John Howe trans.). Hassocks: Harvester Press, 1977, pp. 129–33. First published in French as: 'Cent mille morts par jour', *Le Nouvel Observateur*, 21 December 1966.

——. 'Brazil: The Right to Violence' in *Capitalism in Crisis and Everyday Life* (John Howe trans.). Hassocks: Harvester Press, 1977, pp. 134–40.

——. 'Ce que les écologistes pensent d'eux-mêmes'. *Le Nouvel Observateur*, 22 March 1977.

GORZ, André, and François Châtelet. 'Et si la politique redécouvrait la morale . . . ' (dialogue). *Les Nouvelles littéraires*, 5 May 1977.

GORZ, André. 'Sartre and the Deaf'. *Telos* 33 (1977): 106–08. First published in French as: 'Sartre et les sourds', *Le Nouvel Observateur*, 27 June 1977.

BOSQUET, Michel. 'Qu'est-ce que l'écologie politique?' *Le Sauvage* 43 (July 1977): 14–19.

——. 'La nébuleuse écologique'. *Le Nouvel Observateur*, 22 August 1977.

——. 'Les nouveaux mouvements sociaux. La stratégie de la guérilla'. *Le Nouvel Observateur*, 12 September 1977.

GORZ, André (ed.). *The Division of Labour: The Labour Process and Class-Struggle in Modern Capitalism*. Hassocks: The Harverster Press, 1978.

——. 'Technology, Technicians and Class Struggle' in André Gorz (ed.), *The Division of Labour: The Labour Process and Class-Struggle in Modern Capitalism*. Hassocks: The Harverster Press, 1978, pp. 159–89. Translated as 'Technische Intelligenz und kapitalistische Arbeitsteilung' (translated from the English), *Politikon* (Göttingen) 37 (June–July 1971). First published in French as: 'Technique, techniciens et lutte de classes', *Les Temps modernes* 301–02 (August–September 1971): 141–80.

——. 'The Tyranny of the Factory: Today and Tomorrow' in André Gorz (ed.), *The Division of Labour: The Labour Process and Class-Struggle in Modern Capitalism*.

Hassocks: The Harverster Press, 1978. First published in French as: Michel Bosquet, 'The "Prison Factory"', *New Left Review* 73 (May–June 1972): 23–34.

BOSQUET, Michel. 'Une pastille contre le travail'. *Le Nouvel Observateur*, 23 April 1978.

GORZ, André. 'La politique n'est plus dans la politique'. *Le Nouvel Observateur*, 8 May 1978.

BOSQUET, Michel. 'Ce qui nous manque pour être heureux'. *Le Nouvel Observateur*, 11 September 1978.

——. 'Alain Touraine: la révolution culturelle que nous vivons'. *Le Nouvel Observateur*, 8 January 1979.

GORZ, André. 'Les protestants du marxisme'. *Le Nouvel Observateur*, 7 May 1979.

BOSQUET, Michel. 'Herbert Marcuse, professeur de liberté'. *Le Nouvel Observateur*, 6 August 1979.

——. 'Le droit de désobéir'. *Le Nouvel Observateur*, 26 November 1979.

GORZ, André. *Ecology as Politics* (Patsy Vigderman and Jonathan Cloud trans). Boston, MA: South End Press, 1980.

——. 'Introduction: Two Kinds of Ecology' in *Ecology as Politics* (Patsy Vigderman and Jonathan Cloud trans). Boston, MA: South End Press, 1980, pp. 3–9. First published in French as: 'Partage ou crève!' [Share or die!], *Le Sauvage* 12 (April 1974): 10–12.

——. 'Reinventing the Future' in *Ecology as Politics* (Patsy Vigderman and Jonathan Cloud trans). Boston, MA: South End Press, 1980, pp. 55–64. First published in French as: 'Réinventer l'avenir', *Le Nouvel Observateur*, 4 March 1974.

——. 'Labor and "Quality of life"' in *Ecology as Politics* (Patsy Vigderman and Jonathan Cloud trans). Boston, MA: South End Press, 1980, pp. 130–145.

——. '1. Medicine and Illness' and '2. Health and Society' in *Ecology as Politics* (Patsy Vigderman and Jonathan Cloud trans). Boston, MA: South End Press, 1980, pp. 149–80.

——. 'Ecology and Freedom' in *Ecology as Politics* (Patsy Vigderman and Jonathan Cloud trans). Boston, MA: South End Press, 1980.

——. 'From Nuclear Electricity to Electric Fascism' in *Ecology as Politics* (Patsy Vigderman and Jonathan Cloud trans). Boston, MA: South End Press, 1980.

——. 'Science and Class: The Case of Medicine' in *Ecology as Politics* (Patsy Vigderman and Jonathan Cloud trans). Boston, MA: South End Press, 1980. First published in French as: Michel Bosquet, 'Une médecine de classe', *Lumière et vie* 127 (April 1976): 31–43.

——. 'Wir können mehr machen mit weniger'. *Konkret* (Hamburg) 16 (1980).

——. 'Le travail est devenu un expédient', interview by Philippe Gavi. *Libération*, 28 April 1980.

——. 'Les adieux d'André Gorz au prolétariat', interview by Michel Contat and François George. *Le Monde*, 12 October 1980.

GORZ, André, and Rudolf Bahro. *Ökonomie, Ökologie. Zweite sozialistische Konferenz* (13–15 February 1981). Hamburg: VSA-Verlag, 1981.

BOSQUET, Michel. 'La dynamite d'Edgar Morin'. *Le Nouvel Observateur*, 5 January 1981.

——. 'Plutôt rouge que mort'. *Le Nouvel Observateur*, 21 November 1981.

GORZ, André. *Farewell to the Working Class: An Essay on Post-industrial Socialism* (Mike Sonenscher trans.). London: Pluto Press, 1982. First published in French as: *Adieux au prolétariat*. Paris: Galilée, 1980. Augmented edition: Paris: Seuil, 1981.

——. 'Respekt für ein solches Verhalten?' (interview). *Der Spiegel* 4 (25 January 1982).

BOSQUET, Michel. 'Le PS n'existe plus'. *Le Nouvel Observateur*, 6 February 1982.

GORZ, André. 'Was ist denn schon Freiheit. Antwort an Rudolf Bahro'. *Die Tageszeitung* (1 March 1982).

——. 'Friedensbewegung—keine europäische Solidarität?', interview by Claus Leggewie. *Links* (special edition: 'Zeitung zum Frankfurter Friedenskongress 17–20 June 1982') (June 1982): 8.

——. 'Sur deux fronts'. *Les Temps modernes* 435 (October 1982): 646–50.

BOSQUET, Michel. 'La grève de Maurice Pagat'. *Le Nouvel Observateur*, 11 December 1982.

GORZ, André. 'Automation et crise de la société du travail'. *Infordoc* 404 (February 1984): 17.

——. 'Au-delà de la société du travail'. *Virages* (Brussels) 2 (April 1984): 8–12.

——. 'Ne pas confondre activité autonome et travail salarié'. *Autogestions* 19 (1985): 17–19.

——. 'Die Zukunft der Arbeit', interview by Thomas Kluge and Thomas Jahn in Winfried Hammann and Thomas Kluge (eds), *In Zukunft. Berichte über den Wandel des Fortschritts*. Hamburg: Rowohlt, 1985, pp. 213–39.

——. *Paths to Paradise: On the Liberation from Work* (Malcolm Imrie trans.). London: Pluto Press, 1985. First published in French as: *Les Chemins du paradis. L'agonie du capital*. Paris: Galilée, 1983.

——. 'The American Model and the Future of the Left'. *Telos* 64 (Summer 1985): 117–21.

——. 'Allocation universelle: version de droite et version de gauche'. *La Revue nouvelle* 81 (April 1985): 419–28.

——. 'Quelle paix? Quelle Europe?'. *Lettre internationale* 7 (September 1985): 11–16.

——. 'Socialisme: thèmes pour demain'. *Les Temps modernes* 471 (October 1985): 431–45.

——. 'Richtziele für eine Neugestaltung des Wohlfahrtsstaates' in Michael Opielka and Ilona Ostner (eds), *Umbau des Sozialstaates*. Essen: Klartext Verlag, 1986, pp. 137–48.

——. 'Garantierte Grundversorgung aus rechter und linker Sicht' in Michael Opielka and Georg Vobruba (eds), *Das garantierte Grundeinkommen. Entwicklung und Perspektiven einer Forderung*. Frankfurt: Fischer Taschenbuch Verlag, 1986, pp. 53–62.

——. 'Plus dangereux que Tchernobyl: La Hague'. *Le Nouvel Observateur*, 9 May 1986.

——. 'La plus grande liberté possible' (debate with Peter Glotz and Tilman Fichter). *Les Temps modernes* 483 (October 1986).

——. *The Traitor* (Richard Howard trans.). London: Verso Books, [Second Edition] 1989.

——. *Critique of Economic Reason* (Gillian Handyside and Chris Turner trans). London: Verso Books, 1989. First published in French as: *Métamorphoses du travail. Quête du sens. Critique de la raison économique*. Paris: Galilée, 1988.

——. 'Des zentralen Konfliktes alte und neue Akteure' in Helga Grebing et al. (eds), *Sozialismus in Europa. Bilanz und Perspektiven. Festschrift für Willy Brandt*. Essen: Klartext Verlag, 1989, pp. 67–76.

——. 'A Land of Cockayne?' (interview). *New Statesman and Society*, 12 May 1989, pp. 25–31.

——. 'Sozialismus, Ökologie und kultureller Umbruch'. *Neue Gesellschaft. Frankfurter Hefte* 8 (August 1989): 732–8.

——. 'Une redistribution plus équitable du travail est nécessaire'. *Partenaires* 7 (September 1990): 26–8.

——. 'Droite/gauche. Essai de rédéfinition'. *Revue du MAUSS* 14 (1991): 20.

——. 'On the Difference between Society and Community, and Why Basic Income Cannot by Itself Confer Full Membership of Either' in Philippe Van Parijs (ed.), *Arguing for Basic Income: Ethical Foundations for a Radical Reform*. London: Verso Books, 1992, pp. 178–84.

——. 'Vers une civilisation du temps libéré', interview by Frédéric Audren. *Pantagruel* 4 (Summer 1992): 6–17.

——. *Capitalism, Socialism, Ecology* (Chris Turner trans.). London: Verso Books, 1994.

——. 'Revenu minimum et citoyenneté'. *Futuribles* 184 (February 1994): 59.

——. 'A Sociology of the Subject' in Jon Clark and Marco Diani (eds), *Alain Touraine: Consensus and Controversy*. London: Falmer Press, 1996.

——. 'Revenu de citoyenneté et pluralité des fins légitimes'. *Transversales Science Culture* 40 (July–August 1996): 6–8.

GORZ, André, and Jacques Robin. 'Forger un autre avenir'. *Le Monde*, 8 October 1996.

GORZ, André. 'Gorz, bourreau du travail', interview by Robert Maggiori and Jean-Baptiste Marongiu. *Libération* 25 (September 1997).

——. 'Misères du présent, richesse du possible', interview by Carlo Vercellone, Patrick Dieuaide and Pierre Peronnet. *Alice* 1 (Autumn 1998): 31–5.

——. *Reclaiming Work: Beyond the Wage-Based Society* (Chris Turner trans.). Cambridge: Polity Press, 1999. First published in French as: *Misères du present. Richesse du possible*. Paris: Galilée, 1997.

——. 'Oficios del saber y del trabajo', interview by Michel Zlotowski in December 1998. *Clarín* (Buenos Aires) (21 February 1999), supplement.

——. 'La personne devient une entreprise. Note sur le travail de production de soi'. *EcoRev* 7 (Winter 2001): 8.

—— and Jean-Marie Vincent. 'Dialogue avec André Gorz'. *Variations* 1 (2001): 9–18.

—— and Jacques Robin. 'Forger un autre avenir'; 'Welches Wissen? Welche Gesellschaft?' in Andreas Poltermann (ed.), *Gut zu wissen. Links zur Wissensgesellschaft*. Münster: Westphälisches Dampfboot, 2002, pp. 15–35.

GORZ, André. 'Valeur et richesse: le divorce'. *Transversales Science Culture* 3 (July–September 2002): 47.

——. *L'Immatériel*. Paris: Galilée, 2003.

——. 'La valeur du capital immatériel est une fiction boursière', interview by Denis Clerc and Christophe Fourel. *Alternatives économiques* 212 (March 2003): 68.

——. 'Wa(h)re Arbeit' in Tatjana Freytag and Marcus Hawel (eds), *Arbeit und Utopie. Oskar Negt zum 70. Geburtstag*. Frankfurt: Humanities Online, 2004, pp. 29–37.

——. 'Économie de la connaissance, exploitation des savoirs', interview by Carlo Vercellone and Yann Moulier-Boutang. *Multitudes* 15 (Winter 2004): 205–16.

——. *Wissen, Wert und Kapital. Zur Kritik der Wissensökonomie*. Zurich: Rotpunkt, [2004]2005. Revised and augmented German edition of *L'Immatériel*.

——. 'A crise e o êxodo da sociedade salarial', interview by Sonia Montaño. *Cadernos IHU Idéas* 31 (2005).

——. 'Lettre à François George'. *Les Temps modernes* 632–4 (July–October 2005): 59.

——. 'Authenticité et valeur dans la première philosophie de Sartre'. *Les Temps modernes* 632–4 (July–October 2005): 627.

——. 'L'écologie politique, une éthique de la libération', interview by Marc Robert. *EcoRev* 21 (Autumn–Winter 2005).

——. 'Vidensøkonomi & kapitalismens krise?', interview by Niels Fastrup. *Social Kritik* 107 (December 2006).

——. 'Où va l'écologie?', interview by Gilles Anquetil. *Le Nouvel Observateur*, 14 December 2006.

——. 'Seid realistisch—verlangt das Unmögliche' in Andreas Exner, Werner Rätz and Birgit Zenker (eds), *Grundeinkommen. Soziale Sicherheit ohne Arbeit*. Vienna: Deuticke Verlag, 2007, pp. 70–8.

——. 'Penser l'exode de la société du travail et de la marchandise'. *Mouvements* 50 (June–August 2007): 104.

——. 'Le travail dans la sortie du capitalisme'. *EcoRev'* 28 (Autumn 2007): 8–15.

——. *Le Traître* suivi de *Le Vieillissement*. Paris: Gallimard 'Collection Folio essais', [2005]2008.

——. 'La sortie du capitalisme a déjà commencé' in *Manifeste Utopia*. Lyon: Parangon, 2008, pp. 5–14.

——. *Letter to D.: A Love Story* (Julie Rose trans.). Cambridge: Polity Press, [2006]2009.

——. *The Immaterial: Knowledge, Value and Capital* (Chris Turner trans.). London: Seagull Books, 2010.

——. *Ecologica* (Chris Turner trans.). London: Seagull Books, 2010.

——. 'Political Ecology between Expertocracy and Self-Limitation' in *Ecologica* (Chris Turner trans.). London: Seagull Books, 2010, pp. 43–76. First published in French as: 'L'écologie politique entre expertocratie et autolimitation', *Actuel Marx* 12 (1992): 15-29.

——. 'Vie morte (extraits)'. *La Règle du jeu* 45 (January 2011): 167–9.

——. 'Nous sommes moins vieux qu'il y a vingt ans' (title ascribed by the editors) in Christophe Fourel (ed.), *André Gorz. Un penseur pour le XXIe siècle*. Paris: La Découverte, 2012, pp. 268–74.

——. ' "Je n'existe pas." Note sur le journalisme' (*c*.1960) in Christophe Fourel (ed.), *André Gorz en personne*. Lormont: Le Bord de l'eau, 2013.

——. *Bâtir la civilisation du temps libéré*. Paris: Les liens qui libèrent/Le Monde diplomatique, 2013.

——. 'Leur écologie et la nôtre' (1974) in *Bâtir la civilisation du temps libéré*. Paris: Les liens qui libèrent/Le Monde diplomatique, 2013, pp. 11–19.

——. 'Pourquoi la société salariale a besoin de nouveaux valets' (1990) in *Bâtir la civilisation du temps libéré*. Paris: Les liens qui libèrent/Le Monde diplomatique, 2013, pp. 21–45.

——. 'Bâtir la civilisation du temps libéré' (1993) in *Bâtir la civilisation du temps libéré*. Paris: Les liens qui libèrent/Le Monde diplomatique, 2013, pp. 47–57.

——. *Le Fil rouge de l'écologie. Entretiens inédits en français* (Willy Gianinazzi ed., Erich Hörl after.). Paris: Éditions de l'EHESS, 2015.

——. 'La vie, la nature, la technique' in *Le Fil rouge de l'écologie. Entretiens inédits en français* (Willy Gianinazzi ed., Erich Hörl after.). Paris: Éditions de l'EHESS, 2015, pp. 19–81. Augmented translation of ' "Archäologie" des philosophischen Fadens.

Die Entpackung der verpackten Philosophie', interview with Erich Hörl, *Kurswechsel* [Vienna] 3 (1990): 5–36.

——. 'Le savoir, la valeur, le capital' in *Le Fil rouge de l'écologie. Entretiens inédits en français* (Willy Gianinazzi ed., Erich Hörl after.). Paris: Éditions de l'EHESS, 2015, pp. 83–90. First published in German as: 'Wissen, Wert, Kapital', interview with Thomas Schaffroth, *Die Wochenzeitung* (Zurich) (26 June 2003).

——. 'Vers la multiactivité' in *Le Fil rouge de l'écologie. Entretiens inédits en français* (Willy Gianinazzi ed., Erich Hörl after.). Paris: Éditions de l'EHESS, 2015, pp. 93–100. First published in Spanish as 'Ócio revolucionário', interview with Vladimir Safatle, *Folha de São Paulo, Ilustríssima* (supplement) (30 January 2005).

——. '*André Gorz intellectuel et journaliste. Lettre à une étudiante (1967)*'. *EcoRev'* 46 (Summer 2018): 131–7.

——. *Penser l'avenir. Entretien avec François Noudelmann*. Paris: La Découverte, 2019.

——. *Leur écologie et la nôtre. Anthologie d'écologie politique* (Françoise Gollain and Willy Gianinazzi eds). Paris: Seuil, 2020.

OTHER SOURCES

ADAM, Gérard. 'Où en est le débat sur "la nouvelle classe ouvrière"? État des travaux'. *Revue française de science politique* 18 (5) (1968): 1003–23.

ALCALÁ, Julio Antonio García. 'Un modelo en la oposición al franquismo. Las organizaciones Frente (FLP-EOC-ESWA)', VOL. 1. MA thesis, Universidad Complutense, Madrid, 1997.

ALIER, Joan Martínez. 'La confluence dans l'éco-socialisme' in Jacques Bidet and Jacques Texier (eds), *L'Idée du socialisme a-t-elle un avenir?* Paris: PUF, 1992, pp. 181–93.

ALTWEGG, Jürg. 'Gegen Entfremdung. André Gorz zum siebzigsten Geburtstag' (Interview). *Frankfurter Allgemeine Zeitung*, 9 February 1993.

ANDERSON, Perry. *Considerations on Western Marxism*. London: New Left Books, 1979.

ANONYMOUS. 'Gorz, technocrate ou utopiste?'. *Cash* 5 (January 1987): 2.

APOTHÉLOZ, Charles. 'Idéologie et mystification' (1949) in *Cris et écrits. Textes sur le théâtre, 1944–1982*. Lausanne: Payot, 1990.

ARNSPERGER, Christian. 'Revenu de base, économie soutenable et alternatives monétaires'. *L'Économie politique* 67 (July 2015): 34–49.

AZAÏS, Christian, Antonella Corsani and Patrick Dieuaide (eds). *Vers un capitalisme cognitif. Entre mutations du travail et territoires*. Paris: L'Harmattan, 2001.

BAHRO, Rudolf. 'Rapallo. Warum eigentlich nicht?'. *Der Spiegel* 6 (8 February 1982).

BARBIN, Adeline. *André Gorz. Travail, économie et liberté*. Chasseneuil-du-Poitou: CNDP, 2013.

BARONIAN, Laurent, and Carlo Vercellone. 'Monnaie du commun et revenu social garanti'. *Terrains Théories* 1 (2015).

BAROT, Emmanuel (ed.). *Sartre et le marxisme*. Paris: La Dispute, 2011.

BARRET, Nicolas. *Les Citoyens du Monde, 1948–1951*. MA thesis, University Paris I, 1992.

BAUDET, Marie-Béatrice. 'Les réflexions d'André Gorz et de Guy Aznar ont ouvert le débat'. *Le Monde*, 10 November 1993.

BAUDRILLARD, Jean. *The Consumer Society: Myths and Structures* (Chris Turner trans.). London: Sage Publications, 1998.

BECK, Robert. 'Apogée et déclin de la Saint Lundi dans la France du XIXe siècle'. *Revue d'histoire du XIXe siècle* 29 (2004): 153–71.

BÉGOUT, Bruce. *La Découverte du quotidien*. Paris: Allia, 2005.

BENSAÏD, Daniel, and Henri Weber. *Mai 68: une répétition générale*. Paris: Maspero, 1968.

BENTON, Ted. 'Marxism and Natural Limits: An Ecological Critique and Reconstruction'. *New Left Review* 187 (Nov–Dec 1989): 51–86.

BISCHOFF, Manfred. 'L'humanité a-t-elle toujours "travaillé"?'. *Théologiques* 3 (2) (1995): 45–69.

BLANCHOT, Maurice. 'The Terror of Identification' in *Friendship* (Elizabeth Rottenberg trans.). Stanford, CA: Stanford University Press, 1997, pp. 208–16. First published in French as: 'La passion de l'indifférence', *La Nouvelle Revue française* 67 (July 1958): 93–101.

BOLTANSKI, Luc. 'America, America . . . '. *Actes de la recherche en sciences sociales* 38 (May 1981): 19–41.

——, and Ève Chiapello. *The New Spirit of Capitalism* (Gregory Elliott trans.). London: Verso Books, 2007 [1999].

BOOKCHIN, Murray. 'André Gorz, *Ecology as Politics*'. *Telos* 46 (21 December 1980): 177–90.

BOSCHETTI, Anna. *The Intellectual Enterprise: Sartre and Les Temps modernes*. Evanston, IL: Northwestern University Press, 1988.

BOURG, Dominique. *Les Scénarios de l'écologie*. Paris: Hachette, 1996.

BOVARD, René. 'Situation de l'objecteur de conscience dans le monde'. *Peuple du monde*, 21 May 1949.

——. 'Citoyen du monde'. *Suisse contemporaine* 9 (9 September 1949).

BOWRING, Finn. *André Gorz and the Sartrean Legacy: Arguments for a Person-Centred Social Theory*. London: MacMillan, 2000.

——. 'The Writer's Malady: André Gorz, 1923–2007'. *Radical Philosophy* 148 (March–April 2008): 52.

BRÉCHON, Pierre. 'L'individualisation progresse, mais pas l'individualisme'. *Le Monde*, 25 April 2009.

BROCA, Sébastien. 'Du logiciel libre aux théories de l'intelligence collective'. *Revue TIC&Société* 2 (2) 2008: 81–101. Available at: ticetsociete.revues.org/451 (last accessed: 27 July 2022).

BUACHE, Freddy. *Derrière l'écran. Entretiens avec Christophe Gallaz et Jean-François Amiguet*. Lausanne: L'Âge d'homme, 2009.

CAMARGO, Silvio. 'Experiência social e crítica em André Gorz e Axel Honneth'. *Revista brasileira de ciências sociais* 74 (October 2010): 107–93.

CANNON, Betty. *Sartre and Psychoanalysis: An Existentialist Challenge to Clinical Metatheory*. Lawrence: University Press of Kansas, 1991.

CASTORIADIS, Cornelius. 'The Diversionists'. *Telos* 33 (1977): 102–06. First published in French as: 'Les divertisseurs', *Le Nouvel Observateur* (20 June 1977).

——. 'Reply to André Gorz'. *Telos* 33 (1977): 108–09. First published in French as: 'Réponse à André Gorz', *Le Nouvel Observateur* (4 July 1977).

——. *The Imaginary Institution of Society* (Kathleen Blamey trans.). Cambridge: Polity Press, 1997 [1975].

——, and Daniel Cohn-Bendit. *De l'écologie à l'autonomie*. Paris: Seuil, 1981.

CAYROL, Roland. 'Nouvel *Express* et *Nouvel Observateur*'. *Revue française de science politique* 16 (3) (1966): 493–520.

CELAN, Paul. *Die Gedichte*. Frankfurt: Suhrkamp, 2003.

CHAMBRE, Henri. *Le Marxisme en Union Soviétique*. Paris: Seuil, 1955.

CHASSAGNE, Alexis, and Gaston Montracher. *La Fin du travail*. Paris: Stock, 1978.

CICCARIELLO-Maher, George. 'Detached Irony Towards the Rest: Working-Class One-Sidedness from Sorel to Tronti'. *The Commoner* 11 (Spring 2006): 54–73.

CINGOLANI, Patrick. *Révolutions précaires. Essai sur l'avenir de l'émancipation*. Paris: La Découverte, 2014.

COHN-BENDIT, Daniel. 'Freiheit und politische Ökologie. Ein Gespräch mit Daniel Cohn-Bendit über André Gorz'. *Berliner Debatte Initial* 4 (2013): 67–72.

COLOZZA, Roberto. 'Une affinité intellectuelle, une proximité politique. Lelio Basso, Gilles Martinet et la "deuxième gauche" '. *Histoire@Politique* 16 (January–April 2012): 1–12 (available at: histoire-politique.fr; last accessed: 25 July 2022).

COMBESQUE, Marie Agnès. *Ça suffit! Histoire du mouvement des chômeurs*. Paris: Plon, 1998.

CONTAT, Michel, and Thomas Ferenczi. 'Un entretien avec André Gorz'. *Le Monde*, 14 April 1992.

——. 'André Gorz. Le philosophe et sa femme'. *Le Monde*, 27 October 2006.

——. 'André Gorz, "Morel" et Sartre' in Christophe Fourel (ed.), *André Gorz en personne*. Lormont: Le Bord de l'eau, 2013, pp. 29–38.

CORNUZ, Jeanlouis. 'D'une lecture faite en classe'. *Études de lettres* 2, 1 (3) (July–September 1958): 95–103.

DAGAN, Yaël. 'Les mots du sionisme. Retour aux sources'. *Mil neuf cent. Revue d'histoire intellectuelle* 27 (2009): 133–46.

DAHRENDORF, Ralf. 'Im Entschwinden der Arbeitsgesellschaft'. *Merkur* 8 (1980): 749–60.

——. 'Die Arbeitsgesellschaft ist am Ende'. *Die Zeit* (26 November 1982).

DAMBERT, Dominique, and Didier Adès. 'Vive le "social business"!' *Le Monde*, 12 January 2010.

DANIEL, Jean. *L'Ère des ruptures*, Paris: Grasset, 1979.

——. 'Partir avec elle'. *Le Nouvel Observateur*, 27 September 2007.

DA SILVA, Josué Pereira. *André Gorz. Trabalho e política*. São Paulo: Annablume, 2002.

DE FOUCAULD, Jean-Baptiste. 'Gorz et le temps choisi, un débat inachevé' in Christophe Fourel (ed.), *André Gorz. Un penseur pour le XXIe siècle*. Paris: La Découverte, 2012, pp. 147–62.

DE GAULEJAC, Vincent. *La Société malade de la gestion. Idéologie gestionnaire, pouvoir managérial et harcèlement social*. Paris: Seuil, 2005.

DE LARMINAT, Astrid. 'L'amour se bonifie avec l'âge'. *Le Figaro*, 14 December 2006.

DEJOURS, Christophe. *Souffrance en France. La banalisation de l'injustice sociale*. Paris: Seuil, 1998.

DELPORTE, Christian. '*L'Express*, Mendès France et la modernité politique (1953–1955)'. *Matériaux pour l'histoire de notre temps* 63–4 (July–December 2001): 96–103.

DESCHAVANNE, Éric, and Pierre-Henri Tavoillot. *Philosophie des âges de la vie*. Paris: Grasset, 2007.

DOMARCHI, Jean. 'Théorie de la valeur et phénoménologie'. *Revue internationale* 2 (January–February 1946).

DUBOIN, Marie-Louise. 'Revenu d'existence ou revenu social?'. *La Grande Relève* (March 2003).

——. 'André Gorz et l'économie distributive' in Christophe Fourel (ed.), *André Gorz. Un penseur pour le XXIe siècle*. Paris: La Découverte, 2012, pp. 125–46.

DUPUY, Jean-Pierre. 'Gorz et Illich' in Alain Caillé and Christophe Fourel (eds), *Sortir du capitalisme. Le scénario Gorz*. Lormont: Le Bord de l'eau, 2013, pp. 99–103.

DUVERGER, Timothée. 'Écologie et autogestion dans les années 1970. Discours croisés d'André Gorz et de Cornelius Castoriadis'. *Écologie et politique* 46 (2013): 139–48.

——. *L'Économie sociale et solidaire. Une histoire de la société civile en France et en Europe de 1968 à nos jours*. Lormont: Le Bord de l'eau, 2016.

FAVROD, Charles-Henri. 'Une étude magistrale d'André Gorz'. *Gazette littéraire*, 29 August 1964.

FORNEROD, Françoise. *Lausanne, le temps des audaces. Les idées, les lettres et les arts de 1945 à 1955*. Lausanne: Payot, 1993.

FOTTORINO, Éric. 'Duflot sur la planète Gorz'. 24 September 2011, Available at: lhemicycle.com/134-duflot-sur-la-planete-gorz (last accessed: 25 July 2022).

FOURASTIÉ, Jean. *Les Trente Glorieuses ou la révolution invisible de 1946 à 1975*. Paris: Fayard, 1979.

FOUREL, Christophe (ed.). *La Nouvelle Économie sociale. Efficacité, solidarité et démocratie*. Paris: Syros, 2001.

———. 'De la politique du temps au revenu citoyen. Itinéraire d'un penseur de l'après-capitalisme', interview by Sarah Troche. *Geste*, 6 October 2009.

——— (ed.). *André Gorz. Un penseur pour le XXIe siècle*. Paris: La Découverte, 2012.

FRANKEL, Boris. *The Post-industrial Utopians*. Madison: University of Wisconsin Press, 1987.

FRÉMION, Yves. *Histoire de la révolution écologiste*. Paris: Hoëbke, 2007.

FUMAGALLI, Andrea. 'Bioeconomics and the valorisation process' in Vladimir Cvijanović, Andrea Fumagalli and Carlo Vercellone (eds), *Cognitive Capitalism and Its Reflections in South-Eastern Europe*. Frankfurt: Peter Lang, 2010, pp. 41–59.

GADREY, Jean, and Florence Jany-Catrice. *Les Nouveaux Indicateurs de richesse*. Paris: La Découverte, 2012 [3rd edition].

GALLAND, Bertil. 'Celui qui feuillète aujourd'hui la collection de *La Gazette littéraire* s'émerveille' in Jean-Pierre Moulin (ed.), *Présence de Franck Jotterand. Recueil de textes*. Lausanne: L'Âge d'homme, 1997, pp. 17–23.

GAUSSEN, Frédéric, and Guy Herzlich. 'L'explosion de colère des étudiants a surprise tous les observateurs'. *Le Monde*, 7 May 1968.

GEORGESCU-Roegen, Nicholas. *The Entropy Law and the Economic Process*. Cambridge MA: Harvard University Press, 1971.

———. 'Energy and Economic Myths'. *The Ecologist* (June and August–September 1975). First published in *La Décroissance. Entropie, écologie, économie* (Jacques Grinevald and Ivo Rens trans and intro.). Paris: Le Sang de la terre/Ellébore, 1995 [1979].

GIANINAZZI, Willy. ' "Vivre une vie qui ne se vit pas". Quand Jean-Marie Vincent et André Gorz débattaient de valeur et subjectivité'. *Variations* 17 (2012). Available at: variations.revues.org/354 (last accessed: 27 July 2022).

———. 'Michel Bosquet ou le journalisme comme compromis' in Christophe Fourel (ed.), *André Gorz en personne*. Lormont: Le Bord de l'eau, 2013, pp. 81–6.

———. 'Penser global, agir local. Histoire d'une idée'. *EcoRev'* 46 (Summer 2018): 19–29.

GINTIS, Herbert. 'The New Working Class and Revolutionary Youth'. *Socialist Revolution* 3 (May 1970): 13–43.

——. 'Critique de l'illichisme'. *Les Temps modernes* 314–15 (September–October 1972): 525–57.

GLUCKSMANN, André. *Stratégie de la révolution*. Paris: Christian Bourgois, 1968.

GOLLAIN, Françoise. *Une critique du travail. Entre écologie et socialisme*. Paris: La Découverte, 2000.

——. 'L'apport d'André Gorz au débat sur le capitalisme cognitif'. *Revue du MAUSS* 35 (2010): 541–58.

——. 'André Gorz était-il un écologiste?' *Écologie et politique* 44 (2012): 1–15.

——. 'André Gorz, affects et philosophie' in Christophe Fourel (ed.), *André Gorz en personne*. Lormont: Le Bord de l'eau, 2013, pp. 63–74.

——. Introduction to Françoise Gollain (ed.), *André Gorz. Pour une pensée de l'écosocialisme*. Neuvy-en-Champagne: Le Passager clandestin, 2014, pp. 9–56.

——. 'André Gorz, vers l'inconditionnalité du revenu'. *L'Économie politique* 67 (July 2015): 52–64.

——. 'André Gorz: Wage Labour, Free Time and Ecological Reconstruction'. *Green Letters* 20 (2) (2016): 127–39. Available at: https://bit.ly/3KK7sLB (last accessed: 27 July 2022). First published in French as: 'André Gorz ou le refus de la domination du travail', *Entropia* 2 (Spring 2007): 63–79.

——. *André Gorz, une philosophie de l'émancipation*. Paris: L'Harmattan, 2018.

GREENSPAN, Alan. 'Risk transfer and financial stability'. 5 May 2005. Available at: federalreserve.gov/newsevents/speech/2005speech.htm (last accessed on 18 February 2022).

GRINEVALD, Jacques. 'Nicholas Georgescu-Roegen et le "message terrestre" de la décroissance'. *Entropia* 10 (Spring 2011): 135–54.

GRUMBACH, Tiennot. 'En cherchant l'unité de la politique et de la vie'. *Les Temps modernes* 307 (February 1972): 1215–16.

GRUNDMANN, Reiner. 'The Ecological Challenge to Marxism'. *New Left Review* 187 (May–June 1991): 103–20.

——. *Marxism and Ecology*. Oxford: Clarendon Press, 1991.

GUILLON, Claude and Yves Le Bonniec. *Suicide, mode d'emploi. Histoire, technique, actualité*. Paris: Éditions Alain Moreau, 1982.

HAEGLER, Rolf Paul. *Histoire et idéologie du mondialisme*. Zurich: Europa Verlag, 1972.

HANDWERKER, Marian (director). *André Gorz* (film). Belgium: La Confédération des syndicats chrétiens, September 1990.

HARRIBEY, Jean-Marie. 'Marxisme écologique ou écologie politique marxienne' in Jacques Bidet and Eustache Kouvélakis (eds), *Dictionnaire Marx contemporain*. Paris: PUF, 2001, pp. 183–200.

——. 'Le revenu d'existence ou l'impensé sur le travail'. *Le Monde*, 20 October 2014. Available at: lemonde.fr (last accessed: 27 July 2022).

HEINZE, Rolf G., and Claus Offe (eds). *Formen der Eigenarbeit. Theorie, Empirie, Vorschläge*. Opladen: Westdeutscher Verlag, 1990.

HÉRITIER, Pierre. *Nouvelle croissance et emploi*. Paris: Syros, 1988.

HERVÉ, Alain. 'La genèse des amis de la Terre'. *L'Écologiste* 21 (December–March 2007): 14.

HIMANEN, Pekka. *The Hacker Ethic and the Spirit of the Information Age*. London: Martin Secker & Warburg, 2001.

HORN, Gerd-Rainer. 'The Changing Nature of the European Working Class: The Rise and Fall of the "New Working Class" (France, Italy, Spain, Czechoslovakia)' in Carole Fink, Philipp Gassert and Detlef Junker (eds), *1968: The World Transformed*. Cambridge: Cambridge University Press, 1998, pp. 351–71.

HOWARD, Dick. 'New situation, new strategy: Serge Mallet and André Gorz' in Dick Howard and Karl Klare (eds), *The Unknown Dimension: European Marxism since Lenin*. New York: Basic Books, 1972, pp. 388–413.

——. 'André Gorz & the Philosophical Foundation of the Political'. *Logos* 12 (3) (2013).

HUNNIUS, Gerry (ed.). *Participatory Democracy for Canada: Workers' Control and Community Control*. Montreal: Black Rose Books, 1971.

HURET, Romain. *The Experts' War on Poverty: Social Research and the Welfare Agenda in Postwar America*. Ithaca, NY: Cornell University Press, 2019.

HYAFIL, Jean-Éric. 'Le revenu universel, rémunération du bien commun'. *Le Monde*, 7 November 2014. Available at: lemonde.fr (last accessed: 27 July 2022).

ILLICH, Ivan. 'Pour retrouver la vie'. *Le Nouvel Observateur*, 11 September 1973.

——. 'A Constitution for Cultural Revolution' in *Celebration of Awareness: A Call for Institutional Revolution*. Harmondsworth: Penguin Books, 1980.

——. 'School: The Sacred Cow' in *Celebration of Awareness: A Call for Institutional Revolution*. Harmondsworth: Penguin Books, 1980.

JACOB, Jean. *Histoire de l'écologie politique*. Paris: Albin Michel, 1999.

JAMET, Michel. *Les Défis de L'Express*. Paris: Cerf, 1981.

JAPPE, Anselm. 'André Gorz et la critique de la valeur' in Alain Caillé and Christophe Fourel (eds), *Sortir du capitalisme. Le scénario Gorz*. Lormont: Le Bord de l'eau, 2013, pp. 161–9.

JEANNERET, Pierre. *Popistes. Histoire du parti ouvrier et populaire vaudois. 1943–2001*. Lausanne: Éditions d'en bas, 2002.

JULLIARD, Jacques. 'Save the University'. *Partisan Review* 38(3) (Summer 1971). First published in French as: 'Sauver l'Université', *Le Nouvel Observateur*, 4 May 1970.

———. 'L'utopie au purgatoire?' *Le Nouvel Observateur*, 10 March 1980.

———. *Autonomie ouvrière. Études sur le sydicalisme d'action directe.* Paris: Seuil/ Gallimard, 1988.

———. 'Les passions d'André Gorz'. *Le Nouvel Observateur*, 27 September 2007.

———. *Les Gauches françaises. Histoire, politique et imaginaire, 1762–2012.* Paris: Flammarion, 2012.

———. *Le Choc Simone Weil.* Paris: Flammarion, 2014.

KEMPF, Hervé. 'Brice Lalonde. Le dandy de l'écologie'. *Le Monde*, 11 December 2007.

———. *Comment les riches détruisent la planète.* Paris: Seuil, 2007.

LA TAPEUSE. 'Les noeuds gorziens ou là où il y a de la gêne, il n'y a pas de plaisir'. *Cash* 5 (April 1987): 24–6.

LALONDE, Brice. 'Court traité imagé sur les écologies'. *Le Sauvage* 43 (July 1977): 51–4.

LANDAU, David. 'French Socialist Blasts Unionism'. *The Harvard Crimson*, 13 November 1970.

LANZMANN, Claude. 'Pour Horst, Gérard. André Gorz, Michel Bosquet'. *Les Temps modernes* 645–6 (September 2007): 2.

———. *Le Lièvre de Patagonie. Mémoires.* Paris: Gallimard, 2009.

LAVILLE, Jean-Louis. 'Penser le changement social' in Alain Caillé and Christophe Fourel (eds), *Sortir du capitalisme. Le scénario Gorz.* Lormont: Le Bord de l'eau, 2013.

LE GOFF, Jean-Pierre, *Mai 68. L'héritage impossible.* Paris: La Découverte, 1998.

LECLERC, Michel-Édouard. 'André Gorz: la mort d'un philosophe'. 2 October 2007. Available at: michel-edouard-leclerc.com (last accessed: 25 July 2022).

LEGGEWIE, Claus. 'A Laboratory of Postindustrial Society' in Carole Fink, Philipp Gassert and Detlef Junker (eds), *1968: The World Transformed.* Cambridge: Cambridge University Press, 1998.

LEMIEUX, Cyril (ed.). *La Subjectivité journalistique. Onze leçons sur le rôle de l'individualité dans la production de l'information.* Paris: Éditions de l'EHESS, 2010.

LEVY, Andrea. *Reframing Socialism from the Fifties to the Fin-de-siècle: The Intellectual Odyssey of André Gorz.* MA thesis, Montreal, Concordia University, 1998.

LIPIETZ, Alain. 'André Gorz et notre jeunesse'. *Multitudes* 31 (2008): 163–9.

LIPOVETSKY, Gilles. *L'Ère du vide. Essais sur l'individualisme contemporain.* Paris: Gallimard, 1983.

LITTLE, Adrian. *The Political Thought of André Gorz.* New York: Routledge, 1996.

LUCBERT, Manuel. 'L'aile gauche du parti en quête d'une "nouvelle société" '. *Le Monde*, 15 May 1970.

LUKÁCS, Georg. *History and Class Consciousness: Studies in Marxist Dialectics*. Boston, MA: MIT Press, 1972.

MACINTYRE, Ben. 'In Life, in Death, in Love'. *The Times*, 18 October 2007.

MAFFESOLI, Michel. *The Time of the Tribes: The Decline of Individualism in Mass Society*. London: SAGE Publications, 1995.

MAIRE, Edmond. 'Le mouvement ouvrier face aux idéologies de crise'. *Le Monde*, 21–22 August 1980.

MALLET, Serge. 'Un réformisme révolutionnaire'. *France Observateur*, 21 May 1964.

——. 'L'idole des étudiants rebelles: Herbert Marcuse'. *Le Nouvel Observateur*, 8 May 1968.

——. 'Mai-juin 68: première grève pour la gestion' in *La Nouvelle classe ouvrière*. Paris: Seuil, 1969 [2nd edn].

——. *The New Working Class*. Nottingham: Spokesman Books, 1977.

MANACH, Yves Le. *Bye bye turbin. Suivi de Salauds! On les connaît vos usines, vos partis et vos syndicats*. Paris: Champ libre, 1973.

MANDEL, Ernest. *Marxist Economic Theory*. Delhi: Aakar Books, 2008.

MARAZZI, Christian. *The Violence of Financial Capitalism*. Los Angeles: Semiotext(e), 2010.

——. *Capital and Affects: The Politics of the Language Economy*. Semiotext(e)/Foreign Agents, 2011 [1994].

MARCUSE, Herbert. 'Libertad y agresión en la sociedad tecnológica' in Erich Fromm, Irving L. Horowitz, Herbert Marcuse, Victor Flores Olea and André Gorz, *La Sociedad industrial contemporánea*. Mexico City: Siglo Veintiuno, 1968, pp. 60–89.

MARCUSE, Herbert, et al. 'Écologie et révolution'. *Le Nouvel Observateur*, 19 June 1972.

——. *One-Dimensional Man*. London: Abacus, 1972.

——. 'Socialisme ou barbarie', interview by Jean Daniel and Michel Bosquet of 15 June 1972. *Le Nouvel Observateur*, 8 January 1973.

——. *An Essay on Liberation*. Harmondsworth: Penguin Books, 1973.

MARGLIN, Stephen. 'What do bosses Do?' in André Gorz (ed.), *The Division of Labour. The Labour Process and Class-Struggle in Modern Capitalism*. Hassocks: The Harverster Press, 1978, pp. 13–54.

MARONGIU, Jean-Baptiste, and Frédérique Roussel. 'Aux noms de l'amour'. *Libération*, 5 October 2006.

MARX, Karl. *Grundrisse* (Martin Nicolaus trans.). Harmondsworth: Penguin Books in association with *New Left Review*, 1973.

——. *Capital*, VOL. 1 (Ben Fowkes trans.). Harmondsworth: Penguin Books, 1976.

——. *Capital*, VOL. 3 (Ben Fowkes trans.). London: Penguin Books, 1991.

MASCHINO, Maurice. 'La morale de l'histoire'. *Gazette littéraire* (supplement to the *Gazette de Lausanne*), 10 October 1959.

MASTRORILLI, Carlos P., and Fernando Alvarez. *Marcuse Sartre Nizan Gorz y el Tercer Mundo*. Buenos Aires: Carlos Pérez Editor, 1969.

MÉDA, Dominique. 'La fin de la valeur "travail" ' in *Le Travail, quel avenir?* Paris: Gallimard, 1997.

———. *La Mystique de la croissance. Comment s'en libérer*. Paris: Flammarion, 2013.

MERCURE, Daniel, and Jan Spurk (eds). *Le Travail dans l'histoire de la pensée occidentale*. Quebec: Presses de l'université Laval, 2003.

MERETZ, Stefan. 'André Gorz und der Wissenskommunismus' in Hans Leo Krämer (ed.), *Der Horizont unserer Handlungen: den Zusammenbruch des Kapitalismus denken*. Saarbrücken: Kooperationsstelle Wissenschaft und Arbeitswelt, 2013, pp. 111–19.

MERGENDAHL, Charles. *La Route aux étoiles* [*Don't Wait up for Spring*] (translated and adapted by G. Bosquet [alias Gérard Horst]). Lausanne: Marguerat, 1947.

MERLEAU-PONTY, Maurice. *Phenomenology of Perception*. London: Routledge & Kegan Paul, 1962.

MICHAUD, Dominique Allan. *L'Avenir de la société alternative. Les idées 1968–1990*. Paris: L'Harmattan, 1989.

MOREAU, Jean. 'La nouvelle extrême-gauche'. *Le Nouvel Observateur*, 26 October 1970.

MORIN, Edgar. *Autocritique*. Paris: Seuil, 1959.

———. 'Intellectuels. Critique du mythe et mythe de la critique'. *Arguments* 20 (Oct–Dec 1960).

———, Claude Lefort and Jean-Marc Coudray [Cornelius Castoriadis]. *Mai 1968: la brèche. Premières réflexions sur les événements*. Paris: Fayard, 1968.

MOTHÉ, Daniel. *L'Utopie du temps libre*. Paris: Esprit, 1977.

———. 'Faut-il réduire le temps du travail?'. *Autogestions* 19 (1985): 15–17.

MOULIER-BOUTANG, Yann. 'André Gorz, pour mémoire'. *Multitudes* 31 (Winter 2007): 159–60.

———. *Cognitive Capitalism*. Chichester: Polity Press, 2012 [2007].

MOULIN, Jean-Pierre. 'Les Faux-nez à Paris'. *Gazette littéraire* (supplement to the *Gazette de Lausanne*), 2 July 1949.

———. 'Jean-Pierre Moulin, un "Amant américain" à Paris', interview by Jean-Jacques Roth. *Le Nouveau Quotidien*, 3 January 1993.

MUNDHENK, Michael. 'Appropriating Life-History through Autobiographical Writing. André Gorz's *The Traitor*, a Dialectical Inquiry into the Self'. *Prose Studies: History, Theory, Criticism* 8(2) (1985): 81–96.

Münster, Arno. *Sartre et la morale*. Paris: L'Harmattan, 2007.

Negri, Antonio, and Jean-Marie Vincent. 'Paradoxes autour du travail'. *Futur antérieur* 10 (April 1992): 5.

Negt, Oskar. *Lebendige Arbeit, enteignete Zeit. Politische und kulturelle Dimensionen des Kampfes um die Arbeitszeit*. Frankfurt: Campus Verlag, 1984.

——. 'Aus produktiver Phantasie. Ein revolutionärer Realist unserer Zeit' in Hans Leo Krämer and Claus Leggewie (eds), *Wege ins Reich der Freiheit*. Berlin: Rotbuch Verlag, 1989, pp. 54–73.

Noirot, Paul, Jean-Marie Vincent, Manuel Ballestero and André Gorz. 'Sujet, structures, science et action politique. Discussion'. *Démocratie nouvelle* 4 (April 1967): 58.

Nora, Pierre. 'Aliénation' in *Le Débat, Les Idées en France 1945–1988*. Paris: Gallimard, 1989, pp. 493–500.

Offe, Claus. 'Arbeit als soziologische Schlüsselkategorie?' in Joachim Matthes (ed.), *Krise der Arbeitsgesellschaft*? Frankfurt/New York: Campus Verlag, 1983, pp. 38–65.

Olivier, Philippe [André Glucksmann]. 'Syndicats, comité(s) de lutte, comités de chaîne'. *Les Temps modernes* 310 bis (May 1972): 34–56.

Ory, Pascal (ed.). *Nouvelle histoire des idées politiques*. Paris: Hachette, 1989.

Paris, Robert. 'En deçà du marxisme'. *Les Temps modernes* 240 (May 1966): 1983–2002.

Pessis, Céline (ed.). *Survivre et vivre. Critique de la science, naissance de l'écologie*. Montreuil: L'Échappée, 2014.

Pinto, Louis. 'Un théoricien du *Nouvel Observateur*' in *L'Intelligence en action: Le Nouvel Observateur*. Paris: Métailié, 1984.

Pohier, Jacques. *La Mort opportune. Les Droits des vivants sur leur fin de vie*. Paris: Seuil, 1998.

Postone, Moishe. *Time, Labor and Social Domination*. Cambridge: Cambridge University Press, 2003 [1993].

Poulot, Denis. *Le Sublime ou le travailleur comme il est en 1870, et ce qu'il peut être*. Paris: Maspero, 1980 [1870].

Rabant, Claude. 'Un choix renversant' in Max Bensasson and Annick Feissel (eds), *La Question du choix inconscient. Déterminisme et responsabilité du sujet*. Marseille: Éditions du Hasard, 1997, pp. 37–45.

Raddatz, Fritz. 'Im Nebel eines neuen Monte Verità. André Gorz über das Ende der Arbeitsgesellschaft und die Zukunft der Linken'. *Die Zeit*, 22 November 1991.

Rémy, Jacqueline. *Le 'Nouvel Observateur'. 50 ans de passions*. Paris: Pygmalion, 2014.

Reynaud, Jean-Daniel. 'La nouvelle classe ouvrière. La technologie et l'histoire'. *Revue française de science politique* 22 (3) (1972): 529–42.

Rifkin, Jeremy. *The Zero Marginal Cost Society*. London: Palgrave Macmillan, 2014.

RIUTORT, Philippe. 'Le journalisme au service de l'économie. Les conditions d'émergence de l'information économique en France à partir des années 50'. *Actes de la recherche en sciences sociales* 131–2 (March 2000): 41–55.

ROSANVALLON, Pierre. 'Formation et désintégration de la galaxie "auto" ' in Paul Dumouchel and Jean-Pierre Dupuy (eds), *L'Auto-organisation. De la physique au politique* (*Colloque de Cerisy, 10–17 juin 1981*). Paris: Seuil, 1983, pp. 456–65.

ROSS, Kristin. *May 68 and Its Afterlives*. Chicago: Chicago University Press, 2002.

ROSZAK, Theodore. *The Making of a Counter-culture: Reflections on the Technocratic Society and its Youthful Opposition*. Berkeley: University of California Press, 1969.

ROUSSEL, Frédérique. 'André Gorz, dernière lettre à D.' *Libération*, 25 September 2007.

ROUSSELET, Jean. *L'Allergie au travail*. Paris: Seuil, 1978 [1974].

SANTOS, Ariovaldo. 'Gorz e o inquietante adeus ao proletariado' in Josué Pereira da Silva and Iram Jácome Rodrigues (eds), *André Gorz e seus criticos*. São Paulo: Annablume, 2006, pp. 127–39.

SARTRE, Jean-Paul. 'C'est pour tous que sonne le glas'. *Servir*, 24 June 1948.

——. 'Jean-Paul Sartre ouvre un dialogue'. *Peuple du monde*, 18 June 1949.

——. *Being and Nothingness*. London: Methuen, 1958.

——. 'Les bastilles de Raymond Aron'. *Le Nouvel Observateur*, 19 June 1968.

——. 'Masses, spontanéité, parti'. *Les Temps modernes* 282 (January 1970): 1043–63.

——. 'A Plea for Intellectuals' in *Between Existentialism and Marxism*. London: Verso Books, 1983.

——. *Critique of Dialectical Reason* (Alan Sheridan-Smith trans.). London: Verso Books, 2004. First published in French as: *Critique de la raison dialectique*. Paris: Gallimard, 1960.

SARTRE, Jean-Paul, and Benny Lévy. *L'Espoir maintenant. Les entretiens de 1980*. Paris: Verdier, 1991.

SHEPARD, Paul, and Daniel McKinley (eds). *The Subversive Science: Essays towards an Ecology of Man*. Boston, MA: Houghton Mifflin, 1969.

SIMONNET, Dominique. 'La société dualiste de Michel Bosquet' (interview). *Le Sauvage* 49 (1 January 1978): 20–1.

SOBEL, Richard. 'Travail, liberté et nécessité dans l'utopie communiste. André Gorz, lecteur de Marx'. *Actuel Marx* 46 (2009): 163–76.

SOMMIER, Isabelle. 'Les gauchismes' in Dominique Damamme, Boris Gobille, Frédérique Matonti and Bernard Pudal (eds), *Mai-juin 68*. Ivry-sur-Seine: Éditions de l'Atelier, 2008, pp. 295–305.

STANDING, Guy. *The Precariat: The New Dangerous Class*. London: Bloomsbury Publishing, 2011.

STENKE, Wolfgang. 'Die Wege des André Gorz' in Claus Leggewie and Wolfgang Stenke (eds), *André Gorz und die zweite Linke. Die Aktualität eines fast vergessenen Denkers*. Berlin: Verlag K. Wagenbach, 2017, pp. 10–34.

STEWART, Ramona. . . . *Et le désert autour* [*Desert Town*] (Gérard Horst trans.). Lausanne: Marguerat, 1946.

STILLE, Ugo. 'Marcuse, il teorico della protesta' (interview). *Corriere della Sera*, 5 March 1968.

SUE, Roger. *Renouer le lien social. Liberté, égalité, association*. Paris: Odile Jacob, 2001.

TABET, Alexei. *La Pensée d'Ivan Illich en France. Essai d'histoire intellectuelle*. MA thesis, Université de Paris 1, 2012.

TATMAN, Jeremy. 'A Dialogue with Gorz' in *André Gorz: A Critical Introduction*. London: Pluto Press, 1997.

TINEL, Bruno. '*À quoi servent les patrons?*' *Marglin et les radicaux américains*. Lyon: ENS Éditions, 2004.

TODD, Olivier. *Un fils rebelle*. Paris: Grasset, 1981.

TOPALOV, Christian. *Naissance du chômeur. 1880–1910*. Paris: Albin Michel, 1994.

TOURAINE, Alain. 'Situation du mouvement ouvrier'. *Arguments* 12–13 (January–March 1959).

———. *Le Mouvement de mai ou le communisme utopique*. Paris: Seuil, 1968.

———. *La Société postindustrielle*. Paris: Denoël et Gonthier, 1969.

———. *Return of the Actor: Social Theory in Postindustrial Society*. Minneapolis: University of Minnesota Press, 1988 [1984].

———. 'Die Verweigerung der Integration' in Hans Leo Krämer and Claus Leggewie (eds), *Wege ins Reich der Freiheit*. Berlin: Rotbuch Verlag, 1989, pp. 166–73.

———. 'Le plus imaginatif des penseurs'. *Globe Hebdo* 12 (28 April 1993): 36.

———. 'Itinéraires intellectuels des années 1970'. *Revue française d'histoire des idées politiques* 2 (1995): 394.

TRONTI, Mario. *Nous opéraïstes. Le 'roman de formation' des années soixante en Italie*. Paris/Lausanne: Éditions de l'Éclat/Éditions d'en bas, 2013.

VAN PARIJS, Philippe. 'La porte étroite. Dialogue avec André Gorz'. *Virages* (Brussels) 2 (April 1984): 13–15.

———. 'De la sphère autonome à l'allocation universelle' in Christophe Fourel (ed.), *André Gorz. Un penseur pour le XXIe siècle*. Paris: La Découverte, 2012, pp. 163–77.

VANDERBORGHT, Yannick, and Philippe Van Parijs. *L'Allocation universelle*. Paris: La Découverte, 2005.

VANEIGEM, Raoul. *Nous qui désirons sans fin*. Paris: Gallimard, 1998.

VERCELLONE, Carlo (ed.). *Sommes-nous sortis du capitalisme industriel?* Paris: La Dispute, 2003.

——. 'André Gorz et la dynamique du capitalisme'. *Sens public* (11–12) (October 2009): 159–75.

VIANNAY, Philippe. *Du bon usage de la France.* Paris: Ramsay, 1988.

VIDAL, Jérôme. 'André Gorz sur la ligne de crête du présent'. *Revue internationale des livres et des idées,* 9 July 2010.

VIEILLE-BLANCHARD, Élodie. *Les Limites à la croissance dans un monde global. Modélisations, prospectives, refutations.* Paris: EHESS, 2011.

VINCENT, Jean-Marie. 'Le théoricisme et sa rectification' in Jean-Marie Vincent, Jean-Marie Brohm, Catherine Colliot-Thélène et al., *Contre Althusser.* Paris: UGE, 1974, pp. 215–59.

——. 'Liberté et socialité'. *Futur antérieur* 2 (Summer 1990): 22–37.

VIRNO, Paolo. 'Quelques notes à propos du "general intellect" '. *Futur antérieur* 10 ([April] 1992).

——. *Mondanità. L'idea di 'Mondo' tra esperienza sensibile e sfera pubblica.* Rome: Manifestolibri, 1994.

VON THADDEN, Elisabeth. 'Von Luft und Liebe'. *Die Zeit,* 20 September 2007.

VOYNET, Dominique. Afterword to Alain Caillé and Christophe Fourel (eds), *Sortir du capitalisme. Le scénario Gorz.* Lormont: Le Bord de l'eau, 2013, pp. 207–09.

WEBER, Florence. *Le Travail à-côté. Une ethnographie des perceptions.* Paris: Éditions de l'EHESS, 2009 [1989].

ZIN, Jean. 'La coopérative municipale'. *EcoRev'* 15 (Winter 2003–04).

——. 'André Gorz, pionnier de l'écologie politique' in Christophe Fourel (ed.), *André Gorz. Un penseur pour le XXIe siècle.* Paris: La Découverte, 2012.

ZOLL, Rainer. *Nouvel individualisme et solidarité quotidienne.* Paris: Kimé, 1992.

ACADEMIC STUDIES OF ANDRÉ GORZ

BIGI, Maëlezig. *Autonomie et critique du travail chez André Gorz.* MA thesis, Université de Paris I, Paris, 2010.

BROOKS, Christopher D. *Exile: An Intellectual Portrait of André Gorz.* MA thesis. Ann Arbor: ProQuest, 2010.

CAILLÉ, Alain, and Christophe Fourel (eds). *Sortir du capitalisme. Le scénario Gorz.* Lormont: Le Bord de l'eau, 2013.

CONTAT, Michel. *André Gorz. Vers la société libérée.* Paris: Textuel/INA, 2009.

DA Silva, Josué Pereira. *André Gorz. Trabalho e política.* São Paulo: Annablume-Fapesp, 2002.

——, and Iram Jácome Rodrigues (eds.). *André Gorz e seus críticos.* São Paulo: Annablume, 2006.

Farah, Philip. *André Gorz e la questione del lavoro.* MA thesis. Bari: Università di Bari, 1997.

Fourel, Christophe (ed.). *André Gorz, en personne.* Lormont: Le Bord de l'eau, 2013.

Fröhlich, Florian. *Eine kurze Einführung in die Theorien von André Gorz.* Munich: Grin Verlag, 2010.

Furtado, Roberto Pereira. 'André Gorz. Trabalho, tempo livre e liberdade'. MA thesis, Universidade federal de Goiás, Goiâna, 2012.

Gomes, Marcelo. 'André Gorz e o século XX. A problemática fundamentação metodológica de Adeus ao Proletariado'. MA thesis, Universidade Estadual Paulista Júlio de Mesquita Filho, São Paulo, 2005. Available at: nea-edicoes.com (last accessed: 13 August 2022).

Guillerot, Nicolas. *Capitalisme et revenu minimum. Réflexions à partir de l'œuvre d'André Gorz.* Mémoire de DEA. Paris: Université Paris-I, 1989.

Häger, André. 'André Gorz und die Verdammnis zur Freiheit. Studien zu Leben und Werk'. MA thesis, Bielefeld, 2018.

Krämer, Hans Leo (ed.). *'Der Horizont unserer Handlungen: den Zusammenbruch des Kapitalismus denken' (André Gorz). Kongress über die Ideen von André Gorz 15. und 16. Februar 2013 in Saarbrücken.* Saarbrücken: Presses universitaires de la Sarre, 2013.

Krämer, Hans Leo and Claus Leggewie (eds.). *Wege ins Reich der Freiheit. André Gorz zum 65. Geburtstag.* Berlin: Rotbuch Verlag, 1989.

Langer, André. 'Pelo êxodo da sociedade salarial. A evolução do conceito de trabalho em André Gorz'. MA thesis, *Cadernos IHU* (São Leopoldo, Rio Grande do Sul) 5 (2004).

Leggewie, Claus, and Wolfgang Stenke (eds.). *André Gorz und die zweite Linke. Die Aktualität eines fast vergessenen Denkers.* Berlin: Verlag K. Wagenbach, 2017.

Lesourt, Enzo. *André Gorz. Portrait du philosophe en contrebandier ou l'écologie politique comme reconquête du sujet.* Paris: L'Harmattan, 2011.

Lodziak, Conrad, and Jeremy Tatman. *André Gorz: A Critical Introduction.* London: Pluto Press, 1997.

Modugno, Cristina Di. 'Il Lavoro e l'utopia. Studio sul pensiero di André Gorz'. MA thesis, Università di Bari, Bari, 1997.

Münster, Arno. *André Gorz ou le socialisme difficile.* Paris: Nouvelles éditions Lignes, 2008.

RICHTER, Mathias, and Inka Thunecke (eds.). *Paradies now: André Gorz, Utopie als Lebensentwurf und Gesellschaftskritik*. Talheimer: Mössingen-Thalheim, 2016.

RIZZI, Graziella. 'La Problematica filosofica e politica di André Gorz'. MA thesis, Università degli Studi, Milan, 1974.

STERNBERG, Alice. 'L'Écologie du monde vécu dans l'œuvre d'André Gorz. L'autonomie au fondement du politique'. MA thesis, Université de Paris-VIII, Saint-Denis, 2014.

VALDIVIELSO, Joaquin. 'La filosofía política de André Gorz. Las sociedades avanzadas y la crisis del productivismo'. MA thesis, Universitat de les Illes Balears, Palma, 2001.

ZWENGEL, Ralf (ed.). *Ohne Proletariat ins Paradies? Zur Aktualität des Denkens von André Gorz*. Essen: Klartext Verlag, 2009.

ARCHIVES

CENAC   Centre pour l'Action non-violente, La Chaux-de-Fonds. Library, Bovard collection, D.600.52, correspondence Gérard Horst-René Bovard (August 1949).

CRLR   University of Lausanne, archives of the Centre de recherche sur les lettres romandes, Dardel collection, Servir file.

GRZ   Institut Mémoires de l'édition contemporaine (IMEC), Caen, André Gorz collection.

HM   University of Frankfurt-am-Main. Library archives, Herbert Marcuse collection, correspondance André Gorz-Herbert Marcuse.

LLB   Fondazione Lelio et Lisli Basso, Rome. Archives, correspondence André Gorz/Gérard Horst-Lelio Basso, 1962-1968.

SEUIL   Institut Mémoires de l'édition contemporaine (IMEC), Caen, Éditions du Seuil collection.

CENAC   Centre pour l'Action non-violente, La Chaux-de-Fonds. Library, Bovard collection, D.600.52, correspondence Gérard Horst-René Bovard (August 1949).

All Gorz's letters taken from GRZ are, in fact, copies he made for it. With the exception of the copies of the correspondence to Walter Riffel, which were photocopied at a later date by their recipient.

INTERVIEWERS AND PERSONAL CORRESPONDENTS

Claude Aucouturier, Dominique Bourg, the late Freddy Buache, Éliane Carr, Lucette Cassemiche, Denis Clerc, the late Gaston Cherpillod, Jacques Delors, the late Charles-Henri Favrod, Christophe Fourel, Françoise Gollain, André Henry, the late Alain Hervé, Erich Hörl, Dick Howard, Jacques Julliard, Hans Leo Krämer, the late Serge Lafaurie, Claus Leggewie, Jacques Maury, Gilles Monod, Jean-Pierre Moulin, Claus Offe, Walter Riffel, Jean Robert, the late Michel Rocard, Oreste Scalzone, Joaquin Valdivielso and Patrick Viveret.

Index of Names

Adler-Karlsson, Gunnar, 238, 271, 289

Adorno, Theodor W., 185, 238, 246, 247n43, 281

Akerman, Nordal, 300

Albert, Michael, 152n2

Alessandrini, Jean-François, 273

Althusser, Louis, 83, 84, 122, 139, 141, 144, 146–7, 347

Amado, Jean, 251

Amendola, Giovanni, 87

Anders, Günther (pseudonym of Günther Siegmund Stern), 165, 321

Anderson, Perry, 87, 223

Angeli, Claude, 128, 130

Angerer, Erika: see Horst, Erika, 3, 352

Antelme, Robert, 121, 125n1

Apel, Karl-Otto, 268

Apothéloz, Charles (known as 'Apoth'), 17, 33–4, 43, 85n29

Arbenz Guzmán, Jacobo, 49, 117

Archimbaud, Aline, 255, 292

Archimbaud, Jacques, 255, 292, 298

Arendt, Hannah, 165, 238, 259, 261, 342

Aristotle, 254–5, 260

Aron, Robert, 45

Aronowitz, Stanley, 154

Asor Rosa, Alberto, 140, 250

Aspe, Bernard, 309

Atlan, Henri, 291

Attali, Jacques, 187, 220, 225, 235, 291, 307

Aubry, Martine, 220, 273, 296, 298

Aucouturier, Claude, 205

Auger, Jean, 93

Auroux, Jean, 220

Axelos, Kostas, 71, 74, 105, 118, 164

Aznar, Guy, 225, 234, 252–3, 270, 291–2

Backmann, René, 126, 128, 129

Bacon, Francis 192

Badiou, Alain, 93, 214

Bahro, Rudolf, 213, 218, 223–4, 236, 241, 281

Bakunin, Mikhail, 136

Barbrook, Richard, 316

Barjonet, André, 96, 136

Baronian, Laurent, 339

Barot, Madeleine, 347

Barou, Jean-Pierre, 146

Barthes, Roland, 179

Basso, Lelio, 54, 86–90, 131, 137

Bataille, Georges, 23, 39n11, 345

Baudrillard, Jean, 75, 151, 177

Beauvoir, Simone de, 27, 30, 31, 45, 79, 82, 121, 148, 228, 343

Béchaux, Cécile, 34

Bégout, Bruce, *ix*

Belleville, Pierre, 96, 98

Ben Barka, Mehdi, 117, 119

Benoist, Alain de, 247

Bensaïd, Norbert, 226

Jeanson, Francis, 27, 63, 85

Jonas, Hans, 194–5

Jones, Barry, 234

Jotterand, Franck, 17, 47, 86, 233

Jouvenel, Bertrand de, 199

Jouvenel, Hugues de, 290

Julião, Francisco, 123, 180

Julien, Claude, 119, 234

Julliard, Jacques, 133, 219, 224–5, 352

July, Serge, 129, 135, 234

Jung, Carl Gustav, *ix*

Jünger, Ernst, 165

Juquin, Pierre, 126, 202

Kallscheuer, Otto, 233–4, 268–9, 272

Kant, Immanuel, 225, 332

Karol, K.S. (Karol Kewes), 51, 54, 89, 110, 117–8, 121, 130

Katheline: see Coya, Katheline, 349, 351

Kautsky, Karl, 136

Keane, John, 267

Keir, Doreen (Dorine), 9, 20–1, 33–4, 43, 45–8, 52, 63–4, 66, 108, 118, 180, 183, 200, 205, 225, 229–33, 345–53

Keir, James, 21

Kepler, Johannes, 322

Keynes, John Maynard, 52, 90, 220, 237, 338

Khruschev, Nikita, 131

Kierkegaard, Søren, 23, 32, 341

Kitzmüller, Erich, 353

Klein, Naomi, , 313

Klein, William, 233

Koestler, Arthur, 352

Kojève, Alexandre, 70

Kosik, Karel, 107

Kouchner, Bernard, 135

Krämer, Hans Leo, 233, 236, 272

Kravetz, Marc, 131–2, 134, 147, 199, 233

Krief, Claude, 54, 109

Krumnow, Frédo, 93

Kuhn, Thomas S., 164

Kurz, Robert, 329–30, 332–3, 335, 338, 342

Kurzweil, Ray, 322

Laborit, Henri, 199, 291

Lacan, Jacques, 230

Lafargue, Paul, 69, 143, 159, 352

Lafaurie, Serge, 50, 54, 85, 110, 128, 345, 352, 353

Lafontaine, Oskar, 235, 272

Laing, Ronald D., 60

Lalonde, Brice, 199–201, 205, 208, 226, 233

Lambert, Jean-Paul, 126, 225, 233

Land, Rainer, 268

Langer, André, 324–5

Laniel, Joseph, 48

Lanzmann, Claude, 85, 178, 228, 232

Lapassade, Georges, 133

Laponche, Bernard, 206, 220, 233

Latouche, Serge, 292, 299, 334, 335, 349

Laville, Jean-Louis, 292, 298

Lazzarato, Maurizio, 309

Leclerc, Édouard, 51–2, 178

Leclerc, Michel-Édouard, 178, 233, 348

Le Dantec, Jean-Pierre, 146

Lefebvre, Henri, 70–1, 101, 107, 122, 125

Lefort, Claude, 65, 66, 86, 136, 140